ETHICS IN HUMAN COMMUNICATION

FOURTH EDITION

North Carolina Wesleyan College Library

Scurry - Drum Collection

Given by:
Dr. Frank Scurry and
Carolina Evangelical
Divinity School

ETHICS IN HUMAN COMMUNICATION

FOURTH EDITION

RICHARD L. JOHANNESEN
Northern Illinois University

Prospect Heights, Illinois

For information about this book, write or call:
Waveland Press, Inc.
P.O. Box 400
Prospect Heights, Illinois 60070
847/634-0081

Copyright © 1996, 1990, 1983, 1975 by Richard L. Johannesen

ISBN 0-88133-904-0

All rights reserved. No part of this book may be reproduced, stored in a retrieval system, or transmitted in any form or by any means without permission in writing from the publisher.

Printed in the United States of America

7   6   5   4

Contents

Preface xi
Acknowledgments xiii

1 Ethical Responsibility in Human Communication 1
Inherency of Potential Ethical Issues 2
The "Sermonic" Dimension of Language 3
Adaptation to the Audience 4
The Importance of Ethics 5
Freedom and Responsibility 6
The Intentional and the Sincere 10
Ethics and Personal Character 11
Implied Ethical Contracts 13
A Hypothetical Example 15
An Approach to Ethical Judgment 15
Notes 19

2 Political Perspectives 23
Four Moralities 23
Degree of Rationality 25
Significant Choice 27
Ground Rules for Political Controversy 30
Democratic Debate as a Procedural Ethic 32
A Synthesis of Textbook Standards 33
Ethical Standards for Governmental Communication 34
Public Confidence in Truthfulness of Public Communication 36
Some Other Political Systems 39
Notes 40

3 Human Nature Perspectives 45
Human Rational Capacity 46
Human Symbol-Using Capacity 48
Kant's Categorical Imperative 50
Reason and Language 51
Humans as Persuaders 51
Communicative Competence and the Ideal Speech Situation 52
An Existentialist Ethic for Communication 54
An Epistemic Ethic 55
Human Capacity for Value Judgment 57
A Humanistic Ethic for Rhetoric 58
Notes 59

4 Dialogical Perspectives 63
Focus of Dialogical Perspectives 64
Dialogue versus Expressive Communication 66
Characteristics of Dialogue 66
Characteristics of Monologue 68
Humans as Persons and Objects 70
Dialogue and Persuasion 71
Conditions and Contexts for Dialogue 72
Dialogical Attitudes in Public and Written Communication 73
Toward an Ethic for Rhetoric 76
Dialogical Ethics and Significant Choice 78
Guidelines for Applying Dialogical Standards 79
Notes 80

5 Situational Perspectives 87
Rogge's Situational Perspective 88
Diggs's Situational Perspective 89
Fletcher's Situation Ethics 89
Alinsky's Situational Perspective 90
Ethical Issues in Social Protest Situations 93
Notes 96

6 Religious, Utilitarian, and Legal Perspectives 99
Religious Perspectives: General Nature 99
A Christian Ethic for Persuasion 99
The Mass Media and Christian Morality 100
Religious Perspectives on Advertising 102
An Ethic for Christian Evangelism 103

The National Religious Broadcasters' Code   104
Oral Roberts's Controversial Fundraising Appeal   105
Several Asiatic and Mid-Eastern Religious Perspectives   106
Shared Perspectives   107
Utilitarian Perspectives: General Nature   107
The Social Utility Approach   108
Legal Perspectives: General Nature   110
Politics and Advertising   111
Problems with Legal Perspectives   113
Notes   114

7 Some Basic Issues   117
Absolute and Relative Standards   117
Maximum or Minimum Standards   118
The End as Justification of Means   119
The Ethics of Lying   121
The Ethics of Intentional Ambiguity and Vagueness   125
Ethics, Emotional Appeals, and Rationality   127
The Truth Standard in Commercial Advertising   129
Ethics and Propaganda   131
Ethics and the Demagogue   134
Ethics and Nonverbal Communication   135
Ethics and Tastefulness   137
Ethics and Ghostwriting   138
Objectivity as an Ethical Standard for News Reporting   140
Secrecy: Personal and Governmental   143
Ethical Responsibilities of Receivers   146
Ethical Responsibilities of Non-Participants   148
Notes   149

8 Interpersonal Communication and Small Group Discussion   157
Condon's Interpersonal Ethic   158
A Contextual Interpersonal Ethic   159
An Ethic for Interpersonal Trust   159
An Ethic for Everyday Conversation   160
A Rhetorical Perspective on Interpersonal Ethics   161
Unfair Tactics in Verbal Conflict   161
Individual Responsibility in Relational Communication   162
Keeping the Conversation Going   163
Ethical Responsibility and Communication Competence   165

A Political Perspective for Small Group Discussion 166
Respect for the Worth of Others 167
Ethical Sensitivity 168
A "Groupthink" Ethic 169
Notes 170

9 Communication in Organizations 173
Negative Attitudes of the Public 173
Assessing Ethical Responsibility 174
Organizations as Cultures 176
The Organization's Ethical Climate 176
Character and Virtue Ethics 177
A Framework for Analyzing Ethics in Organizations 179
A Model of Organizational Integrity 180
Ethical Standards for Communication in Organizations 181
Whistleblowing 185
Ethics for Communication Consulting and Training 186
Ethics in Public Relations 187
Examples of Ethical Problems 190
Cynicism and Relevance 193
Notes 193

10 Formal Codes of Ethics 197
Objections to Formal Codes 198
Developing a Sound Formal Code 199
Codes for Individual Organizations 200
Argumentative Function 201
Character-Depiction Function 202
Advertising Association Codes 203
International Association of Business Communicators 205
Public Relations Society of America Code 206
Ethical Values and Principles in Public Service 210
Codes for Political Campaign Communication 212
Spero's Proposed Code for Televised Political
  Campaign Advertisements 214
Notes 218

11 Feminist Contributions 221
An Ethic of Care: Gilligan, Noddings, Manning,
  Tronto, Wood 222
"Telling It Slant": Women and Lying 230

Rhetoric, Persuasion, Communication, and Mass
    Communication 232
Additional Communication Issues 236
Notes 239

12 Intercultural and Multicultural Communication 243
Sitaram and Cogdell's Ethic 245
Kale's Human Nature Ethic 246
Plagiarism as Culturally Variable 247
Multicultural Communication 249
Ethnic Ethics 250
Modified Universalism 251
Moral Exclusion 252
Racist/Sexist Language and Hate Speech 253
Ethical Guidelines for Intracultural Communication 256
Discarding Rigidity 258
Notes 259

Appendix: Case Studies of Theory and Practice 263
Richard L. Johannesen, "An Ethical Assessment of the
    Reagan Rhetoric: 1981–1982" 265
Richard L. Johannesen, "A Rational World Ethic Versus
    a Narrative Ethic for Political Communication" 285
Richard L. Johannesen, "Virtue Ethics, Character, and
    Political Communication" 297
Clifford G. Christians, "Social Responsibility: Ethics and
    New Technologies" 321

Sources for Further Reading 337

Index 367

Preface

My primary intentions in this book are: (1) to provide information and insights concerning a variety of potential perspectives for making ethical judgments about human communication; (2) to sensitize participants in communication to the inherency of potential ethical issues in the human communication process; (3) to highlight the complexities and difficulties involved in making evaluations of communication ethics; (4) to encourage individuals to develop thoughtfully their own workable approach to assessing communication ethics; and (5) to aid individuals in becoming more discerning evaluators of communication through enhancing their ability to make specifically focused and carefully considered ethical judgments.

Hopefully this book will prove useful in studying ethical implications of varied kinds of human communication, whether that communication is oral or written, whether it is labeled informative, persuasive, expository, argumentative, or rhetorical, whether it is labeled interpersonal, small group, public, or mass.

I do not intend to argue my own case for the merit of one particular ethical perspective or set of standards as the best one. I view my role in this book, as I do in the classroom, as one of providing information, examples, and insights and of raising questions for discussion so that you can make judicious choices among ethical options in developing your own position.

Nevertheless, I am sure that at various points in the book my personal judgments, preferences, and biases are reflected; you may, if you think necessary, discount or make allowances for them. Some judgments and preferences are rather overt and easily detected. Such is the case, for example, in my discussion of public confidence in truthfulness of public communication (chapter 2), my explanation of situational, utilitarian, and legal perspectives (chapters 5 and 6), and my evaluation of the ethics of the communication of former President Reagan (appendix). Other judgments and preferences probably are less overt and less consciously included. If I were asked to state my own preference for the ethical perspectives which I find most useful in judging human communication, I still would favor a combination of the "significant choice" political perspective (in chapter 2) and Martin Buber's dialogical perspective (in chapter 4).

For this fourth edition, I have made a number of major revisions and numerous minor alterations. Two new chapters have been added: chapter 11, "Feminist Contributions"—including an ethic of care—and chapter 12, "Intercultural and Multicultural Communication"—including a discussion of campus "hate speech." The theme of the role of ethical character has been strengthened by adding a relevant section to the chapter on organizational communication (9) and a lengthy case study in the appendix.

Significant revisions have been made, or new sections added, in the chapters on ethical responsibility (1), some basic issues (7), interpersonal and small group communication (8), and communication in organizations (9). Some material from the former chapter on examples for analysis has been dropped while other material has been shifted to other chapters. All chapters have some changes and updating of references. In the bibliography of Sources for Further Reading, while I have dropped many older sources, I have added numerous new ones. The bibliography now contains about 640 items, including a lengthy section on ethics in journalism and mass communication.

As reflected in the index, at various points throughout the book I explore issues and standards especially relevant for the mass media. Among such mass media oriented topics are: formal codes of ethics for commercial advertising, public relations, public opinion polls, and political campaign communication; the "truth" standard in commercial advertising; John Merrill's "deontelic" ethic for journalists; propaganda and the demogogue; ethics of the nonverbal dimensions of communication; religion-based standards for advertising and political campaigning; and "objectivity" as a standard for news reporting. A case study in the appendix explores standards for mass media innovation.

Richard L. Johannesen
DeKalb, Illinois

Acknowledgments

I appreciate the cooperation of various organizations for which I have reprinted part or all of their formal codes of ethics: American Advertising Federation, American Association of Advertising Agencies, Better Business Bureau, Committee on Decent Unbiased Campaign Tactics, Common Cause, International Association of Business Communicators, The Josephson Institute for the Advancement of Ethics, and the Public Relations Society of America. I also wish to acknowledge the thorough and perceptive comments of the late Douglas Ehninger (University of Iowa) who read in its entirety the completed manuscript for the first edition. Published reviews of the third edition provided helpful suggestions for this edition. To Neil and Carol Rowe of Waveland Press, I am grateful for their genuine supportiveness of the third and fourth editions.

Chapter 1

Ethical Responsibility in Human Communication

Values can be viewed as conceptions of The Good or The Desirable that motivate human behavior and that function as criteria in our making of choices and judgments. Concepts such as material success, individualism, efficiency, thrift, freedom, courage, hard work, competition, patriotism, compromise, and punctuality all are value standards that have varying degrees of potency in contemporary American culture. But we probably would not view them primarily as *ethical* standards of right and wrong. Ethical judgments focus more precisely on degrees of rightness and wrongness, virtue and vice, and obligation in human behavior. In condemning someone for being inefficient, conformist, extravagant, lazy, or late, we probably would not also be claiming they are unethical. However, standards such as honesty, promise-keeping, truthfulness, fairness, and humaneness usually *are* used in making ethical judgments of rightness and wrongness in human behavior.

Ethical issues may arise in human behavior whenever that behavior could have significant impact on other persons, when the behavior involves conscious choice of means and ends, and when the behavior can be judged by standards of right and wrong.[1] If there is little possible significant, immediate, or long-term impact of our actions (physical or symbolic) on other humans, matters of ethics normally are viewed as minimally relevant. If we have little or no opportunity for conscious free choice in our behavior, if we feel compelled to do or say something because we are forced or coerced, matters of ethics usually are seen as minimally relevant to *our* actions.

Some philosophers draw distinctions between ethics and morals as concepts. Ethics denotes the general and systematic study of what ought to be the grounds and principles for right and wrong human behavior. Morals (or morality) denotes the practical, specific, generally agreed-upon, culturally transmitted standards of right and wrong. Other philosophers, however, use the terms ethics and morals more or less interchangeably—as will be the case in this book.

Inherency of Potential Ethical Issues

Potential ethical issues are inherent in any instance of communication between humans to the degree that the communication can be judged on a right-wrong dimension, involves possible significant influence on other humans, and to the degree that the communicator consciously chooses specific ends sought and communicative means to achieve those ends. Whether a communicator seeks to present information, increase someone's level of understanding, facilitate independent decision in another person, persuade about important values, demonstrate the existence and relevance of a societal problem, advocate a solution or program of action, or stimulate conflict—potential ethical issues inhere in the communicator's symbolic efforts. Such is the case for most human communication whether it is between two people, in small groups, in the rhetoric of a social movement, in communication from government to citizen, or in an advertising, public relations or political campaign.

Humans are the only animals "that can be meaningfully described as having values," believes social psychologist Milton Rokeach. More specifically, social critic Richard Means contends that the "essence of man par excellence may be *Homo ethicus*, man the maker of ethical judgments."[2] But some persons ask, why worry at all about ethics in human communication? Indeed, to avoid consideration of ethics in communication, such persons may resort to various justifications: (1) Everyone knows that this particular communication technique is unethical, so there is nothing to discuss; (2) since only success matters in communication, ethicality is irrelevant; (3) after all, ethical judgments are simply matters of individual personal opinion anyway, so there are no final answers; and (4) it is presumptuous, perhaps even unethical, to judge the ethics of others.[3]

Tension potentially exists *between* "*is*" and "*ought*," between the actual and the ideal. What everyone is doing and what we judge they ought to do may differ. There may be a conflict between a communication technique we know is successful and the judgment that the technique ought not to be used because it is ethically suspect. We may overemphasize our understanding of the nature and effectiveness of communication techniques, processes, and methods at the expense of concern for the ethical use of such techniques. We should examine not only *how to*, but also *whether we ethically ought to*, employ methods and appeals. The question of "whether to" clearly is one not only of audience adaptation but also one of ethics. We may feel that ethical ideals are not realistically achievable and thus are of little usefulness. But Thomas Nilsen reminds us that "we must always expect a gap between ideals and their attainment, between principles and their application." Nevertheless, he feels that "ideals reflect genuine beliefs, intentions, and aspirations. They reflect what we in our more calm and thoughtful moments think ought to be, however aware we may be of our actual . . . level of achievement. . . . Our ideals provide an ultimate goal, a sense of direction, a general orientation, by which to guide conduct."[4]

How participants in a human communication transaction evaluate the ethics of that transaction, or how outside observers evaluate its ethics, will differ depending upon the ethical standards they employ. Some even may choose to ignore ethical judgments entirely. Nevertheless, *potential* ethical questions are there regardless of how they are resolved or answered.

Whether a communicator wishes it or not, communicatees generally will judge, formally or informally, the communicator's effort in part by those communicatees' relevant ethical standards. If for none other than the pragmatic reason of enhancing chances of success, the communicator would do well to consider the ethical criteria held by his or her audience.

The "Sermonic" Dimension of Language

Richard M. Weaver and Kenneth Burke, two contemporary theorists of rhetoric, share the conviction that, to some degree, all intentional use of language between humans is "sermonic." They believe that the idea that language can be used in a *completely* neutral and objective manner is untenable. They argue that language use (our selection of words) inherently expresses the communicator's choices, attitudes, tendencies, dispositions, and evaluations and thus channels the perceptions both of sender and receiver.[5] "We have no sooner uttered words," says Weaver, "than we have given impulse to other people to look at the world, or some small part of it, in our way. Thus caught up in a great web of inter-communication and inter-influence, we speak as rhetoricians affecting one another for good or ill."[6]

A scholar of human communication with a social science orientation, David Berlo, expresses a similar view: ". . . there is reason to believe that all use of language has a persuasive dimension, that one cannot communicate at all without some attempt to persuade, in one way or another."[7] In their textbook on interpersonal communication, Bobby Patton and Kim Giffin contend, "It is ridiculous to consider language a neutral medium of exchange. Specific words are selected for our use because they do affect behavior."[8]

Weaver, Burke, Berlo, and Patton and Giffin are arguing, then, that every intentional human communication transaction inherently involves *some degree* of persuasive purpose and possible impact. The perspectives for ethical judgment and the fundamental ethical issues discussed in this book pertain to this "sermonic" dimension found in varied forms and types of human communication. Weaver and Burke both argue that all human use of language necessarily involves matters of ethical responsibility.[9]

Adaptation to the Audience

What are the ethics of audience adaptation? Most human communicators seek to secure some kind of response from receivers. To what degree is it ethical for communicators to alter their ideas and proposals in order to adapt to the needs, capacities, desires, and expectations of an audience? To secure acceptance, some communicators adapt to an audience to the extent of so changing their ideas that the idea is no longer really theirs. These communicators merely say what the audience wants them to say regardless of their *own* convictions. On the other hand, some measure of adaptation in language choice, supporting materials, organization, and message transmission to reflect the specific nature of the audience is a crucial part of successful communication. No ironclad rule can be set down here. Communicators must decide the ethical balance point between their idea in its pure form and that idea modified to achieve maximum impact with the audience.

The search is for an appropriate point between two undesirable extremes—the extreme of saying only what the audience desires and will approve and the extreme of complete lack of concern for and understanding of the audience. The search is for an appropriate point between too much adaptation to the audience and not enough. Both extremes are ethically irresponsible. This tension, this search for balance in audience adaptation, can be viewed as an example of Aristotle's Principle of the Golden Mean. For Aristotle, moral virtue usually represents a mean or intermediate point between two vices—the vice of excess and the vice of deficiency. For example, courage is a mean between foolhardiness and cowardice. Generosity is a mean between wastefulness and stinginess. Aristotle denies that the mean is a mathematically precise average or midpoint between extremes. Rather, the mean combines the appropriate amount at the appropriate time toward appropriate people in an appropriate manner for appropriate reasons. The mean is also relative to the person's status, specific situation, and strengths and weaknesses of character. A person generally disposed toward one extreme in an appropriate instance ought to tend toward the other extreme to redress the imbalance.[10]

Develop your own ethical judgment about the ethicality of the following example. Consider presidential candidate Walter Mondale's habit in 1983 of telling widely varied interest groups that *each* group's specific interests are "at the very core of my being." Commented *Newsweek* (October 3, 1983, p. 32): "In a single three-week period, Mondale used this same phrase to express his commitment to civil rights, his concern for quality education, and his fidelity to upholding 'the rights of unions.' Some joke that the core of his being must be very large, divided into small wedges, or rentable on short notice."

The Importance of Ethics

Evidence mounted during the 1980s and 1990s of citizen concern with the decline of ethical behavior, especially of persons in positions of significant public or private responsibility. "What Ever Happened to Ethics?" asked the cover story of *Time* (May 25,1987). "A Nation of Liars?" inquired *U.S. News and World Report* (February 23, 1987). A poll in February 1987 by *U.S. News* and the Cable News Network showed that more than half of the persons surveyed believed that people were less honest than ten years earlier. According to *Time*: "Large sections of the nation's ethical roofing have been sagging badly, from the White House to churches, schools, industries, medical centers, law firms and stock brokerages." *Time* concluded: "Ethics, often dismissed as a prissy Sunday School word, now is at the center of a new national debate." Political commentators and private citizens continued to debate the issue of "character" as it applied to ethics in the public and private lives of President Bill Clinton, Speaker of the House Newt Gingrich, and other political leaders. Magazine articles explored the decline of an appropriate "sense of shame" as a norm in American culture (*Atlantic Monthly*, February 1992, pp. 40–70; *Newsweek*, February 6, 1995, pp. 21–25). A national survey of 3,600 college students at 23 colleges (*Washington Post National Weekly Edition*, December 7–13, 1992, p. 36) revealed that one in six college students had lied on a résumé, job application, or during a job interview; that two out of five had lied to a boss and a third had lied to a customer during the past year; and that one out of five admitted cheating on an exam. *Time* magazine devoted seven pages to the topic of "Lies, Lies, Lies" (October 5, 1992).

"A society without ethics is a society doomed to extinction," argues philosopher S. Jack Odell. According to Odell, the "basic concepts and theories of ethics provide the framework necessary for working out one's own moral or ethical code." Odell believes that "ethical principles are necessary preconditions for the existence of a social community. Without ethical principles it would be impossible for human beings to live in harmony and without fear, despair, hopelessness, anxiety, apprehension, and uncertainty."[11]

A societal or personal system of ethics is not a magic or automatic cure-all for individual or collective ills. What can ethical theory and systematic reflection on ethics contribute? One answer is suggested by philosopher Carl Wellman:

> An ethical system does not solve all one's practical problems, but one cannot choose and act rationally without some explicit or implicit ethical system. An ethical theory does not tell a person what to do in any given situation, but neither is it completely silent; it tells one what to consider in making up one's mind what to do. The practical function of an ethical system is primarily to direct our attention to the relevant considerations, the reasons that determine the rightness or wrongness of any act.[12]

Freedom and Responsibility

Twentieth century culture in the United States emphasizes dual concerns for maximizing latitude of freedom of communication and for promoting responsible exercise of such freedom. The current and future boundaries of freedom of communication in the United States are explored in such works as: *The System of Freedom of Expression*, *Freedom of Speech in the United States*, *Speech and Law in a Free Society*, and *The Law of Public Communication*.[13] Thomas Szasz succinctly describes the interrelated and intertwined nature of freedom and responsibility.[14]

> The crucial moral characteristic of the human condition is the dual experience of freedom of the will and personal responsibility. Since freedom and responsibility are two aspects of the same phenomenon, they invite comparison with the proverbial knife that cuts both ways. One of its edges implies options: we call it freedom. The other implies obligations: we call it responsibility. People like freedom because it gives them mastery over things and people. They dislike responsibility because it constrains them from satisfying their wants. That is why one of the things that characterizes history is the unceasing human effort to maximize freedom and minimize responsibility. But to no avail, for each real increase in human freedom . . . brings with it a proportionate increase in responsibility. Each exhilaration with the power to do good is soon eclipsed by the guilt for having used it to do evil.

The continuing tension between freedom and responsibility emerges both in intimate interpersonal communication and in mass communication. "For there to be *freedom* to converse intimately with another person," assumes William Rawlins, "each party must take *responsibility* for communication behavior." Several mass communication scholars believe: "In an environment where freedom is considered paramount, . . . words such as *accountability* and *responsibility* are often not understood or even heard. Increasingly, however, they are the 'watch words' for today's media. The regulation of media, especially broadcasting, has decreased in recent years, and so the need for ethical and moral responsibility in media has become important."[15]

"UNABOM's Manifesto Poses Ethical Dilemma for Papers" read the headline in the *Washington Post* (July 1, 1995, A3). The serial mail bomb terrorist designated by the FBI as UNABOM had killed three people and wounded 23 in the period 1978–1995. In the summer of 1995 he promised to end his mail bomb attacks on persons (but not necessarily on property) if the *New York Times* and the *Washington Post* published his 35,000 word manifesto that described his criticism of modern technological society. Arguments by the press and law enforcement officials presented pro and con viewpoints concerning the wisdom and ethics of publication. On the one hand, publication possibly could save lives. On the other hand, publication would represent giving in to a person who had set himself above normal moral standards. And publication might set a strong precedent for terrorists to blackmail newspapers into publishing their views, thus infringing on First Amendment rights of freedom of the press.

After extensive consultation with the FBI and the attorney general, on November 19, 1995, the *Washington Post* published the manifesto as an eight-page special insert and split the publication costs with the *New York Times*. Publication again prompted divided reactions from media experts and law enforcement officials. Some applauded it for public safety reasons. Others questioned it both for giving in to terrorist demands and for relying heavily on the views of governmental agencies as to whether (and thus what) to publish (*Post*, Nov. 20, 1995, A1, A12; *Times*, Nov. 20, 1995, A16). Donald E. Graham, the publisher of the *Washington Post* (Nov. 19, 1995, A1, A7), said it was published "for public safety reasons, not journalistic reasons." Also he argued: "This is not a First Amendment issue. This centers on the role of a newspaper as part of a community." The publisher of the *New York Times* (Nov. 19, 1995, A1, B7), Arthur Sulzberger, Jr., concluded: "I'm convinced we're making the right choice between two bad options." Clearly this case illustrates the complex tension in our society between freedom and the responsibility in communication.

After over two decades of advocating the imperative of freedom for journalists and of urging an individual existential journalistic ethic, John Merrill modified some of his views. In his book, *The Dialectic in Journalism: Toward a Responsible Use of Press Freedom*, Merrill[16] insists on "the essentiality of freedom, while counterpoising responsibility as a natural limiting factor. . . . The fundamental dialectical theme of this book is freedom and ethics in critical tension that results in a higher synthesis—the ethical use of freedom." At another point he explains:

> Freedom and responsibility are, in a real sense, contraries of great importance in journalism; they are the tension agents that bring conflict into the dialectic. Freedom clashes with ethics to gain more flexibility and individualism. Ethics conflicts with freedom to supplant personal licentiousness with social concern. Neither ever completely wins the battle, and neither falls completely vanquished. Instead, a reconciliation, a hybridization, a mediation—a *dialectical synthesis*—results.

In developing his ethical stance, Merrill combines aspects of two ethical traditions: *deontological* ethics that bases right and wrong on duty to obey universal and absolute principles; and *teleological* ethics that assess ethicality of acts according to the consequences, such as utility and degree of greatest good for the greatest number in the long run for those affected. Thus Merrill labels his view as "deontelic ethics." Journalists would "begin with basic principles or maxims to which they could reasonably pay allegiance and to which they feel a duty to follow." These fundamental principles are held as normal guides for action, but journalists must "not follow these basic ethical tenets blindly or unthinkingly." Deontelic ethics recognizes "specific, and differing, human situations in which exceptions and modifications of the general principles can be made by the concerned journalist" in light of probable consequences and contextual factors. But such modifications are temporary—"not for always but for a particular time."

As communicators, our ethical responsibilities may stem from a position or role we have earned or been granted, from commitments (promises, pledges, agreements) we have made, from established ethical principles, from relationships we have formed, or from consequences (effects, impacts) of our communication on others. Responsibility includes the elements of fulfilling duties and obligations, of being held accountable as evaluated by agreed-upon standards, and of being accountable to our own conscience. But an essential element of responsible communication, for both sender and receiver, is the exercise of thoughtful and caring judgment. That is, the responsible communicator reflectively analyzes claims, soundly assesses probable consequences, and conscientiously considers relevant values (both abstract principles and personal relationships). In a sense a responsible communicator is *response-able*. She or he exercises the ability to respond (is responsive) to the needs and communication of others in sensitive, thoughtful, fitting ways.[17]

"The sense of ourselves as responsible is at least a necessary condition of self-respect," believes Edmund Pincoffs, a contemporary professor of philosophy. Furthermore he argues, "if doing things with words imposes or incurs responsibilities, then a world in which those responsibilities were not honored would be a world in which it would be increasingly difficult and finally impossible to do things with words. Responsibility for what we say, then, is also responsibility for the integrity of the language."[18] The concern for ethically responsible communication finds apt expression in the words of Dag Hammarskjöld, late Secretary General of the United Nations:[19]

> Respect for the word—to employ it with scrupulous care and an incorruptible heartfelt love of truth—is essential if there is to be any growth in a society or in the human race.
>
> To misuse the word is to show contempt for man. It undermines the bridges and poisons the wells. It causes Man to regress down the long path of his evolution.

The Intentional and the Sincere

Whether communicators seem *intentionally* and *knowingly* to use particular content or techniques is a factor that most of us take into account in judging degree of communication ethicality. If a dubious communication behavior seems to stem more from accident, from an unintentional slip of the tongue, or even from ignorance, often we are less harsh in our ethical assessment. For most of us, it is the intentional use of ethically questionable tactics that merits our harshest condemnation. As an example, Nicholas Rescher believes that there is no moral or ethical issue when persons unintentionally or accidentally use unsound evidence or illogical reasoning. But he sees the intentional use of faulty reasoning as quite different. "Undoubtedly, the person who sets out *deliberately to deceive others* by means of improper reasoning is morally culpable. . . ."[20]

In contrast, it might be contended that in argumentative and persuasive situations, communicators have an ethical obligation to double-check the soundness of their evidence and reasoning before they present it to others; sloppy preparation is not an adequate excuse to lessen the harshness of our ethical judgment. A similar view might be advanced concerning elected or appointed government officials. If they use obscure or jargon-laden language that clouds the accurate and clear representation of ideas, even if that use is not intended to deceive or hide, they are ethically irresponsible. Such officials, according to this view, should be obligated to communicate clearly and accurately with citizens in fulfillment of their governmental duties.

In *Moralities of Everyday Life*, the authors note that usually "there is a close relationship between responsibility and intent—we are responsible for what we intend to do, what we are trying to do." Nevertheless they argue the position that "people are responsible for all that they cause so long as they can see that they cause it and can do otherwise. We may feel responsible only for what we intend; we are responsible for all that we do."[21]

As a related question we can ask, does *sincerity* of intent release a communicator from ethical responsibility concerning means and effects? Could we say that *if* Adolf Hitler's fellow Germans judged him to be sincere, they should not assess the ethics of his persuasion? In such cases, evaluations are probably best carried out if we appraise sincerity and ethicality separately. For example, a communicator sincere in intent may be found to utilize an unethical strategy. Or communication techniques generally considered ethical might be used by an insincere person. Wayne Booth reminds us that "sincerity is more difficult to check and easier to fake than logicality or consistency, and its presence does not, after all, guarantee very much about the speaker's case."[22] And Peter Drucker describes the different meanings of sincerity in Western and Eastern cultures. Westerners view sincerity as "words that are true to convictions and feelings" whereas people from Eastern cultures define sincerity as "actions that are appropriate to a specific relationship and make it harmonious and of optimum mutual benefit."[23]

Ethics and Personal Character

An emphasis on duties, obligations, rules, principles, and the resolution of complex ethical dilemmas has dominated the contemporary philosophy of ethics. This dominant emphasis has been true whether as variations on Immanuel Kant's categorical imperative, on John Rawls's depersonalized veil of ignorance to determine justice, on statements of intrinsic ultimate goods, or on Jeremy Bentham's or John Stuart Mill's utilitarian views. The past several decades, however, have witnessed a growing interest among ethicists in a largely ignored tradition that goes back at least as far as Plato's and Aristotle's philosophies of ethics. This largely bypassed tradition typically is called virtue ethics or character ethics. Most ethicists of virtue or character see that perspective as a crucial complement to the current dominant ethical theories. Ethicists describe virtues variously as deep-rooted dispositions, habits, skills, or traits of character that incline persons to perceive, feel, and act in ethically right and sensitive ways. Also they describe virtues as learned, acquired, cultivated, reinforced, capable of modification, capable of conflicting, and ideally coalesced into a harmonious cluster.

Ethical communication is not simply a series of careful and reflective decisions, instance by instance, to communicate in ethically responsible ways. Deliberate application of ethical rules sometimes is not possible. Pressure may be so great or a deadline so near for a decision that there is not adequate time for careful deliberation. We may be unsure what ethical criteria are relevant or how they apply. The situation may seem so unique that applicable criteria do not readily come to mind. In such times of crisis or uncertainty, our decision concerning ethical communication stems less from deliberation than from our formed "character." Furthermore, our ethical character influences the terms with which we describe a situation and whether we believe the situation contains ethical implications.[24]

Consider the nature of moral character as described by ethicists Richard DeGeorge and Karen Lebacqz. According to DeGeorge:

> As human beings develop, they tend to adopt patterns of actions, and dispositions to act in certain ways. These dispositions, when viewed collectively, are sometimes called character. A person who habitually tends to act as he morally should has a good character. If he resists strong temptation, he has a strong character. If he habitually acts immorally, he has a morally bad character. If despite good intentions he frequently succumbs to temptation, he has a weak character. Because character is formed by conscious actions, in general people are morally responsible for their characters as well as for their individual actions.[25]

Lebacqz believes: "Indeed, when we act, we not only *do* something, we also shape our own character. Our choices about what to do are also choices about whom to be. A single lie does not necessarily make us a liar; but a series of lies may. And so each choice about what to *do* is also a choice about whom to *be*—or, more accurately, whom to become."[26]

In Judeo-Christian or Western cultures, good moral character usually is associated with habitual embodiment of such virtues as courage, temperance, wisdom, justice, fairness, generosity, gentleness, patience, truthfulness, and trustworthiness. Other cultures may praise additional or different virtues that they believe constitute good ethical character. Instilled in us as habitual dispositions to act, these virtues guide the ethics of our communication behavior when careful or clear deliberation is not possible.

In *The Virtuous Journalist*, Klaidman and Beauchamp contend that citizens "should expect good character in our national leaders, and the same expectations are justified for anyone in whom we regularly place trust."[27] The *Wall Street Journal* surveyed dozens of top executives of American companies to see if they would hire Lt. Col. Oliver North (of the Iran-Contra scandal) if he applied for a job. Many executives enthusiastically said they would hire him, but some would place restrictions on his responsibilities. Among those who would refuse to hire him, one especially pinpointed the issue of character, saying "it is a real character flaw when someone is willing to lie, cheat, and steal to accomplish the end of his superiors. That flaw will ultimately hurt the company. It's a character flaw that I would find unacceptable despite the strengths of his loyalty. The integrity flaw outweighs any other."[28] Admittedly, the news media (or anyone) may at times be over-zealous and focus on trivial or irrelevant character traits. But in general the emphasis on moral character in evaluating presidential candidates is central "to what the electorate seems to value most in its presidents—authenticity and honesty."[29]

To aid in assessing the ethical character of any person in a position of responsibility or any person who seeks a position of trust, we can modify guidelines suggested by journalists. Will the recent or current ethically suspect communication behavior probably continue? Does it seem to be habitual? Even if the particular incident seems minor in itself, does it "fit into a familiar pattern that illuminates more serious shortcomings?" If the person does something inconsistent with his or her public image, "is it a small miscue or a sign of hypocrisy?"[30] Rhetorical critic Walter Fisher considers character to be an "organized set of actional tendencies" and observes: "If these tendencies contradict one another, change significantly, or alter in 'strange' ways, the result is a questioning of character. . . . Without this kind of predictability, there is no trust, no community, no rational human order."[31]

I explore implications of character ethics for communication in organizations later in chapter 9, and the role of virtue ethics and character in political communication is examined at length in my essay in the appendix. An excellent historical treatment of the tradition in philosophy of virtue ethics is Nancy Sherman, *The Fabric of Character: Aristotle's Theory of Virtue* (1989).

Implied Ethical Contracts

There are some general unspoken assumptions, some implicit expectations, that seem to characterize most instances of public discourse.[32] The speaker or writer believes that a problem or need exists that can be solved or satisfied through communication with other persons. The communicator also believes that the subject is important to a number of persons whose aid can be sought and that the matter cannot be resolved by himself or herself alone. The subject is perceived as important enough to the communicator that she or he is willing to risk public evaluation, and both communicator and audience are assumed to be willing to open themselves to the possibilities to change—to altering their own views or actions. How should this implied general contract influence a communicator's and receivers' ethical judgments? More precisely, are there some relevant ethical guidelines imbedded in this implied contract? Might one be that dogmatic inflexibility is ethically suspect?

In most public and private communication, a fundamental implied and unspoken assumption is that words can be trusted and people will be truthful. Unless there are reasons to be skeptical, we expect people to mean what they say. Also, even if persons do not know the absolutely certain "ultimate truth" about something, we expect those persons to say what they believe to be true and not to say as true what they believe to be false. An observation by Jeffrey Olen concerning journalism applies equally well to human communication generally. We "don't ordinarily enter into explicit agreements to be truthful with one another. . . . The moral prohibition against lying provides, in effect, an implicit agreement, allowing us to expect the truth from one another." Philosopher Warren Shibles agrees: "Strictly speaking, we usually do not have a contract with people not to lie. It is just implied or assumed that we will not lie." Trust in some degree of truthfulness, argues Sissela Bok in *Lying*, is a *"foundation* of relations among human beings." We must trust the words of others if we are to trust that they will treat us fairly, not harm us, and have our welfare at heart. "If there is no confidence in the truthfulness of others. . . how, then, can they be trusted?" Bok stresses: "*Whatever* matters to human beings, trust is the atmosphere in which it thrives."[33]

Beyond a general implied ethical contract, various types of communication settings, communicator roles, and each specific situation may have unspoken expectations that help define the ethical relationship between communicator and audience.[34] As a professor teaching a college course on communication ethics, I assume (perhaps naively) that students in the course will be honest and truthful with me even more than they might be with some others in other contexts or relationships. Thus I have felt betrayed when this implicit expectation occasionally has been violated through plagiarism in a term paper or cheating on an examination. What is your judgment of the implied ethical contract I assume in my course? Consider another example reflective of role and situation. Our expectations concerning honesty, accuracy, and relevancy of information probably would be different when involved with an American Cancer Society representative persuading us to contribute funds as opposed to a used car dealer persuading us to purchase. If the cancer society representative intentionally employed false data, the ethics of that choice could be condemned because we do not expect a representative of a reputable humanitarian society to use questionable techniques; in such a situation we would be especially vulnerable.

A Hypothetical Example

Imagine that you are an audience member listening to a speaker, call him Mr. Bronson, representing the American Cancer Society. His aim is to persuade you to contribute money to the research efforts sponsored by the American Cancer Society. Suppose that, with one exception, all of the evidence, reasoning, and motivational appeals he employs are valid and above ethical suspicion. But at one point in the speech Mr. Bronson *consciously* chooses to use a set of *false* statistics to scare the audience into believing that, during their lifetime, there is a much greater probability of their getting some form of cancer than there actually is.

To promote analysis of the ethics of this persuasive situation, consider these issues: If the audience, or the society at large, views Mr. Bronson's persuasive end or goal as worthwhile, does the worth of his end justify his use of false statistics as a means to help achieve that end? Does the fact that he *consciously* chose to use false statistics make a difference in your evaluation? If he used the false statistics out of ignorance, or out of failure to check his sources, how might your ethical judgment be altered? Should he be condemned as an unethical *person*, as an unethical *speaker*, or as one who in this instance used a *specific* unethical technique?

Carefully consider the standards you would employ to make your ethical judgment. Are they purely pragmatic? In other words, should Mr. Bronson avoid false statistics because he might get caught? Are they societal in origin? If he gets caught, his credibility as a *representative* would be weakened with this and future audiences. Or his getting caught might weaken the credibility of *other* American Cancer Society representatives.

Should his communication ethics be criticized because he violated an implied agreement of trust and honesty between you and him? Your expectations concerning honesty, accuracy, and relevancy of information probably would be different for him as a representative of the American Cancer Society in contrast to the stereotypical used car dealer. You might not expect a representative of such a humanitarian society to use questionable techniques, and thus you would be especially vulnerable.

An Approach to Ethical Judgment

The ethical analysis of any communication situation may be aided by considering some basic elements. Each element and the interaction among them could be probed in depth and should be described accurately and fairly. A *communicator*, with particular *motives*, attempts to achieve a specific *end* with a specific audience by employing (*intentionally or unintentionally*) communicative *means* or techniques to influence that audience. The communicator may be one person, a representative of a group or organization, or an institutional source. The audience may be one person, several, or many. Note that in using the terms communicator and audience we are emphasizing *primary* roles of participants in communication. In face-to-face communication transactions, such as two-person interaction and small group discussion, a single person may rapidly alternate in roles of communicator and communicatee and may almost simultaneously send and receive messages (verbal and nonverbal). The message may be oral or written, delivered face-to-face or presented through the mass media. The communicator's message and techniques also may have effects on the audience in addition to, or in spite of, the end sought. The entire communication transaction occurs within a *situation* of factors that call forth the communicator's efforts and circumscribe his appropriate choices. Perceived problems, the occasion for communicating, political and cultural norms, and the ideological climate of society are a few such situational factors. Other situational factors will be discussed in chapter 5. The communication attempt also occurs within an *ethical context* of value standards held by the audience, the communicator, and society at large.

What ethical standards should be used by communicator and communicatee in judging choices among communicative techniques, contents, and purposes? What should be the ethical responsibilities of a communicator in contemporary American society? Obviously, answers to these questions are ones we should face squarely. We should formulate meaningful ethical guidelines, not inflexible rules, for our communication behavior and for evaluating the communication of others.

The study of communication ethics should encompass both individual ethics and social ethics. What are the ethical virtues of character and the central ethical standards that should guide individual choices? What are the ethical standards and responsibilities that should guide the communication of organizations and institutions—public and private, corporate, governmental, or professional? For an ethically suspect communication practice, where should individual and collective responsibility be placed? The study of communication ethics should suggest standards both for individual daily and context-bound communication choices and also for institutional/systemic policies and practices.

We should consider the warning of Christina Hoff Sommers in her provocative essay, "Ethics Without Virtue." She condemns moral education as presented in most American universities today for addressing itself "not to the vices and virtues of individuals, but to the moral character of our nation's institutions." "Inevitably the student forms the idea," she argues, "that applying ethics to modern life is mainly a question of learning how to be for or against social and institutional policies. . . . In that sort of ethical climate, a student soon loses sight of himself as a moral agent and begins to see himself as a moral spectator or protojurist. . . . The result of identifying normative ethics with public policy is justification for and reinforcement of moral passivity in the student."[35]

One purpose of this book is to make us more discerning receivers and consumers of communication by encouraging ethical judgments of communication which are specifically focused and carefully considered. In making judgments of the ethics of our own communication and the communication to which we are exposed, our aim should be specific rather than vague assessments, and carefully considered rather than reflex-response, "gut level" reactions.

The following framework of questions is offered as a means of making more systematic and firmly grounded judgments of communication ethics.[36] At the same time we should bear in mind philosopher Stephen Toulmin's observation that "moral reasoning is so complex, and has to cover such a variety of types of situations, that no one logical test . . . can be expected to meet every case."[37] In underscoring the complexity of making ethical judgments, in *The Virtuous Journalist*, Klaidman and Beauchamp reject the "false premise that the world is a tidy place of truth and falsity, right and wrong, without the ragged edges of uncertainty and risk." Rather they argue: "Making moral judgments and handling moral dilemmas require the balancing of often ill-defined competing claims, usually in untidy circumstances."[38]

1. Can I *specify exactly* what ethical criteria, standards, or perspectives are being applied by me or others? What is the concrete grounding of the ethical judgment?
2. Can I justify the *reasonableness* and *relevancy* of these standards for this particular case? Why are these the most appropriate ethical criteria among the potential ones? Why do these take *priority* (at least temporarily) over other relevant ones?

3. Can I indicate clearly in what respects the communication being evaluated *succeeds or fails in measuring up* to the standards? What judgment is justified in this case about the *degree* of ethicality? Is the most appropriate judgment a specifically targeted and narrowly focused one rather than a broad, generalized, and encompassing one?
4. In this case to whom is *ethical responsibility owed*—to which individuals, groups, organizations, or professions? In what ways and to what extent? Which responsibilities take precedence over others? What is the communicator's responsibility to herself or himself and to society-at-large? Are the ones to whom primary responsibilities are owed the ones who most appropriately should decide the ethics of this case?
5. *How do I feel about myself* after this ethical choice? Can I continue to "live with myself" in good conscience? Would I want my parents or spouse to know of this choice?
6. Can the ethicality of this communication be justified as a *coherent reflection of the communicator's personal character*? To what degree is the choice ethically "out of character"?
7. If called upon *in public to justify* the ethics of my communication, how adequately could I do so? What generally accepted reasons or rationale could I appropriately offer?
8. *Are there precedents or similar previous cases* to which I can turn for ethical guidance? Are there significant aspects of this instance that set it apart from all others?
9. How thoroughly have *alternatives been explored* before settling on this particular choice? Might this choice be less ethical than some of the workable but hastily rejected or ignored alternatives? If the only avenue to successful achievement of the communicator's goal requires use of unethical communication techniques, is there a realistic choice (at least temporarily) of *refraining* from communication—of not communicating at all?

Throughout this book we present a variety of starting points and materials to aid in analyzing ethics in human communication. Certainly they are not to be viewed as the "last word" on the subject or as the only possible ones. Rather they should stimulate our thinking and encourage reflective judgment.

In chapters 2 through 6 we explore seven perspectives for ethical assessment of human communication. Each perspective represents a major ethical viewpoint or conceptual "lens" which scholars intentionally, and others often unknowingly, use to analyze specific issues and instances. As categories, these perspectives are not mutually exclusive of each other and they are not in any priority. These perspectives should not be taken as exhaustive of possible stances; probably each of us could think of others. For each perspective, the essential elements—the sources of grounding—for that general perspective are briefly explained. Examples—versions—of each perspective are then analyzed.

In chapter 7, we explore some fundamental ethical issues and problems facing us individually and collectively as communicators. Chapters 8 and 9 discuss standards which have been suggested specifically for interpersonal communication, small group discussion, and communication in organizations. Chapter 10 discusses the pros and cons of formal codes of ethics, together with examples of formal codes from advertising, public relations, and political communication. Chapter 11 surveys some contributions to communication ethics from feminist theory, and chapter 12 examines ethical standards and issues in intercultural and multicultural communication. In an appendix are reprinted essays in which one or more of the ethical perspectives in this book are reflected or applied. The extensive bibliography of Sources for Further Reading is categorized according to the chapters in the book, but it also contains a special section on ethics in mass communication.

Through examination of various perspectives, issues, problems, examples, and case studies, this book seeks to aid students and teachers of human communication. The goal is exploration of ethical responsibilities in contemporary communication—whether that communication is oral or written, whether it is labeled informative, persuasive, or rhetorical, whether it is labeled interpersonal, public, or mass.

Notes

[1] See, for example, Carl Wellman, *Morals and Ethics*, 2d ed. (Englewood Cliffs, NJ: Prentice-Hall, 1988), pp. xiii–xviii, 267.

[2] Milton Rokeach, *The Nature of Human Values* (New York: Macmillan/Free Press, 1973), pp. 13, 20; Richard L. Means, *The Ethical Imperative* (Garden City, NJ: Doubleday, 1969), p. 12.

[3] For one attempt to side-step ethical issues, see Theodore Levitt, "Are Advertising and Marketing Corrupting Society? It's Not Your Worry," *Advertising Age* (October 6, 1958): 89–92; a rebuttal to this position is Clyde Bedell, "To the Extent

Advertising and Marketing are Corrupting Society—You'd Better Worry!" *Advertising Age* (October 27, 1958): 101–2.

[4] Thomas R. Nilsen, *Ethics of Speech Communication*, 2nd ed. (Indianapolis: Bobbs-Merrill, 1974), p. 15.

[5] For elaboration of Kenneth Burke's view see his *The Philosophy of Literary Form* (New York: Vintage paperback, 1957), pp. 121–44; *Permanence and Change* (Indianapolis: Bobbs-Merrill paperback, 1965), pp. 175–78; *Language as Symbolic Action* (Berkeley: University of California Press, 1966), p. 45.

[6] Richard M. Weaver, "Language Is Sermonic," in *Contemporary Theories of Rhetoric: Selected Readings*, Richard L. Johannesen, ed. (New York: Harper and Row, 1971), especially pp. 175–79.

[7] David K. Berlo, *The Process of Communication* (New York: Holt, Rinehart and Winston, 1960), pp. 9, 12, 234.

[8] Bobby R. Patton and Kim Giffin, *Interpersonal Communication: Basic Text and Readings* (New York: Harper and Row, 1974), p. 313.

[9] Richard M. Weaver, *The Ethics of Rhetoric* (Chicago: Regnery, 1953), pp. 6, 24; Kenneth Burke, *The Rhetoric of Religion* (Boston: Beacon Press, 1961), pp. 41, 187.

[10] This explanation of the Golden Mean is indebted to Clifford G. Christians, Kim B. Rotzoll, and Mark Fackler, *Media Ethics: Cases and Moral Reasoning*, 2d ed. (New York: Longman, 1987), pp. 9–11. Also see Aristotle, *Nichomachean Ethics*, in *The Basic Works of Aristotle*, ed. Richard McKeon (New York: Random House, 1941), pp. 952–64 (1103a–1109b).

[11] Odell in John C. Merrill and S. Jack Odell, *Philosophy and Journalism* (New York: Longman, 1983), pp. 2, 95.

[12] Wellman, *Morals and Ethics*, 2d ed., p. 305.

[13] See, for example: Thomas I. Emerson, *The System of Freedom of Expression* (New York: Random House, 1970); Franklyn S. Haiman, *Speech and Law in a Free Society* (Chicago: University of Chicago Press, 1981); Thomas L. Tedford, *Freedom of Speech in the United States*, 2d ed. (New York: McGraw-Hill, 1993); Kent R. Middleton and Bill F. Chamberlin, *The Law of Public Communication*, 3rd ed. (New York: Longman, 1994).

[14] Thomas Szasz, *The Theology of Medicine* (Baton Rouge: Louisiana State University Press, 1977), p. xiii.

[15] William K. Rawlins, "Individual Responsibility in Relational Communication," in *Communication in Transition*, Mary S. Mander, ed. (New York: Praeger, 1983), p. 153; Ray Eldon Heibert, Donald F. Ungurait, and Thomas W. Bohn, *Mass Media IV* (New York: Longman, 1985), p. 611. Also see Thomas W. Cooper, et al., eds., *Communication Ethics and Global Change* (New York: Longman, 1989).

[16] John C. Merrill, *The Dialectic in Journalism: Toward a Responsible Use of Press Freedom* (Baton Rouge: Louisiana State University Press, 1989), pp. 10–11, 37–39, 197–202, 214.

[17] This discussion of responsibility is based on: J. Roland Pennock, "The Problem of Responsibility," in *Nomos III: Responsibility*, Carl J. Friedrich, ed. (New York: Liberal Arts Press, 1960), pp. 3–27; Ludwig Freund, "Responsibility—Definitions, Distinctions, and Applications in Various Contexts," in *Ibid.*, pp. 28–42; H. Richard Niebuhr, *The Responsible Self* (New York: Harper and Row, 1963), pp. 47–89, 151–54; Edmund L. Pincoffs, "On Being Responsible for What One Says," paper presented at Speech Communication Association convention, Houston, December 1975; Kurt Baier, "Responsibility and Freedom," in *Ethics and Society*, Richard T.

DeGeorge, ed. (Garden City, NY: Anchor Books, 1966), pp. 49–84. Also see Michael S. Pritchard, *On Becoming Responsible* (Lawrence: University Press of Kansas, 1991).

[18] Pincoffs, "On Being Responsible for What One Says."

[19] Dag Hammarskjöld, *Markings* (New York: Alfred A. Knopf, 1964), p. 112.

[20] Nicholas Rescher, *Dialectics: A Controversy-Oriented Approach to the Theory of Knowledge* (Albany: State University of New York Press, 1977), pp. 78–82; also see Glen H. Stamp and Mark L. Knapp, "The Construct of Intent in Interpersonal Communication," *Quarterly Journal of Speech*, 76 (August 1990): 282–99.

[21] John Sabini and Maury Silver, *Moralities of Everyday Life* (New York: Oxford University Press, 1982), pp. 65–66.

[22] Wayne C. Booth, *Modern Dogma and the Rhetoric of Assent* (Notre Dame: University of Notre Dame Press, 1974); also see Arnold M. Ludwig, *The Importance of Lying* (Springfield, IL: Charles C. Thomas, 1965), p. 227.

[23] Peter Drucker, *The Changing World of the Executive* (New York: Times Books, 1982), p. 249.

[24] Karen Lebacqz, *Professional Ethics* (Nashville: Abingdon Press, 1985), pp. 77–91; Steven Klaidman and Tom L. Beauchamp, *The Virtuous Journalist* (New York: Oxford University Press, 1987), pp. 17–20; Stanley Hauerwas, *Truthfulness and Tragedy* (Notre Dame: University of Notre Dame Press, 1977), pp. 20, 29.

[25] Richard DeGeorge, *Business Ethics*, 3rd ed. (New York: Macmillan, 1990), p. 94.

[26] Lebacqz, p. 83.

[27] Klaidman and Beauchamp, p. 17

[28] "Oliver North, Businessman? Many Bosses Say That He's Their Kind of Employee," *The Wall Street Journal*, July 14, 1987, Eastern Edition, sec. 2, p. 35.

[29] Paul Taylor, "Our People-Magazined Race for the Presidency," *Washington Post National Weekly Edition*, November 2, 1987, p. 23; also see Broder, "Latest departed candidate."

[30] Jonathan Alter, "The Search for Personal Flaws," *Newsweek*, October 19, 1987, p. 79.

[31] Walter R. Fisher, *Communication as Narration* (Columbia: University of South Carolina Press, 1987), pp. 47, 147–48. Also see Jody Palmour, *On Moral Character: A Practical guide to Aristotle's Virtues and Vices* (Washington, DC: Archon Institute for Leadership Development, 1987).

[32] Roderick P. Hart, Gustav W. Friedrich, and Barry Brummett, *Public Communication*, 2d ed. (New York: Harper and Row, 1983), pp. 13–15; Caroll Arnold, *Criticism of Oral Rhetoric* (Columbus, OH: Chas. E. Merrill, 1974), pp.38–43.

[33] Jeffrey Olen, *Ethics in Journalism* (Englewood Cliffs, NJ: Prentice-Hall, 1988), pp. 2–4; Warren Shibles, *Lying* (Whitewater, WI: Language Press, 1985), p. 145; Sissela Bok, *Lying* (New York: Vintage Books, 1979), pp. 32–33.

[34] For elaboration of this viewpoint see Olen, *Ethics in Journalism*, pp. 4–31, 79–80, 101–2; B. J. Diggs, "Persuasion and Ethics," *Quarterly Journal of Speech* 50 (December 1964), 359–73; Robert D. Murphy, *Mass Communication and Human Interaction* (Boston: Houghton Mifflin, 1977), pp. 81–104; Kathleen Hall Jamieson, *Dirty Politics* (New York: Oxford University Press, 1992), p. 59; James E. Porter, "The Role of Law, Politics, and Ethics in Corporate Composing: Toward a Practical Ethics for Professional Writing," in *Professional Communication*,

Nancy R. Blyler and Charlette Thralls, eds. (Newbury Park, CA: Sage, 1993), p. 134.

[35] Christina Hoff Sommers, "Ethics without Virtue: Moral Education in America," *The American Scholar*, 53 (Summer 1984), pp. 381–89. Also see Celeste Michelle Condit, "Crafting Virtue: The Rhetorical Construction of Public Morality," *Quarterly Journal of Speech*, 73 (February 1987), pp. 1–17; Christians, et al., *Media Ethics*, 2d ed., pp. 19–20; W. Lance Bennett, "Communication and Social Responsibility," *Quarterly Journal of Speech*, 71 (August 1985), pp. 259–88; Clifford G. Christians, "A Theory of Normative Technology," in *Technological Transformation: Contextual and Conceptual Implications* (Dordrecht: Kluwer Academic Publishers, 1981), pp. 123–39.

[36] For some of these questions I have freely adapted the discussions of H. Eugene Goodwin, *Groping for Ethics in Journalism*, 2d ed. (Ames: Iowa State University Press, 1987), pp. 14–15; Christians, et al., *Media Ethics*, 2d ed., pp. 17–20; C. Perelman and L. Olbrechts-Tyteca, *The New Rhetoric*, trans. John Wilkinson and Purcell Weaver (Notre Dame: University of Notre Dame Press, 1969), pp. 25, 483.

[37] Stephen Toulmin, *An Examination of the Place of Reason in Ethics* (England: Cambridge University Press, 1950), p. 148.

[38] Klaidman and Beauchamp, *The Virtuous Journalist*, p. 20.

Chapter 2

Political Perspectives

A political system (system of government) usually contains within its ideology an implicit and explicit set of values and procedures accepted as crucial to the health and growth of that governmental system. Once these essential political values are identified for a political system, they can be employed as criteria for evaluating the ethics of communicative means and ends within that particular system. The assumption is that communication should foster realization of these values and that communication techniques and tactics which retard, subvert, or circumvent these fundamental political values should be condemned as unethical.

As used here, the scope of the label "political perspective" ranges far beyond just the communication of presidents, politicians, political campaigns, or a particular political party. Any communication on public issues and public policy broadly defined, whether military, economic, social, or political, whether national, state, or local, could be assessed by one or more of the following political perspectives.

Naturally each different system of government could embody differing values leading to differing ethical judgments. Within the context of American representative democracy, for instance, various analysts pinpoint values and procedures they view as fundamental to optimum functioning of our political system and, thus, as values which can guide ethical scrutiny of communication therein.

Four Moralities

In proposing "An Ethical Basis of Communication," Karl Wallace develops a political perspective.[1] He isolates four values which he believes are basic to the welfare of our political system: respect, or belief in the dignity and worth of the individual; fairness, or belief in equality of opportunity; freedom coupled with responsible exercise of freedom; and belief in each person's ability to understand the nature of democracy. Citizens, to implement these values, should promote freedom of speech, press, and assembly, should encourage general diffusion of information necessary for decision making, and should insure width and diversity of public channels of communication. Wallace outlines four "moralities" or ethical guidelines rooted in these democratic values. These are statements of communication behavior necessary to foster the values.

First, we should develop the *habit of search* stemming from recognition that during the moments we are communicating we are the primary, if not the sole, source of arguments and information on the subject at hand. Our message should reflect thorough knowledge of our subject, sensitivity to relevant issues and implications, awareness of essential and trustworthy opinions and facts, and awareness that most public issues are complex rather than one-sided. As an individual test for this ethical guideline we could ask ourselves: Can I answer squarely, without evasion, any relevant question a hearer or reader might ask?

Second, we should cultivate the *habit of justice* by selecting and presenting fact and opinion fairly. The communicator, according to Wallace, should not distort or conceal data which his audience would need in justly evaluating his argument. The communicator should avoid substituting emotionally loaded language and guilt-by-association for sound argument. As a personal test we can ask: In the selection and presentation of my materials, am I giving my audience the opportunity of making fair judgments?

Third, communicators should habitually *prefer public to private motivations*. Responsible public communicators should uniformly reveal the sources of their information and opinion. We should assist our audience in weighing any special bias, prejudices, and self-centered motivations inherent in source material. As the test question we can ask: Have I concealed information about either my source materials or my own motives which, if revealed, would damage my case?

Finally, Wallace urges us to cultivate the *habit of respect for dissent* by allowing and encouraging diversity of argument and opinion. A communicator will seek cooperation and compromise where appropriate and justified by conscience. But Wallace feels we should not "sacrifice principle to compromise," and we should "prefer facing conflict to accepting appeasement." He offers as a test question: Can

I freely admit the force of opposing evidence and argument and still advocate a position which represents my convictions?

To aid our analysis of Wallace's ethical guidelines, we will suggest several questions. Where might points of ambiguity arise in application of these standards? To what extent are these four ethical standards actually observed by contemporary communicators, such as in political campaigning, advertising, and public relations? Wallace's guidelines seem designed primarily for scrutiny of public communication, such as a public speech, newspaper editorial, or political advertisement. To what degree are these "moralities" also appropriate for ethical assessment of private, interpersonal communication, such as an interview, problem-solving small group discussion, dormitory "bull session," or letter between friends? A good source to stimulate thought on this question is Ernest Bormann's examination of ethical implications of small group discussion in *Small Group Communication*. Bormann relies heavily on Wallace's insights and perspectives.[2]

Wallace also stresses consideration of both means and ends. He is concerned that we have exalted the end of success in communication over the means used to achieve it. Of special importance is his fear that communicators' unconcern for use of ethical techniques and appeals may undermine confidence by breeding distrust and suspicion. To what degree should we believe that the fostering of public confidence in the truthfulness of public communication is a necessary goal for our society?

Degree of Rationality

Franklyn Haiman offers one version of a "degree of rationality" political perspective for judging communication ethics. The fundamental democratic value upon which he bases his approach is enhancement of the human capacity to reason logically. He believes a prime necessity for the adequate functioning of our political system is encouragement of this human rational capacity. The ethical standard advocated by Haiman is the degree of rationality, the degree of conscious free choice, reflected in and promoted by any specific communication technique or appeal.[3]

Condemned as unethical in Haiman's view (particularly in political campaigning, governmental communication, and advertising) are techniques which influence the receiver "by short-circuiting his conscious thought processes and planting suggestions or exerting pressures on the periphery of his consciousness which are intended to produce automatic, non-reflective behavior." Haiman sees these techniques as unethical communicative approaches which attempt to circumvent the human "mind and reason in order to elicit non-reflective, semi-conscious, or unconscious responses." What are some examples from contemporary politics and advertising that probably would fail Haiman's suggested test for ethical communication?

Along with some critics, Haiman suspects the ethics of motivational and emotional appeal as a persuasive technique. But unlike some, he carefully attempts to describe conditions under which such appeals may be considered ethical. As a guide, Haiman suggests that "there is no more effective way in the long run" to motivate a person than to help him consciously focus on emotions, needs, values, and desires which are relevant to the issue at hand and "to show him, clearly and rationally, how he can best fulfill them." But as a basic principle he emphasizes "that to the extent that a persuader seeks to gain uncritical acceptance of his views, whatever extent that may be, he is in violation of democratic ideals."

We can consider several questions related to a political perspective such as Haiman's. Should we believe that emotional appeals are inherently unethical or that they should be judged in the context of how and why they are used? Do all emotional appeals short-circuit human logical reasoning processes? How easy is it to label an appeal as either logical or emotional? How might logical and emotional appeals be intertwined in one argument?

In two writings about a decade later than his initial formulations, Haiman modified his degree-of-rationality political perspective to take into account specific situational justifications for the ethical use of various techniques of the rhetoric of protest and confrontation.[4]

Another version of a degree-of-rationality political perspective comes from Arthur Kruger. That "people can think for themselves and govern themselves intelligently" are basic democratic values presumed by Kruger. From this assumption he derives a stringent standard for judging the ethics of persuasion: "A conclusion must be justified by relevant and sufficient evidence and . . . one who believes rationally tempers his acceptance of a conclusion in accordance with the kind of evidence offered to support it. If there is no evidence or if the evidence conflicts, he suspends judgment." Any persuasive technique which "by-passes or demeans reason" is unethical.[5]

Kruger is particularly severe in his ethical castigation of persuasion which relies on *pathos*, or appeals to emotions, motives, drives, and desires, and on appeals stemming from a persuader's *ethos*, or image of credibility with an audience. He does allow a precisely defined role for emotion. A communicator is ethical when demonstrating (through sound evidence and reasoning) a link between a reasonable proposal and fulfillment of relevant motives and values through that proposal. But his central ethical position is strict: "Persuasion by ethos or pathos either eliminates, obscures, distorts, or actually does violence to reason and hence by its very nature is incompatible with the rational ideal."

Pathos, or emotional appeal, is described by Kruger as "a form of suggestion that plays on hidden desires, frustrations, hostilities, and prejudices" and as an appeal "to basic wants, to the hate object or the love object, to prejudice." As a definition, how psychologically adequate is this description? How might a contemporary social psychologist define emotion?[6] Consider to what degree we should accept or reject Kruger's dictum: "Man must be taught to reflect, to analyze and evaluate, and to this end he must learn to check and control his emotions." With reference to advertising, for example, Samuel Smith contends that it is "not the primary function of advertising to educate or to develop the reasoning power."[7]

Significant Choice

In his book, *Ethics of Speech Communication*, and in several essays, Thomas Nilsen propounds an essentially political perspective for judging communication ethics.[8] Values essential to the optimum functioning of American democracy are the intrinsic worth of the human personality, reason as an instrument of individual and societal development, self-determination as the means to individual fulfillment, and human realization of individual potentialities. Necessary democratic procedures include unrestricted debate and discussion; varied forms of public address, parliamentary procedure, and legal procedure; freedom of inquiry, criticism, and choice; and publicly defined rules of evidence and tests of reasoning.

From this basis Nilsen develops ethical guidelines, not fixed criteria, for a view which he labels "significant choice." The ethical touchstone, he believes, should be "the degree of free, informed, and critical choice" which is fostered by communication on matters significant to us. Ethical communication techniques are those which foster significant choice.

> It is choice making that is voluntary, free from physical or mental coercion. It is choice based on the best information available when

the decision must be made. It includes knowledge of various alternatives and the possible long- and short-term consequences of each. It includes awareness of the motivations of those who want to influence, the values they serve, the goals they seek. Voluntary choice also means an awareness of the forces operating within ourselves.[9]

In public discourse, where relationships are relatively impersonal and the issues public, the good is served by communications that preserve and strengthen the processes of democracy, that provide adequate information, diversity of views, and knowledge of alternative choices and their possible consequences. It is served by communications that provide significant debate, applying rational thought to controversial issues, recognizing at the same time the importance and relevance of feeling and personal commitment. Further, the good is served by communications that foster freedom of expression and constructive criticism, that set an example of quality in speech content, in language usage, and in fair play and civility.[10]

The ethical issues are whether the information presented is the most relevant available and is as complete as the particular circumstances make feasible. Further, since selection of material is inevitable, it must be made clear to the listeners what principles of selection are operating, what biases or special interests characterize the speaker, and what purposes are being served by the information given. Definitions must be adequate; statistical units must be defined and the assumptions underlying their use made explicit. The listeners must not be led to believe that they are getting a more complete and accurate picture than they really are. In addition, the subject must be placed in the proper perspective as far as its individual and social importance is concerned. In brief, the speaker must provide for the listener as adequate a grasp of the truth of the situation as is reasonably possible under the circumstances.[11]

Nilsen uses this perspective of significant choice in one of his essays to evaluate the ethics of persuasive techniques employed by professional public relations and advertising men in political campaigns during the 1950s: (1) repetition of "issues" selected more for "impact value" than for inherent significance; (2) the emphasis on attack of the opposition; (3) a manufactured build up toward climax "which has nothing in particular to do with the importance of the issues"; (4) the "appeal beyond politics" to make issues and contests entertaining; (5) the "negative appeal" to arouse citizens *against* an imminent evil rather than *for* something; (6) minimal candidate exposure in public debates, forums, and interviews; (7) "endless repetition of the so-called issue and virtually crowding out competing ideas."

How many of these techniques still are typical of contemporary political campaigning? Should we view any of them as always unethical? In what ways do these techniques seem to violate the democratic values, procedures, and guidelines stressed by Nilsen? To what degree has the ethical level of political campaigning improved or deteriorated in recent years?

In discussing the ethical demands for telling the truth, Nilsen develops a position he terms "the truth of the situation." As a basic assumption, he holds that the "truth of discourse" never is absolute and always is a matter of degree. In communication, the *Truth* in some ultimate and absolute sense is not possible. Such an assumption seems similar to that of contemporary philosophers W. V. Quine and J. S. Ullian who urge our awareness "that we have less than the whole truth about even those matters we understand best. Such awareness can never be misplaced since 'the whole truth' about anything is but a fanciful ideal."[12]

"Although we can only reach an approximation of the truth," Nilsen contends, "this approximation should be as close as possible." For humans to communicate truthfully, some fundamental demands must be met: good intentions; ability to appraise evidence objectively and to employ rigorous reasoning; knowledge of facts, values, purposes and feelings; and, most important, exercise of disinterested good will.[13]

> Every utterance expresses a part of a vastly larger whole of possible meaning. What is relevant from the larger whole of meaning depends upon several things: the needs, desires, and expectations of the auditors; the purposes and value assumptions of both speaker and listeners; the attitudes, needs, and values of the larger community of which the speaker and listeners are a part; the alternatives open; the possible consequences of the various alternatives and the relationship of these consequences to the values of those concerned.[14]

> If a speaker is to tell the truth, he must attempt to arouse in the mind of his listeners as clear, accurate, and complete a picture or conception of his subject as possible. Since he cannot say all there is to say about it, he must select certain parts or aspects to describe; the aspects must be those which are relevant for the listeners—that is, those which will provide the information needed for informed and constructive response. Moreover, since purposes, values, and feelings have much to do with the meanings the speaker intends and the listeners receive, the speaker must make

clear his own values, purposes, and feelings, and adapt his discourse to compensate for the influence that the listeners' values and feelings will have on the meanings they discern in the words used. Again, the truth that needs to be told is determined by what the listeners need to know and feel in order to make the most informed, constructive response. At the level of human interaction truth and values are intertwined. The truth of discourse refers, not simply to empirically verifiable statements, but to a complex pattern of meanings relating a listener to some part of the world he experiences.[15]

Kathleen Hall Jamieson employs a type of significant-choice political perspective in her book, *Dirty Politics: Deception, Distraction, and Democracy*.[16] In her chapter on argument, engagement, and accountability in political discourse, she posits two preconditions for citizens to make adequate ethical judgments about political communication: "the time to consider options and with it the ability of a conscious agent to grant informed consent." She believes: "In two centuries of political speech we have developed norms for appropriate discourse and additionally some sense of the ideal to which it should aspire." Ethical political argument, Jamieson contends, should allow differing sides to be heard, should be scrutinized for accuracy, relevance, and fairness of evidence, should not distort evidence from its context, should allow a right of reply for persons attacked, should grant the integrity and goodwill of opponents, should assume that advocates must take responsibility for their claims, should avoid name-calling, guilt by association, and other personalized attacks, and should strive toward consensus as much as possible.

Ground Rules for Political Controversy

Sidney Hook presents a framework for evaluating the ethics of public communication on societal controversies, including political campaign persuasion and the rhetoric of protest.[17] Rooted in the values of our democratic society, his political perspective condemns as unethical communication techniques which "tend to poison instead of refreshen" the life blood of that system. Such techniques, Hook feels, characteristically aim, not at establishing the truth or making a case, but merely at discrediting persons. He questions the ethics of communication tactics which suppress relevant evidence, which foster refusal to listen to opposing views, and which fanatically make the holding of a particular idea synonymous with patriotism.

What might be an instance where a method questioned by Hook would be ethically justifiable? What might be an example where the issue is the qualifications and competency of a person? What might be conditions under which it would be ethical to suppress relevant evidence?

Hook elaborates ten "ground rules" or ethical guidelines for scrutinizing communication on controversial public issues. In abbreviated form they are as follows:

1. Nothing and no one is immune from criticism.
2. Anyone involved in a controversy has an intellectual responsibility to inform himself of the available facts.
3. Criticism should be directed first at policies, and against persons only when they are responsible for policies, and against their motives or against their purposes only when there is some independent evidence of their character, not derived from the consequences of their policies.
4. Because certain words are legally permissible, they are not therefore morally permissible.
5. Before impugning an opponent's motives, even when they legitimately may be impugned, answer his arguments.
6. Do not treat an opponent of a policy as if he were therefore a personal enemy of the country or a concealed enemy of democracy.
7. Since a good cause may be defended by bad arguments, after answering those bad or invalid arguments, present positive evidence in behalf of your own position, or for your own alternatives.
8. Do not hesitate to admit lack of knowledge or to suspend judgment if the evidence is not decisive either way.
9. Only in pure logic and mathematics and not in human affairs can you demonstrate that something is impossible. Because something is logically possible, it is not therefore probable. The phrase "it is not impossible" really is a preface to an irrelevant statement about human affairs. In human affairs, especially in politics, the question always is one of the balance of probabilities. The evidence of probabilities must include more than abstract possibilities.
10. When we are looking for truth of fact or wisdom of policy, the cardinal sin is refusal to discuss, or the taking of action that blocks discussion, especially when it takes the form of violence.

Consider the following questions as aids in your assessment of Hook's ground rules. In what ways do you agree or disagree with his suggested standards? To what extent, for example, should the axiom "nothing and no one is immune from criticism" apply to criticism of a president's foreign policy in time of declared war? In what ways did the communication tactics of specific Establishment spokesmen and radical protesters during 1964–70 violate the tenth standard? What ethical justification, if any, might there be for communication techniques which block discussion?

Hook urges that ethical standards for judging societal controversy be enforced not by law but by voluntary self-discipline. To what degree do you feel that the ethics of public communication can or should be enforced by law? Examine the adequacy and/or necessity of such legal enforcement of ethics as regulations governing advertising set by the Federal Trade Commission and the Federal Communications Commission.

Democratic Debate as a Procedural Ethic

Dennis G. Day does not base his political perspective on any particular set of substantive values which are goals essential to our democratic system. Rather his ultimate democratic value, and hence his basic ethical standard, is a procedural one.[18] He believes that our democratic political philosophy does not specify the nature (values sought) of the Good Life; instead it provides a procedural framework within which each person may strive to actualize his individual conception of that life. Debate as "the confrontation of opposing ideas and beliefs for the purpose of decision" is the fundamental procedure. "Democracy is a commitment to means, not ends," says Day. "Democratic society accepts certain ends, i. e., decisions, because they have been arrived at by democratic means."[19]

From this procedural value stems the primary ethical standard for judging public communication within our political system: promotion of "full confrontation of opposing opinions, arguments, and information relevant to a decision." In what ways do you agree or disagree with Day's suggested ethical view? To what degree can or should such a view be enforced by law? To what extent should his standard apply to public communication in nonpolitical fields such as religion, advertising, public relations, and education?

Day accepts as compatible with his view the four "moralities" proposed by Karl Wallace (discussed earlier in this chapter). In what ways does Wallace's perspective seem to harmonize or conflict with Day's perspective? In contrast, Day questions the adequacy of Edward Rogge's situational perspective (to be discussed in chapter 5) and of Franklyn Haiman's "degree of rationality" approach (discussed earlier in this chapter). Day argues, for instance, that the "ethics of democratic discourse do not allow a prejudgment of the reasonableness of discourse as a condition of its expression." He elaborates:

> The ethics of democratic discourse require a commitment to debate, not a commitment to reason. In practice, the appeal to reason often proves to be the most effective technique in debate, and thus we tend to think of debate as "reasoned discourse." But the essential feature of debate is the confrontation of ideas. We may have appeals to reason without having debate, and we may have debate without appeals to reason.[20]

A Synthesis of Textbook Standards

Traditional American textbook discussions of the ethics of persuasion, communication, and argument often include lists of standards suggested for evaluating the ethicality of an instance of persuasion. Such criteria sometimes are rooted, implicitly if not explicitly, in what we earlier in this chapter described as a type of political perspective. That is, the criteria stem from a commitment to values and procedures deemed essential to the health and growth of the American political-governmental system of representative democracy.

What follows is my synthesis and adaptation of a number of such typical traditional lists of ethical criteria for persuasion.[21] Within the context of our own society, the following criteria are not necessarily the only or best ones possible; they are suggested as general guidelines rather than inflexible rules; and they may stimulate discussion on the complexity of judging the ethics of communication. Consider, for example, under what circumstances there may be justifiable exceptions to some of these criteria. How might other cultures and other governmental systems embrace basic values that lead to quite different standards for communication ethics? Also bear in mind that one difficulty in applying these criteria in concrete situations stems from different standards and meanings people may have for such key terms as: distort, falsify, rational, reasonable, conceal, misrepresent, irrelevant, and deceive.

1. Do not use false, fabricated, misrepresented, distorted, or irrelevant evidence to support arguments or claims.
2. Do not intentionally use unsupported, misleading, or illogical reasoning.
3. Do not represent yourself as informed or as an "expert" on a subject when you are not.
4. Do not use irrelevant appeals to divert attention or scrutiny from the issue at hand. Among the appeals that commonly serve such a purpose are: "smear" attacks on an opponent's character; appeals to hatred and bigotry; derogatory insinuations—innuendos; God and Devil terms that cause intense but unreflective positive or negative reactions.
5. Do not ask your audience to link your idea or proposal to emotion-laden values, motives, or goals to which it actually is not related.
6. Do not deceive your audience by concealing your real purpose, by concealing self-interest, by concealing the group you represent, or by concealing your position as an advocate of a viewpoint.
7. Do not distort, hide, or misrepresent the number, scope, intensity, or undesirable features of consequences or effects.
8. Do not use "emotional appeals" that lack a supporting basis of evidence or reasoning, or that would not be accepted if the audience had time and opportunity to examine the subject themselves.
9. Do not over-simplify complex, gradation-laden situations into simplistic two-valued, either-or, polar views or choices.
10. Do not pretend certainty where tentativeness and degrees of probability would be more accurate.
11. Do not advocate something in which you do not believe yourself.

Ethical Standards for Governmental Communication

Directly or indirectly, daily we are exposed to governmental communication in various forms. The president appeals on national television for public support of a domestic economic program or of a diplomatic treaty. A federal official publicly condemns the efforts of a social protest movement as a threat to national security. A government bureaucrat announces a new regulation and presents reasons to justify it. A federal official contends that information requested by a citizen-action group cannot be revealed for national security reasons. A state governor defends a proposed tax increase.

What ethical criteria should we apply to assess the many forms of governmental communication? Obviously the various political perspectives discussed in this chapter could be used to evaluate such communication. And other perspectives or sets of criteria yet to be presented in this book might have application. Here I will summarize two sets of criteria that you may find especially useful and appropriate as you evaluate governmental communication.

Some guidelines for assessing the ethical responsibility of governmental communication have been suggested by Dennis Gouran.[22]

1. The deliberate falsification of information released to the public, especially under circumstances involving the general welfare, is inappropriate and irresponsible.
2. The classification of government documents for the purpose of deceiving or otherwise keeping the public uninformed on matters affecting private citizens' well-being is inappropriate and irresponsible.
3. The deliberate use of official news sources for the purpose of obscuring embarrassing and deceitful governmental acts is inappropriate and irresponsible.
4. Criticism of the press for the purpose of assuring that governmental acts are viewed only in favorable terms is inappropriate and irresponsible.
5. Deliberate attempts by governmental agents to suppress or otherwise interfere with an individual's legitimate exercise of free expression within the limits defined by our courts are inappropriate and irresponsible.
6. Overt and covert governmental acts designed to misrepresent a political candidate's, or any other citizen's, character or position or to violate said individual's rights are inappropriate and irresponsible.
7. Language employed by governmental figures for the purpose of deliberately obscuring the activity or idea it represents is inappropriate and irresponsible.

A series of principles to govern statements by public officials that might stifle citizen dissent and protest have been developed and applied by Ted Finan and Stewart Macaulay. They view these principles as moral or ethical (rather than legal) obligations for government officials when publicly commenting on citizen social protest efforts.[23]

1. Statements are improper when they encourage citizens to retaliate against protestors by ostracizing them, denying them jobs, physically attacking them, etc.
2. Care should be taken to avoid misstatements since they impede rational understanding and decision.
3. Comments should be justified by reliable data and sound reasoning. Statements should not be asserted as certain when they merely are probable or possible. "Statements should contain whatever qualifications are required to make them accurate."
4. Criticism of dissent should be coupled "with a reminder that protest and dissent are a vital part of the American tradition."
5. A statement should not be made when the "risks of suppressing dissent or inciting violence" are too great when balanced against the purpose of the statement.

Public Confidence in Truthfulness of Public Communication

Whether the public communication takes the form of messages from government to governed, political candidate to voter, news media to citizen, or advertiser to consumer, at least a minimal degree of mutual confidence and trust is desirable. Yet now we witness a crisis in public confidence in truthfulness of public communication. By truthfulness as used here we do not mean an ultimate, absolutely certain truth. We are speaking of public confidence in reliable information in the form of accurate data and highly probable conclusions. Such public confidence generally is viewed as a value or goal integral to the optimum functioning of American representative democracy, but it is a goal being less and less attained.

Democratic decision making through vigorous public debate and responsible functioning of our economic system assume maximum access to accurate and trustworthy information. Strong democratic processes, for example, are rooted in adequacy of information, diversity of viewpoints, and knowledge of potential strengths, weaknesses, and effects of alternative choices. These requisites for responsible communication in our political system have been stressed by several of the "political perspectives" already examined.

Weakening of public trust in communication from the government, political candidates, news media, and advertisers is evident. Citizens today complain more and more of "managed news" and a "credibility gap" in communication from the federal government. Statements made by the federal government as factual and dependable on one occasion have a way of becoming "inoperative" on a later occasion. Citizens tend to dismiss as untrue, without analysis, much governmental communication. During political campaigns voters also dismiss many speeches and political advertisements, often characterized by gross hyperbole, as "mere campaign oratory." They have so little confidence in campaign persuasion that they feel a substantial portion of it is not worthy of careful scrutiny.

What are some of the actual and potential consequences flowing from weakened public confidence in truthfulness of public communication? Sincere human communication is thwarted and democratic decision-making processes are hampered. Alienation from the "system" and polarization of attitudes increase. Distrust and suspicion poison a widening variety of human communication relationships. Observed J. Michael Sproule in 1980:[24]

> . . . When people are misled they distrust the sources that have deceived them. If the majority of a society's information sources behave without concern for honest communication, then all communication is weakened. Trust in sources is a necessary condition for verbal communication. Insofar as this trust is lost, language itself is undermined. Without willingness to believe on the part of the receiver, the source's language loses its integrity, and people become divided and alienated.

In *Presidential Secrecy and Deception*, John Orman describes some of the societal instability resulting from weakened public confidence.

> When trust within the political system decreases, support for the regime also decreases; therefore widespread presidential lying can weaken the foundations of a stable political system. Moreover, presidential lying interferes with accountability because citizens cannot be sure when the president is stating his or her views and accomplishments accurately, and thus the citizens have a difficult time determining whether they hold the president accountable.

Orman also notes, however, some persons argue that the expectations of our political system "assume that a fair amount of deception will occur" and that "it is only when deception becomes blatant, chronic, and coercive that the norms of democratic practice are violated." At length in his book, Orman argues that "presidential deception is one of the prime characteristics of the modern presidency" and that it has, indeed, become "blatant, chronic, and coercive."[25]

Humbuggery and Manipulation is F. G. Bailey's analysis of the art of leadership—primarily political leadership. One of Bailey's main arguments is that "no leader can survive as a leader without deceiving others (followers no less than opponents) and without deliberately doing to others what he would prefer not having done to himself." Bailey summarizes his view:

> Leaders are not the virtuous people they claim to be: they put politics before statesmanship; they distort facts and oversimplify issues; they promise what no one could deliver; and they are liars. But I have also insisted that leaders, if they are to be effective, have no choice in the matter. They could not be virtuous (in the sense of morally excellent) and be leaders at the same time. I do not mean that a leader should necessarily behave immorally. . . . I mean only that he must have the imagination (and—a paradox—the moral courage) to set himself above and beyond established values and beliefs if it is necessary to do so to attain his ends.

To what degree do you accept Bailey's viewpoint? You may want to read his book to determine whether he believes that leaders must lie and deceive routinely or only occasionally.[26] From his viewpoint, Bailey seems to describe not only what *is* but also what *ought to be* the case for effective leadership. Why might you agree with the former but not the latter?

We should combat the growing assumption, by us or by others, that most public communication *inherently* is untrustworthy. We should reject as detrimentally cynical the premise of nationally known newsman, I. F. Stone, that "every government is run by liars and nothing they say should be believed."[27] Just because a communication is of a certain type or comes from a certain source (government, candidate, news media, advertiser), it must not be rejected *automatically, without evaluation*, as tainted or untruthful. Nevertheless, today there is a tendency, for example, "to disbelieve the government even when it is telling the truth."[28]

Clearly, always we should exercise caution in acceptance and care in evaluation. Using the best evidence available to us, we should reach a reflective judgment of a message. But to condemn a message as untruthful *solely* because it stems from a suspect source and *before directly* assessing it is to exhibit decision-making behavior detrimental to our political system. In another context, philosopher Henry Johnstone, Jr., reminds us, "It is rational to *consider* whether one has been taken in; it is irrational to conclude automatically in all cases that one *has* been."[29] Rejection of the message, if such be our judgment, should come *after*, not before, our understanding and evaluation of it. As with a defendant in a courtroom, an instance of public communication should be presumed ethically innocent until we, or experts we acknowledge, have proven it guilty.

Some Other Political Systems

Other political systems to some extent espouse fundamental values differing from those central to representative democracy. Thus, they may present different frames of reference for assessing the ethics of communication within that system and may view as ethical techniques which we judge unethical.

In Germany, under Hitler's Nazi influence, the ends of national survival and National Socialism justified any persuasive means.[30] The soundness of political persuasion was measured, not by objective truth, but solely by effectiveness of results. Nazi persuasion frequently reflected either-or oversimplification, inconsistency, questionable premises, faulty analogies, innuendo, and appeals to power, fear, and hate. Joseph Goebbels, the Minister of Propaganda, felt that lies were useful when they could not be disproved and that the source of propaganda should be concealed when revelation might risk failure. Hitler's own oratory, not bounded by logic, plausibility or accuracy, reveals lies, slander, verbal smokescreens to conceal intent, and scapegoat counterattacks. Immediately we recognize that some of these communication tactics characterize public discourse on the contemporary American political scene. These tactics are not generally accepted as ethical in the context of our political values.

Communism in the former Union of Soviet Socialist Republics (USSR) espoused values which gave a special ethical slant to communication techniques and purposes within Soviet society.[31] Values propagated include supreme love of nation, trust in the Party, hatred toward enemies specified by the Party, and promotion of class strife. A communicator need not be impartial and display an objective concern for events. He may, for example, define terms to suit his purposes rather than the facts and he may introduce spurious or irrelevant issues. In the Soviet communist perspective, words were tools to achieve Party approved ends, not means to communicate in the search for truth. Communist ethical standards for judging communication flowed from and were subordinated to the interest of the class struggle as formulated by the Party.

In most communication situations in the kingdom of Burundi in Central Africa, practical and esthetic values take precedence over logical criteria. If they work, lies, distortion, evasion, and irrelevant emotional appeals are ethical. Anthropologist Ethel Albert describes the Burundi political perspective as follows:

> Reliance upon appeals to the emotions as the chief technique of rhetoric is taken for granted as right. . . . There are no reservations about the desirability of flattery, untruths, taking advantage of weakness of character or profiting from others' misfortune. Whatever works is good, and esthetic-emotive values are higher in the hierarchy than moral or logical principles in speech and other behavior.[32],,

The approach to communication ethics of the Burundi society seems to be somewhat similar to those of any preindustrial societies. "In preindustrial societies honorifics, taboos, propriety, and ritual are more important controls over what is said than is any formal criterion of logic or empirical observation."[33] Lest we believe that the concern for ethical communication judged by an objective truth standard characteristic of American representative democracy is duplicated in most other political systems, we should realize that our standard represents a minority viewpoint. Ithiel de Sola Pool concludes: "Fairness, however, compels us to note that a greater concern for the consequences of statements than for their correspondence to some criterion of objective truth has characterized not only modern totalitarians, but most human societies. The democratic liberal tradition is the unusual one in this respect, not the totalitarian one."[34]

Notes

[1] Karl R. Wallace, "An Ethical Basis of Communication," *The Speech Teacher* 4 (January 1955): 1–9.

[2] Ernest G. Bormann, *Small Group Communication: Theory and Practice*, 3rd ed. (New York: Harper and Row, 1990), chapter 11.

[3] Franklyn S. Haiman develops his "degree of rationality" political perspective in two sources: "Democratic Ethics and the Hidden Persuaders," *Quarterly Journal of Speech* 44 (December 1958): 385–92; "A Re-Examination of the Ethics of Persuasion," *Central States Speech Journal* 3 (March 1952): 4–9.

[4] Franklyn S. Haiman, "The Rhetoric of the Streets: Some Legal and Ethical Considerations," *Quarterly Journal of Speech* 52 (April 1967): 99–114. "The Rhetoric of 1968: A Farewell to Rational Discourse," reprinted in Richard L. Johannesen, *Ethics in Human Communication*, 2d ed. (Prospect Heights. IL: Waveland Press, 1983), pp. 177–90.

[5] Arthur N. Kruger, "The Ethics of Persuasion: A Re-Examination," *The Speech Teacher* 16 (November 1967): 295–305. Also see Kruger, "Debate and Speech Communication." *Southern Speech Communication Journal* 39 (Spring 1974): 233–40.

[6] For an article taking direct issue with several of Kruger's basic assumptions and definitions, see Alfred A. Funk, "Logical and Emotional Proofs: A Counter-View," *The Speech Teacher* 17 (September 1968): 210–17. Concerning the appropriateness of dichotomizing between rational and emotional appeals see Gary Cronkhite, *Persuasion: Speech and Behavioral Change* (Indianapolis: Bobbs-Merrill, 1969), chapter 4.

[7] Samuel V. Smith, "Advertising in Perspective," in *Ethics and Standards in American Business*, Joseph W. Towle, ed. (Boston: Houghton Mifflin, 1965), pp. 174–75.

[8] Thomas R. Nilsen's viewpoint of "significant choice" is elaborated in his *Ethics of Speech Communication*, 2d ed. (Indianapolis: Bobbs-Merrill, 1974); "Free Speech, Persuasion and the Democratic Process," *Quarterly Journal of Speech* 44 (October 1958): 235–43; "Ethics and Argument," in *Perspectives on Argument* Gerald R. Miller and Thomas R. Nilsen, eds. (Chicago: Scott, Foresman, 1966), pp. 176–97; "The Ethics of Persuasion and the Marketplace of Ideas Concept," in *The Ethics of Controversy: Politics and Protest*, Donn W. Parson and Wil Linkugel, eds. (Lawrence, KS: The House of Usher, 1968), pp. 7–49.

[9] Nilsen, *Ethics of Speech Communication*, p. 45.

[10] *Ibid.*, p. 18.

[11] *Ibid.*, p. 72.

[12] W. V. Quine and J. S. Ullian, *The Web of Belief* (New York: Random House, 1970), p. 90.

[13] Nilsen, *Ethics of Speech Communication*, ch. 2.

[14] *Ibid.*, p. 34.

[15] *Ibid*, p. 27.

[16] Kathleen Hall Jamieson, *Dirty Politics: Deception, Distraction, and Democracy* (New York: Oxford University Press, 1992), pp. 203–36.

[17] Sidney Hook, "The Ethics of Political Controversy," in *The Ethics of Controversy*, Parson and Linkugel. eds., pp. 50–71. For a much briefer earlier version see Hook, "The Ethics of Controversy," *The New Leader* (February 1, 1954), pp. 12–14. This 1954 version is reprinted in Hook, *Philosophy and Public Policy* (Carbondale: Southern Illinois University Press, 1980), pp. 117–23.

[18] Day specifically rejects the applicability as ethical criteria for communication of the eight democratic values advocated by Ralph T. Eubanks and Virgil L. Baker in their article, "Toward an Axiology of Rhetoric," *Quarterly Journal of Speech* 47 (April 1962): 157–68.

[19] Dennis G. Day, "The Ethics of Democratic Debate," *Central States Speech Journal* 17 (February 1966): 5–14.

[20] *Ibid*, pp. 9–10.

[21] For example, see: E. Christian Buehler and Wil A. Linkugel, *Speech Communication for the Contemporary Student*, 3rd ed. (New York: Harper and Row, 1975), pp. 30–36; Robert T. Oliver, *The Psychology of Persuasive Speech*, 2d ed. (New York: Longmans, Green, 1957). pp. 20–34; Wayne Minnick, *The Art of Persuasion*, 2d ed. (Boston: Houghton Mifflin, 1968), pp. 278–87; Henry Ewbank

and J. Jeffery Auer, *Discussion and Debate*, 2d ed. (New York: Appleton-Century-Crofts, 1951). pp. 255–58; Bert E. Bradley, *Fundamentals of Speech Communication*, 5th ed. (Dubuque, IA: William C. Brown Co., 1988), pp. 23–31; Robert C. Jeffrey and Owen Peterson, *Speech: A Text With Adapted Readings*, 3rd ed. (New York: Harper and Row, 1980), ch. 1.

[22] A detailed discussion of these guidelines is in Dennis Gouran, "Guidelines for the Analysis of Responsibility in Governmental Communication," in *Teaching About Doublespeak*, Daniel Dieterich, ed. (Urbana, IL: National Council of Teachers of English, 1976), pp. 20–31. Also see W. J. Cody and Richardson R. Lynn, *Honest Government: An Ethics Guide for Public Service* (Westport, CT: Praeger, 1992).

[23] Ted Finan and Stewart Macaulay, "Freedom of Dissent: The Vietnam Protests and the Words of Public Officials," *Wisconsin Law Review*, V. 1966 (Summer 1966): 632–723, espec. 677, 695–97.

[24] J. Michael Sproule, *Argument* (New York: McGraw-Hill, 1980), p 282.

[25] John M. Orman, *Presidential Secrecy and Deception: Beyond the Power to Persuade* (Westport, CT: Greenwood Press, 1980), pp. 4–7.

[26] F. G. Bailey, *Humbuggery and Manipulation: The Art of Leadership* (Ithaca, NY: Cornell University Press, 1988), pp. ix–xiii, 2, 7, 10, 168–75.

[27] Reported in *Newsweek*, November 19, 1973, p. 139B.

[28] David Wise, *The Politics of Lying: Government Deception, Secrecy, and Power* (New York: Random House, 1973), p. 345.

[29] Henry W. Johnstone. Jr., "Rationality and Rhetoric in Philosophy," *Quarterly Journal of Speech* 59 (December 1973): 387. Thomas M. Frank and Edward Weisband emphasize: "Among reasonable men it is customary and, indeed, necessary to presume that a person means what he says. Where this presumption fails, the resultant loss of credibility shuts the disbelieved individual off from normal social intercourse and leads him and those with whom he deals to miscalculations and chaos. So, too, when a state speaks." *Word Politics: Verbal Strategy Among the Superpowers* (New York: Oxford University Press, 1971), pp. 120–21.

[30] Adolf Hitler, *Mein Kampf*, trans. Ralph Manheim (Boston: Houghton Mifflin, 1943), pp. 80–81, 106–7, 177–79, 231–32, 342; Z. A. B. Zeman, *Nazi Propaganda* (London: Oxford University Press, 1964), pp. 25–26, 37, 86; Ernest K. Bramstead, *Goebbels and National Socialist Propaganda* (East Lansing: Michigan State University Press, 1965), pp. 56, 174, 193–95, 455–57; Ross Scanlan, "Adolf Hitler and the Technique of Mass Brainwashing," in *The Rhetorical Idiom*, Donald Bryant, ed. (Ithaca. NY: Cornell University Press, 1958). pp. 201–20; Haig Bosmajian, "Nazi Persuasion and the Crowd Mentality," *Western Speech* 29 (Spring 1965): 68–78; Leonard W. Doob, "Goebbels' Principles of Propaganda." *Public Opinion Quarterly* 14 (1950): 419–42; Adolf Hitler, *My New Order*, ed. with commentary by Raoul de Roussy de Sales (New York: Reynal and Hitchcock, 1941), pp. xiv, 7–9.

[31] Jack H. Butler, "Russian Rhetoric: A Discipline Manipulated by Communism," *Quarterly Journal of Speech* 50 (October 1964): 229–39; Robert T. Oliver, *Culture and Communication* (Springfield, IL: Charles C. Thomas, 1962), pp. 88, 104; Alex Inkeles, *Public Opinion in Soviet Russia: A Study in Mass Persuasion* (Cambridge: Harvard University Press, 1962), pp. 6, 22–25, 123, 317–20, 325–27, 337–38; Stefan Possony, *Wordsmanship: Semantics as a Communist Weapon* (Washington, DC: U.S. Government Printing Office, 1961), pp. 2, 14–15; Ithiel de Sola Pool, "Communication in Totalitarian Societies," in Pool, et al., eds., *Handbook of Communication* (Chicago: Rand-McNally, 1973), pp 466–68; Paul Kecskemeti, "Propaganda," in

Handbook of Communication, pp. 849–50; V.M. Tepljuk, "The Soviet Union: Professional Responsibility in Mass Media," in *Communication Ethics and Global Change*, Thomas W. Cooper, et al., eds. (New York: Longman, 1989), pp. 109–23. Also see Richard DeGeorge, *Soviet Ethics and Morality* (Ann Arbor: University of Michigan Press, 1969).

[32] Ethel M. Albert, "'Rhetoric,' 'Logic,' and 'Poetics' in Burundi: Culture Patterning of Speech Behavior," *American Anthropologist*, Special Issue 66, Part 2 (December 1964): 35–54.

[33] Pool, "Communication in Totalitarian Societies," p. 467.

[34] *Ibid*, p. 467.

Chapter 3

Human Nature Perspectives

Human nature perspectives, as considered here, focus on the *essence* of human nature. Answers are sought to the question: What makes a human essentially human? Unique characteristics of human nature which set humans apart from animals are identified. Such characteristics then can be employed as standards for judging the ethics of human communication. The assumption is that uniquely human attributes should be enhanced, thereby promoting fulfillment of maximum individual potential. A determination could be made of the degree to which a communicator's appeals and techniques either foster or undermine the development of a fundamental human characteristic. In light of such criteria, a technique which *de*humanizes, makes a person less than human, is unethical.

Any particular characteristically human attribute could be used in a largely absolute way to assess the ethics of communication regardless of situation, culture, religion, or governmental form. In taking such an absolutist view it could be argued that a human is essentially human no matter the context. Wherever found, a person might be assumed to possess the uniquely human attribute(s) worthy of nurture. Christopher Lyle Johnstone observes that a difficulty in most human nature "approaches to communication ethics is that they are inclined to concentrate upon only one aspect of human nature (e.g. reason, symbolism, persuadability, etc.) at the expense of other equally essential aspects (e.g. imagination, the capacity for humor, curiosity, etc.)."[1]

Skepticism concerning the use of human nature as a basis for ethical norms comes from philosopher Kai Nielsen: "Even if we were to find certain characteristics that all humans, and only humans, possess this of itself would not establish anything of a normative nature; it would not follow that it would be a good thing to have that yearning satisfied. We often 'yearn' for what is not good. . . . It may be that we ought to try to develop potentialities not yet distinctive of the human animal."[2]

Human Rational Capacity

Aristotle's view of human nature, as interpreted and applied by Lawrence Flynn, provides one perspective for evaluating the ethics of communication.[3] Aristotle, according to Flynn, emphasized the capacity for reason as a uniquely human attribute. (Note that the stress on reason here is related more to human nature than to the values central to any particular political system, such as in Haiman's "degree of rationality" approach examined in chapter 2.) A truly human act, from Aristotle's viewpoint, stems from a rational person who is conscious of what he or she does and freely chooses to do it. The ethics of communication are judged by the interrelated criteria of (1) communicator intent, (2) nature of the means employed, and (3) accompanying circumstances as these three factors combine to enhance or undermine human rationality and choice-making ability. While Aristotle apparently held some human actions to be unethical inherently, other human behaviors depend for their ethicality on the above mentioned criteria. But Aristotle did reject the notion that the end justifies the means when the means is unethical. Thus, a worthy end or intent would not justify the use of unethical communicative means.

A much more recent interpretation of Aristotle's ethical standards for rhetoric is provided by Robert Rowland and Deanna Womack.[4] Their analysis of Aristotle's *Rhetoric*, *Nicomachean Ethics*, and *Politics* leads them to refute as partial and oversimplified the view that Aristotle advocated use only of rational appeals and condemned as unethical any use of emotional or nonlogical appeals. Also they question the interpretation that claims Aristotle took a stance wherein achievement of effect was paramount and any emotional appeals that might promote success were approved.

According to Rowland and Womack, Aristotle did assume that the capacity for rationality is a defining characteristic of humans and thus a necessary part of rhetoric. But Aristotle also recognized the emotional nature of humans and believed that emotional appeal is necessary to motivate humans to good actions. Logic by itself normally will not energize people to act. Emotional appeal by itself risks becoming extreme in intensity, thus undercutting the role of reason. Especially ethically suspect are appeals to our "vegetative appetites" such as sex and hunger. In contrast, other emotions, such as fear or anger, involve cognitive, reflective, responses to situations and thus are more susceptible to the influence of reason. Both reason and emotion can be used unethically. Deceptive practices, whether logical or emotional, are unethical for Aristotle because, in Rowland and Womack's words, "reason cannot function without accurate information."

As an art or theory of discovering all available means of persuasion for a given situation, rhetoric is morally neutral in Aristotle's view. But as application or practice, rhetoric becomes in varying degrees either ethical or unethical. In Rowland and Womack's interpretation of Aristotle, ethical rhetoric as practice represents a mean or balance between the extremes of pure logic and of irrational appeals to our animal instincts, to nonreflective emotional states, or to harmful passions. Their interpretation would seem to point toward an Aristotelian ethic for rhetoric summarized as follows: The sound, relevant, integrated use of both reason and emotion in the service of practical wisdom and the general public good.

Several writers on the ethics of advertising suggest the applicability of perspectives rooted in the human rational capacity. Thomas Garrett argues that a person becomes more truly human in proportion as his or her behavior becomes more conscious and reflective.[5] Because of the human capacity for reason and because of the equally distinctive fact of human dependence on other people for development of potential, Garrett suggests there are several ethical obligations. As humans we are obliged, among other things, to behave rationally ourselves, to help others behave rationally, and to provide truthful information. Suggestive advertising, in Garrett's view, is that which seeks to bypass human powers of reason or to some degree render them inoperative. Such advertising is unethical not just because it uses emotional appeal, feels Garrett, but because it demeans a fundamental human attribute and makes people less than human.

Clarence Walton observes that some critics employ a philosophical model of man which identifies three components of human nature as vital elements to be considered in evaluating the ethics of marketing practices: (1) human capability for rational judgment; (2) human capacity for exercising free options among defined alternatives; and (3) human motivation to serve primarily selfish interests or interests of others.[6] Advertising and marketing tactics could be judged, according to this framework, by the degree to which they undermine the human capacity for rational decision, constrict free choice among alternatives, and foster largely selfish interests.

Should perspectives stressing human rational capacity be applied in judging the ethics of advertising and public relations? Why or why not? What are some examples of advertisements or sales approaches which clearly seem to be ethical (or unethical) when evaluated by this perspective?

Human Symbol-Using Capacity

In a tentative, probing spirit, Henry Wieman and Otis Walter offer another human nature perspective for scrutinizing communication ethics. They find the "unique nature of the human being" rooted in "two complicated and interlocking processes which generate all capacities that we call 'human'. . ."[7] In these capacities, they contend, "should lie the ultimate standard of ethics" for assessing human communication.

One fundamentally human attribute, according to Wieman and Walter, is the symbol-using capacity. This capacity, some might say compulsion, to transform the raw data of sensory experience into symbols is viewed as uniquely human. Not only can we convert immediate sensory data into symbols, we also can use symbols to refer to other symbols (such as conceptions of goals, values, ideals) and to pass on accumulated knowledge and insight from one generation to another. This power of symbolization, believe Wieman and Walter, is responsible for the genesis and continued growth of the human personality and for the creative works of humanity.

A second peculiarly human quality, and one which provides a principle to guide our ethical use of symbols, is the "unique need of human beings for other human beings." This need, labeled by Wieman and Walter as "appreciative understanding," is more than the gregariousness of animals. It stimulates development of the "mind" and "self" as human conceptions. Fulfillment of the need for mutual appreciative understanding does not mean, they note, approval of everything someone else does or says. "One cannot, however, justly disapprove anything until after one has first achieved an understanding of it."

The ethical standard advocated by Wieman and Walter is clear: communication is ethical to the degree that it enhances human symbol-using capacity, fulfills the need for mutual appreciative understanding, and promotes mutuality of control and influence. Such communication requires, in part, valid and honest evidence and reasoning along with solutions which are of most benefit to humanity. To what extent can their suggested standard be functionally and unambiguously applied? What might be some examples of communication which would be ethical by this standard but which would be condemned as unethical by criteria and perspectives outlined elsewhere in this book?

Various contemporary scholars share the assumption of Wieman and Walter that the capacity to use symbols is a uniquely human trait. In her *Philosophy in a New Key*, Susanne Langer argues that "symbolism is the recognized key to that mental life which is characteristically human and above the level of sheer animality." She believes that the basic "need of symbolization, . . . which other creatures probably do not have," is obvious in humans, functions continuously, and is the fundamental process of the human mind.[8]

Kenneth Burke, in *Language as Symbolic Action*, makes the human symbol-using capacity the foundation of his definition of man: "Man is the symbol-using (symbol-making, symbol-misusing) animal, inventor of the negative (or moralized by the negative), separated from his natural condition by instruments of his own making, goaded by the spirit of hierarchy (or moved by the sense of order), and rotten with perfection." In another book Burke asserts that the function of rhetoric is to induce "cooperation in beings that by nature respond to symbols."[9] In *Philosophy of Rhetoric*, I. A. Richards assumes that language is "no mere signalling system. . . . It is the instrument of all our distinctively human development, of everything in which we go beyond the other animals."[10]

Evidence is accumulating, however, based on research with chimpanzees and gorillas who have learned non-oral languages (such as gestural sign language used by the deaf), that *symbol generation and utilization*, as opposed to rote learning of signals, *may not be* a solely human ability. The status of the debate on this issue remains unresolved. The evidence and research methods of studies showing that chimpanzees essentially have a humanlike symbolic capacity have been both vigorously attacked and stoutly defended. If the capacity for symbol using eventually is proven to be a characteristic which humans share to a significant degree with at least some other animals, what might be the implications of continuing to use it as a standard for assessing the ethics of human communication? Because its uniqueness is diminished, should it play a very minimal role in evaluation of communication ethics?[11] Because some animals seem to share this important and creative ability, should we broaden our concern for ethical communication to include such animals?[12]

Theodore Levitt uses a human nature position to *defend* advertising techniques often viewed by others as ethically suspect. While admitting that the line between distortion and falsehood is difficult to establish, his central argument is that "embellishment and distortion are among advertising's legitimate and socially desirable purposes; and that illegitimacy in advertising consists only of falsification with larcenous intent." Levitt grounds his defense in a "pervasive, . . . *universal*, characteristic of human nature—the human audience *demands* symbolic interpretation of everything it sees and knows. If it doesn't get it, it will return a verdict of 'no interest.'" Because Levitt sees humans essentially as symbolizers, as converters of raw sensory experience through symbolic interpretation to satisfy needs, he can justify "legitimate" embellishment and distortion. He contends:

> Many of the so-called distortions of advertising, product design, and packaging may be viewed as a paradigm of the many responses that man makes to the conditions of survival in the environment. Without distortion, embellishment, and elaboration, life would be drab, dull, anguished, and at its existential worst.[13]

Kant's Categorical Imperative

To better understand several of the following versions of a human nature perspective, a brief discussion of Immanuel Kant's Categorical Imperative is in order.[14] An eighteenth-century German philosopher, Kant believed that the uniquely human capacity was a sense of conscience (moral will, moral reason). To varying degrees, in Kant's view, all humans possess a sense of right and wrong; universal moral law as apprehended by conscience must be obeyed by all rational beings. Moral imperatives inherent in human nature are categorical—without conditions, exceptions, or extenuating circumstances. A lie, for example, always is unethical. Moral imperatives are right in themselves, not because of their consequences. Kant's is a deontological or duty-bound ethic.

As touchstones to guide ethical behavior, Kant presented two forms of his Categorical Imperative. First: "Act only on that maxim which you can at the same time will to become a universal law." We must ask ourselves, is the ethical principle which I am using to justify my choice a principle that I would want everyone to follow in similar situations? Is the ethical standard that I am following in a particular case one which I would agree should apply to everyone? Second: "Always act so that you treat humanity, whether in your own person or in another, as an end, and never merely as a means." Humans must not be treated simply or solely as things (means to an end), but always also as persons worthy of dignity and respect in themselves.

Reason and Language

An analysis of Bertrand Russell's philosophy by Donald Torrence indicates that Russell adopts a human nature perspective in suggesting ethical standards for human communication.[15] While Russell admits that humans are animals with passions and impulses, Russell also contends that humans possess certain characteristics which in degree are distinctively human. One uniquely human trait is the capacity for reason based on intelligence and imagination. Rational behavior, in Russell's view, involves belief based on sound evidence; nonrational behavior (not necessarily irrational behavior) involves belief rooted in desires and without a foundation of evidence. A second uniquely human trait, according to Russell, is the ability to use language. "We may say. . . . without exaggeration, that language is a human prerogative, and probably the chief habit in which we are superior to 'dumb' animals."[16]

With these ontological premises as a background, Torrence extracts from Russell's philosophy the major ethical guidelines Russell would apply to the human use of language to influence other humans. Russell contends: First, an advocate never should state or imply that the proposition advocated embodies the absolute truth. Opinions and beliefs should be held tentatively rather than dogmatically and always "with a consciousness that new evidence may at any moment lead to their abandonment."[17] Second, if a proposition is subject to scientific proof, to proof by evidence and reasoning, then appeals to desire and emotion should be avoided in seeking its acceptance. Third, if a proposition is not subject to proof by evidence and reasoning, then appeals to emotion and desire are acceptable and necessary. In using such appeals, as in all human behavior, "The supreme moral rule should, therefore, be: *Act so as to produce harmonious rather than discordant desires.*"[18] Communication should promote social cooperation rather than conflict. Finally, Russell would deem persuasion emphasizing one rather than multiple sides of an issue to be ethical. But he also would urge promotion of opportunities for all sides of a controversy to be heard.

Humans as Persuaders

"What is distinctively human at the most fundamental level is the capacity to persuade and be persuaded." Assuming this basic premise, contemporary philosopher Henry W. Johnstone, Jr., develops an ethic for rhetoric (persuasion).[19] Other specifications of the essence of human nature (language-using, political, rational, etc.), Johnstone believes, presuppose the capacity for persuasion. He also believes that what is distinctively human ought to be fostered and perpetuated. Johnstone wants to locate an ethic for rhetoric in the rhetorical process itself. He wants to avoid evaluating the ethics of persuasion by standards external to persuasion, standards derived from the surrounding culture, religion, or political system.

As the foundation of his ethic for rhetoric, Johnstone offers his Basic Imperative: "So act in each instance as to encourage, rather than suppress, the capacity to persuade and be persuaded, whether the capacity in question is yours or another's." Responsible rhetoric is a self-perpetuating rhetoric. People should not employ persuasion to block or foreclose persuasive responses on the part of others. Sullen obedience, inarticulate anger, and refusal to continue listening are examples of such blocking tactics. Tactics like these are "dehumanizing and immoral" because they break the chain of persuasion.

The most ethically responsible rhetoric, in Johnstone's view, is that which addresses others "with love." The spirit of love in persuasion, he believes, means that we are not motivated primarily by selfish personal interests. Instead, when persuading "with love" we respect the truth, respect the other persons participating, and respect those participants' need to know the truth.

Flowing from his Basic Imperative, Johnstone presents duties to ourselves and to others. These duties are ethical standards for assessing an instance of persuasion. Toward ourselves we have the duties of resoluteness and openness. *Resoluteness* means that I must not agree with or give in to the arguments or appeals of others in an unthinking, uncritical, automatic fashion. I must advocate my own position and use my own capacities for persuasion to assess propositions urged by others. *Openness* means I must listen carefully to ideas others present and must not be impassive, self-centered, or simply turn a deaf ear. Toward others we have the duties of gentleness and compassion. *Gentleness* means that I must address others through persuasion rather than violence, either physical violence or symbolic coercive violence. *Compassion* means that I must listen to others more for the sake of their own welfare and interests than for the sake of my own interests.

Communicative Competence and the Ideal Speech Situation

The German philosopher and social critic, Jürgen Habermas, is working toward a comprehensive theory of "communicative competence." How language, as a distinctively human capacity, functions to foster mutual understanding, shared knowledge, mutual trust, and interpersonal relationships is a major focus of his theory. The details of his complex theory, and various shortcomings of it, can be examined in several secondary sources.[20] But for our purposes, two central concepts of his theory of communicative competence have potential as standards for ethical communication. You are urged to consider to what degree these two views might appropriately function as ethical guides.[21]

Habermas identifies four assumptions that underlie all normal human communication. For everyday communication to function smoothly and without question, each participant must assume that the communication of other participants meets these four expectations. While any particular utterance may stress only one expectation, all four assumptions are present to some degree. First, participants assume that all statements made are capable of being comprehended; statements are in a grammatical and semantical form capable of being understood by others. Second, participants assume that the statements are true representations of existing, agreed-upon, factual states of affairs. Third, participants assume that statements sincerely and accurately reflect the actual intentions of others. Fourth, participants assume that statements are appropriate; that is, they are in harmony with relevant shared social values and rules. Could we, then, adapt Habermas and suggest that ethical communication aiming at mutual understanding and trust must meet the tests of comprehensibility, truth, sincerity, and appropriateness?

Habermas also outlines four constituent elements of what he terms the "ideal speech situation," the system where communication is free from (or minimally subject to) constraints and distortions. For both private and public communication, the ideal speech situation can be approximated when four requirements are met. First, participants must have equal opportunity to initiate and continue communicative acts. Second, participants must have equal opportunity to present arguments, explanations, interpretations, and justifications; no significant opinions should go unexamined. Third, participants must have equal opportunity to honestly express personal intentions, feelings, and attitudes. Fourth, participants must have equal opportunity to present directive statements that forbid, permit, command, etc. In an attempt to adapt Habermas's view, we could explore how adequately these four elements of the ideal speech situation might serve as ethical standards for communication.

In *Moral Consciousness and Communicative Action*, Habermas emphasizes the fundamental ethical principles of justice and solidarity.[22] Justice requires equal respect and equal rights for individuals while solidarity demands "empathy and concern for the well-being of one's neighbor." These principles are rooted in the fact that humans are unique in the social and communicative construction of their "selves." At another point Habermas cites Thomas McCarthy's revision of Kant's Categorical Imperative as fitting the theory of communicative action: "Rather than ascribing as valid to all others any maxim that I will to be a universal law, I must submit my maxim to all others for purposes of discursively testing its claims to universality. The emphasis shifts from what each can will without contradiction to be a universal law, to what all can will in agreement to be a universal norm." In Seyla Benhabib's words, the "core idea behind communicative ethics" is the "generation of reasonable agreement about moral principles via an open-ended moral conversation."

An Existentialist Ethic for Communication

An analysis by Karlyn Campbell of the axiological assumptions (values and ethics) basic to the philosophy of Jean-Paul Sartre reveals a human nature framework for assessing communication ethics.[23] Sartre assumes that the capacity to use language is peculiarly human. This is the ability to employ symbols to name or interact with sensory reality, to define and negate, and to abstract or transcend. Human symbol use should promote formation of groups which lessen the isolation of individuals, increase their range of behavior, engage them in decision making, and capitalize upon their unique capacities.

Within Sartre's existentialist philosophy, according to Campbell, are explicit ethical principles applicable in judging human behavior generally and communication specifically.[24] The highest good is "authenticity" and communication which fosters its achievement. Since there is no *a priori* truth or predetermined human nature to function as justification for action, the authentic person admits that complete certainty is impossible, that decisions are more tentative than final, and that no act or policy is ever wholly satisfactory. The authentic human sees life as a process demanding constant action, choice, and revision. The fact that all persons have the capacity, in any situation, to act, choose, and change should be publicly proclaimed. Other people, in light of these responsibilities, should be treated not as objects to be moved or managed, but as subjects capable of decision and action.

Based on her own extensive analysis of Sartre's views on the functions of language in communication, Barbara Warnick summarizes Sartrean ethical guidelines to judge any act of communication.[25] Guided by the spirit of generosity, a communicator will foster situations in which audiences can arrive at their own choices; the communicator functions as a catalyst or facilitator for choice making. Sartre would, believes Warnick, judge a communication act through such questions as: (1) Does the discourse primarily serve the communicator's self-interest and selfish cause, or does it primarily foster the audience's freedom? (2) Does the message explore and expand alternatives, or does it narrow and eliminate them? (3) Is the communicator's purpose to pose problems or to provide solutions? (4) Is the communicator dogmatically committed to or overly ego-involved in the message, or has he or she withdrawn sufficiently to facilitate the audience's participation and response?

An Epistemic Ethic

Epistemology is the study of the origin, nature, methods, and limits of human knowledge. If rhetoric is viewed broadly as intentional human attempts to influence through symbols, one traditional conception of rhetoric's function is to describe it as transmitting or utilizing knowledge (facts, reality) previously discovered or derived through other processes (science, religion, philosophy). According to this view, reality exists "out there" completely independent of humans. Reality simply is waiting to be discovered and transmitted by humans as facts in a completely neutral, objective manner, or as raw material to achieve a persuasive purpose.

In contrast, some contemporary scholars of rhetoric develop a conception of *rhetoric as epistemic, rhetoric as generative of knowledge*.[26] They are exploring the extent to which rhetoric functions to *construct* or *create* reality. According to this view, the only meaningful reality for humans is a symbolically, rhetorically, constructed reality. Humans *in interaction* with their environment (empirical phenomena, concepts, other humans) *give or create* the significance and meaning of the sensations they experience. Some scholars even describe the doing of science as a process of symbolically constructing reality. Richard Gregg summarizes the "rhetoric as epistemic" viewpoint in its most inclusive sense: "All areas of knowledge are human symbolic constructs guided by various human purposes in light of various needs. There are some areas, of course, where objectives or procedures are more clearly defined or agreed upon than others, or where there can be clearly established authoritative bodies which legitimate knowledge claims."[27]

Although he acknowledges a number of useful conceptions of rhetoric, Barry Brummett believes that in a fundamental sense rhetoric best is viewed as "advocacy of realities." He asserts a significant ethical implication of such a stance. Thus, rhetoric in process is doubly ethical: it is the result of a choice on the part of the rhetor as to the reality advocated and the method of doing so, and it urges choice rather than complete and necessary acceptance on the part of the audience. Truth which is rhetorically made encourages choice and awareness of alternative realities.[28]

Robert Scott argues that one unique capacity of humans is their ability to *generate or create* knowledge *in and during* the actual process of communication (Scott uses the term rhetoric as equivalent to persuasion.) Communication, he believes, is not *solely* the *transmission* of knowledge somehow previously established or of prior immutable truth. Truth is contingent and derives from communication interaction in the form of cooperative inquiry. He explains: "Insofar as we can say that there is truth in human affairs, it is in time; it can be the result of a process of interaction at a given moment. Thus rhetoric may be viewed not as a matter of giving effectiveness to truth but of creating truth."[29]

While the rhetoric-as-epistemic view admits no *a priori* knowledge, or no reality completely independent of humans, Scott does not believe that this particular type of relativism necessitates abandonment of ethical and logical standards. "Relativism, supposedly, means a standardless society, or at least a maze of differing standards, and thus a cacophony of disparate, and likely selfish, interests. Rather than a standardless society, which is the same as saying no society at all, relativism indicates circumstances in which standards have to be established cooperatively and renewed repeatedly."[30]

From these assumptions about a uniquely human capacity, Scott derives three ethical guidelines for judging communication. First, we should tolerate divergence of viewpoints and the right of others to self-expression. We spoil our own potentiality for *knowing*, says Scott, if we fail to respect the integrity of the expression of others. Second, we should consciously strive toward maximum participation in the communication transaction at hand. "Inaction, the failure to take on the burden of participating in the development of contingent truth," Scott believes, "ought to be considered ethical failure." Third, in our own communication we should strive to achieve good consequences. But also we should accept responsibility for all undesired and undesirable consequences of our communication so far as they can be known.

How adequate are Scott's suggested ethical guidelines as criteria for assessing both interpersonal and public communication? How easily could they be applied in concrete situations? Note that Scott's first guideline is one also proposed in some of the political perspectives examined in chapter 2, specifically those of Wallace, Nilsen, and Day. This commonality illustrates again, as with the rationality criterion, that a specific ethical standard may become associated with several ethical perspectives. In fact, Scott's second ethical guideline is one also associated with "presentness" as a characteristic of the dialogical perspective to be discussed in chapter 4.

Human Capacity for Value Judgment

The capacity to create and sustain values and to apply them in rendering value judgments is seen by Ralph Eubanks as the central characteristic of human nature.[31] Our "essential nature" is that of the "valuing creature." Humans strive to fulfill their personalities through the values they advocate and embody. For Eubanks, to live as a human being "is to choose between better and worse on the basis of values." Such beliefs lead Eubanks "inexorably" to a human nature perspective on symbolic behavior.

What ethical standards for communication behavior stem from this viewpoint? First, Eubanks endorses the second form of Immanuel Kant's Categorical Imperative: "Act so as to treat humanity, whether in your own person or that of another, always as an end and never as a means only."[32] Second, to promote the "primacy of the person" in our communication transactions, we should adhere to the "civilizing values" of *health, creativity, wisdom, love, freedom with justice, courage,* and *order.*

Third, in our communication we should respect the imperative of *civility.* In our verbal and nonverbal symbolic behavior, we should exemplify the so-called "dialogical" attitudes of genuineness, directness, nonpossessive warmth, and so forth. (This dialogical stance will be explained at length in the following chapter). Civility requires that we avoid communication practices that "violate the intrinsic worth" of other people, practices such as deception, verbal obscenity, and irrelevant attacks on an opponent's character.

Fourth, the "ethical demand of *veracity*, or truthfulness," is crucial. Through communication we not only transmit established knowledge, but we also create or construct knowledge. Eubanks favorably cites the "epistemic ethic" proposed by Robert Scott (and previously explained in this chapter). A "major affront to human dignity" Eubanks believes, would be the violation of the "very process by which wisdom is transmitted and knowledge generated. . . ." Hiding the truth, falsifying evidence, or using faulty reasoning are among the tactics condemned as unethical.

A Humanistic Ethic for Rhetoric

The "commitment to the idea that humanness is good—that human nature has worth," is the starting point for Christopher Lyle Johnstone's "humane ethic" for rhetoric.[33] Such a commitment assumes that we should seek out, nurture, and actualize the multiple essential elements of human nature. Our choices of communication means and ends can be assessed for ethicality, in general, by the degree to which they humanize or dehumanize us. By "rhetorical" Johnstone means "those dimensions of discourse that function to induce judgment or provoke decision," those communicative elements that influence a receiver's "coming-to-judgment." Rhetoric offers "grounds for legitimate choice" by combining feeling, imagining, inference making, and value judgment. Johnstone, too, sees rhetoric as having an epistemic function, a function of generating reliable knowledge in and through the rhetorical process. Human nature flowers at its fullest not in isolation but in relationship and interaction with the environment and other humans.

Based on these fundamental assumptions, Johnstone develops a humanistic ethical stance applicable to rhetoric. He describes a "general sense" of the obligations of such an ethic.

> To be *humane* suggests that one's conduct is guided by a respect for and a tenderness toward others' beings. It suggests a prizing of these beings and a desire to protect and nourish them. In the first instance, therefore, a humanist ethic requires that the individual be responsive in his or her actions to the impact they might

have on the humanity of those affected by the act. It demands, finally, that one conduct oneself so as to maximize opportunities for cultivating in oneself and in others an awareness and appreciation of humanness.

As an ethical orientation appropriate for evaluating the "attitudes" of participants in communication, Johnstone endorses the "dialogical" stance that we will explore in the following chapter. Such a spirit of dialogue is characterized in part by such qualities as mutuality, open-heartedness, directness, spontaneity, honesty, lack of pretense, nonmanipulative intent, and loving responsibility of one human for another.

What ethical guidelines does Johnstone offer to assess the ethicality of the "content" of rhetoric? How should we assess the ethics of the evidence, reasoning, and appeals we use to justify the choices we advocate? Humane rhetoric should include in its arguments "an analysis of the human foundations of the values argued from." "A humanizing argument," he believes, "will articulate the fundamental commitments upon which it draws. . . ." Concludes Johnstone:

> The "good reasons" upon which choice can be made, therefore, will articulate, clarify, and affirm those human features that are most to be valued: our resourcefulness, our capacity for loving, our receptiveness to and inclination toward beauty, our emotional resilience and range of sensitivities, our capacities for foresight and self-control, our imagination, our curiosity, our capacity for wonder, our powers of passionate attachment, to name but a few. These are features that humanists have always embraced. These are among the characteristics of human nature that must be known and prized if we are to live humane lives.

Notes

[1] Christopher Lyle Johnstone, "Ethics, Wisdom, and the Mission of Contemporary Rhetoric: The Realization of Human Being," *Central States Speech Journal*, 32 (Fall 1981): 180, n. 12.

[2] Kai Nielsen, "On Taking Human Nature as the Basis for Morality," *Social Research*, 29 (Summer 1962): 157–77.

[3] Lawrence J. Flynn, S.J., "The Aristotelian Basis for the Ethics of Speaking," *The Speech Teacher*, 6 (September 1957): 179–87.

[4] Robert C. Rowland and Deanna Womack, "Aristotle's View of Ethical Rhetoric," *Rhetoric Society Quarterly*, XV (Winter-Spring, 1985): 13–32.

[5] Thomas M. Garrett, S.J., *An Introduction to Some Ethical Problems of Modern American Advertising* (Rome: The Gregorian University Press, 1961), pp. 39–47.

[6] Clarence C. Walton, "Ethical Theory, Societal Expectations and Marketing Practices," in *Speaking of Advertising*, John S. Wright and Daniel S. Warner, eds. (New York: McGraw-Hill, 1963), pp. 359–373.

[7] Henry N. Wieman and Otis M. Walter, "Toward an Analysis of Ethics for Rhetoric," *Quarterly Journal of Speech* 43 (October 1957): 266–70. For another version see Otis M. Walter and Robert L. Scott, *Thinking and Speaking*, 4th ed. (New York: Macmillan, 1979), pp. 235–39. For an application to mass media ethics, see Jerry Harvill, "Oikonomia: The Journalist as Steward," *Journal of Mass Media Ethics*, 3, no. 1, (1988): 65–76.

[8] Susanne Langer, *Philosophy in a New Key* (New York: New American Library Mentor Book, 1948), pp. 34, 45.

[9] Kenneth Burke, *Language as Symbolic Action* (Berkeley: University of California Press, 1966), pp. 3–22; Burke, *A Rhetoric of Motives* (New York: Prentice-Hall, 1950), p. 43.

[10] I. A. Richards, *The Philosophy of Rhetoric* (New York: Oxford University Press Galaxy Book, 1965), p. 131.

[11] For analyses, including ones denying that chimpanzees have demonstrated a human capacity for symbol use, see: Charlton Laird, "A Nonhuman Being Can Learn Language," *College Composition and Communication*, 23 (May 1972): 142–54; Eugene Linden, *Apes, Men, and Language* (New York: *Saturday Review*/Dutton, 1974); "Symposium on Language and Communication," in *The Great Ideas Today 1975* (Chicago: Encyclopaedia Britannica, 1975), pp. 6–100; Fred C. C. Peng, ed., *Sign Language and Language Acquisition in Man and Ape* (Boulder, CO: Westview Press, 1978); Geoffrey Bourne, ed., *Progress in Ape Research* (New York: Academic Press, 1977); Thomas Sebeok and Jean Umiker-Sebeok, eds., *Speaking of Apes: A Critical Anthology of Two-Way Communication with Man* (Bloomington: Indiana University Press, 1980); Linda Haupe and Meridith Richards, "Defining Man Through Language: A Theoretical and Historical Perspective," *Pavlovian Journal of Biological Science*, 14 (October-December 1979): 234–42; Thomas A. Sebeok and Robert Rosenthal, eds., *The Clever Hans Phenomenon: Communication With Horses, Whales, Apes, and People* (New York: New York Academy of Sciences, 1981), pp. 26–129; David Premack, *Gavangi! Or the Future History of the Animal Language Controversy* (Cambridge, MA: MIT Press, 1986). A relevant theory developed by Frank E. X. Dance is that the capacity for spoken language, not symbolism in general or language in general, is the uniquely human attribute. Dance, "A Speech Theory of Human Communication," in Dance, ed., *Human Communication Theory: Comparative Essays* (New York: Harper & Row, 1982), pp. 120–46.

[12] Social scientists R. Harré and P. F. Secord take this latter position. *The Explanation of Social Behavior* (Totowa, NJ: Littlefield, Adams and Co., 1973), p. 96.

[13] Theodore Levitt, "The Morality (?) of Advertising," *Harvard Business Review* (July-August 1972): 84–92. Reprinted in Lee Thayer, et al., eds., *Ethics, Morality, and the Media* (New York: Hastings House, 1980), pp. 184–96.

[14] This discussion is based upon Radoslav A. Tsanoff, *Ethics*, Rev. Ed. (NY: Harper & Row, 1955), pp. 107, 167–68; Brendan E. A. Liddell, *Kant on the Foundation of Morality* (Bloomington: Indiana University Press, 1970), pp. 42–49, 119–20, 133, 155–57, 200, 227, 247; Clifford G. Christians, Kim B. Rotzoll, and Mark Fackler, *Media Ethics*, 2d. ed., (New York: Longman, 1987), pp. 11–12.

[15] Donald L. Torrence, "A Philosophy for Rhetoric from Bertrand Russell," *Quarterly Journal of Speech* 45 (April 1959): 153–65.

[16] Bertrand Russell, *An Outline of Philosophy* (London: G. Allen and Unwin, 1927), p. 47.
[17] Bertrand Russell, *Unpopular Essays* (New York: Simon and Schuster, 1950), p. 15.
[18] Russell, *Outline of Philosophy*, p. 242.
[19] Henry W. Johnstone, Jr., "Toward an Ethics for Rhetoric," *Communication*, 6, no. 2 (1981): 305–14. Also see Johnstone, *Validity and Rhetoric in Philosophical Argument* (University Park, PA: Dialogue Press of Man and the World, 1978), pp. 41–43, 84–85, 133; Molly Wertheimer, "Johnstone's Versions of Rhetoric," *Dimensions of Argument*, eds. George Ziegelmueller and Jack Rhodes (Annandale. VA: Speech Communication Association, 1981), pp. 865–74; Johnstone, Jr., "Bilaterality in Argument and Communication," in *Advances in Argumentation Theory and Research*, eds. J. Robert Cox and Charles A. Willard (Carbondale: Southern Illinois University Press, 1982), pp. 95–103.
[20] See, for example, Thomas McCarthy, *The Critical Theory of Jürgen Habermas* (Cambridge, MD: MIT Press, 1978); Jane Braaten, *Habermas's Critical Theory of Society* (New York: State University of New York press, 1991); Larry J. Ray, *Rethinking Critical Theory* (Newbury Park, CA: Sage, 1993).
[21] The sources drawn upon for the following descriptions are: Jürgen Habermas, *Communication and the Evolution of Society*, trans. Thomas McCarthy (Boston: Beacon Press, 1979), ch. 1; Thomas McCarthy, "Translator's Introduction," in Jürgen Habermas, *Legitimation Crisis* (Boston: Beacon Press, 1975), pp. vii–xxiv; Brant R. Burleson and Susan L. Kline, "Habermas's Theory of Communication: A Critical Explication," *Quarterly Journal of Speech* 65 (December 1979): 412–28; Thomas Farrell, "The Ideality of Meaning of Argument: A Revision of Habermas," in *Dimensions of Argument*, Ziegelmueller and Rhodes, eds., pp. 905–26; Susan L. Kline, "The Ideal Speech Situation: A Discussion of Its Presuppositions," in *Ibid.*, pp. 927–39. Also see Habermas, *Legitimation Crisis*, pp. 95, 120; Ronald Beiner, *Political Judgment* (Chicago: University of Chicago Press, 1983), pp. 25–30; J. Torpey, "Ethics and Critical Theory: From Horkheimer to Habermas," *Telos*, 69 (Fall 1986): 68–84.
[22] Jürgen Habermas, *Moral Consciousness and Communicative Action*, trans. Christian Lenhardt and Shierry Weber Nicholson (Cambridge, MA: MIT Press, 1990), pp. 56–67, 200. Also see Seyla Benhabib and Fred Dallmayr, eds., *The Communicative Ethics Controversy* (Cambridge, MA: Mit press, 1990), espec. p. 345; Kenneth Baynes, "Communicative Ethics, the Public Sphere, and Communication Media," *Critical Studies in Mass Communication*, 11 (December 1994): 315–26; Niels Thomassen, *Communicative Ethics in Theory and Practice* (New York: St. Martin's Press, 1992).
[23] Karlyn Kohrs Campbell, "The Rhetorical Implications of the Axiology of Jean-Paul Sartre," *Western Speech* 35 (Summer 1971): 155–61.
[24] See, for example, Jean-Paul Sartre, "Existentialism Is a Humanism," in Walter Kaufman, ed., *Existentialism from Dostoyevsky to Sartre* (Gloucester: Peter Smith, 1956), pp. 287–311. Also see Linda A. Bell, *Sartre's Ethics of Authenticity* (Tuscaloosa: University of Alabama Press, 1989).
[25] Barbara Warnick, "Jean-Paul Sartre: The Functions of Language in Rhetorical Interaction," Ph.D. dissertation, University of Michigan. 1977, pp. 57–91.
[26] Richard B. Gregg, "Rhetoric and Knowing: The Search for Perspective," *Central States Speech Journal*, 32 (Fall 1981): 133–44; C. Jack Orr, "How Shall We Say:

'Reality Is Socially Constructed Through Communication?'" *Central States Speech Journal*, 29 (Winter 1978): 263–74; Michael C. Leff, "In Search of Ariadne's Thread: A Review of the Recent Literature on Rhetorical Theory," *Central States Speech Journal*, 29 (Summer 1978): 73–91; Walter Weimer, "Science as a Rhetorical Transaction," *Philosophy and Rhetoric*, 10 (Winter 1977): 1–19; Peter L. Berger and Thomas Luckman, *The Social Construction of Reality* (Garden City, NY: Doubleday, 1966), pp. 38, 89, 96, 119–20, 140–42; Richard Gregg, *Symbolic Inducement and Knowing* (Columbia: University of South Carolina Press, 1984); Richard A. Cherwitz and James W. Hikens, *Communication and Knowledge* (Columbia: University of South Carolina Press, 1986).

[27] Gregg, "Rhetoric and Knowing," 141.

[28] Barry Brummett, "Some Implications of 'Process' or 'Intersubjectivity': Postmodern Rhetoric," *Philosophy and Rhetoric*, 9 (Winter 1976): 21–51.

[29] Robert L. Scott, "On Viewing Rhetoric as Epistemic," *Central States Speech Journal*, 18 (February 1967): 9–17.

[30] Scott, "On Viewing Rhetoric as Epistemic: Ten Years Later," *Central States Speech Journal*, 27 (Winter 1976): 258–66. Also see Jeffrey L. Bineham, "From Within the Looking-Glass: The Ontology of Consensus Theory—Bineham's Rejoinder," *Communication Studies*, 49 (Fall 1989): 182–88.

[31] Ralph T. Eubanks, "Reflections on the Moral Dimension of Communication," *Southern Speech Communication Journal*, 45 (Spring 1980): 297–312. Also see Eubanks, "Axiological Issues in Rhetorical Inquiry," *Southern Speech Communication Journal*, 44 (Fall 1978): 11–24; Virgil L. Baker and Ralph T. Eubanks, *Speech in Personal and Public Affairs* (New York: David Makay Co., 1965), preface and ch. 6.

[32] Immanuel Kant, *Fundamental Principles of the Metaphysics of Morals*, trans. Thomas Abbott (Indianapolis, IN: Library of Liberal Arts/Bobbs-Merrill. 1949), p. 46.

[33] Christopher Lyle Johnstone, "Ethics, Wisdom, and the Mission of Contemporary Rhetoric: The Realization of Human Being." *Central States Speech Journal*, 32 (Fall 1981): 177–88.

Chapter 4

Dialogical Perspectives

The term "dialogue" apparently means many things to many people. In the political arena we hear the give and take of debate labeled the public dialogue. Religious leaders of divergent faiths exchange views in ecumenical dialogue. Educational experts encourage classroom dialogue through group discussion and question and answer. Classicists examine Plato's dialogues and dramatists write dialogue for their plays. Communication researchers remind us that human communication is not a one-way transmission but a two-way dialogic transaction. And race relations experts urge expanded dialogue between whites and nonwhites.

Another view of dialogue has emerged from such fields as philosophy, psychiatry, psychology, and religion.[1] The outline and details of this view presently are only broadly and flexibly defined. Proponents discuss the concept of communication as dialogue, often contrasting it with the concept of communication as monologue. Various of the central characteristics of dialogical communication are treated by various scholars under a variety of labels: authentic communication, facilitative communication, therapeutic communication, nondirective therapy, presence, participation, existential communication, encounter, self-disclosing communication, actualizing communication, supportive communication, helping relationship, caring relationship, and loving relationship. So, too, various labels are used to designate the features of monological communication: defensive communication, manipulative communication, inauthentic communication, directive communication, etc.

Focus of Dialogical Perspectives

Dialogical perspectives for evaluating communication ethics focus on the *attitudes toward each other* held by the participants in a communication transaction. Participant attitudes are viewed as an index of the ethical level of that communication. The assumption is that some attitudes (characteristic of dialogue) are more fully human, humane, and facilitative of self-fulfillment than are other attitudes (characteristic of monologue). Dialogical attitudes are held to best nurture and actualize each individual's capacities and potentials, whatever they are. The techniques and presentation of a communication participant could be scrutinized to determine the degree to which they reveal ethical dialogical attitudes or unethical monological attitudes toward other participants.

Among contemporary existentialist philosophers, Martin Buber is the primary one who places the concept of dialogue at the heart of his view of human communication and existence. His writings on dialogue have served as a stimulus for other scholars.[2] Another existentialist philosopher who finds dialogue, or its equivalent, fundamental to our understanding of humanity is Karl Jaspers.[3] The principle of dialogue appears in the conceptions of desirable human communication described by such psychologists and psychiatrists as Carl Rogers, Eric Fromm, Paul Tournier, Jack Gibb, Everett Shostrom, Sidney Jourard, David Johnson, and Abraham Maslow.[4] Other scholars, such as Reuel Howe, Georges Gusdorf, Milton Mayeroff, John Powell, and Floyd Matson and Ashley Montagu, also elaborate some features of the concept.[5]

Martin Buber's analysis of two primary human relationships or attitudes, I-Thou and I-It, significantly influenced the concept of communication as dialogue. According to Buber, the fundamental fact of human existence is "man with man," person communicating with person. Interaction between humans through dialogue promotes development of self, personality, and knowledge. For Buber, meaning and our sense of "self" are constructed only in the realm of the "between" of relationships; our becoming "persons" rather than self-centered individuals arises only in the "between" of dialogic relationships.

In the I-Thou or dialogical relationship, the attitudes and behavior of each communication participant are characterized by such qualities as mutuality, open-heartedness, directness, honesty, spontaneity, frankness, lack of pretense, nonmanipulative intent, communion, intensity, and love in the sense of responsibility of one human for another.[6] In dialogue, although interested in being understood and perhaps in influencing, a communicator does not attempt to *impose* his or her own truth or view on another and is not interested in bolstering his or her own ego or self-image. Each person in a dialogic relationship is accepted as a unique individual. One becomes totally aware of the other person rather than functioning as an observer or onlooker.

The essential movement in dialogue, according to Buber, is turning toward, outgoing to, and reaching for the other. And a basic element in dialogue is "seeing the other" or "experiencing the other side." A person also does not forego his or her own convictions and views, but strives to understand those of others and avoids imposing his or her own on others. For Buber, the increasing difficulty of achieving genuine dialogue between humans of divergent beliefs represents the central problem for the fate of humankind.

Carl Rogers provides a second major influence for the concept of communication as dialogue. Differences between the views of Rogers and Buber are debated.[7] Nevertheless, the processes characteristic of Rogers's client-centered, nondirective approach to psychotherapy, of his person-centered view of communication, are similar in important respects to Buber's conception of dialogic communication. In fact, after extensive comparison, Maurice Friedman concludes: "Rogers's emphases upon the I-Thou relationship in therapy, healing through meeting, acceptance, empathy, unconditional positive regard, and congruence are not only compatible with Buber's philosophy of dialogue but could be strengthened, clarified, and made more consistent within that framework."[8] In Rogers's language, therapists who are "transparently real" or are "congruent" are genuine and honest in expressing their feelings at the moment toward the client, realizing that those feelings expressed must be relevant to the relationship. Through "empathic understanding" the therapist attempts to assume the internal frame of reference of the client and attempts to perceive both the world and the client through the client's own eyes. Although temporarily setting aside their own ideas and values, complete therapist-client identification does not occur, for therapists ultimately retain their own sense of personhood and self-identity.

The therapist holds "unconditional positive regard" for the patient; this is a generally nonevaluative, nonjudgmental attitude which actively accepts the patient as a worthy human being for whom the counselor has genuine respect. The therapist exhibits a nonpossessive caring and prizes the client's feelings and opinions. He or she trusts clients and sees them as individual persons having worth in their own right. While the therapist may offer negative "reactions" to the client, expressing the therapist's personal viewpoint toward the client's behavior or beliefs, the therapist avoids "evaluations" which condemn the fundamental worth of the client as a human being or which apply to the client a set of external, absolute, value standards.

Dialogue versus Expressive Communication

Some writers imply that Buber's and Rogers's views of communication are synonymous with "expressive" communication. In expressive communication, the writers contend, we always reveal every gut feeling, do our own thing, do what comes naturally, let the chips fall where they may, and are totally honest without considering the consequences to others in the situation.[9] However, Rogers makes clear that congruence or transparency does not mean simply expressing every feeling or attitude experienced at the moment in a relationship. Rogers's description of congruence explicitly excludes expression of feelings that are irrelevant or inappropriate to that particular relationship or situation.[10] Buber's view of dialogue clearly would exclude unrestrained expressivism. Dialogue involves a genuine concern for the welfare and fulfillment of the other and a conscious choice making in response to the demands of specified situations. For example, dialogue requires sensitivity to the role responsibilities of such relationships as teacher-pupil, therapist-client, doctor-patient, clergy-parishioner, and parent-child.[11]

Characteristics of Dialogue

We now can summarize the characteristics of dialogue fundamental to the process. These are the major attitudinal dimensions which most scholars writing on dialogue, under various labels, identify to some degree as typifying communication as dialogue. In this summary, I have relied heavily on Martin Buber's terminology and explanations.[12]

Remember that dialogue manifests itself more as a stance, orientation, or bearing in communication rather than as a specific method, technique, or format. We can speak of an attitude of dialogue in human communication. As categories, these characteristics are not mutually exclusive, not completely separate from each other; there may be margins of overlap. Other writers might choose different language to describe essentially the same characteristics. Furthermore, the categories are not intended in any particular rank order of importance.

There is another important point to bear in mind. Even the characteristics of dialogue can be abused and used irresponsibly. Blunt honesty, for example, could be employed to humiliate others in order to satisfy our own ego and sense of self-importance.

Authenticity. One is direct, honest, and straightforward in communicating all information and feelings that are *relevant and legitimate* for the subject at hand. But we avoid simply letting ourselves go and saying everything that comes to mind. We strive to avoid facade, projecting a false image, or "seeming" to be something we are not. The communication filters formed by inappropriate or deceptive roles are minimized. But the legitimate expectations of an appropriate role can be honestly fulfilled. In judging appropriateness, we would consider both our own needs and those of other participants.

Inclusion. One attempts to "see the other," to "experience the other side," to "imagine the real," the reality of the other's viewpoint. Without giving up our own convictions or views, without yielding our own ground or sense of self, we imagine an event or feeling from the side of the other. We attempt to understand factually and emotionally the other's experience.

Confirmation. We express nonpossessive warmth for the other. The other person is valued for his or her worth and integrity as a human. A partner in dialogue is affirmed as a person, not merely tolerated, even though we oppose her or him on some specific matter. Others are confirmed in their right to their individuality, to their personal views. Confirmation involves our desire to assist others to maximize their potential, to become what they can become. The spirit of mutual trust is promoted. We affirm others as unique persons without necessarily approving of their behavior or views.

Presentness. Participants in a dialogue must give full concentration to bringing their total and authentic beings to the encounter. They must demonstrate willingness to become fully involved with each other by taking time, avoiding distraction, being communicatively accessible, and risking attachment. One avoids being an onlooker who simply takes in what is presented or an observer who analyzes. Rather, what is said to us enters meaningfully into our life; we set aside the armor used to thwart the signs of personal address. The dialogic person listens receptively and attentively and responds readily and totally. We are willing to reveal ourselves to others in ways appropriate to the relationship and to receive their revelation.

Spirit of Mutual Equality. Although society may rank participants in dialogue as of unequal status or accomplishment, and although the roles appropriate to each partner may differ, participants themselves view each other as persons rather than as objects, as things, to be exploited or manipulated for selfish satisfaction. The exercise of power or superiority is avoided. Participants do not impose their opinion, cause, or will. In dialogic communication, agreement of the listener with the speaker's aim is secondary to independent, self-deciding participation. Participants aid each other in making responsible decisions regardless of whether the decision be favorable or unfavorable to the particular view presented.

Supportive Climate. One encourages the other to communicate. One allows free expression, seeks understanding, and avoids value judgments that stifle. One shows desire and capacity to listen without anticipating, interfering, competing, refuting, or warping meanings into preconceived interpretations. Assumptions and prejudgments are minimized.

Characteristics of Monologue

In elaborating their view of communication as dialogue, many writers discuss the concept of communication as monologue. To illuminate dialogue, they contrast it with monologue as a usually undesirable type of human communication. Monologue frequently is equated with persuasion and propaganda. Such an equation is open to debate depending upon how persuasion and propaganda are defined. The relation of ethics and propaganda will be examined in chapter 7. Matson and Montagu contend that "the field of communication is today more than ever a battleground contested by two opposing conceptual forces—those of *monologue* and *dialogue*."[13]

At the minimum, a human treated as an It in monologue simply is observed, classified, measured, or analyzed as an object, not encountered as a whole person.[14] The communication is nonpersonal or impersonal. More frequently, according to Buber, the I-It relation, or monological communication, is characterized in varying degrees by self-centeredness, deception, pretense, display, appearance, artifice, using, profit, unapproachableness, seduction, domination, exploitation, and manipulation.[15] Communicators manipulate others for their own selfish ends. They aim at power over people and view them as objects for enjoyment or as things through which to profit. The monological communicator is interested in the personal attributes of receivers only to the extent that he or she can capitalize on those attributes to achieve selfish ends. In monologue we are primarily concerned with what others think of us, with prestige and authority, with display of our own feelings, with display of power, and with molding others in our own image.

Buber describes typical examples of monologue disguised as dialogue.

> A *debate* in which the thoughts are not expressed in the way in which they existed in the mind but in the speaking are so pointed that they may strike home in the sharpest way, and moreover without the men that are spoken to being regarded in any way present as persons; a *conversation* characterized by the need neither to communicate something, nor to learn something, nor to influence someone, nor to come into connexion with someone, but solely by the desire to have one's own self-reliance confirmed by marking the impression that is made, or if it has become unsteady to have it strengthened; a *friendly chat* in which each regards himself as absolute and legitimate and the other as relativized and questionable; a *lover's talk* in which both partners alike enjoy their own glorious soul and their precious experience—what an underworld of faceless spectres of dialogue![16]

Writers such as Matson and Montagu, Howe, Gusdorf, Gibb, Shostrom, Jaspers, Meerloo, Greenagel and Rudinow use much the same vocabulary as Buber to explain the nature of monologue.[17] A person employing monologue seeks to command, coerce, manipulate, conquer, dazzle, deceive, or exploit. Other persons are viewed as "things" to be exploited solely for the communicator's self-serving purpose; they are not taken seriously as persons. Choices are narrowed and consequences are obscured. Focus is on the communicator's message, not on the audience's real needs. The core values, goals, and policies espoused by the communicator are impervious to influence exerted by receivers. Audience feedback is used only to further the communicator's purpose. An honest response from a receiver is not wanted or is precluded. Monological communicators persistently strive to impose their truth or program on others; they have the superior attitude that they must coerce people to yield to what they believe others ought to know. Monologue lacks a spirit of mutual trust, and it displays a defensive attitude of self-justification.

Buber believes that some I-It relations in the form of an impersonal type of monologue often are unavoidable in human life (such as in routine, perfunctory, interactions). For example, in impersonal, pragmatic exchanges of information (that Buber terms "technical dialogue") where understanding of each other as unique individuals is not expected or appropriate, dialogue would not be the goal. In Buber's view, I-It relations, especially in the form of exploitative monologue, become evil when they predominate our life and increasingly shut out dialogue. In contrast, Howe contends that any monologue (nondialogue) relation always is unethical because it exploits.[18]

In his article "On Using People," Don Marietta questions the view that human communication never should be of the I-It type and never should reflect attitudes of participants being "used" as things and means.[19] He rejects misinterpretations of the second version of Kant's Categorical Imperative that urge us to treat others and ourselves always as ends and never as means. Rather, Kant said humans should not be treated "merely" (or solely) as means. He argues that some institutionalized communication transactions, such as buying cigars from a salesperson at a drug store counter, do not ethically demand full dialogue. As minimal ethical standards, such routine and relatively impersonal interactions demand honesty and civility. But making all human relationships as personal as marriage or close friendship "would be intolerable." In all human communication, contends Marietta, persons should not be used solely as means. In communication a person is ethically justified in using another person as a means "if the relationship is such that the used person is not prevented from realizing his own ends in that relationship." For Marietta, a communicator ethically could "use" another person to satisfy his or her own ends as long as the other person also has the opportunity to satisfy his or her own ends, and as long as the other person is not systematically subjected to harm in areas of psychological vulnerability.

Humans as Persons and Objects

John Stewart suggests characteristics of both personal and impersonal communication in which we relate to others primarily as persons or primarily as objects.[20] Persons each are unique biologically and psychologically, are actors capable of choice among means and ends, are beings whose feelings and emotions are not readily measurable and quantifiable, and are reflective in the sense of being aware of life's meaning and time-flow. In contrast, when we communicate with others primarily as objects, we see them as essentially similar and interchangeable, as responding without choice to external stimuli, as measurable and quantifiable in all important respects, and as unreflective and unaware of their "self" or their "place" in human existence. In addition, Stewart argues that only persons are *addressable*, while objects are not. Objects can be *talked about* and even animals can be *talked to*. But only persons can be *talked with*. Only persons can engage in mutually responsive communication.

Stewart contends, however, that not all objectifying communication is undesirable. For some relationships, dialogic communication is not possible, appropriate, or expected. But while not all our communication can be dialogic, believes Stewart, more of it could be. Stewart concludes:[21]

> The ethic which emerges from this perspective on persons is grounded in response-ability. Since each communication contact has person-building potential, ethical communication is communication which promotes realization of that potential. Such communication is responsive, attentive to and concretely guided by as much as possible of one's own and the other's humanness, that is, uniqueness, choice-making, more-than-spatiotemporal aspects, and reflexivity.

Dialogue and Persuasion

Some writers on the nature of monologue, by equating monologue and persuasion, contend that all attempts at persuasion are unethical. Is it inherently unethical to attempt to persuade others, to ask them to adopt your viewpoint?

Buber, and some others to varying degrees, believe that even in dialogue we may express disagreement with other persons, may seek to influence them, or may attempt to suggest the inadequacy of what those persons are believing or doing. But always, according to Buber, the communicative influence must be exerted in a noncoercive, nonmanipulative manner that respects the free choice and individuality of the receiver.[22]

In a speech in 1953 in Frankfurt, Germany, Martin Buber, himself a Jew of German origin, reflected the dialogic attitudes of inclusion and confirmation toward Germans who participated in, who ignored, or who resisted Nazi atrocities. Buber stood his own ground in condemning those who committed atrocities while at the same time attempting to understand the circumstances and motives of those who knew of atrocities but did not resist or those who were uninformed but did not investigate rumors.[23]

Persuaders could, I contend, present their best advice for solution to a problem in as sound and influential a way as possible, always admitting that it may not be the only solution and that ultimately the audience has the right of independent choice. A communicator can advise rather than coerce or command.[24] While the communicator may express judgments of policies and behaviors, judgments of the intrinsic worth of audience members *as persons* are avoided.

Richard M. Weaver feels that all humans are "born rhetoricians" who by nature desire to persuade and be persuaded. "We all need," says Weaver, "to have things pointed out to us, things stressed in our own interest."[25] Monologue is most properly viewed as only *one* (although usually unethical and undesirable) species of persuasion; monologue, I would contend, should not be equated with *all* types of persuasion.

Some scholars perceive dialogue and monologue as mutually exclusive opposites. Certainly Matson and Montagu describe them as polar phenomena. Buber, however, sees any human relationship as involving greater or lesser degrees of dialogical and monological attitudes. He rejects a conception of communication as either all dialogic or all monologic, and he realizes that "pure" dialogue seldom occurs.[26]

Conditions and Contexts for Dialogue

Under what conditions and in what communication contexts and situations can dialogue function most effectively? We could speculate that dialogue seems most likely to develop in private, two-person, face-to-face, oral communication settings that extend, even intermittently, over lengthy periods of time. If this is true, dialogue would most frequently occur in such relationships as husband-wife, parent-child, doctor-patient, psychotherapist-client, counselor-counselee, clergy-parishioner, continuing small-group discussions, and sensitivity-training sessions.

Privacy seems desirable for dialogue, but perhaps not absolutely necessary. The time factor would appear important; a great amount of time usually is necessary for the maturation of dialogue. While dialogue may be most likely when only two people are involved, it would seem possible for dialogue to occur in small groups. Although face-to-face oral communication seems requisite for optimum dialogue, communicators can reflect dialogical attitudes toward receivers in writing or in mass media situations.

Within the context of small group communication, Gibb identifies characteristics of "supportive" (dialogical) and "defensive" (monological) communication which enhance or undermine the group's efficiency.[27] In supportive communication, the speaker's attitudes toward other group members are those of factual objectivity, cooperativeness, concern for others as persons, openmindedness, honesty, genuineness, empathy, equality, and willingness to delay judgment. In defensive communication, by contrast, speaker attitudes are those of negativism, quick judgmentalism, control, manipulation for personal gain, superiority in knowledge and values, deception, unconcern, aloofness, and dogmatism.

Buber believes that dialogue to some degree is possible in virtually any realm of human interaction. Buber, Howe, Jaspers, and Rogers specifically discuss the possibility of dialogue in such fields and settings as politics, business, education, and labor-management negotiations.[28] Indeed, several scholars have advocated the desirability of a diological ethical approach to guide the public relations practices of organizations. At length they describe how ethical public relations practice should embody attitudes of dialogue rather than monologue.[29] You are urged to read these provocative arguments and judge for yourself how adequately they have made their case for the applicability of dialogue to public relations.

Despite the unplanned nature of dialogue, and although "genuine dialogue cannot be arranged beforehand," Buber believes nevertheless that "one can hold oneself free and open for it" and can be "at its disposal."[30] Perhaps this is what Thomas Nilsen means by choosing to open ourselves to dialogue. "I can choose whether I will consider the other's self-determining choice more important than his acceptance of mine; I can choose whether I will turn to the other and seek to meet him; to perceive him in his wholeness and uniqueness; I can choose whether I will value him as a person above all else. I can choose to try to relate to him as honestly as I can rather than put on a front so that he cannot relate to me."[31]

Dialogical Attitudes in Public and Written Communication

Dialogue flowers most easily in private, interpersonal communication settings. But public communicators (in speeches, essays, editorials, and mass media appeals) *could* hold and reflect honest, sincere dialogical attitudes toward their audiences.[32] In fact, public communicators in speech or writing often do reveal varying degrees of dialogue or monologue. Several textbooks on written rhetoric advocate insights from Carl Rogers.[33] Mahatma Gandhi, the famous advocate of nonviolent political change in India, reflected major attitudinal elements of dialogue in a public address to an international conference.[34]

Consider the somewhat monological attitudes which a newspaper reader perceived in the nationally syndicated opinion column of Carl Rowan.[35]

> Carl Rowan so often writes as if there can be just no viewpoint other than his own. His recent column on amnesty was a case in point. I am not writing to take issue with his position, but to chide him for his attitude toward those who disagree with him. . . . Let Rowan plump for his convictions. . . . But let him refrain from disparagement—to the point of contempt—toward those who disagree with him.

A more recent example of monological arrogance was Secretary of State James Baker's explanation in 1990 of the need to send American troops to the Gulf War: "To bring it down to the average American citizen, let me say it means jobs." Syndicated news colunmist Mona Charen wondered: "Bring it 'down to the average American'? Is that how this administration sees the people? Too simpleminded or too selfish to understand anything beyond their pocketbooks?"[36]

Several scholars of rhetoric explore monological and dialogical communicator attitudes toward audience from the metaphorical vantage point of rhetoric as love.[37] Richard M. Weaver analyzes Plato's *Phaedrus* from a rhetorical viewpoint and concludes that, among other things, it is a commentary on rhetoric in the guise of the metaphor of love. Weaver's perception of the *Phaedrus* allows him to explain three kinds of lovers (the non-lover, evil lover, and the noble lover), which he in turn equates with the neutral speaker, the evil speaker, and the noble speaker.[38] Each of the lover-speakers exhibits characteristic attitudes toward the audience. The neutral speaker's attitudes are prudence, disinterest, objectivity, moderation, blandness, and cold rationality. The evil or base speaker reflects attitudes of exploitation, domination, possessiveness, selfishness, superiority, deception, manipulation, and defensiveness. The evil communicator, according to Weaver, frequently subverts clear definition, causal reasoning, and an "honest examination of alternatives" by "discussing only one side of an issue, by mentioning cause without consequence or consequence without cause, acts without agents or agents without agency. . . ." The noble speaker described by Weaver exalts the intrinsic worth of the audience and reflects essentially dialogical attitudes: respect, concern, selflessness, involvement, and a genuine desire to help the audience actualize its potentials and ideals.

Through the metaphorical prism of love, Wayne Brockriede probes the nature of argumentation and of arguers as lovers. Using a sexual metaphor, Brockriede identifies three stances of arguer toward other arguers: rape, seduction, and love.[39] Several writers supplement Brockriede's analysis by suggesting additional stances: flirtation, romance, and lust. Emory Griffin develops categories roughly similar to those of Weaver and Brockriede: nonlover, smother lover, legalistic lover, flirt, seducer, rapist, and true lover.[40] (See my later discussion of Griffin's view in chapter 6.)

The rhetorical rapist, according to Brockriede, assumes a unilateral relationship with the audience, sees them as objects, victims or inferior human beings, and intends to manipulate or violate them. The rapist's attitudes toward the audience are superiority, domination, coercion, and contempt. The attitudes of rhetorical rape often manifest themselves, feels Brockriede, in the courtroom, political campaign, business meeting, legislative chamber, and competitive intercollegiate debate.

The rhetorical seducer, according to Brockriede, is often found in the fields of politics and advertising, and also assumes a unilateral relationship with the audience. The rhetorical seducer's attitudinal tone is deceptive, insincere, charming, beguiling, and indifferent to the identity, integrity, and rationality of the audience. Characteristically, says Brockriede, the rhetorical seducer employs logical fallacies (such as begging the question and the red herring), misuses evidence (such as withholding information and quoting out of context), and bedazzles with appeals, language, and presentation which lower the audience's reflective guard.

In contrast, the rhetorical lover represents the desirable (dialogical) argumentative stance. A bilateral or power parity relationship is sought by the rhetorical lover who views the audience as persons rather than objects or victims. The attitudes of speaker toward audience characterizing the rhetorical lover are equality, respect, willingness to risk self-change, openness to new ideas and arguments, and a genuine desire to promote free choice in the audience. Brockriede believes that the attitudes of rhetorical love frequently are found in communication between friends, actual lovers, philosophers, and scientists.

Literary critics such as Wayne Booth, Walker Gibson, and Northrop Frye offer additional insights concerning communicator attitudes which are essentially dialogical or monological. "Rhetorical stance," according to Wayne Booth, represents a "proper balance" among "the available arguments about the subject itself, the interests and peculiarities of the audience, and the voice, the implied character of the speaker."[41] Three unbalanced or undesirable stances, in Booth's estimation, are those of the pedant, the advertiser, and the entertainer. The pedant ignores or undervalues the audience and focuses on the subject. In the pedantic stance the speaker's attitudes toward audience are the take-it-or-leave-it ones of neutrality and indifference. The advertiser undervalues the subject and overvalues pure effect with audience. The speaker in the advertiser's stance, with a success-at-all-costs orientation, reflects attitudes of exploitation and pandering. The speaker in the entertainer's stance is willing to "sacrifice substance to personality and charm"; the attitudes are self-aggrandizement and egocentricity.

Tough style, sweet style, and stuffy style are three extreme types of contemporary American prose condemned by Walker Gibson as undesirable because they lack genuine respect for the feelings of the audience.[42] When employing a tough style the speaker's tone is egocentric, brow-beating, no-nonsense, domineering, curt, covertly intimate, intense, and often omniscient. The sweet style, frequently found in advertisements, finds a speaker revealing attitudes of condescension, solicitousness, cuteness, and covert intimacy. A speaker in the stuffy style, with a message-centered orientation, shows toward the audience attitudes which are impersonal, cold, standoffish, unfeeling, objective, and nonjudgmental.

Northrop Frye distinguishes between "genuine speech" and "bastard speech," both of which reflect characteristic speaker attitudes toward the audience.[43] Genuine speech, which takes pains to express itself clearly and carefully and which grows from a spirit of community, finds the speaker addressing the audience on a basis of equality stemming from shared humanity. Bastard speech, which employs unexamined clichés addressed to the reflexes of the audience rather than to their intelligence or emotions, reflects attitudes of egotism and of exploitation of selfish audience needs and resentments.

Toward an Ethic for Rhetoric

Some contemporary conceptions of mature and responsible rhetoric or argument appear similar at a number of points to a dialogic ethic. The conceptions further open the possibility that dialogic attitudes may be applicable to some degree, or in part, in public communication. To stimulate discussion of this possibility, I offer here my synthesis of standards for sound and ethical rhetoric derived from

Dialogical Perspectives

Douglas Ehninger, Walter Fisher, Wayne Brockriede, and Henry W. Johnstone, Jr.[44]

1. Ethical rhetoric serves the ends of self-discovery, social knowledge, or public action more than personal ambition.
2. Ethical rhetoric avoids intolerance and acknowledges audience freedom of choice and freedom of assent.
3. Ethical rhetoric is reflexive in including self-scrutiny of one's own evidence, reasoning, and motives.
4. Ethical rhetoric is attentive to data through use of accurate, complete, and relevant evidence and reasoning and through use of appropriate field-dependent tests for soundness of evidence and reasoning.
5. Ethical rhetoric is bilateral. Bilaterality includes mutuality of personal and intellectual risk, openness to the possibility of self-change, and openness to scrutiny by others.
6. Ethical rhetoric is self-perpetuating. Disagreement on a subject leaves open the possibility of deliberation on other subjects and of later deliberation on the disputed subject. Also, human capacities for persuasion, in ourselves and in others, are nurtured through what Henry W. Johnstone terms the habits of resoluteness, openness, gentleness, and compassion. (See my summary in chapter 3.)
7. Ethical rhetoric embodies an attitude of reasonableness. Reasonableness includes willingness to present reasons in support of our views, tolerance of presentation of reasons by others, respect for the intrinsic worth of the other person as a human, and avoidance of personalizing the controversy.
8. Ethical rhetoric manifests what Walter R. Fisher terms the "logic of good reasons." Such a logic of value judgment embodies five key questions. (a) What are the implicit and explicit values embedded in a message? (b) Are the values appropriate to the nature of the decision that the message bears upon? (c) What would be the effects of adhering to the values in regard to one's concept of oneself, to one's behavior, to one's relationships with others and society, and to the processes of rhetorical transaction? (d) Are the values confirmed or validated in one's personal experience, in the lives or statements of others whom one admires and respects, and/or in a conception of the best audience that one can conceive? (e) Even if an immediate need for belief or action has been demonstrated, would an outside observer/critic assess

the values offered or assumed in the message as the ideal basis for human conduct?

Dialogical Ethics and Significant Choice

Some scholars advocate that dialogue, as a more desirable type of communication behavior, should be *substituted* for persuasion. Such a position usually is taken when persuasion is defined as wholly equatable with unethical monologue. Other scholars, in contrast, see dialogue as a *supplement* to traditional theory, practice, and ethics of persuasion.

Although Thomas Nilsen's *Ethics of Speech Communication* primarily develops a political perspective centering on the concept of "significant choice" (see our earlier discussion in chapter 2), he also offers some supplementary dialogical standards for assessing the ethics of interpersonal communication. Nilsen feels interpersonal communication, where "the impact of personality on personality is more immediate" than in public communication, must meet the ethical standards both of significant choice and of dialogue.[45] "Morally right speech," says Nilsen, "is that which opens up channels for mind to reach mind, heart to reach heart." Such speech creates conditions "in which the personality can function most freely and fully." Nilsen believes that ethical interpersonal communication fosters the dignity of the individual personality, optimizes the sharing of thought and feeling, promotes feelings of belonging and acceptance, and fosters cooperation and mutual respect.

Nilsen suggests that the following attitudes be encouraged for achievement of ethical interpersonal communication: (1) respect for a person as a person regardless of age, status, or relationship to the speaker; (2) respect for the other person's ideas, feelings, intentions, and integrity; (3) permissiveness, objectivity, and openmindedness which encourage freedom of expression; (4) respect for evidence and the rational weighing of alternatives; and (5) careful and empathic listening prior to agreeing or disagreeing.

Paul Keller and Charles Brown offer a dialogical perspective for interpersonal communication as a supplement to more traditional political perspectives for judging the ethics of persuasion.[46] In fact, they build their view in part on Nilsen's analysis of values fundamental to the American political system. As basic democratic values they adhere to the intrinsic worth of the human personality and the process of self-determination as means of individual fulfillment. They see "signs concerning the attitude of speaker and listener toward each other" as more valid ethical indexes than are indications of loyalty to rationality or to some conception of universal truth.

Keller and Brown would demand that a speaker be sensitive to listener freedom of choice and be willing to tolerate a listener response contrary to the one sought. If a speaker attempts to influence others and the suggestion or advice is rejected by listeners, the speaker is unethical to the degree that his subsequent communication with them reflects such attitudes as anger, despondency, appeal of sympathy, withdrawal, or unconcern. Ethical standards for interpersonal communication are violated, believe Keller and Brown, to the degree that a speaker shows hostility toward listeners or in some way tries to subjugate them.

In her article on "Nixon and the Strategy of Avoidance," Karen Rasmussen applies standards of significant choice, dialogue, and rhetorical seduction to evaluate the ethics of Richard M. Nixon's public communication during the 1972 presidential campaign. You may wish to develop your own assessment of how adequately and appropriately she applies these standards.[47]

Guidelines for Applying Dialogical Standards

A human communication ethic rooted in dialogical perspectives has been attacked as unrealistic, unnecessary, and even as harmful.[48] Keller defends a dialogical communication ethic as possible and pragmatically useful in improving the human condition.[49]

Note that when two basic dialogical attitudes come into conflict, situational factors (such as will be discussed in chapter 5) may influence ethical judgment. A choice may have to be made and a temporary hierarchy of priorities established. In a specific communication situation, for example, the attitude of concern for the psychological welfare of a close friend might take precedence over an attitude of total frankness and blunt honesty. We each probably could think of other such examples.[50]

Remember that communicator attitudes toward receivers are revealed *both* through verbal elements (word choice, overt meaning) *and* through nonverbal elements (eye contact, facial expression, gestures, posture, vocal tone and quality, etc.). Consider whether dialogical and monological attitudes seem most clearly and easily revealed through verbal or nonverbal cues.

John Makay and William Brown list ten conditions for dialogue which we also might use as ethical guides for determining the degree to which dialogical attitudes reveal themselves in a human communication transaction.[51]

1. Human involvement from a felt need to communicate
2. An atmosphere of openness, freedom, and responsibility
3. Dealing with the *real* issues and ideas relevant to the communicator
4. Appreciation of individual differences and uniqueness
5. Acceptance of disagreement and conflict with the desire to resolve them
6. Effective feedback and use of feedback
7. Mutual respect and, hopefully, trust
8. Sincerity and honesty in attitudes toward communication
9. A positive attitude for understanding and learning
10. A willingness to admit error and allow persuasion

The ethical standard implied in most conceptions of communication as dialogue seems clear. Human communication achieves maximum ethicality in appropriate situations to the degree that it reflects and fosters participant attitudes of authenticity, inclusion, confirmation, presentness, mutual equality, and supportiveness. A communicator's choices in seeking understanding or influence can be assessed for the extent to which they reveal dialogical attitudes, impersonal attitudes, or unethical exploitative monological attitudes.[52]

Notes

[1] For an earlier analysis than appears in this chapter, see Richard L. Johannesen, "The Emerging Concept of Communication as Dialogue," *Quarterly Journal of Speech*, 57 (December 1971): 373–82. For additional analyses, see John Stewart, "Foundations of Dialogic Communication," *Quarterly Journal of Speech*, 64 (April 1978): 183–201; John Poulakos, "The Components of Dialogue," *Western Speech*, 38 (Summer 1974); 199–212. A textbook that synthesizes and applies the perspective discussed in this chapter is T. Dean Thomlison, *Toward Interpersonal Dialogue* (New York: Longman, 1982). Also see Ronald C. Arnett, *Communication and Community: Implications of Martin Buber's Dialogue* (Carbondale: Southern Illinois University Press, 1986); Rob Anderson, Kenneth R. Cissna, and Ronald C. Arnett, eds., *The Reach of Dialogue: Confirmation, Voice, and Community* (Creskill, NJ: Hampton Press, 1994).

[2] The major works by Martin Buber relevant to communication as dialogue are: *I and Thou*, trans. Ronald Gregor Smith, 2d ed. (New York: Scribners, 1958): *Between Man and Man*, trans. Ronald Gregor Smith (New York: Macmillan paperback, 1965), especially pp. 1–39, 83–103; *The Knowledge of Man*, ed. Maurice S. Friedman, trans. Friedman and Ronald Gregor Smith (New York: Harper and Row, 1965), especially pp. 72–88, 110–20, 166–84; and *Pointing the Way*, trans. Maurice S. Friedman (New York: Harper Torchbook, 1963), especially 83, 206, 220–39. The standard analysis of Buber's concept of dialogue is Maurice S. Friedman, *Martin Buber: The Life of Dialogue* (New York: Harper Torchbook, 1960), especially 57–97, 123–26, 176–83.

See also Paul E. Pfuetze, *Self, Society, Existence: Human Nature and Dialogue in the Thought of George Herbert Mead and Martin Buber* (New York: Harper Torchbook, 1961), pp. 139–206.

3 Among the works of Karl Jaspers, see particularly *Philosophy*, trans. E. B. Ashton, vol. 2 (Chicago: University of Chicago Press, 1970), pp. 56–69, 76–77, 97, 101.

4 Among the works of Carl Rogers, see *Client-Centered Therapy* (Boston: Houghton Mifflin, 1951), pp. 19–64; *On Becoming a Person* (Boston: Houghton Mifflin, 1961), pp. 16–22, 31–69, 126–158, 338–46, 356–59; Rogers and Barry Stevens, *Person to Person* (Lafayette, CA: Real People Press, 1967), pp. 88–103; "The Necessary and Sufficient Conditions of Therapeutic Personality Change," *Journal of Consulting Psychology*, 21 (February 1957): 95–103. For the other sources see: Eric Fromm, *The Art of Loving* (New York: Harper, 1956), pp. 7–31; Paul Tournier, *The Meaning of Persons*, trans. Edwin Hudson (New York: Harper and Row, 1957), pp. 123–59, 191, 196, 203, 209; Jack R. Gibb, "Defensive Communication," *Journal of Communication*, 11 (September 1961): 141–48; Everett L. Shostrom, *Man, the Manipulator* (New York: Bantam Books, 1968); Sidney M. Jourard, *The Transparent Self*, 2d ed. (Princeton, NJ: Van Nostrand, 1971); David W. Johnson, *Reaching Out: Interpersonal Effectiveness and Self Actualization*, 2d ed. (Englewood Cliffs, NJ: Prentice-Hall, 1981); Abraham Maslow, *Motivation and Personality*, 2d ed. (New York: Harper and Row, 1970), ch. 11; Maslow, *Toward a Psychology of Being*, 2d ed. (Princeton, NJ: Van Nostrand Insight Book, 1968), chs. 6 and 7; Maslow, *The Farther Reaches of Human Nature* (New York: Viking, 1971), pp. 17–18, 41–73, 260–66, 347.

5 Reuel Howe, *The Miracle of Dialogue* (New York: Seabury Press, 1963), pp. 6, 36–83; Georges Gusdorf, *Speaking (La Parole)*, trans. Paul T. Brockelman (Evanston, IL: Northwestern University Press, 1965), pp. 57, 84–85, 101–4; Milton Mayeroff, *On Caring* (New York: Harper and Row, 1971); John Powell, S.J., *Why Am I Afraid to Tell You Who I Am?* (Chicago: Argus Communications, 1969); Floyd Matson and Ashley Montagu, eds., *The Human Dialogue* (New York: Free Press, 1967), pp. 1–11.

6 This description of Buber's conception is based on: Buber, *Between Man and Man*, pp. 5–10, 20–21, 82, 96–101; Buber, *Knowledge of Man*, pp. 76–77, 86; Buber, *Pointing the Way*, p. 222; Friedman, *Martin Buber*, pp. 57, 81–89, 97, 180–81.

7 Ronald C. Arnett, "Toward a Phenomenological Dialogue," *Western Journal of Speech Communication*, 45 (Summer 1981): 201–12; Rob Anderson, "Phenomenological Dialogue, Humanistic Psychology, and Pseudo-Walls: A Response and Extension," *Western Journal of Speech Communication*, 46 (Fall 1982): 344–57; accompanied by a reply by Arnett, "Rogers and Buber: Similarities, Yet Fundamental Differences": 358–72; Ronald C. Arnett, "What is Dialogic Communication? Friedman's Contributions and Clarification," *Person-Centered Review*, 4 (February 1989): 42–60.

8 See, for example, Rogers, *Client-Centered Therapy*, pp. 19–64; Rogers, *On Becoming a Person*, pp. 16–22, 31–69, 126–58, 338–46; 356–59; Rogers and Stevens, *Person to Person*, pp. 88–103; Rogers in Buber, *The Knowledge of Man*, p. 170; Rogers, *A Way of Being* (Boston: Houghton Mifflin, 1980), chs. 1, 6, 7; Maurice Friedman, "Carl Rogers and Martin Buber: Self Actualization and Dialogue," *Person-Centered Review*, 1 (November 1986): 409–35.

[9] Roderick P. Hart and Don M. Burks, "Rhetorical Sensitivity and Social Interaction," *Speech Monographs*, 38 (June 1972): 76, 84, 87, 89–90. For a contrasting view, see Allan Sillars, "Expression and Control in Human Interaction," *Western Speech* 38 (Fall 1974): 269–277. Also see Donald K. Darnell and Wayne Brockriede, *Persons Communicating* (Englewood Cliffs, NJ: Prentice-Hall, 1976), chs. 2, 11, 12. For a critique of Hart and Burks's mistaken equating of dialogue and expressive communication, see Gerald Fulkerson, "The Ethics of Interpersonal Influence: A Critique of the Rhetorical Sensitivity Construct," *Journal of Communication and Religion*, 13 (1990): 1–14.

[10] Rogers, *On Becoming a Person*, pp. 51, 61, 118.

[11] Buber, *Knowledge of Man*, pp. 31–33, 75–77, 85–86, 171–73; Buber, *I and Thou*, pp. 131–34; Buber, *Between Man and Man*, pp. 95–101; Buber in Sydney and Beatrice Rome, eds., *Philosophical Interrogations* (New York: Holt, Rinehart and Winston, 1964), p. 66. Also see three books by Maurice Friedman: *The Hidden Human Image* (New York: Delacorte, 1974), pp. 274–85; *Touchstones of Reality* (New York: Durton, 1972), p. 307; *To Deny Our Nothingness* (New York: Delacorte, 1967), p. 25; and Donald L. Berry, *Mutuality: The Vision of Martin Buber* (Albany: State University of New York Press, 1983), pp. 41–68.

[12] See the writings by Martin Buber and Carl Rogers cited in prior footnotes. For typical summaries from a psychological viewpoint, see Dean C. Barnlund, *Interpersonal Communication: Survey and Studies* (Boston: Houghton Mifflin, 1968), pp. 637–40; Charles B. Truax and Robert B. Carkuff, *Toward Effective Counseling and Psychotherapy* (Chicago: Aldine, 1967), pp. 23–43, 58–60, 68–69, 141. For interpretations of Buber on dialogue, see Maurice Friedman's two books: *Touchstones of Reality*, chs. 16, 17, 18; *To Deny Our Nothingness*, chs. 16, 19. Also see Alexander S. Kohanski, *An Analytical Interpretation of Martin Buber's I and Thou* (Woodbury, NY: Barron's Educational Series, 1975). Bear in mind that Buber also describes the communication relationship of a human I with God, the Eternal Thou. His view of dialogic I-Thou communication between humans derives from his assumptions about the nature and significance of human communication with God and God with humans. See Buber, *I and Thou*, pp. 75–120; Friedman, *Martin Buber*, chs. XII, XXIV, XXV; Kohanski, *Analytical Interpretation of Martin Buber's I and Thou*, pp. 100–147.

[13] Matson and Montagu, *The Human Dialogue*, p. viii.

[14] Kohanski, *Analytical Interpretation of Martin Buber's I and Thou*, pp. 48, 168, 174.

[15] This description of the I-It relation is based on Buber, *I and Thou*, pp. 34, 38, 43, 60, 105, 107; Buber, *Knowledge of Man*, pp. 82–83; *Between Man and Man*, pp. 19–20, 23, 29–30, 95; Friedman, *Martin Buber*, pp. 57–58, 63, 82, 123–24, 180.

[16] Buber, *Between Man and Man*, pp. 19–20.

[17] Matson and Montagu, *The Human Dialogue*, pp. 3–10; Howe, *The Miracle of Dialogue*, pp. 18–56, 84–88; Gusdorf, *Speaking*, pp. 106–8; Gibb, "Defensive Communication"; Shostrom, *Man, the Manipulator*; Jaspers, *Philosophy*, Vol. 2, pp. 49, 60, 80–84, 90; Joost Meerloo, *Conversation and Communication* (New York: International Universities Press, 1952), pp. 94–97, 133–43; Frank Greenagel, "Manipulation and the Cult of Communication in Contemporary Industry," in *Communication-Spectrum* 7, Lee Thayer, ed. (National Society for the Study of Communication, 1968), pp. 237–45; Joel Rudinow, "Manipulation," *Ethics*, 88 (July 1978): 338–347.

[18] Buber, *I and Thou*, pp. 34, 46, 48; Buber, *Between Man and Man*, p. 19; Ronald C. Arnett, *Dwell in Peace: Applying Nonviolence to Everyday Relationships* (Elgin, IL: Brethren Press, 1980). pp. 129–31; Howe, *Miracle of Dialogue*, pp. 38–39.

[19] Don E. Marietta, "On Using People," *Ethics*, 82 (April 1972): 232–38. Also see Arthur Flemming, "Using a Man as a Means," *Ethics*, 88 (July 1978): 283–298; for a contrasting view, see John R. S. Wilson, "In One Another's Power," *Ibid.*; 299–315. Nancy Davis, "Using Persons and Common Sense," *Ethics*, 94 (April 1984): 387–406.

[20] John Stewart, ed., *Bridges Not Walls*, 6th ed. (New York: McGraw-Hill, 1995), pp. 15–22; Stewart and Carol Logan, *Together: Communicating Interpersonally*, 4th ed. (New York: McGraw-Hill, 1993), ch. 1.

[21] John Stewart, "Communication, Ethics, and Relativism: An Interpersonal Perspective," paper presented at Speech Communication Association convention, New York City, November 1980.

[22] Buber, *Knowledge of Man*, pp. 69-79. See also Rogers, *On Becoming a Person*, p. 358; Shostrom, *Man, the Manipulator*, p. 51; Gerard Egan, *Encounter: Group Processes for Interpersonal Growth* (Belmont, CA: Wadsworth, 1970), pp. 266–68.

[23] Buber, *Pointing the Way*, pp. 232–33; Arnett, *Dwell in Peace*, pp. 114–16.

[24] On the "advisory" function of rhetoric see Karl R. Wallace, "Rhetoric and Advising," *Southern Speech Journal* 29 (Summer 1964): 279–84; Walter R. Fisher, "Advisory Rhetoric," *Western Speech* 29 (Spring 1965): 114–19; B. J. Diggs, "Persuasion and Ethics," *Quarterly Journal of Speech* 50 (December 1964): especially 363–64.

[25] Richard M. Weaver, "Language Is Sermonic," in Richard L. Johannesen, ed., *Contemporary Theories of Rhetoric: Selected Readings* (New York: Harper and Row, 1971), pp. 175–76.

[26] Buber, *Between Man and Man*, pp. 36, 97.

[27] Gibb, "Defensive Communication."

[28] Buber, *Between Man and Man*, pp. 34–39; Buber, *I and Thou*, pp. 47–50, 131–33; Howe, *Miracle of Dialogue*, pp. 3–17, 69, 105–52; Jaspers, *Philosophy*, Vol. 2, pp. 82–93; Rogers, *Client-Centered Therapy*, pp. 278–427; Rogers, *Freedom to Learn* (Columbus, OH: Charles Merrill, 1969). For an example, see Eric M. Eisenberg and H. L. Goodall, Jr., *Organizational Communication: Balancing Creativity and Constraint* (New York: St. Martin's Press, 1993), pp. 40–44.

[29] Ron Pearson, "Business Ethics as Communication Ethics: Public Relations Practice and the Idea of Dialogue," in *Public Relations Theory*, Carl H. Botan and Vincent Hazelton, Jr., eds. (Hillsdale, NJ: Erlbaum, 1989), pp. 111–31; Pearson, "Beyond Ethical Relativism in Public Relations: Coorientation, Rules and the Idea of Communication Symmetry," in *Public Relations Research Annual*, Vol. 1, James E. Grunig and Larissa A. Grunig, eds. (Hillsdale, NJ: Erlbaum, 1989), pp. 67–86; Carl Botan, "A Human Nature Approach to Image and Ethics in International Public Relations," *Journal of Public Relations Research*, 5 (1993): 71–81.

[30] Buber, *Knowledge of Man*, p. 87; Buber, *Pointing the Way*, p. 206.

[31] Thomas R. Nilsen, "Dialogue and Group Process," paper presented at the 1969 convention of the Speech Association of America.

[32] For one innovative discussion, see George E. Yoos, "A Revision of the Concept of Ethical Appeal," *Philosophy and Rhetoric*, 12 (Winter 1979): 41–58.

[33] Richard E. Young, et al., *Rhetoric: Discovery and Change* (New York: Harcourt, Brace and World, 1970), ch. 12; Maxine Hairston, *A Contemporary Rhetoric*, 3rd ed. (Boston: Houghton Mifflin, 1982). For a critical view of Rogers, see Phyllis Lassner, "Feminist Responses to Rogerian Argument," *Rhetoric Review*, 8 (Spring 1990): 220–31.

[34] Michael J. Beatty, et al., "Elements of Dialogic Communication in Gandhi's Second Round Table Conference Address," *Southern Speech Communication Journal*, XLIV (Summer 1979): 386–98. Also see V. V. Ramana Murti, "Buber's Dialogue and Gandhi's Satyagraha," *Journal of the History of Ideas*, 24 (1968): 605–13. For other discussions of dialogic attitudes in formal communication settings, see Donald G. Douglas, "Cordell Hull and the Implementation of the 'Good Neighbor Policy'," *Western Speech*, 34 (Fall 1970): 288–99; William D. Thompson and Gordon C. Bennett, *Dialogue Preaching: The Shared Sermon* (Valley Forge, PA: Judson Press, 1969); Gary L. Cronkhite, *Public Speaking and Critical Listening* (Menlo Park, CA: Benjamin/Cummings, 1978), pp. 36–43.

[35] Kathleen Kaufman, letter to the editor, Chicago *Daily News*, April 23, 1973.

[36] Mona Charen, "Unfamiliarity Breeds Contempt for Modest George," *Chicago Tribune*, November 19, 1990, sec. 1, p. 21.

[37] The following discussion of the views of rhetorical theorists and literary critics is adapted from a more extensive examination of speaker attitude toward audience as a conceptual framework for rhetorical criticism: Richard L. Johannesen, "Attitude of Speaker Toward Audience: A Significant Concept for Contemporary Rhetorical Theory and Criticism," *Central States Speech Journal* 25 (Summer 1974).

[38] Richard M. Weaver, *The Ethics of Rhetoric* (Chicago: Regnery, 1953), pp. 3–26.

[39] Wayne Brockriede, "Arguers as Lovers," *Philosophy and Rhetoric* 5 (Winter 1972): 1–11.

[40] Darnell and Brockriede, *Persons Communicating* pp. 162–169; Karen Rasmussen, "Nixon and the Strategy of Avoidance," *Central States Speech Journal*, 24 (Fall 1973): 193–202; Emory A. Griffin, *The Mind Changers: The Art of Christian Persuasion* (Wheaton, IL: Tyndale House, 1976), ch. 3.

[41] Wayne Booth, "The Rhetorical Stance," *College Composition and Communication* 14 (October 1963): 139–45.

[42] Walker Gibson, *Tough, Sweet, and Stuffy: An Essay on Modern American Prose Styles* (Bloomington: Indiana University Press, 1966).

[43] Northrop Frye, *The Well-Tempered Critic* (Bloomington: Indiana University Press, 1966), pp. 13–51.

[44] Douglas Ehninger, "Argument as Method: Its Nature, Its Limitations and Its Uses," *Speech Monographs*, 37 (June 1970): 101–10; Darnell and Brockriede, *Persons Communicating*, chs. 7, 11; Walter R. Fisher, "Toward a Logic of Good Reasons," *Quarterly Journal of Speech*, 64 (December 1978): 376–84; Fisher, "Rationality and the Logic of Good Reasons," *Philosophy and Rhetoric*, 13 (Spring 1980): 121–130; Henry W. Johnstone, Jr., "Towards an Ethics of Rhetoric," *Communication*, 6, no. 2 (1981): 305–14; Johnstone, Jr., *Validity and Rhetoric in Philosophical Argument* (University Park, PA: The Dialogue Press of Man and the World, 1978), chs. 11, 17; Johnstone, Jr., "Bilaterality in Argument and Communication," in *Advances in Argumentation Theory and Research*, eds. J. Robert Cox and Charles A. Willard (Carbondale: Southern Illinois University Press, 1982), pp. 95–102.

[45] Thomas R. Nilsen, *Ethics of Speech Communication*, 2d ed. (Indianapolis: Bobbs-Merrill, 1974), pp. 19, 88–94.

[46] Paul W. Keller and Charles T. Brown, "An Interpersonal Ethic for Communication," *Journal of Communication*, 18 (March 1968): 73–81. A later expanded version is Brown and Keller, *Monologue to Dialogue An Exploration of Interpersonal Communication*, 2d ed. (Englewood Cliffs, NJ: Prentice-Hall, 1979), ch. 11.

[47] Karen Rasmussen, "Nixon and the Strategy of Avoidance." *Central States Speech Journal*, 24 (Fall 1973): 193–202.

[48] Alan Scult, "Dialogue and Dichotomy: Some Problems in Martin Buber's Philosophy of Interpersonal Communication," paper presented at Speech Communication Association convention, Anaheim, CA, Nov. 1981; Gerald M. Phillips and Nancy J. Metzger, *Intimate Communication* (Boston: Allyn and Bacon, 1976), chs. 1, 11; Phillips, "Rhetoric and Its Alternatives as Bases for Examination of Intimate Communication," *Communication Quarterly*, 24 (Winter 1976): 11–23.

[49] Paul W. Keller, "Interpersonal Dissent and the Ethics of Dialogue," *Communication*, 6, no. 2 (1981): 287–304; Brown and Keller, *Monologue to Dialogue*, 2d ed., pp. 304–8. Also see Beverly A. Gaw, "Rhetoric and Its Alternatives as Bases for Examination of Intimate Communication: A Humanist Response," *Communication Quarterly*, 26 (Winter 1978): 13–20.

[50] For a discussion of a situation illustrating that, "depending on context, monologue may have positive or negative properties," see Karen Rasmussen, "Inconsistency in Campbell's *Rhetoric*: Explanation and Implication," *Quarterly Journal of Speech* 60 (April 1974): 198–99.

[51] John J. Makay and William R. Brown, *The Rhetorical Dialogue* (Dubuque, IA: William C. Brown Co., 1972), p. 27. For a detailed discussion of these conditions, see John J. Makay and Beverly A. Gaw, *Personal and Interpersonal Communication: Dialogue with the Self and with Others* (Columbus, OH: Charles E. Merrill Co., 1975), ch. 8.

[52] Cissna and Anderson draw primarily on Buber but also on the works of Mikhail Bakhtin and Hans-Georg Gadamer to identify the following characteristics of dialogue: immediacy or presence; emergent unanticipated consequences; recognition of "strange otherness"; collaborative orientation; vulnerability; mutual implication; temporal flow; and genuineness and authenticity. Kenneth R. Cissna and Rob Anderson, "Communication and the Ground of Dialogue," in *The Reach of Dialogue*. Anderson, Cissna, and Arnett, eds., pp. 9–30.

Chapter 5

Situational Perspectives

Situational perspectives focus regularly and primarily on the *elements of the specific communication situation at hand*. Virtually all perspectives (those mentioned in this book and others) make some allowances, on rare occasion, for the modified application of ethical criteria due to special circumstances. However, an extreme situational perspective routinely makes judgments only in light of *each different context*. Criteria from broad political, human nature, dialogical, or religious perspectives are minimized; absolute and universal standards are avoided.

Among the concrete situational or contextual factors that may be relevant to making a purely situational ethical evaluation are: (1) the role or function of the communicator for the audience (listeners or readers); (2) audience standards concerning reasonableness and appropriateness; (3) degree of audience awareness of the communicator's techniques; (4) degree of urgency for implementation of the communicator's proposal; (5) audience goals and values; (6) audience standards for ethical communication.

Two analysts of communication ethics offer their negative judgments of an extreme or "pure" situational perspective. "When the matter of ethics" is reduced to pure situationism, argues John Merrill, "it loses all meaning as ethics." "If every case is different, if every situation demands a different standard, if there are no absolutes in ethics, then we should scrap the whole subject . . . and simply be satisfied that each person run his life by his whims or 'considerations' which may change from situation to situation."[1] Bert Bradley concludes:[2]

> It appears . . . that situation ethics has an unsettling ability to justify a number of diverse decisions. It is not difficult to see how

situation ethics can be used to rationalize, either consciously or unconsciously, decisions and actions that stem from selfish and evasive origins.

An extremely vulnerable aspect of situation ethics is that it requires a high degree of sophistication in reasoning, objectivity in analysis, and an unusual breadth of perspective to exist in combination within a single individual. These attributes rarely occur singly in human beings.

Rogge's Situational Perspective

Edward Rogge develops a largely situational perspective in which ethics of communication are not to be measured against any "timeless, universal set of standards." Ethical criteria should, says Rogge, "vary as factors in the speech situation vary, . . . as the necessity for implementation of the persuader's proposal varies, . . . as his degree of leadership varies."[3]

A number of situational ethical judgments of communication derive from Rogge's analysis. It could be argued that unlabeled hyperbole (unidentified extreme exaggeration) is ethical in a political campaign (we have come to expect it as part of the game)[4] but is unethical in a classroom lecture. It could be argued that imperiled national security might justify use of otherwise unethical communication techniques (recollect the rationale given for the coverup of the Watergate break-in and the secret American bombing of Cambodia). It could be argued that an acknowledged leader has the responsibility in some situations to rally support, and thus could employ emotional appeals which circumvent human processes of rational choice. Rogge contends: "To insist that such speeches must be evaluated by how accurately the speaker used the methods of reasoning, or how frequently he short-circuited thinking, seems irrelevant. One of the functions of the leader is to overcome apathy."

In extending Rogge's viewpoint, it could be argued that a communicator may ethically employ techniques such as suggestion, innuendo, guilt-by-association, or unfounded name-calling as long as the audience both recognizes the use of such methods and approves of that use. Rogge specifically admits that "suggestion, if willingly submitted to by a majority of persuadees, is an ethical method of persuasion." In what ways should we agree or disagree with Rogge's situational perspective? How adequate and dependable a guide for ethical assessment of communication is a situational perspective?

Diggs's Situational Perspective

B. J. Diggs offers a partially situational perspective. He primarily focuses on the "contextual character of the ethical standards" which should govern persuasion.[5] Diggs believes that a persuader's role or position, as defined by the specific situation, audience and society, should determine what criteria are appropriate for judging the ethics of means and ends. In trying to persuade us, a friend, lawyer, or salesperson each would be subject to somewhat different ethical standards. Even generally accepted universal or societal ethical norms, says Diggs, often depend for their interpretation and application on the nature of the persuader's specific role with the audience.

Within his situational viewpoint stressing the nature of a persuader's specific role, Diggs suggests various guidelines for assessment of ethics, We should consider the degree to which we or another person: (1) has a *right* to communicate on the subject (has adequate knowledge of the subject and of audience needs and responsibilities); (2) has an *obligation* to communicate on the subject (perhaps due to role or possession of vitally needed information); (3) uses morally right communicative means; (4) urges the wise and right course; (5) and demonstrates good reasons for adopting the view advocated.[6] How valuable as guidelines are these considerations suggested by Diggs?

Diggs also notes that the receiver or persuadee can share in the blame for unethical persuasion. Being gullible, *too* open-minded, or being too closed-minded, Diggs argues, can allow the success of unethical persuasion. Do you agree with Diggs? Who should bear the prime responsibility for the ethical level of persuasion in a society—the persuader, the audience, or both?

Fletcher's Situation Ethics

In 1966, Joseph Fletcher, a professor of social ethics at an Episcopal theological school, published his controversial book, *Situation Ethics: The New Morality*.[7] One premise of his Christian situation ethics is that ethical judgments of human behavior, including communication, should be made in light of specific situational factors rather than according to prescriptive or absolute standards. Another premise of his Christian situation ethics is that there is *one* absolute ethical criterion to guide situational evaluations—namely, *love* for fellow humans in the form of genuine affection for them and concern for their welfare. This loving relationship is similar in some respects to attitudes characteristic of dialogue as examined previously in chapter 4.[8]

To aid in the ethical evaluation of human behavior, Fletcher outlines four general situational elements which easily could be used to judge communication ethics: What is the end or goal sought? What means or methods are used to achieve the end? What motive(s) generate the effort? What are the foreseeable immediate and remote consequences of the end and means?[9]

Two quotations summarize Fletcher's concept of Christian situation ethics. "The situationist enters into every decision-making situation armed with the ethical maxims of his community and its heritage, and he treats them with respect as illuminators of his problems. Just the same he is prepared in any situation to compromise them or set them aside in the situation if love seems better served by doing so."

> Christian situation ethics has only one norm or principle or law . . . that is binding and unexceptionable, always good and right regardless of the circumstances. That is "love"—the *agape* of the summary commandment to love God and the neighbor. Everything else without exception, all laws and rules and principles and ideals and norms, are only *contingent*, only valid *if they happen* to serve love in any situation.[10]

Alinsky's Situational Perspective

In *Rules for Radicals*, Saul Alinsky, a noted community organizer, presents an essentially situational perspective for evaluating the ethics of communication and persuasion as forces for societal change. He does espouse the democratic political values of equality, justice, peace, cooperation, educational and economic opportunity, freedom, right of dissent, and the preciousness of human life.[11] But Alinsky constantly stresses that situational and contextual ethical judgments of communication are necessary for actualizing these goals. The communicator persuading in behalf of significant societal change, believes Alinsky, must view truth and all values as relative.[12] In the revised edition of *Reveille for Radicals*, Alinsky argues pragmatically: "We must accept open-ended systems of ethics and values, not only to meet constantly changing conditions but also to keep changing ourselves, in order to survive in the fluid society that lies ahead of us. Such systems must be workable in the world *as it is* and not unrealistically aimed toward the world *as we would like it to be*."[13]

Alinsky develops eleven rules for ethical judgment of means and ends, including communicative means and ends, in societal agitation and protest.[14] Note the distinctly situational nature of many of these rules, particularly the third, fourth, fifth, and eighth. To what extent should we accept Alinsky's view as a desirable and workable ethical perspective? In paraphrased and condensed form, Alinsky's rules are:

1. One's concern with the ethics of means and ends varies inversely with one's personal interest in the issue. When our interest is minimal or when we are far from the scene of conflict, we can afford the luxury of morality.
2. The judgment of the ethics of means is dependent upon the political position of those sitting in judgment. (For illustration of this variability, refer to the diverse political perspectives which we examined in chapter 2.)
3. In war the end justifies almost any means. Alinsky does not mean solely military combat. "A war is not an intellectual debate, and in the war against social evils there are no rules of fair play."[15]
4. Judgment must be made in the context of the times in which the action occurred and not from any other chronological vantage point.
5. Concern with ethics increases with the number of means available and vice versa. Moral questions may enter when we have the opportunity to choose among equally effective alternative means.
6. The less important the end desired, the more one can afford to engage in ethical evaluations of means.
7. Generally, success or failure is a mighty determinant of ethics. A successful outcome may allow the suspect means to be rationalized as ethical.
8. The morality of a means depends upon whether the means is being employed at a time of imminent defeat or imminent victory. The same means used when victory is assured may be judged immoral, but when used in desperate circumstances may be acceptable.
9. Any effective means automatically is judged by the opposition as unethical.
10. You do what you can with what you have and clothe it with moral garments. Leaders such as Churchill, Gandhi, Lincoln, and Jefferson always covered naked self-interest in the clothing of "moral principles" such as "freedom," "equality of humankind," "a law higher than man-made law," and so on.

11. Goals must be phrased in powerful general terms such as "Liberty, Equality, Fraternity," "Of the Common Welfare," "Pursuit of Happiness," or "Bread and Peace." (In this connection we profitably might examine the contemporary use of slogans and phrases which reflect potent value commitments: Duty, Honor, Country; Law and Order; Law and Order with Justice; Freedom Now!; All Power to the People; Peace with Honor.)[16]

Alinsky also offers a number of "rules" for utilizing "power tactics" to aid the "have-nots" in taking power away from the "haves." In most cases, these rules can be applied to tactics and techniques of protest communication. Apart from the situational perspective in which they are rooted, what might be some other ethical perspectives and sets of standards which appropriately could be applied to assess the ethics of these rules? Do *you* believe that any of these rules or tactics are unethical and, if so, why? Alinsky discusses these rules at length in *Rules for Radicals*; they are presented here in condensed and partially paraphrased form.[17]

1. Power is not only what you have but what the enemy thinks you have.
2. Never go outside the experience of your people.
3. Whenever possible go outside the experience of the enemy. Attempt to cause confusion, fear, and retreat.
4. Make the enemy live up to their own book of rules. They will be unable to do so and you can expose them.
5. Ridicule is man's most potent weapon. The opposition finds it almost impossible to counterattack ridicule, is infuriated, and then overreacts to your advantage.
6. A good tactic is one that your people enjoy.
7. A tactic that drags on too long becomes a drag.
8. Keep the pressure on, with different tactics and actions.
9. The threat is usually more terrifying than the thing itself.
10. The major premise for tactics is the development of operations that will maintain a constant pressure on the opposition.
11. If you push a negative hard and deep enough it will break through into its counterside. Mistakes made by the enemy can be converted to your advantage.
12. The price of a successful attack is a constructive alternative. If the opposition finally admits the problem, you must have a solution ready.

13. Pick the target, freeze it, personalize it, and polarize it. Select your target from the many available, constantly focus on it, attack a concrete person who represents the opposing institution, and force a choice between all good and all bad.

Ethical Issues in Social Protest Situations

Is the use of so-called "obscene" and "profane" words ethical in some public communication situations? In American culture, such words often are viewed as acceptable (if not ethical) in certain clearly specified private or semiprivate communication settings. Such words are not severely frowned upon, for instance, in an Army barracks, in some family settings, and between some close friends.

But what of public communication settings in such forms as public speeches, newspaper editorials, and argumentative essays? During the 1960s and 1970s, communicators who engaged in social protest often utilized obscenity and profanity to express deep emotion or to further some more ultimate goal. What ethical judgment should be made of such use in protest and according to what standards? Sidney Hook,[18] as part of his political perspective (discussed in chapter 2), judged as unethical the use of obscenity in protest "by certain radical student groups" because such language is "incompatible with the whole process of democracy, and tends to destroy it." To what extent would you agree or disagree with this judgment?

J. Dan Rothwell concludes his analysis of the serious functions which obscenity can serve in protest rhetoric with this provocative summary:

> Neither denunciation nor suppression of its use is an adequate response to the fact of verbal obscenity; the students of rhetoric must seek to understand the purposes and effects of this rhetorical strategy. Despite centuries of negative criticism, verbal obscenity has become a more frequent rhetorical device. It is successful in creating attention, in discrediting an enemy, in provoking violence, in fostering identification, and in providing catharsis. . . . Hoping it will go away will not make it so. It is time to accept verbal obscenity as a significant rhetorical device and help discover appropriate responses to its use.[19]

Communicators whose aim is persuasion usually seek to generate between themselves and their audience an end-state variously described as consensus, agreement, or identification. But on occasion some communicators see *promotion of conflict*, *unrest*, and *tension* as desirable for a healthy and growing society. In specific situations, such communicators view aggressive, abrasive, nonconciliatory (sometimes coercive) techniques of protest rhetoric as pragmatically and ethically justifiable.[20] Franklyn Haiman, in his lecture, "The Rhetoric of 1968: A Farewell to Rational Discourse," not only describes the characteristics of contemporary protest rhetoric but also assesses the effectiveness of such rhetoric and uses a largely situational perspective to justify much of it ethically.[21]

Herbert W. Simons argues that "inciting or exacerbating conflict may be just as ethical as working at preventing, managing, or resolving it." Rather than assuming that coercive and confrontative rhetoric necessarily is evil, Simons urges that we evaluate users of such rhetoric open-mindedly "in light of the ends they sought to achieve, the conditions under which they took action, and the consequences of their acts on themselves, on other interested parties, and on the system as a whole."[22]

Kenneth Keniston contends that under "many circumstances" people should "deliberately create" psychological conflict "within those whose behavior belies their professed values" and social conflict "between those who condone or ignore injustice and those who wish to correct it." He argues that "the value of conflict cannot be judged apart from its contexts, objects, and results."[23]

Protesters often present an ethical rationale for their use of extreme rhetorical tactics. Frequently they argue that society must be awakened to a crucial problem, that the true evil nature of an opponent must be exposed, or that the traditional channels and types of public communication and decision making are inadequate for certain groups or in certain contexts. This latter point concerning the inadequacy of traditional modes of public persuasion is an assumption held by many protesters and by some analysts of confrontation rhetoric. It is an assumption sometimes used for ethical justification without accompanying evidence that this assumption is true in a given instance.[24]

As proof of the inadequacy of traditional channels and types of public communication and decision making, and thus as support for the ethicality of extreme and less traditional persuasive techniques, practitioners and analysts of confrontation rhetoric sometimes cite one or more of the following reasons.

1. Traditional methods are too slow and cumbersome to meet pressing societal problems.

2. Some segments of the citizenry do not have ready access to the traditional channels, perhaps due to high cost, ethnic discrimination, or Establishment control.
3. The Establishment simply refuses to listen. (Note that some protesters assume that an answer of "no" can be taken as absolute proof of refusal to listen; they assume that willingness to listen is proven only by acceptance of *their* viewpoint.)
4. The Establishment cannot be trusted. (Note that mutual trust is a basic element in many traditional modes of communication.)
5. Traditional modes have become masks for perpetuating injustice. When delay of decision is the Establishment goal, for example, a "study committee" is appointed to "investigate" the problem.
6. Some citizens lack facility with words and must turn to nonverbal and fragmentary means to symbolize their grievance. (Note that skill in word use is a requisite for effective utilization of most traditional channels.)
7. Traditional modes emphasize reasoned discourse which today seems increasingly irrelevant to the great moral issues. (Note that rationality and reasonableness are assumed in the Anglo-American heritage of rhetorical theory. See the discussion of this point in chapter 7.)
8. Traditional modes lead to negotiation and compromise, which are unacceptable outcomes in light of the protesters' "nonnegotiable" demands and clear perception of moral truth. Protesters would be co-opted by the assumption of conciliation inherent in traditional rhetoric.

In what ways would you agree or disagree with the above reasons as support for the ethics of extreme protest rhetoric? What concrete ethical guidelines *should be* used as most appropriate for scrutinizing the rhetoric of social protest and confrontation? For instance, are the situational and political perspectives more appropriate than the human nature and dialogical perspectives? Why? What are other alternatives?

"Moralistic preferences for order, civility, rationality, and decorum are still merely preferences. Such preferences may mask injustice, ignore the marginalized, and even become rationales for the powerful." These assumptions by Steven Goldzwig undergird his defense of such "demagogic" strategies and tactics as threats, shattering of consensus, polarization, vilification, and conspiracy appeals as sometimes necessary, effective, and ethical modes of agitation in social protest efforts.[25]

He urges development and application of new ethical standards to more adequately evaluate the ethics of social protest agitation. As one suggestion, he proposes suspending ethical judgment of a "demagogue" until the "ultimate purpose" of the suspect tactic can be determined. An additional possibility is to employ a "situational ethic in which hyperbole, emotional appeals, suggestion, innuendo, name-calling, and guilt by association" might be viewed in a more favorable ethical light under certain circumstances. Consideration of "ends, means, motives, short- and long-term consequences, the duty to communicate or not to communicate, and the employment of good reasons" are among Goldzwig's possible relevant ethical criteria.

Notes

[1] John C. Merrill, *The Imperative of Freedom* (New York: Hastings House, 1974), chs. 8–10, espec. pp. 170–73.

[2] Bert E. Bradley, *Fundamentals of Speech Communication: The Credibility of Ideas*, 3rd ed. (Dubuque, IA: William C. Brown Co., 1981), pp. 27–29.

[3] Edward Rogge, "Evaluating the Ethics of a Speaker in a Democracy," *Quarterly Journal of Speech*, 45 (December 1959): 419–25.

[4] Doris Graber, "Political Communication," in *Communication Yearbook 2*, ed. Brent, Ruben (New Brunswick, NJ: Transaction Books, 1978), p. 417.

[5] B. J. Diggs, "Persuasion and Ethics," *Quarterly Journal of Speech*, 50 (December 1964): 359–73; For a response by Howard H. Martin questioning some facets of Diggs's position, and for Diggs's reply, see *Quarterly Journal of Speech*, 51 (October 1965): 329–33.

[6] On the concept of "good reasons," see Karl R. Wallace, "The Substance of Rhetoric: Good Reasons," *Quarterly Journal of Speech*, 49 (October 1963): 239–49; Walter R. Fisher, "Toward a Logic of Good Reasons," *Ibid.*, 64 (December 1978): 376–84.

[7] Joseph Fletcher, *Situation Ethics: The New Morality* (Philadelphia: Westminster Press, 1966). See also Fletcher, *Moral Responsibility: Situation Ethics at Work* (Philadelphia: Westminster Press, 1967). For some pro and con evaluations of Fletcher's view, see Harvey Cox, ed., *The Situation Ethics Debate* (Philadelphia: Westminster Press, 1968).

[8] For example, Fletcher, *Situation Ethics*, pp. 51, 79, 103.

[9] *Ibid.*, pp. 127–28.

[10] *Ibid.*, pp. 26, 30.

[11] Saul D. Alinsky, *Rules for Radicals: A Practical Primer for Realistic Radicals* (New York: Random House, 1971), pp. xxiv, 3, 12, 22, 46–47. For further evaluation of Alinsky's position on social agitation, see the interview with him in *Playboy*, March 1972, pp. 59–79, 169–78.

[12] Alinsky, *Rules for Radicals*, pp. 7, 11–12, 79.

[13] Saul D. Alinsky, *Reveille for Radicals* (New York: Vintage Books, 1969), p. 207.

[14] Alinsky, *Rules for Radicals*, pp. 24–47.

[15] Alinsky, *Reveille for Radicals*, pp. 132–33.

[16] For a penetrating analysis of the persuasive functions of potent value concepts ("god terms" and "devil terms"), see Richard M. Weaver, *The Ethics of Rhetoric* (Chicago: Regnery, 1953), chapter 9.

[17] Alinsky, *Rules for Radicals*, pp. 126–164.

[18] Sidney Hook, "The Ethics of Political Controversy," in *The Ethics of Controversy: Politics and Protest*, Donn W. Parson and Wil Linkugel, eds. (Lawrence, KS: The House of Usher, 1968), p. 61. Also see Thomas R. Nilsen, *Ethics of Speech Communication*, 2d ed. (Indianapolis: Bobbs-Merrill, 1972), pp. 65–68.

[19] J. Dan Rothwell, "Verbal Obscenity: Time for Second Thoughts," *Western Speech* 35 (Fall 1971): 231–42. Also see Haig Bosmajian, "Obscenity and Protest," in *Dissent: Symbolic Behavior and Rhetorical Strategies*, Haig Bosmajian, ed. (Boston: Allyn and Bacon, 1972), pp. 294–306; J. Dan Rothwell, *Telling It Like It Isn't* (Englewood Cliffs, NJ: Prentice-Hall 1982), ch. 4.

[20] See, for example, Herbert W. Simons, "Persuasion in Social Conflicts: A Critique of Prevailing Conceptions and a Framework for Future Research," *Speech Monographs* 39 (November 1972): especially 238–40; Parke G. Burgess, "Crisis Rhetoric: Coercion vs. Force," *Quarterly Journal of Speech* 59 (February 1973): especially 69–73; Franklyn S. Haiman, "The Rhetoric of the Streets: Some Legal and Ethical implications," *Quarterly Journal of Speech* 53 (April 1967): 99–114; Alinsky, *Rules for Radicals*, pp. 59, 62; Kenneth Keniston, *Youth and Dissent* (New York: Harvest Book, 1971), pp. 319, 336, 388–89.

[21] Haiman's lecture is reprinted in Johannesen, *Ethics in Human Communication*, 2d ed, pp. 177–90. On the nature and characteristics of protest and confrontation rhetoric, see, for example, John W. Bowers, Donovan Ochs, and Richard J. Jensen, *The Rhetoric of Agitation and Control*, 2d ed. (Prospect Heights, IL: Waveland Press, 1993); Charles Stewart, et al., *Persuasion and Social Movements*, 3rd ed. (Prospect Heights, IL: Waveland Press, 1994).

[22] Simons, "Persuasion in Social Conflicts," pp. 238–40.

[23] Keniston, *Youth and Dissent*, p. 319.

[24] For two efforts to document the existence of this assumed inadequacy of traditional channels and types of public persuasion, see Howard Zinn, *Disobedience and Democracy* (New York: Vintage Books, 1968), pp. 7, 53–68, 105; Ruth McGaffey, "A Critical Look at the Marketplace of Ideas," *The Speech Teacher* 21 (March 1972); 115–22.

[25] Steven R. Goldzwig, "A Social Movement Perspective on Demagoguery: Achieving Symbolic Realignment," *Communication Studies*, 40 (Fall 1989): 202–28.

Chapter 6

Religious, Utilitarian, and Legal Perspectives

Religious Perspectives: General Nature

Various world religions emphasize moral and spiritual values, guidelines, and rules that can be employed as standards for evaluating the ethics of communication. One source for ethical criteria would be the sacred literature of a particular religion, such as the Bible, Koran, or Talmud.[1] Furthermore, interpretations stemming from a religion may present standards for ethical communication.

The Old Testament clearly admonishes Jews and Christians against use of lies and slander. The Lord commands Moses, "You shall not steal, or deal falsely, nor lie to one another." The Psalmist reports, "Let not slander be established in the land." In the New Testament, Christians are told, "Let everyone speak the truth with his neighbor. . . ." Jesus warns, "I tell you, on the day of judgment men will render account for every careless word they utter; for by your words you will be justified and by your words you will be condemned."[2]

A Christian Ethic for Persuasion

The source of human religiousness is a person's creation in the image of God. This premise underlies a religious perspective on persuasion and communication developed by Charles Veenstra and Daryl Vander Kooi.[3] Because humans are created in God's image, they are endowed with a uniquely human capacity for ethical judgment, they honor God through worship and the quality of their relationships with other persons, and they have the capacities for creative thought and communication not possessed by other creatures. Veenstra and Vander Kooi derive a number of "principles" for a Christian ethic of persuasion and communication. First, humans deserve full respect as reflections of God's image. We should communicate with others in the same loving and respectful spirit we worship God.

Second, honesty should be practiced in all aspects of persuasion. Persuaders should be open with audiences concerning their intentions and accurate with audiences concerning all facts relevant to ideas, policies, or products.

> Honesty necessitates careful documentation of facts, solid information, cogent reasoning, clear statistics, quoting within context, appropriate emotional appeals, use of genuine experts, etc. If the persuader fully respects the persuadee, he will not try to bypass the persuadee's ability to think, to weigh alternatives, to choose, since these abilities make up part of the image of God in that persuadee.

However, the requirement for honesty does not demand full and complete disclosure at all times. Tactfulness and sensitivity to others' feelings should guide implementation of the principle of honesty. In addition, receivers of communication have the ethical responsibility to be honest in their feedback, that is, in their expression of interest and attention, of feelings, of judgments, and of disagreements.

Third, only the best language should be employed. As a guiding question, they ask: "Is this the best language I can use to show respect for the image of God in a person?" Profanity and obscenity clearly would be unethical. Fourth, the genuine needs of an audience should be determined and an attempt made to meet those real needs. Needs should not be manufactured where none actually exist. Appeals to genuine needs should not be confused with appeals to audience wants and preferences. Fifth, communication techniques and appeals should be appropriate for the subject, participants, and situation. Techniques and appeals should be relevant to the genuine needs being addressed. In Christian evangelism, for example, conversion should stem from commitment of both heart and mind, from both emotional and logical appeals.

The Mass Media and Christian Morality

"Authentic Christian morality" is a concept developed by Kyle Haselden as a standard for evaluating the morality of communication, especially mass communication.[4] Two other possible "Christian" standards are examined by Haselden and rejected: Christian legalism and Christian situation ethics. Christian legalism, according to Haselden, assumes that the Ten Commandments, the teaching of Jesus and his disciples, and church doctrines derived from them, provide a "detailed, inflexible, always appropriate moral code" which is "adequate for all times, places, persons, and circumstances." This legalist approach fails, he argues, because it externalizes and mechanizes morality, takes a negative, restrictive, static stance, emphasizes trivialities, predetermines the range of future decisions, and "precludes the working of the Holy Spirit."

In chapter 5 we examined the nature of Joseph Fletcher's Christian situation ethics in which love is the sole standard to be used in judging what is ethical in the context of each specific, unique, situation. Haselden finds this view defective because it too easily fosters unprincipled behavior, unrealistically disconnects each act and situation from tradition, law and revelation, and utilizes an inadequate definition of love simply as benevolence or good will.

Authentic Christian morality, according to Haselden, strives to secure the freedom, the latitude of choice, necessary to transform people into persons (as opposed to treating them as things, animals, or machines). God's will for humans, as exemplified in Jesus Christ, stresses love as the force leading to the experience of oneness. But this love goes beyond simple benevolence to include sexual, aesthetic, and parental love. Indeed this love combines and transforms all of these into a oneness within appropriate ethical guidelines. Haselden also contends that "it is not possible to be a genuine Christian without participating in authentic morality" and that "it is possible to participate in genuine morality without being a Christian or even a theist."

Haselden applies ethical criteria rooted in his concept of authentic Christian morality. In the course of his ethical scrutiny, he assesses the degree of morality of various mass media: books, magazines, radio, television, films, and commercial advertising.[5] Concerning the philosophy that guides the commercial advertising industry, Haselden concludes that it is "antithetical to almost everything we have been taught as Christians." As guidelines for exploring ethical issues in mass communication, Haselden suggests several sets of questions.[6]

> Are we really concerned about the effect of that medium on people or are we concerned about its effect on things secondary to people? Does our deepest focus fall on the national image, static customs, honored institutions, memories of how much better things and people were in the old days, organized religion, our personal fear of painful change, or on people? . . .

So the question that we should ask about the impact of the media of mass communication on our society is whether they help people become persons or prevent their being persons. Do they facilitate and promote man's emergence as true man—integrated, independent, and responsible—or do they transform man into a receptacle, a puppet, an echo?

Do modern forms of communication help man to be his full self? Do they discover and encourage the unfolding of his latent possibilities? Or, do they reduce all men to a stale pattern of conformity, blighting those individual traits that add charm and possibility to the whole society? Does mass communication inevitably mean the emergence of a mass mind, an intellectual ant heap, an amorphous religiosity, and a collective ethic? Will the media eventually standardize all human behavior at the level of the lowest conduct in the society, or will they enrich the general tone and character of the people?

Religious Perspectives on Advertising

John McMillin contends that the first responsibility of an advertiser is not to either business or society but rather to God and to principles higher than self, society, or business.[7] Thus, advertisers are responsible to multiple neighbors—to owners, employees, clients, customers, and the general public. Second, they have a responsibility for objective truth. Third, they are responsible for preparing advertising messages with a sense of respect for their audience. Finally, argues McMillin, advertisers are responsible for seeking product improvements.

In 1962 a committee of the Illinois Synod of the Presbyterian Church published a statement on "Ethics in Advertising."[8] As a foundation for their ethical guidelines, from a Christian viewpoint they describe the essential characteristics of human nature, the purposes of human life, and the values and obligations stemming from such nature and purposes. They differentiate between "factual truth" that can be verified through empirical observation and demonstration and "impressionistic truth" that employs feeling and imagination to go beyond but not violate the facts. "Truth is greater than mere facts," but cannot be "contrary to fact." Anyone who attempts to persuade the public should employ both kinds of truth but should avoid presentations that misrepresent or mislead. Based on the remainder of their discussion, it is possible to extract and summarize a number of ethical standards for advertising.

1. Advertising methods should not dull perception and judgment through harassing or wearing down the mind.

2. Appeals should be to "higher" emotions and desires rather than to "lower" ones such as vanity, status, false images of happiness, self-indulgence, or lust for power.
3. Products advertised should meet genuine needs in consumers' lives, "not artificially stimulated needs." Extravagant consumption should not be stimulated merely to create a larger market. Products actually should provide increased comfort, convenience, or service.
4. Merits and features of products should be presented honestly rather than distorting the facts while barely remaining "within the legal limits of the truth."
5. Appeals should be in good taste. Some appeals in bad taste would be sensationalism to create false impressions, blatant sounds that irritate in order to capture attention, or words and pictures that debase, exploit, or mock things we commonly accept as private or sacred.
6. Advertising methods should be fair and honorable rather than unfair and dishonorable. To be avoided are unfounded comparisons; claims for added features or ingredients that exaggerate far beyond their actual performance; comparisons that degrade other products through implication; animation or dramatization that creates false impressions; exaggerated claims that exploit consumer ignorance or insult their intelligence.

An Ethic for Christian Evangelism

An ethic for the Christian who seeks to persuade others to commit themselves to Christianity has been developed by Emory Griffin.[9] Employing the metaphorical imagery of love and courtship, he finds in the Bible, in Plato's *Phaedrus*, and in Soren Kierkegaard's *Philosophical Fragments* bases for his viewpoint. Griffin describes the communication practices of the ethical Christian lover-persuader and of various unethical lover-persuaders. Each type of persuader is described in part by the degree to which they implement the twin requirements of *love* (genuine concern for the consequences of an act upon other persons) and *justice* (adherence to universal rules of Christian conduct).

The *true lover*, the ethical Christian persuader, is both loving and just. Such persuaders care more about the welfare of others than about their own egos. They use appeals that respect the human rights of others, including the right to say no. The *non-lover* attempts to avoid persuasion by taking a nonmanipulative, detached, uninvolved stance. Indeed, Griffin sees this type as even more unethical than various false lovers because non-lovers are uncaring about their own beliefs or about other persons.

Various types of false lover-persuaders deny to others the free choice of whether to accept Christ. The *flirt* sees people simply as souls to be counted. The evangelist "who is more concerned about getting another scalp" for his or her collection than for the welfare of others exemplifies the Christian flirt. The *seducer* employs deception, flattery, and irrelevant appeals to success, money, patriotism, popularity, or comfort to entice the audience. Because the religious seducer induces decisions for the wrong reasons, she or he is unethical. The *rapist* uses psychological coercion virtually to force a commitment. Intense emotional appeals, such as to guilt, effectively "remove the element of conscious choice." The *smother lover* overwhelms others with love, so much so that he or she will not take no for an answer. Smother lovers believe that they know what is best for everyone else, treat everyone identically, and ignore the uniqueness of each person. Their persuasion is unethical, believes Griffin, because it fails to respect the free choice of others. Finally, the *legalistic lover* lacks genuine love and persuades purely "out of a sense of obligation or duty." The legalistic lover may go through the motions when there is no genuine need, when he or she no longer feels personally motivated, or even when relevant human needs are being ignored.

The National Religious Broadcasters' Code

"America's scandal-plagued religious broadcasters adopted a rigorous set of ethical and financial guidelines Wednesday in an attempt to restore public confidence in the integrity of the $2 billion-a-year television and radio evangelism industry." Thus began a column by Bruce Buursma, the religion reporter for the *Chicago Tribune* (February 4, 1985, sec. 1, p. 5; also see February 7, 1985, sec. 1, p. 3). At their annual meeting the National Religious Broadcasters' Commission on Ethics and Financial Integrity adopted a stringent code to govern members of the association. Of special interest for a discussion of communication ethics are the following standards excerpted from the Commission By-Laws: (1) all requests for financial support shall be made in an ethical and dignified manner; (2) every appeal for funds should be directed toward motivating the believers to participate in

Christian ministries as a part of Biblical responsibilities; (3) the trust relationship between donor and fundraiser requires that funds collected be used for the intended purpose and not be absorbed by excessive fundraising costs; (4) appeals for funds shall not be associated with material objects which are inconsistent with the spiritual purposes of the appeal (would you consider plastic statues of Jesus or Mary, so-called prayer handkerchiefs, "blessed" water, or stones with "spiritual" healing power to be consistent or appropriate?); (5) fundraising appeals must communicate realistic expectations to the donor of what the donor's gift will accomplish within the limits of the organization's ministry; (6) incentives and premiums offered by a ministry must be presented in a manner that is clear and factual to avoid misleading the donor.

Oral Roberts's Controversial Fundraising Appeal

On two weekends in January 1987, evangelist Oral Roberts recounted on his syndicated television program an encounter with God the previous year. God told him that Roberts would not be allowed to live beyond March 1987 unless he raised $8 million to be used for 69 scholarships for medical students at Oral Roberts University to allow them to serve in medical clinics overseas. In an emotion-laden plea to his viewers, Roberts asked: "Will you help me extend my life?" Roberts's chief spokeswoman, Jan Dargatz, defended Roberts's motives to reporters but conceded that his "methods have hit the fan." Dargatz said that Roberts sincerely believed the fund drive was a do-or-die effort" and believed it "from the very core of his being." The Rev. John Wolf, senior minister of Tulsa's All Souls Unitarian Church, condemned the appeal as "emotional blackmail" and as an "act of desperation" (Account taken from Bruce Buursma, *Chicago Tribune*, January 17, 1987, sec. 1, pp. 1, 10). Another news report revealed that in 1986 Roberts had made a similar appeal. Roberts told a Dallas audience that his "life is on the line" and that God "would take me this year" if he did not raise necessary funds to finance "holy missionary teams." "Because if I don't do it," Roberts said, "I'm going to be gone before the year is out. I'll be with the Father. I know it as much as I'm standing here." Roberts failed to raise the necessary money (*Chicago Tribune*, February 26, 1987, sec. 1, p. 4).

Now attempt to assess the ethicality of Roberts's appeals. Particularly bring to bear the ethic for Christian evangelism developed by

Emory Griffin. Is Roberts's appeal best characterized as that of the true lover, non-lover, flirt, seducer, rapist, smother lover, or legalistic lover? Why? Also apply any of the relevant standards of the National Religious Broadcasters. How might versions of the human nature or the dialogical ethical perspectives apply? What about the issues of conscious intent, sincerity, habits of character, and good ends justifying dubious means? How might these issues influence your ethical evaluations? Finally, consider the Christian ethic for persuasion proposed by Veenstra and Vander Kooi. How relevant is it and how might it apply?

Several Asiatic and Mid-Eastern Religious Perspectives

Several oriental religions also provide examples of religious perspectives for accepting or shunning certain communication appeals.[10] The Confucian religion generally has tended to shun emotional appeals and stress fact and logic. But within the Confucian religious mainstream, various tributaries and rivulets have occurred. A sixteenth-century scholar named Yulgok developed a view which approved appeals to any or all of seven passions (joy, anger, sorrow, fear, love, hatred, and desire) as means of persuading people to adopt the four principles of charity, duty to neighbors, propriety, and wisdom. The School of Rites, a sixteenth-century variation of Confucianism, emphasized ritualistic patterns of human behavior. Thus depth of understanding, the policy advocated, and the facts of the matter were less crucial than proper modes of procedure. Taoist religion stresses empathy and insight, rather than reason and logic, as roads to truth. Citing facts and demonstrating logical conclusions are minimized in favor of feeling and intuition. In Buddhism a number of sacred truths that seekers of morality must follow center on ethical communication: avoid anger, gossip and boasting; avoid quarreling; avoid lies and false speech; employ words that give peace; and speak with a pure mind.

The theocratic state of Iran is a "God-fearing" state in which the unity of God, humankind, and nature is assumed. It is, as Thomas Cooper describes it, a state in which Allah is supreme and all human-made laws are void. International laws governing communication and codes of ethics are irrelevant; the role of the media becomes "commanding to the right and prohibiting the wrong." Cooper observes: "This doctrine subjugates all media to the purpose of preparing the next generation for their role as Muslims. Media become strictly a cultural and educational tool that propagates a comprehensively organized religious ethic, one that governs all legal, political, and social subsystems of Muslim society. Always on guard against sacrilegious tendencies of foreign media . . . , the operative code of Iranian mass media is . . . undiluted Muslim ethics."[11]

Shared Perspectives

J. Vernon Jensen examines the ancient Eastern and Western religions of Hinduism, Buddhism, Taiosm, Confucianism, Judaism, Christianity, and Islam and finds that, despite significant differences in core values, views of the deity, and sacred truths, these seven world religions share some commonalities concerning communication ethics.[12] Generally, these religions stress individual responsibilities more than rights, and they typically employ negatively worded statements to identify specifically what not to do. Jensen isolates a core of six ethical standards for communication held in common by these religious traditions: (1) tell the truth and avoid lies; (2) do not slander anyone; (3) do not blaspheme, dishonor, and profane the sacred persons, symbols, or rituals central to the religion; (4) avoid communication that demeans other persons or life in general by being "evil, shameful, foolish, clever, cunning, glib, or vain"; (5) aim habitually to embody ethical virtues in your character as preparation for ethical communication and aim to become trustworthy—to earn trust; and (6) go beyond traditional notions of communicating to inform, persuade, and please in order to to aim at "edifying" others, that is, showing them how close to excellence humans can become. Jensen argues in conclusion: "One need not be a 'believer' to appreciate the power of the values expressed in these various traditions, and with a reasonable amount of filtering, we would learn from them to our benefit."

Utilitarian Perspectives: General Nature

Utilitarianism is a type of teleological or consequentialist ethics; evaluation of consequences is the test. Utilitarian perspectives emphasize criteria of usefulness, pleasure, and happiness to assess communication ethics. Wayne Brockriede synthesizes one standard for ethical rhetoric from the influential utilitarian view of English philosopher Jeremy Bentham: "good reasons, supported by specific and abundant evidence, free from fallacies, expressed in clear language, and showing that the given proposal will probably promote the greatest happiness of the greatest number of people."[13] Thomas Hearn points to ambiguity lurking in the phrase "the greatest happiness of the greatest number." On the one hand, it could mean that, after considering everyone's interests, we do what will produce the most good, the greatest happiness. On the other hand, it could mean that we should benefit the maximum number of persons. Says Hearn, "the formula may require that one should do *the most good*, or that one should benefit *the most persons*. Depending on which version of the principle is adopted, different answers are obtained about what is to be done in certain moral situations."[14]

The utilitarian standard for evaluating communicative means and ends could be phrased as a question: Does the technique or goal promote the greatest good for the greatest number in the long run? Bear in mind that the utilitarian perspective usually is applied in combination with other perspectives. The definition of "good" often is derived from religious, political, human nature, or other vantage points. The standard(s) or value(s) that provide the substance for the concept of "good" often are rooted in such other perspectives. Also remember that some utilitarian perspectives, such as the one next described, could be viewed as a partly situational perspective (as discussed in chapter 5) or as a type of political perspective (as discussed in chapter 2). Later utilitarians expanded the concept of happiness to encompass such intrinsically worthy values as friendship, health, and knowledge.

The Social Utility Approach

In a number of sources, William S. Howell (sometimes with Winston Brembeck) has developed a "social utility" approach to communication ethics. Howell offers this approach as applicable for both public persuasion and for intimate communication, for both communication *within* a given culture and for intercultural communication *between* people of different cultures.[15]

This social utility approach stresses usefulness to the people affected and the survival potential for groups involved. Ethically adequate communication, for Howell, "assesses the short-range and long-range consequences of the communicative act, including the benefits to and negative effects on the group and on particular individuals." Ethical communication should "benefit most of the people involved" with "minimum harm to individuals." Standards of "benefit" and of "harm" are rooted in a "culture's ongoing value system, and thus can be described as *cultural-specific*. What is useful in one culture may well be detrimental in another." Among the questions that might be asked in applying the social utility approach are: Is there a revealed or concealed penalty to be paid? Could injury to one or a few individuals outweigh group gains?

That the ethics of communication is a function of context is an assumption basic to Howell's view. Universal standards for communication ethics are inappropriate. "Circumstances and people exert powerful influences. To say it differently, applied ethics constitute a necessarily open system. The environment, the situation, the timing of an interaction, human relationships, all affect the way ethical standards are applied." While not approving universal standards, Howell claims that the social utility approach is a framework that can be applied universally.

Howell suggests six criteria that should be met by any useful and workable system of communication ethics. First, the system protects the fabric of its culture. A society's intricately woven fabric of values and basic assumptions should be preserved. "Whatever strengthens or protects the fabric of a culture is ethical. What strains, weakens, or tears it is unethical." Second, ethical responsibilities are shared by both communicator and communicatee. "What the receiver does with the message he receives can contribute as much to the ethical qualities of a communication as the intent and strategies of the sender." Third, it must be both pragmatic and idealistic, both workable and desirable. "Operationally, ideals are useful as goals, to establish directions that are necessary to effect change." But, Howell believes, "instead of trying to assess only the *goodness* of an ideal, let the further criterion, 'Does it work?' be emphasized." The ideal is operationally effective if it modifies behavior significantly in the direction of the moral goal it embodies. Fourth, the system of ethics is sensitive to the gap between verbalization and action, between words and deeds. It must allow "for the human capacity to say one thing and do something else." Fifth, it accepts relativity in the application of ethical principles, even when a principle is almost universally agreed to. The ethics of communication is a function of context. Sixth, social utility is the standard to be considered in every ethical decision.

Legal Perspectives: General Nature

A legal perspective would take the general position that illegal human communication behavior also is unethical. That which is not specifically illegal is viewed as ethical. In other words, legality and ethicality are made synonymous. Such an approach certainly has the advantage of allowing simple ethical decisions. We would only need to measure communication techniques against current laws and regulations to determine whether a technique is ethical. We might, for example, turn for ethical guidance to the regulations governing advertising set forth by the Federal Trade Commission or the Federal Communications Commission. Or we might use Supreme Court criteria, or state legislation, defining obscenity, pornography, libel, or slander to judge whether a particular message is unethical on those grounds.

However, many people would feel uneasy with this legalistic approach to communication ethics. They would contend that obviously there are some things that presently are legal but that are ethically dubious. And some social protestors for civil rights and against the Vietnam War during the 1960s and 1970s admitted that their actions then were illegal but contended they were justifiable on ethical and moral grounds. Richard DeGeorge and Joseph Pichler, contemporary philosophers, contend that "morality is broader than legality. Not everything that is immoral can or should be made illegal."[16] Chief Justice Warren Burger spoke for a unanimous Supreme Court in 1974 in the case of *Miami Herald v. Tornillo*. "A responsible press is an undoubtedly desirable goal, but press responsibility is not mandated by the Constitution and like many other virtues it cannot be legislated."

How should we answer the question, to what degree can or should we enforce ethical standards for communication through government law or regulation? What degrees of soundness might there be in two old but seemingly contrary sayings? "You can't legislate morality." "There ought to be a law." In twentieth-century society in the United States, very few ethical standards for communication are codified in governmental laws or regulations. As indicated earlier, F.C.C. or F.T.C. regulations on the content of advertising and laws and court decisions on obscenity and libel represent the governmental approach. But such examples are rare compared to the large number of laws and court decisions specifying the boundaries of freedom of speech and press in our society. Rather, our society applies ethical standards for communication through the more indirect avenues of group consensus, social pressure, persuasion, and formal-but-voluntary codes of ethics.

Politics and Advertising

On occasion, proposals are made to pass legislation that would promote ethical political campaign communication by regulating the content of political speeches, politically sponsored television programs, televised political advertisements, or the reporting of public opinion polls. For example, without mentioning possible conflicts with freedom-of-speech provisions of the First Amendment, Brembeck and Howell maintain that government regulation "of the content of politically sponsored programs could safeguard against unethical and vicious practices."[17]

In the mid-1970s, the New York state legislature passed a Fair Campaigning Code that prohibited attacks on candidates based on race, sex, religion, or ethnic background and prohibited misrepresentations of a candidate's qualifications, position, or party affiliation. In January 1976, the U.S. Supreme Court, by a summary action, affirmed a lower court decision that these provisions of the New York code were unconstitutional under the First Amendment, were overbroad and vague in meaning and possible application, and created a substantial "chill" that probably would deter use of protected free speech.[18]

Robert Spero explains that unethical content of televised political advertisements presently cannot be banned or regulated through government law because it is viewed as ideological or political speech protected by the First Amendment. "When political speech turns up in the form of a television commercial, freedom of speech is extended implicitly to whatever the candidate wishes to say or show, no matter how false, deceptive, misleading, or unfair it may be."[19]

As part of its Code of Professional Ethics and Procedures, the American Association of Public Opinion Research has established "standards for minimal disclosure" to guide professional public opinion pollsters in conducting polls and presenting results. Consider whether these standards appropriately might be applied to news media in reporting polls and to politicians in publicizing poll results:

1. Who sponsored the survey and who conducted it
2. The exact wording of the questions asked, including the text of any preceding instruction or explanation to the interviewer or respondent that might reasonably be expected to affect the response
3. A definition of the population under study and a description of the sampling frame used to identify this population
4. A description of the sampling selection procedure, giving a clear indication of the method by which the respondents were selected by the researcher, or whether the respondents were entirely self-selected

5. Size of sample and, if applicable, completion rates and information on eligibility criteria and screening procedures
6. A discussion of the findings, including, if appropriate, estimates of sampling error, and a description of any weighting or estimating procedures used
7. Which results are based on parts of the sample, rather than the total sample
8. Method, location, and dates of the data collection

Actually an earlier version of these standards formed the basis for a "Truth-in-Polling Act" proposed numerous times but never passed in the U.S. House of Representatives—a law intended to govern news media reports of polls.[20]

In considering cultural factors in advertising, anthropologist Jules Henry contends that modern commercial advertisers operate on the assumptions that "truth" not only is what sells and what they want people to believe, but also that "truth is that which is not legally false." "Legally innocent prevarication" is the phrase coined by Henry to label statements which, "though not legally untrue, misrepresent by implication."[21] Ivan Preston examines "puffery" in commercial advertising in his book, *The Great American Blow-Up*. He explains: "By legal definition, puffery is advertising or other sales representations which praise the item to be sold with subjective opinions, superlatives, or exaggerations, vaguely and generally, stating no specific facts." Although presently legally nondeceptive, Preston argues that virtually all puffery is false by implication. As one remedy, he advocates removal of puffery (legalized deception) from the marketplace by making puffery illegal.[22]

Concerning advertising ethics, Burton Leiser believes that because "the law does not always conform with standards of moral right," advertisers who are "concerned with doing what is right need not set the limits of their conduct at the bounds" set by the law. Harold Williams issues a reminder to his professional advertising colleagues.[23]

> What is legal and what is ethical are not synonymous, and neither are what is legal and what is honest. We tend to resort to legality often as our guideline. This is in effect what happens when we turn to the lawyers for confirmation that a course of action is an appropriate one.
>
> We must recognize that we are getting a legal opinion, but not necessarily an ethical or moral one. The public, the public advo-

cates, and many of the legislative and administrative authorities recognize it even if we do not.

In analyzing the need for a public ethic in mass communication, E. S. Safford, a publisher, concludes:[24]

> Good character or good taste are not functions of an imposed regulatory system. The value standards of a society must come from agreed-upon ethical commitments and not from imposed legislation. The communication gatekeepers, the organizations, the systems and the people who are responsible for distributing information, opinions, and ideas must come to grips with concepts, not legal interpretations. If national cultural goals can be agreed upon, then ethical commitments will eliminate the need for legal definitions and regulatory tests.

Problems with Legal Perspectives

John Stuart Mill, the nineteenth-century British utilitarian philosopher and a leading advocate of maximum freedom of speech, identified a number of public communication practices that he felt were ethically dubious. Included in his catalogue of ethically suspect techniques were: hiding of facts and arguments; misstating elements of a case; misrepresenting an opponent's views; invective or name-calling; sarcasm; unfair personal attacks; stigmatizing opponents unfairly as bad or immoral. Nevertheless, Mill felt that the law should not "presume to interfere with this controversial misconduct." For Mill, "law and authority have no business" regulating such communication behavior.[25]

Consider the following five problems that may result from attempts to enforce ethical standards for communication through government laws and regulations.[26] First, oversimplified and superficial judgments may be made of complex situations. Second, regulation of unethical communication techniques may have a harmful "chilling effect" on use of other less ethically doubtful techniques. People feel less free to speak their minds for fear of legal action. Third, legal regulation of the content of communication may undermine human capacities for communication and reason by violating our right to learn the maximum we are capable of learning, by narrowing our range of choices, and by constricting our access to ideas and knowledge. Fourth, legal regulation tends to remove from receivers, the audience, the necessity for choice and judgment. Rather than fostering mutually shared ethical responsibilities for communication, regulation tends to focus responsibility on the communicator while minimizing audience responsibility. Finally, governmental regulation of almost anything, including communication content, has a tendency to expand to include ever-widening spheres of behavior, spheres that most citizens might not want regulated by law.

Franklyn Haiman, scholar of the First Amendment and communication ethics, explores where our society should "draw the line against writing morality into law" for both physical and communicative behaviors.[27] He proposes three criteria as guides. First, a "moral standard concerning a particular behavior" should be codified in legislation only when there is a "near-unanimous consensus in society that the conduct in question is immoral." Second, laws that codify ethical standards must embody credibility and fairness by being realistically enforceable and by not being subject to capricious or unequal enforcement. Finally: "A free society will always draw the line between what it considers immoral and what it makes illegal as close as possible to the more serious, direct, immediate, and physical of the harms, and it will leave to the operations of social pressure, education, and self-restraint the control of behaviors whose harm to others is less serious, less direct, less immediate, and less physical." Consider the adequacy of Haiman's guidelines. Describe, if you can, a type of communication that you believe not only to be unethical but also should be regulated by law. How well would the communication you condemn as unethical, and the law regulating it, measure up to the three tests? What revisions or modifications of Haiman's guidelines might you suggest? Why?

Notes

[1] Concerning the influence of Moslem religion on Arab persuasive techniques, see H. Samuel Hamod, "Arab and Moslem Rhetorical Theory and Practice," *Central States Speech Journal*, 14 (May 1963): 97–102; also see Allen Merriam, "Rhetoric and the Islamic Tradition," *Today's Speech*, 22 (Winter 1974): 43–49.

[2] All quotations are from the Revised Standard Version. See Leviticus, 19:11; Psalms, 140:11; Proverbs, 21:6; Psalms, 59:12; Zechariah, 8:16; Ephesians, 4:25; Matthew, 12:36–37.

[3] Charles D. Veenstra and Daryl Vander Kooi, "Ethical Foundations for 'Religious' Persuasion: A Biblical View," *Religious Communication Today*, 1 (September 1979): 43–48; for a more extensive development of this position, see Veenstra, "A Reformed Theological Ethics of Speech Communication," unpublished Ph.D. dissertation, University of Nebraska, 1981, ch. 4.

[4] Kyle Haselden, *Morality and the Mass Media* (Nashville, TN: Broadman Press, 1968), espec. chs. 1, 2, and 10.

[5] *Ibid.*, chs. 3, 6, 7, 8.

[6] *Ibid.*, pp. 36, 41, 43.

[7] John E. McMillin, "Ethics in Advertising," in *Speaking of Advertising*, John S. Wright and Daniel S. Warner. (New York: McGraw-Hill, 1963), pp. 453–58.

[8] Donald G. Hileman, et al., "Ethics in Advertising," reprinted in *Advertising's Role in Society*, John S. Wright and John E. Mertes, eds. (St. Paul, MN: West Publishing Co., 1974), pp. 259–64.

[9] Emory A. Griffin, *The Mind Changers: The Art of Christian Persuasion* (Wheaton, IL: Tyndale House, 1976), ch. 3. For an extensive discussion of ethical issues and standards for evangelistic persuasion, see the entire issue of *Cultic Studies Journal*, 2 (Fall/Winter 1985).

[10] Robert T. Oliver, *Culture and Communication* (Springfield, IL: Charles C. Thomas, 1962), pp. 111–17, 133–35. Also see Oliver, *Communication and Culture in Ancient India and China* (Syracuse. NY: Syracuse University Press. 1971), pp. 76–77, 124, 145–49, 176, 181, 193; D. Lawrence Kincaid. ed., *Communication Theory: Eastern and Western Perspectives* (San Diego, CA: Academic Press, 1987); William G. Kirkwood, "Truthfulness as a Standard for Speech in Ancient India," *Southern Communication Journal*, LIV (Spring 1989): 213–34; Arnold D. Hunt, Maeie T. Crotty, and Robert B. Crotty, *Ethics of World Religions*, Revised Ed. (San Diego: Greenhaven Press, 1991), pp. 136, 141, 144–46.

[11] Thomas W. Cooper, *Communication Ethics and Global Change* (New York: Longman, 1989), p. 253. In this book also see Hamid Mowlana, "Communication, Ethics, and the Islamic Tradition," pp. 137–46.

[12] J. Vernon Jensen, "Ancient Eastern and Western Religions as Guides for Contemporary Communication Ethics," in *Proceedings of the Second National Communication Ethics Conference, June 11–14, 1992*, James A. Jaksa, ed. (Annandale, VA: Speech Communication Association, 1992), pp. 58–67.

[13] Wayne E. Brockriede, "Bentham's Philosophy of Rhetoric." *Speech Monographs*, 23 (November 1956): 235–46.

[14] Thomas K. Hearn, Jr., ed., *Studies in Utilitarianism* (New York: Meredith, 1971), p. 10. This anthology reprints the classic statements on utilitarianism by Jeremy Bentham and John Stuart Mill as well as more recent interpretations.

[15] Winston L. Brembeck and William S. Howell, *Persuasion: A Means of Social Influence*, 2d ed. (Englewood Cliffs, NJ: Prentice-Hall, 1976), ch. 10; Howell, *The Empathic Communicator* (Copyright 1982, reissued 1986 by Waveland Press, Prospect Heights, IL), ch. 8; Howell, "Foreward," in *Ethical Perspectives and Critical Issues in Intercultural Communication*, Nobleza, Asuncion-Lande, ed. (Falls Church, VA: Speech Communication Association, n.d.) pp. viii–x; Howell, "Ethics of Intercultural Communication," paper presented at Speech Communication Association convention, November 15, 1981. See also, Patricia Freeman, "An Ethical Evaluation of the Persuasive Strategies of Glenn W. Turner of Turner Enterprises," *Southern Speech Communication Journal*, 38 (Summer 1973): 347–61, where Freeman uses the "social utility" perspective as one basis for ethical judgment.

[16] Richard T. DeGeorge and Joseph A. Pichler, eds., *Ethics, Free Enterprise, and Public Policy* (New York: Oxford University Press, 1978), p. 7.

[17] Brembeck and Howell, *Persuasion*, 2d ed., p. 344.

[18] *United States Law Week*, 44 (January 13, 1976): 3390.

[19] Robert Spero, *The Duping of the American Voter: Dishonesty and Deception in Presidential Television Advertising* (New York: Lippincott and Crowell, 1980), ch. 9.

[20] *Code of Professional Ethics and Practices and AAPOR's Procedures*, (Ann Arbor, MI: American Association of Public Opinion Research, 1991), pp. 4–5; Lucien N. Nedzi, "Public Opinion Polls: Will Legislation Help?" *Public Opinion Quarterly*, 35 (1971): 336–41.

[21] Jules Henry, *Culture Against Man* (New York: Random House, 1963), ch. III.

[22] Ivan Preston, *The Great American Blow-Up: Puffery in Advertising and Selling* (Madison: University of Wisconsin Press, 1975), espec. pp. 6–8, 17, 188–89.

[23] Harold M. Williams, "What Do We Do Now, Boss? Marketing and Advertising," *Vital Speeches of the Day*, 40 (February 15, 1974): 285–88; Burton M. Leiser, "The Ethics of Advertising," in *Ethics, Free Enterprise, and Public Policy*, DeGeorge and Pichler, eds., p. 181.

[24] E. S. Safford, "The Need for a Public Ethic in Mass Communication," in *Ethics, Morality and the Media*, Lee Thayer, et al., eds. (New York: Hastings House, 1980), p. 149.

[25] John Stuart Mill, *On Liberty* (New York: Appleton-Century-Crofts, 1947), pp. 53–54. Also see Franklyn S. Haiman, *Speech and Law in a Free Society* (Chicago: University of Chicago Press, 1981), pp. 232–33.

[26] Sidney Hook, "The Ethics of Political Controversy," in *The Ethics of Controversy: Politics and Protest*, Donn Parson and Wil Linkugel, eds. (Lawrence, KS: The House of Usher, 1968), p. 53; Kyle Haselden, *Morality and the Mass Media*, chs. 4, 5, 9; Lee Thayer, "Ethics, Morality, and the Media," in *Ethics, Morality and the Media*, Thayer, et al., eds., pp. 16, 39–40; Haiman, *Speech and Law in a Free Society*, pp. 207–208, 277–278.

[27] Franklyn S. Haiman, *"Speech Acts" and the First Amendment* (Carbondale: Southern Illinois University Press, 1993), pp. 81–86.

Chapter 7

Some Basic Issues

In previous chapters we surveyed seven potential perspectives for evaluating the ethics of human communication—the religious, utilitarian, legal, political, human nature, dialogical, and situational perspectives. With this information in hand, we now examine a variety of questions which underscore difficult issues related to ethical problems in human communication. As creators of messages, and as receivers constantly bombarded with complex verbal and nonverbal messages, we continually face resolution of one or another of these fundamental issues. We hope that the raising of these issues will stimulate you to consider them at length on your own to reach your own position on them.

Absolute and Relative Standards

To what degree should ethical criteria for judging human communication be *inflexible*, *universal*, and *absolute* or to what degree should they be *flexible*, *situation-bound*, and *relative*?[1] Surely the more absolute our standards are the easier it is to render simple, clear-cut judgments. But in matters of human interaction and public decision making, the ethics of communicative means and ends seldom are simple. Several cautions probably are worth remembering. Usually the choice is not between an absolute standard or an extremely relativistic one; for most of us most of the time the applicable ethical standard is one which to *some degree* is relative and context-bound.[2]

Should ethical criteria be more stringent for communication aimed at children as opposed to adults? Should ethical standards for public communication differ between peacetime and time of declared war? Should ethical standards vary for communication in different fields, such as advertising, education, law, politics, and religion? Jurgen Ruesch argues that at present "there is no single set of ethical rules that control communication." Instead, he contends, "we have to specify what purposes the communication serves."[3] Based on this assumption, Ruesch suggests that differing sets of ethical standards might have to apply for such different areas as: (1) the interpretive, manipulative, and exhortative communication of advertisers, propagandists, and public relations experts; (2) the representational communication of scientists; (3) the political communication of government and candidates; and (4) the personal communication of individuals.

Also worth remembering is the fact that ethical criteria which we *assume* to be obviously appropriate and valid may be viewed as irrelevant by *other persons*. Consider the following observation concerning some of the ethical and value standards implied in assumptions central to our view of communication in Anglo-American and Western European culture.[4]

> When we think of influencing people, we think of free men who have the right to cast free ballots; we think of rational beings, beset by emotionalism, but finally "available" to persuasion that is factually and logically sound. We think of propositions that are worthy of discussion because they are based on probabilities, concerning which various speakers may reasonably present various interpretations. And with our emphasis on the sovereignty of the people and the doctrine of the "greatest good for the greatest number," we accept (sometimes with bad grace) the conclusion finally rendered by majority vote. It is honestly and fundamentally difficult for us to realize that *no single one of these presumptions is universal.* . . . It is my belief that we shall have to stop using rhetoric in the singular and commence using it in the plural.

In making ethical evaluations of communication, probably we should avoid snap judgments, carefully examine the relevant circumstances to determine which might influence our judgment and to what degree, consider the welfare of everyone involved, and utilize the ethical perspectives most appropriate for the instance.

Maximum or Minimum Standards

Should guidelines for assessing the ethics of human communication be stated as *minimum* criteria to be met in order to maintain ethicality? Or should they be stated as *maximum* ideals we are *obliged* to strive for? After surveying scholars representing both views, Thomas

Nilsen offers his belief that communicators have an obligation to follow the "optimific" standard—to follow the better of two "good" criteria.[5] What is *your* view? Ethicists also discuss ethical behavior termed *superogatory*. Superogatory ethical communication would be above and beyond the call of duty. Such behavior, while ethically desirable, is not required.

As a related question, is it best to phrase guidelines for ethical communication in a negative, "thou-shalt-not," fashion or in affirmative, positive language?[6] For example, instead of saying "do not make unsupported attacks on your opponent," would it be better to say "support any attacks made on your opponent"? Or instead of saying "do not distort or falsify evidence," would it be more desirable to say "present only factual evidence and present it in its true form and context"? It could be argued that negative wording leaves unclear whether *inaction and passivity* are ethical or whether only positive action which promotes achievement of maximum standards is ethical.[7]

The End as Justification of Means

In assessing the ethics of human communication, does the *end* justify the *means*? Does the necessity of achieving a goal widely acknowledged as worthwhile justify the use of ethically questionable techniques? A number of scholars remind us that the communicative means employed can have impacts and effects on audience thought and decision-making habits apart from and in addition to the specific end which the communicator seeks. No matter the purpose they serve, the arguments, appeals, structure, and language we choose do shape the audience's values, thinking habits, language patterns, and level of trust.[8]

Concerning advertising and public relations, John Marston contends that a "good end cannot be held to justify a bad means. . . . Public relations, like democracy itself, is a way of achieving agreement through understanding and persuasion. The way is just as important as the ends sought at any particular moment by fallible human beings; and indeed it may be more important, because democracy lives by the road it travels."[9] Because advertising is so powerful and widespread, semanticist S. I. Hayakawa believes "it influences more than our choice of products; it also influences our patterns of evaluation. It can either increase or decrease the degree of sanity with which people respond to words."[10]

"The kinds of persuasion exercised on people are important elements in their logical and moral training." This contention is central to the view of B. J. Diggs in his essay on "Persuasion and Ethics."[11] Robert Oliver expands a similar line of reasoning. "An audience that is induced to accept shoddy reasoning or falsification of facts to support a right conclusion has, at the same time, suffered the adverse effect of becoming habituated to false pleading." This process, feels Oliver, probably would make "listeners more vulnerable, on another occasion, to demagoguery exercised in a bad cause."[12]

To say that the end does not *always* justify the means is different from saying that ends *never* justify means. The communicator's goal probably best is considered as one of a number of potentially relevant ethical criteria from among which the most appropriate standards (perspectives) are selected. Under some circumstances, such as threat to physical survival, the goal of personal or national security *temporarily* may take precedence over other criteria. Arthur Sylvester, former Assistant Secretary of Defense for Public Affairs, evoked divided citizen reactions with his assertion that "it is the government's inherent right to lie if necessary to save itself when faced with nuclear disaster; that is basic."[13]

In general, however, we best can make mature ethical assessments by evaluating the ethics of communicative techniques *apart* from the worth and morality of the communicator's specific goal. We can strive to judge the ethics of means and ends *separately*. In some cases we may find ethical communication tactics employed to achieve an unethical goal. In other cases unethical techniques may be used in the service of an entirely ethical goal. On this point, Winston Brembeck and William S. Howell offer a worthwhile warning. "Methods themselves must meet many ethical standards (for example, humanitarian and social). The zealous proponent of a good cause must continually review his methods to be sure that he is not slipping into practices he himself would condemn when used for a 'lesser' purpose."[14]

Although discussed in the context of journalistic ethics, the six questions suggested by Warren Bovée can serve as useful probes to unravel the degree of ethicality embedded in almost any particular means-end relationship.[15] Here are the questions in paraphrased form: (1) Is the means truly unethical/morally evil or just distasteful, unpopular, unwise, or ineffective? (2) Is the end truly good or does it simply appear good to us because we desire it? (3) Is it probable that the ethically bad or suspect means actually will achieve the good end? (4) Is the same good achievable using other more ethical means if only we are willing to be creative, patient, determined, and skillful? (5) Is the good end clearly and overwhelmingly better than the probable bad effects of the means used to attain it? Bad means require justification whereas good means do not. (6) Will the use of the unethical means to achieve a good end withstand the test of publicity? Could the use of the unethical means be justified to those most affected by them or to those most capable of impartially judging them?

The Ethics of Lying

Is it ever ethical to lie? To this question, some people would respond with a resounding no, never! Others would respond with less certainty. Some would say that it depends upon the meaning or definition of a lie. Some would say it depends upon the intent and circumstances of the lie. For example, if we are telling a "little white lie" to spare the feelings of a friend who at the moment is emotionally unstable, that communication may not be defined as a "real" lie or may be viewed as justified by intent and circumstances.

Making ethical judgments of lies often is a complex rather than a simple matter. No detailed and exhaustive treatment will be presented here. Instead I simply will sketch some issues, viewpoints, and sources that should be useful to you in investigating the subject further. Contemporary philosopher Charles Fried contends that lying (asserting as true what we believe to be false) always is wrong because it demonstrates disrespect for persons as beings capable of rational judgments and of free and intentional choice. At the same time, Fried believes that "withholding a truth which another needs may be perfectly permissible" because withholding truth is not defined as lying. Utilitarian Carl Wellman observes that the "most useful rule for any society to have is not simply, 'Acts of lying are always wrong,' but something more like, 'Lying is wrong except to save a human life or to spare hurt feelings over unimportant matters.'"[16]

What do we mean by a lie? What is the nature and scope of the human behavior we term lying? Here are two views of the nature and boundaries of lying. George Yoos reminds us that definitions of a lie are culture-bound. Interpretations of what a lie is and expectations concerning appropriateness of deceptive behavior differ from society to society. At length Yoos describes a broad spectrum of behavior that can be termed lying.[17]

> Our looks, our actions, and even our silence can lie. Reports, promises, and even apologies lie. We lie by implication and sug-

gestion. What is first needed in order to understand the phenomena of lying is to analyze the wide variety of deliberate deceptions that take place by means of speech acts other than the giving of information, for to lie is not just to say only what is clear-cut and false. An analysis of lying involves, among other things, an analysis of motives, beliefs, and intentions. In sum, lying is not just simply misinforming or inaccurately reporting what it is that is the case. Lying extends to all sorts of statements and behaviors that may be misleading, deceptive, and confusing.

In *Lying: Moral Choice in Public and Private Life*, Sissela Bok distinguishes between intentional deception and intentional lying. Deception is the larger, more encompassing, category of which lying is a sub-category. When we "communicate messages meant to mislead" others, to "make them believe what we ourselves do not believe," then we are engaged in intentional deception. Deception may come not only through words but also through gestures, disguise, action and inaction, and even silence. Bok defines a lie as "any intentionally deceptive message which is *stated*."[18] Although lies usually are oral or written, they could be in other symbol systems such as Morse code or sign language. In her book, she explores the functioning and assessment of lying in varied contexts: white lies; lies in a crisis or for the public good; lying to liars and to enemies; lying to protect confidentiality; lying for the welfare of others; lies in social science research on humans; lies to the sick and dying.

Bok argues that lying always carries an "initial negative weight," that "truthful statements are preferable to lies in the absence of special considerations," and that "lying requires explanation, whereas truth ordinarily does not." Her fundamental assumption is that trust in some degree of truthfulness is a *"foundation* of relations among human beings; when this trust shatters or wears away, institutions collapse . . . *Whatever* matters to human beings, trust is the atmosphere in which it thrives."[19]

The "moral presumption against lying," contends Joseph Kupfer, rests on two lines of argument that demonstrate ultimate negative effects on the "character" of the liar. First, lying causes immediate restriction of the freedom of the deceived. Lying inclines the liar toward a general disrespect for persons—toward abuse of the uniquely human capacity for language as necessary for understanding and reflective choice. Second, lying involves the self-contradiction of "repudiating in speech what we believe." Liars disguise their "real selves" from others by contradicting their real beliefs and thus who they really are. This self-opposition threatens the integration or coherence of the liar's personality. By disguising the self, the liar rejects an opportunity for self-knowledge; reactions of others useful for self-definition are possible only in response to truthful self-disclosure of beliefs. Both of the negative effects on the liar—an attitude of disrespect for persons and a threat to coherence of personality—weaken the moral character of the liar.[20]

Lies, says Bok, add to the power of the liar and diminish the power of those deceived by altering their choices in several ways. First, the lie may obscure or hide some objective the deceived person sought. Second, the lie may obscure or eliminate relevant alternatives that should be considered. Third, the lie may misinform concerning benefits and costs of probable consequences. Finally, lies may mislead concerning the level of confidence or certainty we should have about our choice.

What excuses typically are offered to make a particular lie permissible? What excuses do we offer to minimize, or even remove, the blame for something that normally would be a fault? Sometimes we contend that what is labeled a fault is not actually one. Sometimes we admit that a fault happened, but argue that we are not responsible for it and thus not blameworthy. Sometimes we are bold enough to admit both that the fault happened and that we are responsible, but we argue we still are not blameworthy because we did it in the name of some higher good. Among the higher goods frequently used to justify a lie are: avoiding harm to ourselves or others; producing benefits for others; promoting fairness and justice; and protecting the truth by counteracting another lie, by furthering some more important truth, or by preserving the confidence of others in our own truthfulness. Consider when and how often you have heard the following rationalizations for cheating, described by J. Barton Bowyer, also applied to excuse lying: (1) I need it; (2) they deserve it; (3) it won't matter anyway; and (4) no one will know anyhow.[21]

At one point, Bok outlines a three-level procedure for determining whether a lie is justifiable. The justification procedure moves from the private to public spheres to foster increasing assurance that the lie is justified.[22] First, we scrutinize our own conscience through internal testing to ensure that the decision is carefully weighed. Second, we examine precedents, consult with friends, elders and colleagues, and seek the advice, directly or through their writings, of experts on ethics. Third, and most crucial, Bok contends that there should be opportunity for public debate among the public at large. For example, public scrutiny might occur prior to policy decisions such as use of deception in experiments on human subjects, entrapment by police in "sting" operations, or use of unmarked police cars to trap speeders. The decision, or potential decision, to deceive deliberately should be scrutinized by reasonable persons of all allegiances, including representatives of those potentially to be effected. In the course of such public debate, the availability of alternative non-deceptive means must be explored. The moral reasons for and against the lie should be evaluated from the viewpoint of the deceived and others affected by it. From the viewpoint of reasonable people outside the specific deceptive situation, additional potential harms should be weighed: an uncondemned liar may find lying all the easier on subsequent occasions; observers may be encouraged to imitate the lying; essential trust central to the human communication process may seriously be weakened.

In *The Varnished Truth: Truth Telling and Deceiving in Ordinary Life*, David Nyberg takes issue with many of the assumptions and arguments by Sissela Bok and takes a much broader view of the necessity and ethicality of some lying and deception.[23] Nyberg considers deception to be "normal rather than abnormal" and to be "an essential property of language and not merely some kind of perversion of it." It is not a question, in his view, of whether deception ever is acceptable but rather "how we may deceive whom about what and for how long." We have not, he argues, "diligently trained ourselves to deceive thoughtfully and judiciously, charitably, humanely, and with discretion." "Truth telling," he contends, "is morally overrated."

For Nyberg, deception is an "essential component of our ability to organize and shape the world, to resolve problems of coordination among individuals who differ, to cope with uncertainty and pain, to be civil and to achieve privacy as needed, to survive as a species, and to flourish as persons." In order to avoid misunderstanding of his position, he does "repudiate all harmfully exploitative deceptions. . . ." But it is a "mistake to despise and reject all other forms of deception, too, just because we have had experience with these contemptible ones." And Nyberg argues that while truth telling is a natural obligation in most voluntary relationships, persons in involuntary relationships have to decide what degree of truth telling is reasonable. You are urged to compare Sissela Bok's *Lying* with Nyberg's *The Varnished Truth* to determine your own position on the issues.

The Ethics of Intentional Ambiguity and Vagueness

Language that is of doubtful or uncertain meaning might be a typical definition of ambiguous language. Ambiguous language legitimately is open to two or more interpretations.[24] Vague language lacks definiteness, explicitness, or preciseness of meaning. Clear communication of intended meaning usually is one major aim of an ethical communicator, whether that person seeks to enhance receiver understanding or seeks to influence belief, attitude, or action. Textbooks on oral and written communication typically warn against ambiguity and vagueness; often they directly or indirectly take the position that intentional ambiguity is an unethical communication tactic. One textbook on argument, for example, condemns as sham or counterfeit proof the use of equivocation, vagueness, and ambiguity because they "are attempts to avoid or circumvent the proof process." A textbook for the beginning course in English admonishes: "The writer is responsible for supplying all the meaning, and he is seriously at fault when he leaves the reader to grope even for a moment."[25]

A somewhat different viewpoint is offered for consideration by Lee Williams and Blaine Goss.[26]

> ... one must be careful not to equate untruthfulness with ambiguity, or to confuse ambiguity in informative speaking with ambiguity in persuasive speaking. To encode a vague message is not necessarily to encode a lie or untruthful statement. Indeed, vagueness is not even a necessary condition for lying to occur, for there are many lies which explicitly identify their referents. We must remember that all words contain some degree of vagueness, and instead of being inherently bad, vagueness, like rhetoric, appears to be an amoral means which can be applied to produce many different ends.

Most people probably would agree that intentional ambiguity is unethical in situations where accurate instruction or efficient transmission of precise information is the acknowledged purpose. Even in most so-called persuasive communication situations, intentional ambiguity would be ethically suspect. However, in some situations communicators may feel that the intentional creation of ambiguity or vagueness is necessary, accepted, expected as normal, and even ethically justified.[27] Such might be the case, for example, in religious discourse, in some advertising, in some legal discourse, in labor-management bargaining, in political campaigning, or in international diplomatic negotiations.

We can itemize a number of specific purposes for which communicators might feel that intentional ambiguity is ethically justified: (1) to heighten receiver attention through puzzlement; (2) to allow flexibility in interpretation of legal concepts; (3) to use ambiguity on secondary issues to allow for precise understanding and agreement on the primary issue; (4) to promote maximum receiver psychological participation in the communication transaction by letting them create their own relevant meanings; (5) to promote maximum latitude for revision of a position in later dealings with opponents or with constituents by avoiding being "locked-in" to a single absolute stance.[28]

In his *Law Dictionary for Non-Lawyers*, Daniel Oran warns against the use of vague language but also explains: "Some legal words have a 'built-in' vagueness. They are used when the writer or speaker does not want to be pinned down. For example, when a law talks about 'reasonable speed' or 'due care,' it is deliberately imprecise about the meaning of the words because it wants the amount of speed allowed or care required to be decided situation-by-situation, rather than by an exact formula."[29] What is your personal assessment of the ethicality of such intentional vagueness? On what ethical grounds would you defend or condemn such vagueness?

In political communication, whether during campaigns or by government officials, several circumstances might be used to justify intentional ambiguity ethically. First, a president, or presidential candidate, often must communicate to multiple audiences through a single message via a mass medium such as television or radio. Different parts of the message may appeal to specific audiences while at the same time intentional ambiguity in some message elements avoids offending any of the audiences.[30] Lewis Froman describes a second circumstance. A candidate "cannot take stands on specific issues because he doesn't know what the specific choices will be until he is faced with the necessity for concrete decision. Also, specific commitments would be too binding in a political process that depends upon negotiation and compromise."[31] Third, groups of voters increasingly make decisions whether to support or oppose a candidate on the basis of that candidate's stand on a single issue of paramount importance to those groups. The candidate's position on a variety of other public issues often is ignored or dismissed. "Single-issue politics" is the phrase frequently used to characterize this trend. A candidate intentionally may be ambiguous on one emotion-packed issue in order to get a fair hearing for stands on many other issues.[32]

In some advertising intentional ambiguity seems to be understood as such by consumers and even accepted by them. Consider possible ethical implications of the advertisement for Noxema Shaving Cream which urged (accompanied by a beautiful woman watching a man shave in rhythm with striptease music): "Take it off. Take it *all* off." Or what about the "sexy" woman in the after-shave cologne advertisement who says, "All my men wear English Leather, or they wear *nothing at all*."

A balanced and flexible view on the ethics of intentional ambiguity and vagueness is offered by Thomas Nilsen.[33]

> This is not to say that vagueness and ambiguity are wrong in themselves. To a certain extent they cannot be avoided. There are also instances of their legitimate use. If a speaker seeks to stimulate his listeners to feelings of national pride (certainly an acceptable purpose if done with prudence), he must realize that for different people different aspects of their national life are cause for pride, and the speaker can rightfully permit each listener to identify with that which is most meaningful to him. Where rigorous thought is needed, however, where decisions are being made on specific issues, such personal interpretations may be highly misleading, and the speaker has an ethical obligation to minimize them. If ambiguity is unavoidable, it should be made explicit. Where vagueness is unavoidable, the speaker should not claim more specificity than the terms warrant.

Ethics, Emotional Appeals, and Rationality

Is the use of so-called "emotional appeals" in communication *inherently* unethical? What should be the ethical standards guiding appeals to an audience's emotions, motives, drives, needs, and desires? Our American culture traditionally has viewed with suspicion the expression of or capitalization on emotion in public communication. Emotionalization in interpersonal communication usually has been judged less harshly. The Aristotelian heritage in rhetorical theory has perpetuated the primacy of reason and logic over emotion in selecting ethical persuasive strategies.[34] On this point you may wish to refer back to the "degree of rationality" political perspective discussed in chapter 2.

One generalization which emerges from contemporary social science research on communication is that receivers of messages find it difficult to categorize appeals or supporting materials as either logical or emotional in exactly the same manner intended by the communicator. Differing audiences may view the same appeal differently. A given technique, such as a set of statistics indicating the high probability of falling victim to cancer during our lifetime, may be perceived as possessing *both* rational and emotional components. On a related point, Ivan Preston observes that although an outside observer may judge an advertising message as irrational, from the viewpoint of the receiving consumer the message may be evaluated as rational in light of his or her own values and goals.[35]

Oliver notes the cultural variability of standards for assessing rationality. "People in separate cultures and separate nations are concerned about *different* problems; and they have different systems of thinking about them. What seems important to us is not necessarily important to everyone. Our logic may not be theirs; our very faith in rationality may be countermatched by their faith in irrationality. What we consider proof of a particular proposition, they may consider irrelevant."[36] "There are many logics," observe John Condon and Fathi Yousef, "each being a system with its own assumptions and consistent in itself, and different cultures will express different logics." They caution us "against criticizing statements from other societies which rely on different authorities, derive from different perceptions of the world, and follow a logic which is different from our own."[37] Marshall McLuhan offers provocative hypotheses concerning the impact of visual, print orientation on Western culture's conception of rationality.[38]

> Connected sequential discourse, which is thought of as rational, is really visual. It has nothing to do with reason as such. Reasoning does not occur on single planes or in continuous, connected fashion. The mind leapfrogs. It puts things together in all sorts of proportions and ratios instantly. To put down thoughts in coded, lineal ways was a discovery of the Greek world. It is not done this way, for example, in the Chinese world. But to deny that the Chinese have access to reason would be ridiculous.

Even within contemporary American culture, there are differing conceptions of what is rational or reasonable.[39] In the context of political communication, Dan Nimmo describes the nature of an ideal rationality that seldom, if ever, occurs.[40] Winston Brembeck and William S. Howell recognize: "Methods of critical thinking are culture bound. Within a culture, approved norms exist that function as universals." They outline values that they believe function as "universals of thoughtful deliberation in America": orderliness; clarity and directness; concreteness and specificity; accuracy; unity and coherence.[41] Other scholars explore the possibility that standards for "reasonable" communication vary between different fields of discourse, such as public issues, philosophy, religion, natural science, law, historiography, or the arts. There may be standards for reasonableness in discourse agreed upon by experts *within* particular fields but that differ *between* fields.[42]

The ethicality of so-called emotional and logical appeals depends primarily on which specific technique is used, in what manner, and in what context. The need to dichotomize communicative appeals into logical or emotional categories does not seem very compelling. A communicative technique can be assessed for ethicality in and of itself regardless of how it is labeled. Note, too, that a specific "emotional appeal" may be viewed as nonrational (different from reason) without necessarily being irrational (contrary to reason).

If we do, nevertheless, wish to evaluate the ethics of a communication technique which we perceive as an "emotional appeal," the following guidelines are suggested within the context of "mainstream" American culture. Assuming that the appeal is ethical in light of other *relevant* perspectives, the "emotional" technique is ethical if it is undergirded by a substructure of sound evidence and reasoning to support it. Presentation of this substructure could accompany the appeal in the message, or the substructure could exist apart from the message and be produced upon the request of a critic. When a *sound* proposal is linked to satisfaction of *relevant* audience emotions, values, and motives, then the appeal probably is ethical. If the audience is asked to view the emotional appeal not as proof or justification but as an *expression* of the communicator's internal emotional state, it probably is ethical. Generally, the emotional appeal is ethically suspect when it functions as *pseudo-proof* giving the appearance of sound evidence or when it functions to short-circuit the receiver's capacity for free, informed, critical choice.[43]

The Truth Standard in Commercial Advertising

Commercial advertising in America typically has been viewed as persuasion that argues a case or demonstrates a claim concerning the actual nature or merit of a product. To such attempts at arguing the quality of a product, ethical standards rooted in truthfulness and rationality have been applied. For instance, are the evidence and reasoning supporting the claim clear, accurate, relevant, and sufficient in quantity? Are the motivational and emotional appeals directly relevant to the product?[44]

But what if the primary purpose of most commercial advertisements, especially on television, is *not* to prove a claim? Then what ethical standards we apply may stem from whatever alternative view we hold of advertising's nature and purpose. In *Advertising Age*, J. R. Carpenter observed: "Specific claims can be argued on the basis of facts. Logic can be questioned. . . . But it is difficult to challenge image, emotion, style. . . ."[45] Some advertisements function primarily to capture and sustain consumer attention, to announce a product, or to create consumer awareness of the name of a product.[46] What ethical criteria are most appropriate for such attention-getting advertisements?

Some analysts view commercial advertising as a type of poetic game.[47] The following poetic techniques are used in combination to invite consumers to participate in a recreational, emotionally satisfying experience: making the commonplace significant; connotation; ambiguity; aesthetically pleasing structure. If there is such a thing as commercial advertising-as-poetic, what ethical standards should we use to judge this kind of poetry?

Neither poets nor advertisers, argues Theodore Levitt, focus on the literal functionality of things they depict. "Instead," he contends, "each celebrates a deep and complex emotion" symbolized through "creative embellishment—a content which cannot be captured by literal description alone." Levitt views advertising as commercial poetry. Neither poetic descriptions nor advertisements make any "pretense of being the things themselves." He admits that there are tasteless and intentionally deceptive advertisements and he condemns advertising that "dulls our senses and assaults our sensibilities." But advertisements are the symbols of human aspirations. "They are not the real thing, nor are they intended to be, nor are they accepted as such by the public."[48]

In *The Responsive Chord*, Tony Schwartz leaves the impression that truth is completely irrelevant as a standard for electronic media, especially for commercial and political television advertisements.[49] He assumes that "the question of truth is largely irrelevant when dealing with electronic media content." Argues Schwartz:

> Electronic communication deals primarily with effects. The problem is that no 'grammar' for electronic media effects has been devised. Electronic media have been viewed merely as extensions of print, and therefore subject to the same grammar and values as

print communication. The patterned auditory and visual information on television or radio is not 'content.' Content is a print term, subject to the truth-falsity issue. Auditory and visual information on television or radio are stimuli that affect a viewer or listener. As stimuli, electronically mediated communication cannot be analyzed in the same way as print 'content.' A whole new set of questions must be asked, and a new theory of communication must be formulated.

Since "truth is a print ethic, not a standard for ethical behavior in electronic communication," Schwartz feels that critics and regulatory agencies should assess the ethics of advertising not by standards of truth and clarity of content but by evaluating effects of advertisements on receivers.[50] He laments, however, that at present we "have no generally agreed-upon social values and/or rules that can be readily applied in judging whether the effects of electronic communication are beneficial."

In a later writing, Schwartz attempts to clarify his position by contending that truth is a relevant but not a major standard for judging electronic media ethics. It is interesting to note, however, that in his evaluation of *political* broadcast advertising, he employs such truth-related standards as accuracy, factual verifiability, and use of a factual foundation to support implications.[51]

Ethics and Propaganda

Is propaganda unethical? The answer to this question in part depends on how propaganda is defined. Numerous, often widely divergent, definitions abound.[52] Originally the term "propaganda" was associated with the efforts of the Roman Catholic Church to persuade people to accept the Church's doctrine. Such efforts were institutionalized in 1622 by Pope Gregory XV when he created the Sacred Congregation for Propagating the Faith. The word propaganda soon came to designate not only institutions seeking to propagate a doctrine but also the doctrine itself and the communication techniques employed.

Today one cluster of definitions of propaganda presents a *neutral* position toward the ethical nature of propaganda. A definition combining the key elements of such neutral views might be: Propaganda is a *campaign* of *mass* persuasion. According to this view, propaganda represents an organized, continuous effort to persuade a mass audience primarily using the mass media.[53] Propaganda thus would include advertising and public relations efforts, national political election campaigns, the persuasive campaigns of some social reform movements, and the organized efforts of national governments to win friends abroad, maintain domestic morale, and undermine an opponent's morale both in hot and cold war. Such a view stresses communication channels and audiences and categorizes propaganda as one species of persuasion. Just as persuasion may be sound or unsound, ethical or unethical, so too may propaganda.

Another cluster of definitions of propaganda takes a *negative* stance toward the ethical nature of propaganda. Definitions in this cluster probably typify the view held by many "average" American citizens. A definition combining the key elements of such negative views might be: Propaganda is the intentional use of suggestion, irrelevant emotional appeals, and pseudo-proof to circumvent human rational decision-making processes.[54] Such a view stresses communication techniques and sees propaganda as *inherently* unethical.

Jacques Ellul, the noted French social and political analyst, has written at length on propaganda. In his book, *Propaganda*, Ellul offers this definition: "A set of methods employed by an organized group that wants to bring about active or passive participation in its actions of a mass of individuals, psychologically unified through psychological manipulations and incorporated in an organization." He does not view propaganda simply as a campaign of mass persuasion. Rather he sees propaganda as so pervasive and powerful in all aspects of contemporary technological societies that it is an injurious "menace which threatens the total human personality."[55]

In a lengthy essay, Ellul focuses precisely on the ethical implications of propaganda.[56] Contrary to the conventional wisdom on the limitations of propaganda, Ellul argues that, even in the long run, the clearest and most obvious factual evidence cannot overcome the self-contained delusional world constructed by modern propaganda. Ellul outlines three reasons why he believes propaganda is so pervasive and potent that it destroys, literally obliterates, any possibility of ethics. First, propaganda is a self-justifying process whereby a descriptive state of what *is* (power) evolves into a value judgment of what *ought* to be (this power is right and just). Second, because propaganda focuses on the instantaneousness of the immediate and the present, it destroys the sense of history (continuity of generations) and of philosophy (critical reflection on experiences) necessary for moral existence. Third, because propaganda undercuts our powers of conscious choice making and because it fosters a situation in which we each remain completely alone while still belonging to a collective mass, it destroys the kinds of mutual, thoughtful, interpersonal communication (reciprocal participation, encounter, dialogue) necessary for building an ethical existence.

Are the traditional "propaganda devices" always to be viewed as unethical? Textbooks in such fields as journalism, speech communication, and social psychology often discuss the traditional list: name-calling, glittering generality, transfer, testimonial, plain folks, card-stacking, and band wagon.[57] Such a list does *not* constitute a sure-fire guide, a "handy dandy" checklist, for exposure of unethical persuasion. The ethics of at least some of these techniques depends on how they are employed in a given context. Let us examine, for instance, the devices of name-calling and of plain folks.

Name-calling involves labeling a person, group, or idea with terms carrying extremely negative or evil meanings. Whether calling an opponent a "card-carrying Communist" would be ethical or unethical would be determined in part by whether the opponent *actually was* a formal, registered member of the Communist Party. The possible contextual nature of judging the ethics of name-calling is suggested by Lawrence Flynn.

> Name-calling may be only harmless banter which bespeaks no evil intent. In political encounters, epithets of a certain indignity pass as accepted maneuvers of the game. Nobody takes them seriously, except perhaps the victim, who attempts to outdo his opponent in the practice of name-calling. On the other hand, an epithet deliberately based on untruth attaches a false label to the victim, and to the perpetrator, a true one. This evil act is calumny.[58]

The plain folks technique stresses humble origins and modest backgrounds shared by the communicator and audience. The communicator emphasizes to his audience, although usually not in these words, that "we're all just plain folks." In his "whistle-stop" speeches to predominantly rural, Republican audiences during the 1948 presidential campaign, Democrat Harry Truman typically used the plain folks appeal in the introductions of his speeches to establish common ground. He used the device to accomplish one of the purposes of the introductory segment of most speeches—namely, establishment of rapport; he did not rely on it for proof in the main body of his speeches. If a politician relied primarily on the plain folks appeal as pseudo-proof in *justifying* the policy he advocated, such usage could be condemned as unethical. Furthermore, Truman really was the kind of person who could legitimately capitalize on his actual plain folks background. A politician of more privileged and patrician background, such as Edward Kennedy, could be condemned for using an unethical technique *if* he were to appeal to farmers and factory workers by saying "you and I are just plain folks."

Ethics and the Demagogue

Today the label "demagogue" frequently is used to render a negative ethical judgment of a communicator. Too often the label is left only vaguely defined; the criteria we are to use to evaluate a person as a demagogue are unspecified. In ancient Greece, a demagogue simply was a leader or orator who championed the cause of the common people.

In the following 1972 description of Governor George Wallace of Alabama, what characteristics are suggested as marks of a demagogue? To what extent should we agree with them as appropriate criteria for judging a demagogue? Should we accept as valid the linkages between each characteristic and the public figure used to illustrate it? Would *you* label Wallace as a demagogue?

> He is the quintessential demagogue, combining the missionary zeal of a Barry Goldwater, the raw pursuit of power of a Kennedy, the expansive populism of a Huey Long, the Chameleon-like adaptability of a Nixon, and the disarmingly blunt, or somewhat crude, appeal of an Archie Bunker.[59]

You now are invited to consider the following five characteristics collectively as possible appropriate guides for determining to what degree a persuader merits the label demagogue.[60]

1. A demagogue wields popular or mass leadership over an extensive number of people.
2. A demagogue exerts primary influence through the medium of the spoken word—through public speaking, whether directly to an audience or via radio or television.
3. A demagogue relies heavily on propaganda defined in the negative sense of intentional use of suggestion, irrelevant emotional appeals, and pseudo-proof to circumvent human rational decision-making processes.
4. A demagogue capitalizes on the availability of a major contemporary social cause or problem.

5. A demagogue is hypocritical; the social cause serves as a front or persuasive leverage point while the actual primary motive is selfish interest and personal gain.

Several cautions are in order in applying these guidelines. A communicator may reflect each of these characteristics to a greater or lesser degree and only in certain instances. A communicator might fulfill only several of these criteria (such as items 1, 2, and 4) and yet not be called a demagogue; characteristics 3 and 5 seem to be central to a conception of a demagogue. How easily and accurately can we usually determine a communicator's *actual* motivations? Should we limit the notion of a demagogue solely to the political arena? An excellent collection of case studies which you may want to examine is Reinhard Luthin's *American Demagogues*.

Ethics and Nonverbal Communication

Nonverbal factors play an important role in the communication process. In a magazine advertisement, for example, the use of certain colors, pictures, layout patterns, and types of print all influence how the words in the advertisement are received. In *The Importance of Lying*, Arnold Ludwig underscores the ethical implications of some dimensions of nonverbal communication: "Lies are not only found in verbal statements. When a person nods affirmatively in response to something he does not believe or when he feigns attention to a conversation he finds boring, he is equally guilty of lying . . . A false shrug of the shoulders, the seductive batting of eyelashes, an eyewink, or a smile may all be employed as nonverbal forms of deception."[61] Silence, too, may carry ethical implications.[62] For instance, if to be responsible in fulfillment of our role or position demands that we speak out on a subject, to remain silent might be judged unethical. On the other hand, if the only way that we can persuade others successfully on a subject is to employ unethical communication techniques or appeals, the ethical decision probably would be to remain silent.

Spiro T. Agnew, when vice president of the United States, catalogued numerous nonverbal elements of television news broadcasts that he felt carried ethical implications: facial expressions, sarcastic tone of voice, raised eyebrow, and vocal inflection.[63] In the context of contemporary American political campaigns, Dan Nimmo questions the ethicality of electronically induced voice compression in radio and television advertisements for candidates. "A slow talking, drawling Southerner can be made to speak at the rate of a clipped New

Englander. A hesitant, shy sounding speaker becomes decisive and assured."[64] The *Journal of Mass Media Ethics*, 6 (no. 3, 1991) contains three essays that examine the ethics of computer digital alteration of photos and video.

In *Harper's* magazine, Earl Shorris condemns as unethical the nonverbal tactics of the *New York Times* in opposing Mrs. Bella Abzug as a candidate for mayor of New York City.[65]

> The *Times*, having announced its preference for almost anyone but Mrs. Abzug in the mayoral election, published a vicious photograph of her taken the night of her winning the endorsement of the New Democratic Coalition. In the photograph, printed on page 1, Mrs. Abzug sits alone on a stage under the New Democratic Coalition banner. There are three empty chairs to her right and five empty chairs to her left. In this forlorn scene the camera literally looks up Mrs. Abzug's dress to show the heavy calves and thighs of an overweight woman in her middle years.
>
> While the editorial judgment may be right, in that Bella Abzug is probably not the best choice or even a good choice for mayor of New York, the photograph is an example of journalism at its lowest. . . .

Do the ethical standards commonly applied to verbal communication apply equally as appropriately to nonverbal elements in communication? Should there be a special ethic for nonverbal communication in place of, or in addition to, the ethical criteria for assessing human use of language? For instance, what ethical standards should govern eye contact, facial expression, tone of voice, or gestures? How should the ethics of silence be judged? In television news coverage or political advertisements, what ethical standards should govern editing out of material, camera angles, or lighting of a person's face as they stimulate accurate or inaccurate meanings and impressions in the viewer?[66]

To further explore ethical standards for nonverbal communication, you are urged to read several sources that are especially rich in extended case studies. The entire issue of the *Journal of Mass Media Ethics*, 2 (Spring/Summer 1987) is devoted to photojournalism ethics. Some contributors suggest concrete ethical guidelines (pp. 34, 71–73). Others discuss photos as claims and the nonobjectivity of photos (pp. 50, 52). A photo as a reflection of the photographer's formed ethical character is probed (p. 9). *Image Ethics* is an anthology of original essays that explore "ethical and moral issues surrounding the use of the camera," especially the "moral rights of those individuals and groups whose images are used by photographers, film-makers, and video producers." This book also highlights the tension between freedom and responsibility: "Photography, film and television confer enormous power to create images that combine verisimilitude and visual impact. . . . These powers are appropriately protected under our Constitution as an essential freedom in a democratic society, but they should also entail responsibilities. There is . . . the need for all concerned to pause and contemplate the moral implications of the images they produce and distribute."[67]

As elements in the human communication process, many nonverbal signals seem unintentional or semiconscious. To the extent that a nonverbal element reflects lack of conscious choice or intent, to that degree should we consider that element as outside the realm of ethical scrutiny? On the other hand, because some nonverbal cues often are less consciously controlled by the communicator than words and because they usually are assumed by receivers to be more believable than words as keys to real sender intent and meaning, should we view nonverbal elements as *better* indexes than words of the ethical level of communication?

Ethics and Tastefulness

Should *tastefulness and tact* be included or excluded as *ethical* criteria for evaluating human communication? Should some communicative tactics be judged *unethical* because, with respect to a given context, they are too candid, obviously inappropriate, tasteless, or tactless? To encourage further exploration of this issue, we will briefly note some views on the subject.[68]

In evaluating the ethics of protest rhetoric characteristic of the late 1960s, Franklyn Haiman reached this conclusion concerning the lack of organization and the aggressive, nonconciliatory tone which typified the style of such rhetoric. "As for the . . . formlessness and abrasiveness, I simply cannot bring myself to mounting an ethical high horse. To me they are strictly matters of taste and changing styles, hardly worthy of serious ethical disputation." Note that Haiman seems to separate matters of taste and of ethical judgment. In judging the ethics of advertising, believes ethicist Richard DeGeorge, "we should distinguish between that which is in poor taste and that which is immoral."[69]

In contrast, in their consideration of the ethics of persuasion, Brembeck and Howell argue:[70]

> Tact is considered by many to be a part of pleasantness and politeness in persuasion, but too superficial to figure in basic

ethics. We believe tact to be of ethical importance because people have no right to injure the feelings of others unnecessarily. When a message might have been implemented in an effective way that would have spared the prestige and ego of a minority group but it did not, it falls short of being ethical.

Most untactful persuasion has become so through carelessness. Tact might well be made another test of ethics and applied continuously in planning and analyzing persuasion.

Concerning matters of ethics and truth in advertising, C. H. Sandage and Vernon Fryburger observe: "There are also advertisements and advertising practices that are in poor taste or inconsiderate of the reader, listener, or viewer. The blatant use of sex symbols, unrestricted references to the most personal of body functions, and excessive repetition are all too common."[71]

Ethics and Ghostwriting

Is a communicator unethical when utilizing a ghostwriter?[72] Can a speaker or writer ethically use a person, or staff, to write his or her message, to write parts of the message, to contribute ideas, or to do research? Nationally prominent figures such as Franklin D. Roosevelt, Adlai E. Stevenson II, John F. Kennedy, Richard M. Nixon, and Ronald Reagan relied heavily on ghostwriters. Rhetorical critics stress that these speakers frequently played an extensive role in the creation of their own speeches. Were they, nevertheless, unethical in using speechwriters? We can analyze the ethics of ghostwriting through exploration of a number of interrelated questions.

First, what is the communicator's intent and what is the audience's degree of awareness? Clearly condemned by some critics is the communicator who deceives the audience by pretending to author his or her own messages when, in fact, they are ghostwritten. However, if the audience is fully aware that ghostwriting is a normal circumstance, such as for presidents, senators, or corporation executives, then no ethical condemnation may be warranted. Everyone seems aware, for example, that certain classes of speakers use ghostwriters and make no pretense of writing all of each of their speeches.

Second, does the communicator use ghostwriters to make himself or herself appear to possess personal qualities which he or she really does not have? Eloquent style, wit, coherence, and incisive ideas are qualities all communicators desire; but some communicators can obtain them only with the aid of ghostwriters. We must consider the extent to which ghostwriters are used to improve a communicator's image without unethically distorting his or her true character.

Third, what is the communicator's role and what are the surrounding circumstances? Pressures of time and duty are invoked to sanction the necessity of ghostwriters for some communicators. In a speech communication course or an English composition course, most people agree that the student is entirely responsible for creating his or her own message. Training in analysis, research, and composition is subverted when a student relies on someone else to do all or part of his or her work. However, the president of the United States, a senator, a college president, or corporation head may, because of job demands and lack of time, be unable to avoid using ghostwriters. But what about a college professor, state senator, or local businessman? Are they unethical when they use a ghostwriter? Should clergy use a ghostwriter? Although a minister has written his or her own sermon, is he or she ethical if he or she repeats the same speech again and again over the years, even though the nature and needs of the congregation change? Some critics would argue that when the president of the United States speaks, not as the head of the executive branch, as in a State of the Union message, but as an individual politician, as in a presidential campaign, he or she should avoid using ghostwriters.

Fourth, to what extent do the communicators actively participate in the writing of their messages? Adlai E. Stevenson II and Franklin D. Roosevelt participated extensively in the writing of their major addresses, even though each of them used a staff of speechwriters. They are not often ethically condemned for employing ghostwriters; their speeches accurately reflected their own style and intellect. But what of the ethics of the speakers who let their ghostwriter research and write the entire speech and then simply deliver it?

Finally, does the communicator accept responsibility for the message he or she presents? Some argue that even if communicators did not write their message, or help write it, they still are ethical as long as they accept responsibility for the ethics and accuracy of its contents. When their statement is criticized, communicators should not disclaim authorship and "pass the buck" to their ghostwriters.

By fully exploring these five issues, we should be able to assess perceptively the ethics of a communicator who employs ghostwriters. Depending on the standards we employ, our judgment may not always be clear-cut. Through such analysis, however, we may avoid oversimplification inherent in most either-or evaluations.[73]

Objectivity as an Ethical Standard for News Reporting

In what ways and to what degree should "objectivity" be a standard for ethical news reporting in the print and electronic media? In their book, *Basic Issues in Mass Communication: A Debate*, Everette Dennis and John Merrill set some of the agenda for exploring this matter. Merrill presents a case for contending that objectivity is *not* possible in journalism, while Dennis suggests methods whereby journalistic practice can be deemed objective.[74] In the Code of Ethics of Sigma Delta Chi, the Society of Professional Journalists, objectivity is a major standard, yet it is left undefined. Some definition of the nature of this concept would seem necessary to determine its appropriateness and workability.[75]

According to James Carey, the practice of objective reporting developed out of a purely commercial motive, namely "the need to serve politically heterogeneous audiences without alienating any significant segment of the audience." The national wire services apparently started the practice by instructing reporters and writers that all copy should be acceptable to both Republican and Democratic subscribers. Subsequently this commercially grounded strategy was "rationalized into a canon of professional competence and an ideology of professional responsibility."[76] Gaye Tuchman argues that the formal news procedures used to promote objectivity "are actually strategies through which newsmen protect themselves from critics" and lay claim to professional status because their "special professional knowledge is not sufficiently respected by news consumers. . . ."[77]

Jorgen Westerstahl advocates a view of objectivity that encompasses factuality, including truthfulness and relevance, and impartiality, including balance/nonpartisanship and neutral presentation. He believes that not all elements apply in all cases, or in equal degree, or in a like manner.[78] A similar view defines an objective report as "detached, unprejudiced, unopinionated, uninvolved, and omniscient." Only the verifiable facts are transmitted, and those in a neutral fashion. Balance is achieved by presenting both sides of a story (thereby assuming that a story has *more* than one side or *only* two sides).[79] According to Robert Hackett:

> This position implies that the journalist and the news media are detached observers, separable from the social reality on which they report; that truth or knowledge depends upon the observer's/journalist's neutrality in relation to the object of study; that the news medium, when "properly used," is neutral and value free, and thus can guarantee the truthfulness of "the message." That is, the news

can potentially transmit an unbiased, transparent, neutral translation of some external reality.[80]

However, these conditions simply are not possible. In varying degrees, inevitable processes of selection, focus, interpretation, and evaluation function to limit the objectivity of a report. Institutional characteristics of news media organizations including the constraints of time/space and the demands for profit and success often cause the media to focus on audience-oriented issues. Individual reporters necessarily reflect their own personal histories (upbringing, education, values, etc.) in selecting the language and images in which to cast the report. The goal of presenting all the facts and nothing but the facts is impossible because the reality or truth of a situation emerges only as humans connect, interpret, and evaluate the empirical facts to give them meaning in some larger context.[81]

While recognizing that subjectivity, selectivity, and incompleteness will always affect news reporting in varying degrees, some scholars and practitioners contend that objectivity is largely achievable. Donald McDonald advocates this view and conceives of objectivity not as the total truth about something and not as absence of all subjectivity, but rather in terms set forth in 1947 by the Hutchins Commission on Freedom of the Press: ". . . a truthful, comprehensive, and intelligent account of the day's events in a context which gives them meaning."[82] Another view depicts objectivity as an attitude, as a sincere and conscious attempt to be factual, unbiased, balanced, and fair. As such, it is a practical goal to aim for but never to meet fully. According to this view, the development of language habits taught by general semanticists, such as Alfred Korzybski and S. I. Hayakawa, can implement this attitude.[83]

Dennis describes a position wherein objectivity is a goal never perfectly achieved, and reporters try to be impartial, factual, and accurate in observation. "The true test is whether reasonable people in the same cultural setting would have similar—if not always the same—perceptions of the event or issue if they were to have done their own reporting." To make journalism as objective as possible, Dennis outlines a program of strategic planning for news organizations. Policies would need to be set that consistently guide the following inquiries: What is worth covering and why? When has enough information been gathered? What is important enough to put in a story and why? What is essential to full and accurate presentation? What words and images will be used—especially to distinguish factual information from the reporter's impressions? What criteria will govern editing? In addition, Dennis urges that a more careful distinction be drawn among three types of stories: (1) descriptive—the basic who, what, where, and when facts of a situation; (2) analytical—focuses on the "forces at work, the competing interests, points of view, possible explanations and interpretations of how and why the situation or event occurred"; (3) consequential—immediate and long-term consequences for individual and community; often involves speculation based on authoritative sources.[84]

In April 1980, the Mexico Declaration (signed by representatives of international and regional journalistic organizations) offered suggestions for an international code of journalistic ethics. Principle X urged dedication to objective reality, whereby

> ... facts are reported conscientiously in their proper context, pointing out their emphasis, with due deployment of the creative capacity of the journalist, so that the public is provided with adequate material to facilitate the formation of an accurate and comprehensive picture of the world in which the origin, nature, and essence of events, processes, and states of affairs are understood as objectively as possible.[85]

In its code of standards and ethics, the *Washington Post* consciously avoids what it terms "endless" arguments about objectivity and substitutes what it believes is a more workable standard, namely, fairness. A fair story includes all significant facts, omits irrelevant information, does not mislead or deceive, and openly reveals the reporter's emotions or biases.[86]

In *Committed Journalism*, Edmund Lambeth describes "authentic interpretation" as an alternative to the "old objectivity":[87]

> Authentic interpretation retains the fidelity to fact central to the "old objectivity" while furnishing perspective and fullness of meaning. It supplies background information unavailable from or omitted by news sources; it translates complex data or terminology so that it can be understood; it provides enough context to allow readers to judge the news for themselves and not be misled; it tells candidly what information is unavoidably missing from a story; and, when necessary, it is explicit enough about methods used to gather the story to let the reader assess its probity and fairness.

Finally, W. Lance Bennett condemns both objectivity and fairness as standards not only because they ultimately are unachievable but also because devotion to them biases news reports in favor of the status quo and official approved viewpoints. Instead he urges the practice of "advocacy" journalism.[88]

So, then, in what ways and to what degree should objectivity be a standard for ethical news reporting?

Secrecy: Personal and Governmental

What is a secret? In her book, *Secrets*, Sissela Bok argues that "anything can be secret as long as it is kept intentionally hidden, set apart in the mind of its keeper as requiring concealment." Bok probes the nature of the concept, examines the need for and the dangers of secrecy, and illuminates varied contexts for secrecy and revelation such as personal relations, gossip, business, government, whistleblowing, leaking of information, social science research, undercover police operations, and investigative journalism. In *Lying*, Bok advocated a negative ethical presumption against all lying—any specific lie needed adequate justification. In *Secrets*, however, Bok holds a "neutral" view of secrecy—not all secrets are wrong and not all secrets need justification. "Secrecy may accompany the most innocent as well as the most lethal acts; it is needed for human survival, yet it enhances every form of abuse."[89]

Bok does explain two assumptions that undergird her analysis of secrecy. First she assumes *equality* as a principle: "Whatever control over secrecy and openness we conclude is legitimate for some individuals should, in the absence of special considerations, be legitimate for all." Her second assumption is the desirability for "*Partial individual control* over the degree of secrecy or openness about personal matters—those indisputably in the private realm." Some individual control over intimate and personal secrets is necessary to protect self-identity, plans and actions, and possessions. "With no control over secrecy and openness, human beings could not remain either sane or free." Admittedly even in private relationships, secrecy as a habit or in a specific case can harm both the keeper and the excluded. An ability to exercise *discretion* is vital for judging the ethicality of secrecy. Discretion is the ability to "discern what is and is not intrusive and injurious," to cope with "the moral questions about what is fair or unfair, truthful or deceptive, helpful or harmful," and to know "when to hold back in order not to bruise" and "when to reach out."[90]

The relationship between secrecy and power occupies a central place in Bok's analysis.[91] Power may be exercised by a person in authority or by one who exercises unscrupulous means; power may be collective in groups or institutions. "When power is joined to secrecy, therefore, and when the practices are of long duration, the danger of spread and abuse and deterioration increases." Concerning personal matters there is a "presumption in favor of individual control over secrecy and openness" and "the burden of proof is on those who would deny them such control." In the cases of collective and institutional power joined with secrecy, the presumption reverses. When those who exercise such power "claim control over secrecy and openness, it is up to them to show why giving them such control is necessary and what kinds of safeguards they propose." For example, there "should be a strong presumption against governmental control over secrecy because of the abuses it can conceal, the power governments exercise, and their special obligations of accountability." The test of public debate and justification applies here to secrecy as it did in *Lying* to practices of institutions. A proposed or actual policy of secrecy should, in principle at least, be capable of public deliberation by reasonable persons, including those who oppose the practice and those who are directly affected by it. You may wish to review the section on lying earlier in this chapter, where the justification procedures Bok proposes are explained.

We turn now to a particular aspect of governmental secrecy—secrecy by the president of the United States. When is presidential secrecy ethical and when is it unethical? In *Presidential Secrecy and Deception*, John Orman presents both a framework of values (a grounding) and suggested guidelines for evaluating the ethicality of presidential secrecy. Orman's view is rooted in the particular "political perspective" of representative democracy—in fundamental values essential for the optimum functioning of our system of governing.

Orman offers five value premises as a framework within which ethical standards should emerge. First, presidential secrecy or deception is unjustified when it is unconstitutional, illegal, or unethical. While such actions may be necessary pragmatically, they are not justified. Unethical presidential actions include systematic lying or deception, "breach of faith" with citizens, valuing power above other values, abusing power, using one's authority to justify immoral acts, or acting out of a motivation for personal material gain. Second, "means and ends must be compatible." A worthy presidential goal does not justify use of ethically suspect means, and the use of ethically acceptable means does not automatically provide justification for a goal. "National security must compete with other goals and values." Third, the argument that "other nations do it" is not by itself sufficient justification for presidential secrecy or deception. Fourth, "if an open and public alternative to the covert policy exists, then the policymaker should select the open and public alternative." While presidential secrecy "is neither all good nor all evil," and while there are legitimate reasons for keeping some presidential actions secret, this value "argues that openness is preferable to secrecy." Fifth, "if a truthful statement or option to a false statement is available, then the president should select the truthful statement." While "a certain amount of deception may be justified to maintain national security" or other competing democratic values, this principle "simply argues that a truthful statement is preferable to deception."[92]

Orman outlines a "system of accountability for presidential secrecy"—implemented through congressional legislation—that would specify the categories of information that the president might be allowed to keep secret from Congress, the press, and the public. These categories comprise legitimate "executive secrets": (1) specific details about ongoing diplomatic negotiations; (2) methods, sources, and technology of secret intelligence-gathering means; (3) defense contingency plans, military plans, troop movements, and weapons research and development especially during times of declared war; (4) details of advice given to the president; and (5) details about the ongoing negotiations of other nations, their covert intelligence means, their defense and weapons plans, and the nature of their executive advice. In contrast, Orman adapts the suggestions of Halperin and Hoffman that other categories of information be required to be *automatically released* by the president to Congress and the public: (1) the fact that Americans are engaged in combat or are about to be; (2) the stationing of American forces abroad; (3) countries in which the United States stores nuclear weapons; (4) financing of foreign combat operations or foreign military forces; (5) commitments to do any of the above or start of negotiations contemplating such commitments; (6) existence, budgets, and functions of intelligence organizations; (7) concepts and costs of weapons systems; and (8) any unlawful action of which any official of the executive branch gains knowledge. Finally, Orman offers guidelines for when a president ethically can lie to protect a secret: (1) to save the nation from a nuclear war; (2) when the lie is the only option to protect the "executive secrets" categorized earlier; (3) to prevent undue alarm in Congress, press, or the public in time of a constitutionally declared war. In Orman's view, there can be no unchallenged and general permission for a president to lie.[93]

How reasonable and workable is Orman's system for the legality and ethicality of presidential secrecy? What additional categories of secrecy do you believe should be specified as unethical—or as ethical?

To what degree is presidential (or governmental) secrecy an area where legality and ethicality necessarily must be synonymous?

Ethical Responsibilities of Receivers

What are our ethical responsibilities as receivers or respondents in communication? An answer to this question may stem in part from the image we hold of the communication process. Receivers would seem to bear little, if any, responsibility if they are viewed as inert, passive, defenseless receptacles, as mindless blotters uncritically accepting arguments and ideas. In contrast, communication can be viewed as a transaction where both senders and receivers bear mutual responsibility to participate actively in the process. This shared responsibility may vary proportionally according to roles. This image of receivers as active participants might suggest a number of responsibilities. Here I will suggest two major responsibilities that perhaps are best captured by the phrases "reasoned skepticism" and "appropriate feedback."[94]

Reasoned skepticism includes a number of elements. It represents a balanced position between the undesirable extremes of being too open-minded, too gullible, on the one hand and being too closed-minded, too dogmatic, on the other. We are not simply unthinking blotters "soaking up" ideas and argument. Rather we should exercise our capacities actively to search for meaning, to analyze and synthesize, to interpret significance, and to judge soundness and worth. We do something to and with the information we receive; we process, interpret, and evaluate it. Also, we should inform ourselves about issues being discussed. We should tolerate, even seek out, divergent and controversial viewpoints, the better to assess what is being presented. We should not be so dogmatic, ego-involved, and defensive about our own views that we are unwilling to take into account (understand, evaluate, and perhaps even accept) the views and data presented by others.

As receivers, we must realize that accurate understanding of a communicator's message may be hindered by our attempt to impose prematurely our own ethical standards on him or her. Our immediate "gut-level" ethical judgments may cause us to distort the intended meaning. Only after reaching an accurate understanding of the sender's ideas can we reasonably evaluate the ethics of his or her communication strategies or purposes.

In this era of public distrust of the truthfulness of public communication, reasoned skepticism also requires that we combat the automatic assumption that most public communication always is untrustworthy. Just because a communication is of a certain type or comes from a certain source (government, candidate, news media, advertiser), it must not automatically, without evaluation, be rejected as tainted or untruthful. Clearly, we must always exercise caution in acceptance and care in evaluation, as emphasized throughout this book. Using the best evidence available to us, we may arrive at our best judgment. However, to condemn a message as untruthful or unethical solely because it stems from a suspect source and before directly assessing it is to exhibit decision-making behavior detrimental to our political, social, and economic system. Rejection of the message; if such be the judgment, must come after, not before, our evaluation of it. As with a defendant in the courtroom, public communication must be presumed ethically innocent until we, or experts we acknowledge, have proved it guilty.

As active participants in the communication process, the feedback we provide to senders needs to be appropriate in a number of senses. Our response, in most situations, should be an honest and accurate reflection of our true comprehension, belief, feeling, or judgment. Otherwise communicators are denied the relevant and accurate information they need to make decisions. If we are participating in communication primarily for purposes other than seriously trying to understand and assess the information and arguments (perhaps to make friends, have fun, be socially congenial), we should reveal our intent to the other participants. It would seem ethically dubious to pretend acceptance of an argument with the actual intent of later condemning it on a more opportune occasion. Likewise it seems ethically dubious to lack understanding of an argument but to pretend to agree with it in order to mask our lack of comprehension.

Our feedback might be verbal or nonverbal, oral or written, immediate or delayed. A response of puzzlement or understanding, of disagreement or agreement, could be reflected through our facial expression, gestures, posture, inquiries, statements during a question-and-answer period, or letters to editors or advertisers. In some cases, because of our special expertise on a subject, we even may have the obligation to respond while other receivers remain silent. We need to decide whether the degree and type of our feedback are appropriate for the subject, audience, and occasion. For instance, to interrupt with questions, or even to heckle, might be appropriate in a few situations but irresponsible in many others.

Ethical Responsibilities of Non-Participants

If both communicators and receivers in communication share ethical responsibilities, what about nonparticipants, third parties, and onlookers? In various of his writings and conference presentations, Kenneth Andersen probes this question and sketches some of the issues involved.[95] Our purpose here in adapting his ideas is not to answer the question at length, but to stimulate your thought on the matter. Nonparticipants as a label might include individuals, a group, or the public-at-large. Such "outsiders" might include an ideal observer or critic.

People not directly involved in a communication situation nevertheless may indirectly or ultimately be affected by that communication. They may have an indirect interest in the effects and ethics of that situation. They may wish, indeed have a responsibility, to intervene in some way to judge the ethics or exert influence, especially if they believe that both communicators and receivers have failed to fulfill their own ethical responsibilities.

Nonparticipants also contribute to the process of creating the larger moral context of ethical expectations within which a particular instance occurs. They have a responsibility of active concern for the general "ethic" of communication that should guide society. Nonparticipants are part of the complex web of communications that characterizes contemporary culture; legitimately they can influence the ethical standards, both minimal and ideal, that exert moral pressure on modern communicators.

Does the "public" have ethical responsibilities for communication? Clifford Christians, a mass media ethicist, examines collective or communal ethical responsibility.[96] He maintains that "vast numbers of persons can share the same general undifferentiated responsibility simultaneously." He grounds his view in a particular conception of human nature with our uniquely human ability to communicate seen both as a fundamental capacity and right. "By collective or communal responsibility," says Christians, "I refer to a broad moral duty by the general public to supervise such social processes as communication."

Notes

[1] See, for example, Eugene Carson Blake, "Should Codes of Ethics in Public Life Be Absolute or Relative?" *Annals of the American Academy of Political and Social Science*, 363 (January 1961): 4–11.

[2] A helpful categorization of types of relativism is John H. Barnsley, *The Social Reality of Ethics: A Comparative Analysis of Moral Codes* (London: Routledge and Kegan Paul, 1972), ch. 9. Also see William B. Gudykunst and Young Yum Kim, *Communicating With Strangers: An Approach to Intercultural Communication* (Reading, MA: Addison-Wesley, 1984), pp. 199–294.

[3] Jurgen Ruesch, "Ethical Issues in Communication," in *Communication: Ethical and Moral Issues*, Lee Thayer, ed. (New York: Gordon and Breach, 1973), pp. 16–17.

[4] Robert T. Oliver, *Culture and Communication* (Springfield IL: Charles C. Thomas, 1962), p. 79.

[5] Thomas R. Nilsen, *Ethics of Speech Communication*, 2d ed. (Indianapolis: Bobbs-Merrill, 1974), pp. 84–87.

[6] For insight on the points made in this paragraph, the author has drawn upon a graduate research paper by David Harold Smith, "Stating Ethical Guidelines for Speech Communication in Positive Terms" (Northern Illinois University, Department of Speech Communication, 1973).

[7] See Hugh Rank, "Watergate and the Language," in *Language and Public Policy*, Hugh Rank, ed. (Urbana, IL: National Council of Teachers of English, 1974), p. 5; Wayne N. Thompson, *The Process of Persuasion* (New York: Harper & Row, 1975), pp. 470–71.

[8] Thomas R. Nilsen, "Free Speech, Persuasion, and the Democratic Process," *Quarterly Journal of Speech*, 44 (October 1958): 235–43; Herbert W. Simons, *Persuasion* (Reading, MA: Addison-Wesley, 1976), pp. 147–49.

[9] John E. Marston, *The Nature of Public Relations* (New York: McGraw-Hill, 1963), pp. 346–59.

[10] S. I. Hayakawa, *Language in Thought and Action*, 4th ed. (New York: Harcourt Brace Jovanovich, 1978), p. 257.

[11] B. J. Diggs, "Persuasion and Ethics," *Quarterly Journal of Speech*, 50 (December 1964): 366.

[12] Robert T. Oliver, *The Psychology of Persuasive Speech*, 2d ed. (New York: Longmans, Green, 1957), p. 26.

[13] *New York Times*, December 7, 1962, p. 5. Also see Arthur Sylvester, "The Government Has the Right to Lie," *Saturday Evening Post*, 240 (November 18, 1967): 10ff.

[14] Winston L. Brembeck and William S. Howell, *Persuasion: A Means of Social Influence*, 2d ed. (Englewood Cliffs, NJ: Prentice-Hall, 1976), p. 239.

[15] Warren G. Bovée, "The End Can Justify the Means—But Rarely," *Journal of Mass Media Ethics*, 6, no. 3 (1991): 135–45.

[16] Charles Fried, *Right and Wrong* (Cambridge,: Harvard University Press, 1978), pp. 9–10, 29, 54–78; Carl Wellman, *Morals and Ethics*, 2d ed. (Englewood Cliffs, NJ: Prentice-Hall, 1988), p. 41.

[17] George Yoos, "Rational Appeal and the Ethics of Advocacy," in *Essays on Classical Rhetoric and Modern Discourse*, Robert Connors, et al., eds. (Carbondale: Southern Illinois University Press, 1984), pp. 82–97. For other explorations of

definition, see Frederick Siegler, "Lying," *American Philosophical Quarterly*, 111 (April 1966): 128–36: Roderick M. Chisholm and Thomas D. Feehan, "The Intent to Deceive," *Journal of Philosophy*, LXXIV (March 1977): 143–59.

[18] Sissela Bok, *Lying: Moral Choice in Public and Private Life* (New York: Vintage Books, 1979), ch. 1. For a much broader and more inclusive conception of lying that includes indirect, unconscious, and habitual lies, see Dwight Bolinger, "Truth is a Linguistic Question," in *Language and Public Policy*, Rank, ed., pp. 161–75.

[19] Bok, *Lying*, ch. 2.

[20] Joseph Kupfer, "The Moral Presumption Against Lying," *Review of Metaphysics*, 36 (September 1982): 103–26; also see Elizabeth Minnick, "Why Not Lie?" *Soundings*, 68 (Winter 1985): 493–509.

[21] Bok, *Lying*, ch. 6; J. Barton Bowyer, *Cheating* (New York: St. Martin's Press, 1982), p. 207.

[22] Bok, *Lying*, ch. 7.

[23] David Nyberg, *The Varnished Truth: Truth Telling and Deceiving in Ordinary Life* (Chicago, University of Chicago Press, 1993), pp. 1–5, 10–11, 25, 78, 114. Also see Arnold M. Ludwig, *The Importance of Lying* (Springfield, IL: Charles C. Thomas, 1965); and Robert L. Wolk and Arthur Henley, *The Right to Lie* (New York: Peter H. Wyden, Inc., 1970).

[24] See, for example, Roger Hufford, "The Dimensions of an Idea: Ambiguity Defined," *Today's Speech*, 14 (April 1966): 4–8; William Empson, *Seven Types of Ambiguity*, 3rd ed. (Edinburgh: T.A. Constable, Ltd., 1947).

[25] Douglas Ehninger, *Influence, Belief, and Argument: An Introduction to Responsible Persuasion* (Glenview, IL: Scott, Foresman, 1974), pp. 113–15; W. Ross Winterowd, *Rhetoric and Writing* (Boston: Allyn and Bacon, 1965), p. 277.

[26] M. Lee Williams and Blaine Goss, "Equivocation: Character Insurance," *Human Communication Research*, 1 (Spring 1975): 265–70.

[27] For discussions of contexts in which intentional ambiguity might be considered necessary, accepted, exacted as normal, or even ethical, see the following sources: Robert T. Oliver, *Culture and Communication* (Springfield, IL: Charles C. Thomas, 1962), pp. 65–69; I. A. Richards, *The Philosophy of Rhetoric* (New York: Oxford University Press Galaxy Book, 1965), p. 40; Raymond E. Anderson, "Kierkegaard's Theory of Communication," *Speech Monographs* 30 (March 1963): 6–7; Fred C. Ikle, "Bargaining and Communication," in *Handbook of Communication*, Ithiel de Sola Pool, et al., eds. (Chicago: Rand-McNally, 1973), pp. 837–40; B. Aubrey Fisher, "The Persuasive Campaign: A Pedagogy for the Contemporary First Course in Speech Communication," *Central States Speech Journal* 20 (Winter 1969): 297–98. Murray Edelman, *The Symbolic Uses of Politics* (Urbana: University of Illinois Press, 1967), pp. 139, 141, 148; John C. Condon, *Semantics and Communication*, 2d ed. (New York: Macmillan, 1975), pp. 114–15; Doris Graber, *Verbal Behavior and Politics* (Urbana: University of Illinois Press, 1976), p. 31.

[28] For example, see Donald N. Levine, *The Flight from Ambiguity* (Chicago: University of Chicago Press, 1985); Eric M. Eisenberg, "Ambiguity as Strategy in Organizational Communication," *Communication Monographs*, 51 (September 1984): 227–42; William Kohlmann, "In Praise of Ambiguity," *Newsweek*, April 1, 1985, pp. 10–11; Chaim Perelman, "The Use and Abuse of Confused Notions," *ETC: A Review of General Semantics*, 36 (1979): 313–324; David Kaufer, "Metaphor and Its Ties to Ambiguity and Vagueness," *Rhetoric Society Quarterly*, 13 (Summer-Fall, 1983): 209–20.

[29] Daniel Oran, *Law Dictionary for Non-Lawyers* (St. Paul, MN: West Publishing Co., 1975), pp. 330–31.

[30] Craig R. Smith, *Orientations to Speech Criticism* (Chicago: Science Research Associates, 1976), p. 11; Tony Schwartz, *The Responsive Chord* (Garden City, NY: Anchor Books, 1974), pp. 96–97.

[31] Lewis A. Froman, Jr., "A Realistic Approach to Campaign Strategies and Tactics," in *Electoral Process*, M. Kent Jennings and L. Harmon Zeigler, eds. (Englewood Cliffs, NJ: Prentice-Hall, 1966), p. 9.

[32] This idea was suggested to the author by Martha O'Grady in her graduate course research paper, "Ambiguity in the American Political and Legal Systems," Northern Illinois University, Department of Communication Studies, 1981.

[33] Nilsen, *Ethics of Speech Communication*, 2d ed., pp. 75–76.

[34] Edwin Black, *Rhetorical Criticism* (New York: Macmillan, 1965), chs. 4 and 5.

[35] Ivan L. Preston, "Theories of Behavior and the Concept of Rationality in Advertising," *Journal of Communication*, 17 (September 1967): 211–22; also see Preston, "Logic and Illogic in the Advertising Process," *Journalism Quarterly*, 44 (Summer 1967): 231–39.

[36] Oliver, *Culture and Communication*, p. 155.

[37] John C. Condon and Fathi Yousef, *An Introduction to Intercultural Communication* (Indianapolis: Bobbs-Merrill, 1975), ch. 10; also see D. Lawrence Kincaid, ed., *Communication Theory: Eastern and Western Perspectives*, (San Diego, CA: Academic Press, 1987).

[38] Interview with Marshall McLuhan in *McLuhan: Hot and Cool*, Gerald E. Stearn, ed. (New York: Dial, 1967), p. 270.

[39] Fern L. Johnson, "A Reformulation of Rationality in Rhetoric," *Central States Speech Journal*, 24 (Winter 1973): 262–71.

[40] Dan Nimmo, *Political Communication and Public Opinion in America* (Santa Monica, CA: Goodyear Pub. Co., 1978), pp. 362–72, 413–14. Also see Robert E. Lane and David O. Sears, *Public Opinion* (Englewood Cliffs, NJ: Prentice-Hall, 1964), ch. 7.

[41] Brembeck and Howell, *Persuasion*, 2d ed., ch. 8.

[42] Stephen Toulmin, et al., *An Introduction to Reasoning* (New York: Macmillan, 1979), espec. chs. 12–17; Richard D. Rieke and Malcolm O. Sillars, *Argumentation and the Decision Making Process*, 2d ed. (Glenview, IL: Scott, Foresman, 1984), chs. 4 and 5; Stephen Toulmin, *The Uses of Argument* (Cambridge, England: Cambridge University Press paperback, 1964), pp. 14–15, 36, 175–76, 182–83, 248; Gidon Gottlieb, *The Logic of Choice* (New York: Macmillan, 1968); Richard E. Crable, *Argumentation as Communication* (Columbus. OH: Charles E. Merrill, 1976), ch. 7. George Yoos argues that ethical standards for advocacy differ between contexts of discourse, such as law, advertising, politics, and love. Yoos, "Rational Appeal and the Ethics of Advocacy," in *Essays on Classical Rhetoric and Modern Discourse*, Connors, et al., eds., p. 111.

[43] See, for example, Barnet Baskerville, "The Illusion of Proof," *Western Speech* 25 (Fall 1961): 236–42. For emphasis on integrating and balancing the use of emotional and rational appeals, see Nilsen, *Ethics of Speech Communication*, 2d ed., pp. 57–59.

[44] Such truth and rationality based standards are reflected throughout the American Association of Advertising Agencies' "Code of Ethics" and throughout the Ameri-

can Advertising Federation's "Advertising Code of American Business." (These codes are reprinted in chapter 10 of this book.) Also see Gunnar Andren, "The Rhetoric of Advertising," *Journal of Communication*, 30 (Autumn 1980): 74–80; Robert Spero, *The Duping of the American Voter* (New York: Lippincott and Crowell, 1980), pp. 5–6; Carl P. Wrighter, *I Can Sell You Anything* (New York: Balantine Books, 1972), ch. 3; Richard M. Weaver, *Life Without Prejudice and Other Essays* (Chicago, Regnery, 1965), pp. 121–28.

[45] J. R. Carpenter, "Voice of the Advertiser," *Advertising Age*, 19 (April 1971): 57. Also see Ivan Preston, *The Great American Blow-Up: Puffery in Advertising and Selling* (Madison: University of Wisconsin Press, 1975); Neil Postman, *Amusing Ourselves To Death* (New York: Viking, 1984), pp. 127–128.

[46] Lawrence W. Rosenfield, et al., *The Communication Experience* (Boston: Allyn and Bacon, 1976), pp. 310–312, 324. Also see Richard DeGeorge, *Business Ethics*, 2d ed. (New York: Macmillan, 1986), pp. 275–80; W. Lance Hayes, "Of That Which We Cannot Write: Some Notes on the Phenomenology of Media," *Quarterly Journal of Speech*, 74 (February 1988): 1–17.

[47] Rosenfield, *Communicative Experience*, pp. 254–83.

[48] Theodore Levitt, "The Morality (?) of Advertising," *Harvard Business Review* (July-August, 1972): 84–92.

[49] Tony Schwartz, *The Responsive Chord* (Garden City, NY: Anchor Books, 1974), pp. 18–22.

[50] Moving beyond the content-oriented view of persuasion ethics advocated in his book, *The Art of Persuasion* (2d ed., 1968), Wayne Minnick more recently advocates a consequences-oriented standard for assessing ethicality of persuasion in both electronic and print mass media. Minnick, "A New Look at the Ethics of Persuasion," *Southern Speech Communication Journal*, 45 (Summer 1980): 352–62.

[51] Tony Schwarz, "Ethics in Political Media Communication," Communication, 6, no. 2 (1981): 213–24. A later book by Schwartz is *Media: The Second God* (New York: Random House, 1981).

[52] One early survey of over forty varied definitions is Frederick E. Lumley, *The Propaganda Menace* (New York: Century, 1933), chapter 2. Also see Erwin Fellows, "Propaganda: History of a Word," *American Speech* 34 (October 1959): 182–189; Fellows, "Propaganda and Communication: A Study in Definitions," *Journalism Quarterly*, 34 (1957): 431–42; Garth Jowett and Victoria O'Donnell, *Propaganda and Persuasion*, 2d ed. (Beverly Hills: Sage, 1992).

[53] For example, see Terrence H. Qualter, *Propaganda and Psychological Warfare* (New York: Random House, 1962), ch. 1; Paul Kecskemeti, "Propaganda," in *Handbook of Communication*, Ithiel de Sola Pool, et al., eds. (Chicago: Rand McNally, 1973), pp. 844–870; Nick Aaron Ford, ed., *Language in Uniform: A Reader on Propaganda* (Indianapolis: Odyssey Press, 1967), pp. vii–viii, 19–20; Thomas M. Garrett, S.J., quoted by Walter Taplin, "Morals," in *Speaking of Advertising*, John S. Wright and Daniel S. Warner, eds. (New York: McGraw-Hill, 1963), p. 336; Brembeck and Howell, *Persuasion*, 2d ed., p. 19.

[54] For example see W. H. Werkmeister, *An Introduction to Critical Thinking*, rev. ed. (Lincoln, NE: Johnson, 1957), ch. 4; Stuart Chase, *Guides to Straight Thinking* (New York: Harper, 1956), chs. 20–21; Roy Paul Madsen, *The Impact of Film* (New York: Macmillan, 1973), pp. 441–44; Nilsen, *Ethics of Speech Communication*, 2d ed., pp. 81–82.

55 Jacques Ellul, *Propaganda* (New York: Vintage Books paperback, 1973), pp. xv, xvii, 38, 61, 174–75, 180, 188, 217.

56 Jacques Ellul, "The Ethics of Propaganda: Propaganda, Innocence, and Amorality," *Communication* 6, no. 2 (1981): 159–77.

57 For the list of propaganda devices as originally explained in 1937 by the Institute for Propaganda Analysis, see *Propaganda Analysis I* (October and November 1937): 1–8. The Institute defined propaganda as "expression of opinion or action by individuals or groups deliberately designed to influence opinions or actions of other individuals or groups with reference to predetermined ends." The original explanation of these devices is reprinted in Ford, ed., *Language in Uniform*, pp. 12–18.

58 Lawrence J. Flynn, S. J., "The Aristotelian Basis for the Ethics of Speaking," *The Speech Teacher* 6 (September 1957): 186–87.

59 Stephan Lesher, "The New Image of George Wallace," *Chicago Tribune*, January 2, 1972, Sec. 1A, p. 1.

60 The basic formulation from which these guidelines have been adapted was first suggested to me by Professor William Conboy of the University of Kansas. These five characteristics generally are compatible with standard scholarly attempts to define a demagogue. For instance, see Reinhard Luthin, *American Demagogues* (reprinted ed., Gloucester, MA: Peter Smith, 1959), pp. ix, 3, 302–19; Barnet Baskerville, "Joseph McCarthy: Briefcase Demagogue," reprinted in *The Rhetoric of the Speaker*, Haig A. Bosmajian, ed. (New York: D.C. Heath, 1967), p. 64; Charles W. Lomas, *The Agitator in American Society* (Englewood Cliffs, NJ: Prentice-Hall, 1968), pp. 18–19; Wayne C. Minnick, *The Art of Persuasion*, 2d ed. (Boston: Houghton Mifflin, 1968), p. 6; G. M. Gilbert, "Dictators and Demagogues," *Journal of Social Issues*, 11, no. 3 (1955): 51–53.

61 Ludwig, *The Importance of Lying*, p. 5.

62 For one survey of research on silence, see Richard L. Johannesen, "The Functions of Silence," *Western Speech*, 38 (Winter 1974): 25–35. Also see Barry Brummett, "Towards a Theory of Silences as a Political Strategy," *Quarterly Journal of Speech*, 66 (October 1980): 289–303; Deborah Tannen and Muriel Saville-Troike, eds., *Perspectives on Silence* (Norwood, NJ: Ablex, 1985); Adam Jaworski, *The Power of Silence: Social and Pragmatic Perspectives* (Newbury Park, CA: Sage, 1993), ch. 4.

63 Spiro T. Agnew, "Television News Coverage," *Vital Speeches of the Day*, December 1, 1969, pp. 98–101.

64 Dan Nimmo, "Ethical Issues in Political Campaign Communication," *Communication* 6, no. 2 (1981): 187–206.

65 Earl Shorris, "The Fourth Estate," *Harpers*, (October 1977), p. 106.

66 Several insights concerning ethical issues in nonverbal communication stem from a graduate course research paper by Deborah H. Lund, "Implications of Ethical Standards in Nonverbal Communication," (Northern Illinois University, Department of Speech Communication, 1973). For additional nonverbal examples that raise ethical issues, see John L. Hulteng, *The Messenger's Motives: Ethical Problems of the News Media*, 2d ed., (Englewood Cliffs, NJ: Prentice-Hall, 1985), ch. 9; E. S. Safford, "The Need for a Public Ethic in Mass Communication," in *Ethics, Morality, and the Mass Media*, Lee Thayer, et al., eds. (New York: Hastings House, 1980), espec. pp. 143–144.

[67] Larry Gross, John Stuart Katz, and Jay Ruby, eds., *Image Ethics: The Moral Rights of Subjects in Photographs, Film, and Television* (New York: Oxford University Press, 1988), pp. v, 32. Also see Paul Lester, *Photojournalism: An Ethical Approach* (Hillsdale, NJ: Erlbaum, 1991).

[68] For some actual examples from newspapers and television that can be judged for their tastelessness and possible unethicality, see Hulteng, *The Messenger's Motives*, 2d ed., ch. 4.

[69] DeGeorge, *Business Ethics*, 2d ed., p. 274.

[70] Winston L. Brembeck and William S. Howell, *Persuasion: A Means of Social Control*, 1st ed. (New York: Prentice-Hall, 1952), p. 462.

[71] C. H. Sandage and Vernon Fryburger, *Advertising Theory and Practice*, 8th ed. (Homewood, IL: Irwin, 1971), ch. 5. Also see William H. Boyenton, "Enter the Ladies—86 Proof: A Study in Advertising Ethics," *Journalism Quarterly*, 44 (Autumn 1967): 445–53.

[72] This section on ethics and ghostwriting is adapted from Richard L. Johannesen, "On Teaching the Social Responsibilities of a Speaker," in Jeffery Auer and Edward B. Jenkinson, eds., *Essays on Teaching Speech in the High School* (Bloomington: Indiana University Press, 1971), pp. 229–31. For one interpretation see Ernest G. Bormann, "The Ethics of Ghostwritten Speeches," *Quarterly Journal of Speech* 47 (October 1961): 262–67.

[73] For some recent relevant sources, see the three essays on ghostwriting in *Communication Education*, 33 (1984): 301–7. Also see Kathleen Hall Jamieson, *Eloquence in an Electronic Age* (New York: Oxford University Press, 1988), pp. 201–37; Martin Medhurst, "Ghostwritten Speeches: Ethics Isn't the Only Lesson," *Communication Education*, 36 (July 1987): 241–49; Matthew Seeger, "Ghostbusting: Exorcising the Great Man Spirit from the Speechwriting Debate," *Communication Education*, 34 (October 1985): 353–58.

[74] Everette E. Dennis and John C. Merrill, *Basic Issues in Mass Communication: A Debate* (New York: Macmillan, 1984), pp. 103–19.

[75] For a thorough theoretical critique of objectivity as a concept (and of its polar companion, bias) see Robert A. Hackett, "Decline of a Paradigm? Bias and Objectivity in News Media Studies," *Critical Studies in Mass Communication*, 1 (September 1984), pp. 229–59.

[76] James W. Carey, "The Communications Revolution and the Professional Communicator," in *The Sociology of Mass Media Communicators* (The Sociological Review: Monograph No. 13), ed. Paul Halmos (Keele, Staffordshire: University of Keele, 1969). pp. 23–38.

[77] Gaye Tuchman, "Objectivity as Strategic Ritual: An Examination of Newsmen's Notions of Objectivity," *American Journal of Sociology*, 77 (January 1972), pp. 660–79; also see Dan Schiller, *Objectivity and the News* (Philadelphia: University of Pennsylvania Press, 1981), pp. 1–11.

[78] Jorgen Westerstahl, "Objective News Reporting: General Premises," *Communication Research*, 10 (July 1983), pp. 403–24.

[79] Dennis and Merrill, *Basic Issues*, pp. 104–106, 111. Also see John Calhoun Merrill, *Existential Journalism* (New York: Hastings House, 1977) pp. 108–15.

[80] Hackett, "Decline of a Paradigm," p. 234.

[81] Hackett, "Decline of a Paradigm," pp. 233–37; Merrill in Dennis and Merrill, *Basic Issues*, pp. 104–10; Carey, "The Communications Revolution," p. 36; Edmund B. Lambeth, *Committed Journalism: An Ethic for the Profession* (Bloomington:

Indiana University Press, 1986), pp. 4–5; also see Theodore Glasser, "The Puzzle of Objectivity," *The Quill* (February 1982): 9–23.

[82] Donald McDonald, "Is Objectivity Possible?" in *Ethics and the Press*, John C. Merrill and Ralph D. Barney, eds. (New York: Hastings House, 1975), pp. 69–88.

[83] See the description of this "attitudinal" view in John C. Merrill and Ralph L. Lowenstein, *Media, Messages, and Men*, 2d ed. (New York: Longman, 1979), pp. 202–14.

[84] Dennis and Merrill, *Basic Issues*, pp. 113–18.

[85] See Kaarle Nordenstreng, *The Mass Media Declaration of UNESCO* (Norwood, NJ: Ablex, 1984), pp. 247, 456.

[86] *The Washington Post* code is reprinted in Bruce M. Swain, *Reporter's Ethics* (Ames: Iowa State University Press, 1978), pp. 131–34.

[87] Lambeth, *Committed Journalism*, p. 74.

[88] W. Lance Bennett, *News: The Politics of Illusion* (New York: Longman, 1988), pp. 105–144.

[89] Sissela Bok, *Secrets: On the Ethics of Concealment and Revelation* (New York: Vintage Books, 1984). Intro. and ch. 1.

[90] Bok, *Secrets*, chs. 2 and 3.

[91] Bok, *Secrets*, chs. 8, 12, 13.

[92] John M. Orman, *Presidential Secrecy and Deception: Beyond the Power to Persuade* (Westport, CT: Greenwood, 1980), pp. 4–7, 165–67.

[93] Orman, *Presidential Secrecy*, pp. 196–205. Also see Morton Halperin and David Hoffman, *Top Secret* (Washington, DC: New Republic Books, 1977), pp. 55–85.

[94] Some of the suggestions in this section derive from the following receiver-oriented sources: Crable, *Argumentation as Communication*, ch. 8; Nilsen, *Ethics of Speech Communication*, 2d ed., pp. 33–34, 74–75; Kenneth E. Andersen, *Persuasion*, 2d ed. (Boston: Allyn and Bacon, 1978), chs. 15, 18; Mary John Smith, *Persuasion and Human Action* (Belmont, CA: Wadsworth, 1982), pp 4–9, 76, 315; Lee Thayer, "Ethics, Morality, and the Media," in *Ethics, Morality and the Media*, Thayer, et al., eds., pp. 14–17, 35–39; Gary L. Cronkhite, "Rhetoric, Communication, and Psycho-Epistemology," in *Rhetoric: A Tradition in Transition*, Walter R. Fisher, ed. (East Lansing: Michigan State University Press, 1974), pp. 261–78; William R. Rivers, et al., *Responsibility in Mass Communication*, 3rd ed. (New York: Harper & Row, 1980), pp. 285–88.

[95] Kenneth E. Andersen, "A Code of Ethics for Speech Communication," *Spectra* (January 1984): 2–3; Andersen, "Communication Ethics: The Non-Participant's Role," *Southern Journal of Speech Communication*, XLIX (Summer 1984): 219–28; Andersen, "The Ethical Role of the 'Non-Participants' in a Communications Activity," unpublished conference presentation; Andersen, "The Role of the Third Party," presented at seminar on communication ethics, Speech Communication Association, November 1986.

[96] Clifford G. Christians, "Can the Public Be Held Accountable?" *Journal of Mass Media Ethics*, 3, no. 1 (1988): 50–58.

Chapter 8

Interpersonal Communication and Small Group Discussion

Interpersonal communication has become a label used to describe a number of different human communication processes; presently it lacks a meaning shared uniformly or precisely among communication scholars.[1] Some simply designate it as one of several "levels" of human communication: intrapersonal (within a single person); interpersonal (between two people); small group (among three to nine people); public (one person to a formal audience); and mass media.

Dean Barnlund describes interpersonal communication as persons in face-to-face encounters in relatively informal social situations sustaining focused interaction through reciprocal exchange of verbal and nonverbal cues. Gerald Miller and his colleagues differentiate between noninterpersonal communication and interpersonal communication. In noninterpersonal communication, information known among participants about each other is primarily of a cultural or of a sociological (group affiliation) nature. In contrast, participants in interpersonal communication ground their perceptions and reactions in the unique psychological characteristics of each other's individual personalities. John Stewart sees the essence of interpersonal communication as centered in the quality of the communication among participants. Participants relate to each other as persons (unique, capable of choice, having feelings, being of inherent worth, and self-reflective) rather than as objects or things (interchangeable, measurable, responding automatically to stimuli, and lacking self-awareness).[2]

Some of the ethical stances we have examined previously in this book obviously can apply to interpersonal communication defined in one of the above ways. The various dialogical perspectives described in chapter 4, although applicable in some degree to public communication, apply primarily to private, face-to-face communication and assume a particular quality or attitude among participants. Human nature and situational perspectives (chapters 3 and 5) would seem applicable both in interpersonal and public settings, and some religious and utilitarian approaches (chapter 6) would appear relevant.

What about the various sets of ethical guidelines that have been developed for public speaking, rhetoric, persuasion, argument, and mass communication? Are these ethical standards also applicable equally and uniformly to interpersonal communication? Or are ethical standards needed that apply uniquely and most appropriately solely to interpersonal communication? We now will survey some examples of criteria and guidelines that either have been offered as ethical standards for interpersonal communication or that might be adapted to serve that purpose.

Condon's Interpersonal Ethic

John Condon explores a wide array of ethical issues that typically emerge in interpersonal communication settings: candor, social harmony, accuracy, deception, consistency of word and act, keeping confidences, and blocking communication. In discussing these ethical themes, Condon stresses that any particular theme may come into conflict with other themes and that we may have to choose one over the other in a given situation. Although Condon does not formulate specific ethical criteria, perhaps we can restate some of his views in the form of potential guidelines that we may want to consider.[3]

1. Be candid and frank in sharing personal beliefs and feelings. Ideally, "we would like *no* to mean *no*; we would like a person who does not understand to say so, and a person who disagrees to express that disagreement directly."
2. In groups or cultures where interdependence is valued over individualism, keeping social relationships harmonious may be more ethical than speaking our minds.
3. Information should be communicated accurately, with minimal loss or distortion of intended meaning.
4. Intentional deception generally is unethical.
5. Verbal and nonverbal cues, words and actions, should be consistent in the meanings they communicate.

6. Usually it is unethical to block intentionally the communication process, such as cutting off persons before they have made their point, changing the subject when the other person obviously has more to say, or nonverbally distracting others from the intended subject.

A Contextual Interpersonal Ethic

In developing what he labels as a "contextual approach" to interpersonal communication ethics, Ronald Arnett takes the position that while some concrete guidelines are necessary in ethical decisions, we simultaneously must remain flexible to the contextual demands of the moment.[4] Our ethical system is established, but it must be open to modification in the circumstances at hand. We should, he suggests, take neither an absolute, dogmatic stance, nor an extremely relativistic, entirely situation-determined stance. From this vantage point, Arnett offers three propositions as ethical standards for interpersonal communication.

Proposition One: we must be open to information reflecting changing conceptions of self and others, but such openness does not imply agreement with those changes, only an attempt to understand the other's perceptual world. We also should be sensitive to our own and others' role responsibilities in concrete situations. *Proposition Two*: the self-actualization or self-fulfillment of participants should be fostered if at all possible; but the "good" decision may require sacrifice of something important to one or more participants. *Proposition Three*: we should take into account our own emotions and feelings, but emotions cannot be the sole guide for behavior. At times the "good" response or action requires doing what does not feel emotionally good. Arnett concludes by stressing that a "contextual ethic does not recognize 'self-actualization' and 'getting in touch with one's feelings' as the primary function of interpersonal communication."

An Ethic for Interpersonal Trust

Central to both public and interpersonal communication is a minimal level of trust among participants. Kim Giffin and Richard Barnes offer an ethic of interpersonal trust based on a particular view of human nature. They assume that while humans are essentially good by nature, there are realistic limits and constricting circumstances that most of the time limit achievement of ideal human potential.[5] An ethic that increases our trust in each other is desirable because our trust of others tends to stimulate their trust of us, because our own self-image can be improved, and because our psychological health is nurtured. They do recognize the dangers of trusting people. Others may use our trust to deceive us; and continued exposure to broken trust breeds alienation from others and declining self-confidence.

Giffin and Barnes present three ethical guidelines for trust in interpersonal communication. First, we should attempt actively to extend our trust of those around us as widely as possible. This is desirable most of the time for most people. Second, "our trust of others should be tentative." Our trust should be offered a little at a time, and we should clarify to others "what we are risking, what we are counting on them to do or be, and what we expect to achieve." Third, trust should not only be given but it also should be earned. "An act of trust is unethical unless the trusted person is trustworthy—it takes two to trust one."

An Ethic for Everyday Conversation

Philosopher H. P. Grice views everyday conversation as one type of purposive, rational, human behavior. He attempts to uncover some of the basic expectations that need to be fulfilled if conversation, whether to exchange information or to attempt influence, is to be adequate.[6] Grice assumes that contributions by participants should be appropriate for the purpose and for the particular stage of the conversation. Grice also outlines various maxims to guide adequate conversation. While he does not state them as ethical criteria, you may want to consider to what degree some or all of them could serve as ethical guidelines for most types of interpersonal communication. They are presented here in adapted and paraphrased form.

Quantity: contributions should present as much information, advice, or argument as is required by current purposes of the conversation, but should not present more than is required. *Quality*: try to make your contributions true; do not say what you believe is false and do not say anything lacking an adequate basis of evidence. *Relation*: be relevant, taking account of the facts that participants may have different standards of relevance and that topics often shift during a conversation. *Manner*: be clear, brief and orderly; avoid intentional ambiguity and obscurity of expression.

A Rhetorical Perspective on Interpersonal Ethics

A rhetorical perspective on interpersonal communication contends that the traditional concepts and principles of rhetoric for public influence apply equally well to intimate and interpersonal communication. Rhetoric is intentionally functional. According to Harold Barrett, the user of rhetoric seeks "to be effective, to get an answer, to be somebody, to be recognized, listened to, validated, understood—to be accepted. . . . The goal of rhetorical interaction, then, is the location of common ground on which to relate successfully."[7] People in interpersonal communication, believes Barrett, should strive to be both effective and ethical, all the while showing respect for the "being" of others—respect for their intrinsic worth as humans.

Barrett describes some "subtly violent" verbal and nonverbal techniques that are ethically objectionable in interpersonal communication. *Scapegoating* involves blaming others for faults or problems that primarily are our own. *Unnecessarily critical condemnation* of others, as a kind of rhetorical assault, leads to guilt feelings and eventual weakening of the persuasive powers of the person criticized. *Coercion* through threats against weaker persons is rhetorical bullying. *Restriction of freedom to choose* could be achieved by withholding information necessary to make a decision or by not revealing a relevant personal feeling. *Lying or deceiving* (as opposed to harmless fibbing) can intentionally or unintentionally cause others personal distress or painful emotional injury. *Violating a trust* harms or destroys relationships.

Unfair Tactics in Verbal Conflict

Disagreement and conflict sometimes occur in intimate and informal interpersonal settings. In such situations, when at least one party may be emotionally vulnerable, individuals often affect each other in direct and powerful ways. When you as a receiver in such a situation decide to respond by expressing strong disagreement, there are some "unfair" tactics of verbal conflict you may want to avoid because they are ethically irresponsible.

The Intimate Enemy: How to Fight Fair in Love and Marriage is a provocative book by George Bach and Peter Wyden. Raymond Ross and Mark Ross have adapted some insights from this book to suggest unfair and unethical tactics of verbal conflict to be avoided.[8] Avoid monopolizing the talk with the intent of preventing others from expressing their own opinion. Avoid entrapment in which you lure someone into saying something that you intend to use later to embarrass or hurt them. Avoid verbally "hitting below the belt" by taking unfair advantage of what you know to be the other person's special psychological vulnerability. Avoid stockpiling or accumulating numerous grievances so that you can overwhelm other persons by dumping complaints on them all at once. Finally, avoid dragging in numerous irrelevant or trivial issues and arguments in order to pile up an advantage.

Individual Responsibility in Relational Communication

As mentioned in chapter 1, William K. Rawlins notes the tension between freedom and responsibility even for interpersonal and intimate communication: "For there to be *freedom* to converse intimately with another person, each party must take *responsibility* for communicative behavior." Rawlins also believes that "disclosing personal thoughts and feelings and speaking freely in a relationship are *rights*, not *obligations*. To allow viable associations to develop, intimates should acknowledge limits in their communication and respect each other's separateness." In part, contends Rawlins, "self-oriented communicative responsibility involves structuring messages that preserve personal privacy and shield self's vulnerabilities. Responsible other-directed communication fosters individuality by respecting others' privacy and protecting others' sensitivities."[9] In exploring an ethic of responsibility for interpersonal communication, Rawlins focuses on four topics: openness, privacy, protection, and deception.

Openness should not be without limits. There should be a "freedom to be open without the compulsion to be 'transparent.'" "Truth-dumping and burdening another with personal affairs" may he harmful because they restrict the other's freedom "by thrusting emotional and cognitive work and/or requirements of confidence on that person." Self-disclosure may restrict the other's choice by creating an expectation or duty to reciprocate. Unrestrained blanket honesty "evades personal responsibility for the effects of one's statements."

Privacy is essential in interpersonal relations and includes both the right to exclude other persons and a recognition of the other's right to privacy. The distinction between privacy and secrecy is an important one. Privacy usually protects behavior that is morally neutral or positively valued. In contrast, "secrecy usually hides something viewed negatively by self and others." Misevaluation of ethicality may occur if a legitimate right of privacy is asserted by a person but others perceive it as devious or deceptive secrecy.

"As intimates become aware of each other's" most private thoughts, feelings, and behaviors, they usually gain "knowledge of sensitive, hurtful issues." Thus, believes Rawlins, "protectiveness is essential for individuals to tolerate the vulnerability accompanying intimacy." The extremes of excessive protectiveness and total expressiveness of feelings both may be harmful to the relationship. "Thus, the tension between candor and restraint must be managed consciously in responsible relational communication."

> While revealing personal information enables other to know self better, telling everything degrades self's privacy and makes self excessively vulnerable. Similarly, self must be candid in order for the other to trust in self's honesty; but self cannot be too blunt or other's privacy and/or feelings may be threatened, thereby diminishing other's trust in self's protection.

Rawlins draws a "basic distinction between duplicity" as a necessary element in social life and "deceit that is unethical or bad." With the "intentions motivating the behavior" as the crucial determinant, Rawlins finds that "benign or white sham is at times necessary to protect others and allow us to get along with them." But "black sham—exploitative and destructive fakery used to take advantage of others—undermines relationships."

In thinking about your own intimate interpersonal relationships, how adequate is the guidance provided by Rawlins's analysis? On what grounds would you rest your decisions about degree of ethical or responsible openness, privacy, protectiveness, and deception? With what aspects of Rawlins's analysis do you especially agree or disagree? Why?

Keeping the Conversation Going

In several of his works, Stanley Deetz develops a communication ethic of "keeping the conversation going." He starts with the assumption that the nature and character of humans are formed in communication interaction. Deetz builds upon the work of the German social critics Jürgen Habermas, Karl Otto Apel, and, especially, Hans-Georg

Gadamer.[10] While Deetz believes that his view is applicable not only to interpersonal communication but also to public discourse, organizational communication, and mass communication, here I will suggest only its applications to interpersonal communication. Genuine conversation aims at "creating mutual understanding through open formation of experience" rather than at self-expression or at making one's view prevail. The focus is on mutual understanding of the subject matter of the conversation. Deetz proposes a guiding ethical principle "based on the very conditions of mutual understanding": "Every communicative act should have as its ethical condition the attempt to keep the conversation—the open development of experience—going." Genuine conversation should be "responsive to the subject matter of the conversation and at the same time help establish conditions for future unrestrained formation of experience"—future minimally constrained communication.

Genuine conversation, says Deetz, can be blocked or distorted, either occasionally or systematically, through a variety of unethical communication practices—practices often reinforced by unquestioned institutional and societal assumptions. *Freezing participants* involves using stereotypes, hardened categories, or frozen labels that shut down or constrict conversation by ignoring individual differences and potential for personal change. In Martin Buber's terminology, viewing a person as an It or an object strips the person of humanity and lessens the obligation to respect that person's rights and character. Or dismissing someone's view without examination simply by labeling the person as racist, sexist, homosexual, Pro-Life, or Pro-Choice constricts the possibility of genuine conversation. *Disqualification* centers on rules or norms that determine who has a right to speak on a subject. Societally formed ideas of "expertise, professional qualification, and specialization" often are used to dismiss a person's views or disqualify the person from speaking. To automatically dismiss a person's idea without examination simply by asserting that "you're no expert," or "you're merely an amateur," or asking "what right do you have. . . ?" may block genuine conversation. In *naturalization*, "one particular view of the subject matter" (from among multiple plausible ones) is "frozen as the way the thing is." Multiple viewpoints or potential for alternatives can be narrowed to one assertion or assumption about the way things or persons "naturally" are as fixed or unquestioned. Unchallenged statements like "that's just the way" that women, or blacks, or Jews "are" function to undermine genuine conversation. *Neutralization* "refers to the process by which value positions become hidden and value-laden activities are treated as if they were value free." Dismissal of a position as a "threat to progress" may be taken as a factual description without thought concerning the often competing values imbedded in differing notions of "progress."

Topical avoidance centers on norms in the relationship or group that prohibit "the discussion of some events or feelings." Conversation is forced to "go around and leave out" taboo topics, and thus valuable discussion of conflicts, emotions, priorities, and perceptions often are denied to participants. *Subjectification of experience* involves the dismissal or trivialization of another person's view as merely "a matter of opinion" and thus so subjective and individualized as not to be appropriate for discussion on an allegedly more factual or reasonable level. *Meaning denial* "happens when one possible interpretation of a statement is both present in the interaction and denied as meant." When you shout at another person during an interaction and yet proclaim that you are not angry, a "message is present and disclaimed; said and not said." The burden of creation of meaning unfairly is shifted entirely to the listener, and you retain "control without responsibility." You might assert irresponsibly that the person should have known you were angry despite what you said to the contrary. *Pacification* occurs when messages function to avoid valuable discussion of conflict, problems, and solutions by downplaying their seriousness or discounting the capacities of individuals to grapple with them. Issues are avoided by describing them as too trivial to warrant discussion or too monumental for us to do anything about them.

Ethical Responsibility and Communication Competence

Ethical responsibility is a fundamental dimension of communication competence in the view developed by Stephen Littlejohn and David Jabusch. Their ethical stance applies, they believe, to persuasion in interpersonal, organizational, and public communication. Littlejohn and Jabusch assume that communicators share the responsibility for the outcomes of the transaction and they center their view on the ethical principles of caring and openness. "*Caring* is concern for the well-being of self and others. It involves a feeling that what happens to others is as important as what happens to self. It is the spirit of good will. *Openness* is a willingness to share information with others and, conversely, an interest in the disclosures of other people. It is, in short, a spirit of honesty."[11]

Emerging from high and low degrees of interaction between the caring and openness orientations of a person are four positions judged as ethical to varying degrees.

Ethical Responsibility. Communicators share responsibility for determining consequences. There is a high degree of completely and honestly shared information and a high degree of concern for the well-being of all participants.

Unshared Responsibility. The communicator assumes total responsibility for consequences of the transaction by maintaining high concern for the well-being of others but withholding or distorting information for what he or she judges to be the best interest of others.

Abdicated Responsibility. The communicator assumes no responsibility and leaves total responsibility for consequences to other participants. While the communicator may share information completely and honestly, he or she lacks concern for the effects of that honesty on others.

Irresponsibility. The communicator not only refuses to assume responsibility but also denies others any opportunity to have control. The communicator not only withholds or distorts relevant information but also shows no concern for consequences and the well-being of others.

"Most of the time," contend Littlejohn and Jabusch, "you will probably have to choose between persuading with unshared responsibility and persuading with shared responsibility." On what grounds might you decide between these two orientations and decide their degree of ethicality? In what ways do you agree or disagree with their ethical viewpoint rooted in caring and openness? Try to think of four stereotypical communication situations that might clearly illustrate each of the four ethical positions.

A Political Perspective for Small Group Discussion

Several writers suggest ethical standards for the type of small group communication which is task-oriented toward reaching a mutually agreeable decision or solving a problem. Ernest Bormann takes a political perspective based on the values central to American representative democracy, especially on the "four moralities" developed by Karl Wallace and examined previously in chapter 2. In summarized and paraphrased form, here are the major ethical guidelines urged by Bormann in two of his writings.[12]

Interpersonal Communication and Small Group Discussion 167

1. Participants should be allowed to make up their own minds without being coerced, duped, or manipulated.
2. Participants should be encouraged to grow and to develop their own potential.
3. Sound reasoning and relevant value judgments are to be encouraged.
4. Conflicts and disagreements that focus on participants as persons rather than on ideas or information should be avoided.
5. Participants who manipulate group members solely or primarily for their own selfish ends are unethical.
6. In the role of advisor, participants should present information honestly, fairly, and accurately. They should reveal their sources. They should allow others to scrutinize their evidence and arguments. Lying is unethical because it breaks the trust necessary for participants to assess information.
7. With respect to external groups or individuals, participants within the group should be committed to defending "true statements of fact, praiseworthy value statements, and sound advice."
8. Participants should communicate with each other as they would want others to communicate with them.
9. Communication practices in the group should be judged within a framework of all relevant values and ethical criteria, not solely or primarily by the worth of the end or goal to be reached. Gandhi's ethical touchstone is sound: "Evil means, even for a good end, produces evil results."

Respect for the Worth of Others

In his book, *Discussion, Conference, and Group Process*, Halbert Gulley supports a basic premise of Thomas Nilsen concerning the concept of The Good basic to our culture: communication that enhances and nurtures human personalities is good; communication that damages, degrades, or stifles human personalities is bad. Gulley identifies a number of guidelines for ethical communication in small group discussions.[13] They are presented below in partially paraphrased form.

1. A communicator has a responsibility for defending the policy decisions of groups in whose deliberations he or she participated.

If the participant cannot, he or she should make the refusal of support clear at the time the decision is reached.

2. A communicator has a responsibility to be well informed and accurate. "To present a few facts as the whole story, tentative findings as firmly established conclusions, or partial understanding as authoritative is to mislead the group."
3. A communicator has a responsibility to encourage actively the comments of others and to seek out all viewpoints, including unpopular ones.
4. A communicator should openly reveal her or his own biases, and should identify her or his sources of information and any prejudices of such sources.
5. "Uninhibited lying, fabrication of evidence, inventing of sources, deliberate misquoting, and falsification of facts are obviously dishonest practices."
6. "The ethical group member does not attempt to manipulate the talk unfairly so that his selfish ends are served and the group wishes frustrated."
7. The ethical communicator avoids use of tactics to intentionally cloud analysis: name-calling, emotionally "loaded" language, guilt-by-association, hasty generalizations, shifting definitions, and oversimplified either-or alternatives.

Ethical Sensitivity

Dennis Gouran urges that "ethical sensitivity" is a leadership function that any small group discussion participant should be willing to perform.[14] "Groups are not always aware of the ethical implications of their decisions. Were a member to call this possibility to the attention of his or her own colleagues, in some instances they might arrive at a different decision." The ethically sensitive group participant seeks to avoid unintentionally unethical decisions and to promote exploration of issues from more than a purely pragmatic viewpoint. Rather than rendering rapid, dogmatic, either-or ethical judgments, the ethically sensitive discussant raises questions about the ethical justifiability of ideas and actions.

Gouran presents five considerations to guide assessment of the degree of ethical responsibility shown in a particular small group decision-making process. (1) Did we show proper concern for those who will be affected by our decision? (2) Did we explore the discussion question as responsibly as we were capable of doing? (3) Did we misrepresent any position or misuse any source of information? (4) Did we say or do anything that might have unnecessarily diminished any participant's sense of self-worth? (5) Was everyone in the group shown the respect due him or her?

A "Groupthink" Ethic

"Groupthink" is the collective label used by social psychologist Irving Janis to describe characteristics of small groups whose processes of problem solving and policy determination typically result in ineffectiveness, low quality decisions, and failure to attain objectives. Janis analyzed the historical records, observers' accounts of conversations, and participants' memoirs for a number of such actual disastrous decisions. He identifies eight main symptoms that characterize "groupthink." Janis simply describes these characteristic processes and does not intend them as ethical standards.[15] Nevertheless, it may be fruitful for us to convert them to ethical guidelines for healthy, humane, reasonable task-oriented small group discussions. How clear, appropriate, and applicable would you consider them to be as potential ethical guidelines?

1. Avoid the "illusion of invulnerability" which fosters "excessive optimism and encourages taking extreme risks."
2. Avoid rationalizations that hinder members from reassessing their basic assumptions before reaffirming commitment to previous decisions.
3. Avoid "an unquestioned belief in the group's inherent morality," a belief that inclines members to "ignore the ethical and moral consequences of their decisions."
4. Avoid stereotyping adversaries' views as "too evil to warrant genuine attempts to negotiate, or as too weak and stupid" to thwart your efforts against them.
5. Avoid pressure that makes members feel disloyal if they express "strong arguments against any of the group's stereotypes, illusions, or commitments."
6. Avoid individual self-censorship that minimizes for each person the importance of his or her own doubts or counterarguments.

7. Avoid a "shared illusion of unanimity concerning judgments conforming to the majority view." This illusion results both from "self-censorship of deviations" and from the "false assumption that silence means consent."
8. Avoid the emergence of "self-appointed mindguards." These are members "who protect the group from adverse information that might shatter their complacency about the effectiveness and morality of their decisions."

Notes

[1] See Joe Ayres, "Four Approaches to Interpersonal Communication," *Western Journal of Speech Communication*, 48 (Fall 1984): 408–40: Mark L. Knapp and Gerald R. Miller, eds., *Handbook of Interpersonal Communication* (Beverly Hills: Sage, 1985), especially see p. 27.

[2] Dean Barnlund, *Interpersonal Communication: Survey and Studies* (Boston: Houghton Mifflin, 1968), pp. 8–10: Gerald R. Miller and Mark Steinberg, *Between People: A New Analysis of Interpersonal Communication* (Chicago: Science Research Associates, 1975), ch. 1: Gerald R. Miller and Michael J. Sunnafrank, "All for One But One Is Not for All: A Conceptual Perspective of Interpersonal Communication," in *Human Communication Theory: Comparative Essays*, Frank E. X. Dance, ed. (New York: Harper & Row, 1982), pp. 220–42: John Stewart and Carol Logan, *Together: Communicating Interpersonally*, 4th ed. (New York: McGraw-Hill, 1991), ch. 1; John Stewart, ed., *Bridges Not Walls*, 6th ed. (New York: McGraw-Hill, 1995), pp. 15–22.

[3] John C. Condon, *Interpersonal Communication* (New York: Macmillan, 1977), ch. 8.

[4] Ronald C. Arnett, "Ethics of Interpersonal Communication Revisited," paper presented at Speech Communication Association convention, Anaheim, CA, November 1981. Also see Arnett, *Communication and Community: Implications of Martin Buber's Dialogue* (Carbondale: Southern Illinois University Press, 1986), ch. 4.

[5] Kim Giffin and Richard E. Barnes, *Trusting Me, Trusting You* (Columbus, OH: Charles E. Merrill, 1976), ch. 7.

[6] H. P. Grice, "Logic and Conversation," in *Understanding Arguments*, Robert J. Fogelin, ed. (New York: Harcourt Brace Jovanovich, 1978), pp. 329–343. For an analysis of Grice's maxims from a feminist theoretical perspective, see Gillian Michell, "Women and Lying" A Pragmatic and Semantic Analysis of 'Telling It Slant'," *Women's Studies International Forum*, 7 (1983): 375–83.

[7] Harold Barrett, *Daring to Be: Love and the Art of Rhetorical Intercourse* (Chicago: Nelson-Hall, 1982), pp. 3–26. For two other rhetorical perspectives, see Marcus L. Ambrester and Glynis Holm Strause, *A Rhetoric of Interpersonal Communication* (Prospect Heights, IL: Waveland Press, 1984); Gerald M. Phillips and Nancy Metzger, *Intimate Communication* (Boston: Allyn and Bacon, 1976).

[8] Raymond S. Ross and Mark G. Ross, *Relating and Interacting* (Englewood Cliffs, NJ: Prentice-Hall, 1982), pp. 77, 138–41.

[9] William K. Rawlins, "Individual Responsibility in Relational Communication," in *Communications in Transition*, Mary S. Mander, ed. (New York: Praeger, 1983): 152–67. Also see Rawlins, "Openness as Problematic in Ongoing Friendships: Two Conversational Dilemmas," *Communication Monographs*, 50 (March 1983): 1–13.

[10] Stanley Deetz, "Reclaiming the Subject Matter as a Guide to Mutual Understanding: Effectiveness and Ethics in Interpersonal Interaction," *Communication Quarterly*, 38 (Summer 1990): 226–43; Deetz, "Keeping the Conversation Going: The Principle of Dialectic Ethics," *Communication* 7, no. 7 (1983): 263–88; Deetz, *Democracy in an Age of Corporate Colonization: Developments in Communication and the Politics of Everyday Life* (Albany: State University of New York Press, 1992), pp. 145–98.

[11] Stephen W. Littlejohn and David M. Jabusch, *Persuasive Transactions* (Glenview, IL: Scott, Foresman, 1987), pp. 12–22; Littlejohn and Jabusch, "Communication Competence: Model and Application." *Journal of Applied Communication Research*, 10 (Spring 1982): 29–37.

[12] Ernest G. Bormann, "Ethical Standards for Interpersonal/Small Group Communication," *Communication* 6, no. 2 (1981): 267–86; Bormann, *Small Group Communication: Theory and Practice*, 3rd ed. (New York: Harper & Row, 1990), ch. 11.

[13] Halbert E. Gulley, *Discussion, Conference, and Group Process*, 2d ed. (New York: Holt, Rinehart and Winston, 1968), pp. 148–52.

[14] Dennis Gouran, *Making Decisions in Groups* (1982; reissue, Prospect Heights, IL: Waveland Press, 1990), pp. 166–67, 227. For Gouran's application of the ethical sensitivity approach, see his "The Watergate Cover-Up: Its Dynamics and Its Implications," *Communication Monographs*, 43 (August 1976): 176–86.

[15] Irving L. Janis, *Victims of Groupthink*, 2d ed. (Boston: Houghton Mifflin, 1982), pp. 174–75. For a case study of groupthink and communication ethics, see Ronald R. Sims, *Ethics and Organizational Decision Making* (Westport, CT: Quorum, 1994), pp. 61–79.

Chapter 9

Communication in Organizations

One role fulfilled by many persons in contemporary American society is that of communicator within a formal organization, whether that be a large corporation, small business, governmental agency, health care organization, or educational institution. Formal organizations themselves communicate with their various publics, whether they be clients, consumers, other organizations, government regulatory agencies, or the public-at-large. Some versions of the ethical perspectives explored in earlier chapters could apply to organizational communication settings, as would some of the previously presented guidelines for ethical interpersonal and small group communication. However, the characteristics of formal organizations pose special constraints and influences on communication ethics.

Negative Attitudes of the Public

Beyond a continuing focus on the ethics of political communication, public concern has risen about ethics of communicators in business and other organizational settings. In one survey of 671 managers, almost 25 percent said that high ethics could hinder a successful career; bending the rules was necessary to survive (*Wall Street Journal*, September 8, 1987). A *Gallup Report* poll (August 1985) found that the standards of honesty and ethics were rated as a combined low/very low for the following: business executives (18 percent), lawyers (30 percent), realtors (31 percent), insurance salespersons (38 percent), advertising practitioners (39 percent). In a national survey during 1993–1994 of over 4,000 employees in businesses (*Ethics Journal*, Fall/Winter 1994), one-fourth of the employees "believed that their companies ignore unethical conduct to meet business objectives, and nearly one employee in six stated that their company overtly encourages misconduct to meet business objectives.

"Has Truth Gone Out of Style?" Walt Harrington of the *Washington Post* examined this question at length in the *Washington Post*'s national weekly edition (January 4–10, 1988). One of his major arguments is that

> people today distrust one another more readily and lie and deceive more willingly for good reason—as a sensible, realistic reaction to lying politicians, bureaucrats and businessmen and, more important, as a reaction to a rising helplessness that has come with the big, anonymous monster we call modern life.
>
> People lie, cheat, steal more today not so much because they don't know right from wrong, but because in big, bureaucratized America, it's harder to do the right thing and easier and easier to do the wrong thing. When people feel deceived by leaders and institutions, it's easier for them to deceive in return.
>
> [We] distrust one another when we are acting in our institutional roles—as politicians, lawyers, journalists, salesmen—because we all know that the institutions we all represent, despite the pieties, often care more for votes, profits or power than for people.

Harrington believes that if public trust in organizations is to be renewed, there must be serious debate on "how huge, cold corporations can win back the faith of workers and customers; how greed can be tempered in business schools, board rooms and labor unions; how admen can worship truth as well as sales; how companies can insist on honesty and fairness in their sales forces; how leaders can be made to see the destructive power of every lie, grand or petty." The topics discussed in this chapter aim to make you a more informed and reflective participant in this debate, especially concerning ethical communication in formal organizations.

Assessing Ethical Responsibility

The complex, impersonal, hierarchical nature of modern organizations presents some difficulties for communication ethics. Indeed, Charles Redding summarizes the view of a number of critics that "there is something *inherently* present in any modern organization that facilitates unethical or immoral conduct."[1] Robert Jackall assumes that modern organizations are "vast systems of organized irresponsibility" that erode "internal and even external standards of morality."[2] What matters most in the organizational world, concludes Jackall:

> is not what a person is but how closely his many personae mesh with the organizational ideal; not his willingness to stand by his actions but his agility in avoiding blame; not what he believes or says but how well he has mastered the ideologies that serve his corporation; not what he stands for but whom he stands with in the labyrinths of his corporation.

How does a member of an organization, or an outsider, determine where responsibility and blame should rest for an unethical communication? Does responsibility and accountability reside at the top with the president, corporate executive officer, or chair of the board? Does it reside with the immediate communicator? What ethical responsibilities should be borne by "relay" persons in an organization? Such relay persons—in between the originator of a message and the receivers—function to link parts of a system, to store information, to stretch and alter the message, and to exert control of information.[3] Is the responsibility to be shared equally—or to varying degrees—by every member of the organization? Would the responsibility most appropriately be placed on the organization or institution itself rather than on specific individuals? Is the responsibility a *negative* one in the sense of an obligation to avoid communication that harms others? Is it an *affirmative* responsibility to communicate actively to help others? On what basis is the responsibility being assigned? Does the person have the *capability* to influence the choice and either does or does not? Does the person's *formal role* specify certain obligations and functions?[4]

In *Political Ethics and Public Office*, Dennis Thompson argues for assessment of individual responsibility within an organizational context, whether the organization be a public service or private enterprise one. The sense of complexity and frustration he describes concerning governmental organizations applies equally well to corporations. "Because many different officials contribute in many different ways to decisions and policies . . . , it is difficult even in principle to identify who is morally responsible for . . . outcomes." It is difficult to locate a person who singlehandedly made the policy or even one whose contribution "is significant enough to warrant credit or blame for it."[5]

Organizations as Cultures

A significant scholarly perspective for studying a formal organization is to conceive of it as a "culture." Just as an anthropologist would study an ethnic or national culture, organizational researchers and consultants frequently describe an organization as a culture.[6] Central components of this culture are the organization's basic values, taken-for-granted assumptions, decision-making rules, managerial styles, organizational heroes and heroines, stories of success and failure, rituals and ceremonies, sense of tradition and loyalty, and accepted topics and methods of communication. Part of an organization's culture may include "a positive or negative approach to moral issues and moral actions," both by individuals and by the organization itself, when dealing with employees, customers, and other organizations.[7] How does an individual mesh his or her personal communication ethic with the ethical norms and expectations of the organization? What if they conflict in a given instance? What if over time the personal and organizational systems of communication ethics become incompatible? When is it ethically responsible for an employee to "blow the whistle" on his or her organization?

The Organization's Ethical Climate

"The types of ethical climates existing in an organization or group influence what ethical conflicts are considered, the process by which such conflicts are resolved, and the characteristics of their resolution."[8] A number of elements have been identified that, taken together, would promote development of a healthy, vigorous ethical climate.[9]

Top management must set a high ethical tone for the entire organization by demonstrating a firm and clear commitment to ethical behavior for all employees. The personal example of their own daily behavior is one way for top management to demonstrate such commitment. Also desirable is development of a formal code of ethics or set of written ethical expectations that explain in clear terms the ethical standards demanded by the organization. Ideally such a code of ethics, even if initially developed solely by top management, will evolve and modify over time through discussion by employees at a number of levels. The organization's ethical expectations must be reinforced not only through prompt, publicized, and appropriate punishment for violation but also through rewards and recognition for consistently or significantly upholding the ethical standards.

Commitment of resources also demonstrates an organization's concern for ethics. Companies can appoint an "ethics officer" or "ethics committee" whose functions are to make sure that ethical considerations are a routine part of major policy decisions and to provide interpretations of ethical guidelines for employees in doubt. An increasing number of organizations are hiring external ethics consultants to advise them on ways of improving the ethical climate. A major commitment of resources is represented by ongoing educational programs to sensitize supervisors and managers at various levels to the ethical dimensions of decisions or procedures and to train them in systematic ways of thinking about ethics (*Business Week*, February 15, 1987, pp. 56–57; *Newsweek*, May 9, 1988, p. 56). Another possibility suggested is a formal and periodic "ethics audit" of overall performance of the organization.[10]

A sense of ethics must be "institutionalized" into the organization.[11] Ethical concerns must be regarded as on a par with economic and pragmatic concerns in decision making. Procedures must be established so that ethical issues automatically are confronted as part of a decision. Opportunities and mechanisms should be established for employees to express their ethical concerns without fear of blocking promotion, demotion, firing, or other retribution. Employee "whistle-blowing" on ethical violations by the organization truly should become rare and a last resort.

> Organizations must consciously act to make ethics a legitimate topic of discussion, not only for those times of crisis when a personal value is challenged or painful competing claims are present, but also to allow employees to fully examine the range of options available, to anticipate pitfalls, and to explore creative ways of resolving their dilemmas.[12]

A 1993–1994 national survey of over 4,000 employees of businesses (*Ethics Journal*, Fall/Winter 1994) revealed that corporation ethics programs do seem to have a significant positive effect on "employees' behavior, as well as their attitudes toward the ethics of fellow employees, management, their companies. . . . The most positive effects were reported in companies which have all three program components—codes of conduct, ethics training, and ethics offices."

Character and Virtue Ethics

Ethical rules, principles, and codes can serve important functions as guides to ethical communication in organizations. But rules, principles, and codes are not enough. "Corporate culture and organizational policy are powerful forces that can mold the ethical spirit of an organization, but they are no substitute for the character of individual employees."[13]

Oliver Williams and Patrick Murphy explore the ethics of virtue as a moral theory for business.[14] They believe that ethical virtues can be shaped by our individual choices and encouraged by the "environments within which we live and work." In developing a proposed decision or policy, a theory of virtue prompts the developer to ask two key questions: What sort of person am I shaping? What sort of organization am I shaping? Moral vision and moral sensitivity—the abilities to "see" ethical implications of actions and communication where others do not—play central roles in virtue theory. However, Williams and Murphy also note that a "business organization can so shape people that they do not 'see' the ethical dimensions of the professional world." They argue: "Underpinned by a theory of virtue, an ethical corporate culture, through an ingrained set of habits and perspectives, trains all those in its purview to see things in a certain way and hence is likely to predispose them toward ethical behavior." In addition, role models have a vital function in a theory of virtue. We are educated and inspired by the behavior of moral role models we encounter directly or by examples of ethical behavior embodied in stories we hear about the organization.[15]

Several scholars suggest clusters of ethical virtues that they believe are especially appropriate for individuals in organizations. In his discussion of the virtues in a professional setting, William May advocates the relevance of virtues such as honesty, respect, benevolence, promise keeping, prudence, perseverance, courage, integrity, concern for the public good, compassion, justice and humility.[16] In *Ethics and Excellence*, Robert Solomon develops an Aristotelian approach that stresses personal character and virtue in a business context.[17] He argues that his approach would encourage the "flourishing" of the individual, the business, and the society not just in the bottom-line sense of success but in the broader promotion of "excellence." At length Solomon discusses "the basic business virtues" of honesty, fairness, trust, and toughness and also the "virtues of the self" within a corporation of honor, loyalty, friendliness, and a sense of shame. Additionally important in his view are caring, compassion, and the "ultimate" virtue of justice.

A Framework for Analyzing Ethics in Organizations

Based on her lengthy interviews of 33 managers representing various functions and levels in companies of varied size and from diverse industries, Barbara Toffler offers an extremely useful framework for systematically thinking about ethics in an organization.[18]

Elements of Ethical Situations. (1) *People*—What relationship do I have with others in terms of closeness of contact and strength of commitment (obligation) to them? How inevitable and how serious will be the harm caused by my action? Am I avoiding the doing of harm simply for fear of being disliked? (2) *Competing Claims* may exist between two or more personal values, between personal values and values of others, between means and ends, and between two or more persons to whom I have an obligation. (3) *Intervention* by me in the lives of others or their intervention in mine can occur where either there is agreement about what is to be done or there is conflict. (4) *Determining Responsibility*—Is the responsibility primarily to do something or to avoid doing something? Is the responsibility primarily of the causal, or capacity, or role type?

Is the choice I am faced with an *ethical issue*—meaning is it easy to name, not influenced by context, clearly involves an ethical matter, addresses the claims of a single person or group who has a "stake" in the choice, addresses the right and wrong of one value, and assumes that persons can do the "right thing" if they want to? Or is the choice I am facing an *ethical dilemma*—meaning is it hard to name, embedded in a specific context, involves disagreement on whether it actually represents an ethical matter, addresses the claims of multiple, often competing, stakeholders, addresses multiple, often competing, values, and assumes that although persons want to do the right thing they are unsure what it is or lack the capacity to do it?

Organizational Factors. (1) Policies, rules, and procedures concerning ethics. (2) Systems that facilitate or impede implementation of these policies and rules. (3) The organization's "culture" of values, beliefs, and sensitivity that may promote or retard ethical behavior. (4) "The way we do things around here." *Individual Factors.* How do I perceive my explicit and implicit roles and the task requirements of my job? What degree of real choice do I perceive in the decision? What are the "stakes" I perceive in my job or in the decision? *Personal Background.* How is my decision influenced by what I was taught or the way I was raised?

A Model of Organizational Integrity

After extensive research with several thousand employees in almost a dozen organizations in the United States, Julie Belle White and Doug Wallace developed an organizational integrity audit from which they derived a Model of Organizational Integrity.[19] Their Integrity Audit identifies ethical-standards characteristic of an ethical organizational climate. "The Model of Organizational Integrity describes organizational 'habits of the heart' which are akin to the personal virtues giving moral muscle to individuals of integrity. Through constant exercise of these habits the group develops the will and ability to handle ethical issues well." Six habits along with specific commitments and practices to implement them comprise the model. Here they are in paraphrased form.

Habit: Solving Ethical Problems Directly and Reflectively. The commitment to take an ethical stance involves taking an ethical viewpoint when discussing issues, being willing individually and collectively to tackle ethical problems, and striving to have the organization's ethical standards reflected in its actual priorities. The commitment to use responsive and responsible processes means seeking help when an ethical problem arises, persistently seeking to solve the ethical problem, considering the means used to solve the ethical problem to be as important as the goal sought, and willingness to accept consequences of ethical decisions (including negative ones). The commitment to dedicate and utilize resources involves spending necessary money, taking sufficient time, and securing necessary information to solve the ethical problem. The commitment to seek options requires the active search for options and the careful consideration of alternative courses of action.

Habit: Interacting Responsibly. The commitment to follow principles of justice and care requires that people be treated both fairly and with sensitivity. The commitment to interact with trust and respect involves showing respect for others' views and striving to trust and be trusted by individuals and groups. The commitment to communicate openly means being honest and open in relationships, freely sharing feelings and ideas, and communicating both good and bad news. The commitment to encourage dissent requires allowing dissent and allowing advocates of diverse ethical views to voice their positions.

Habit: Modeling Integrity. The commitment to have ethical role models throughout the organization demands that "the head of the organization publicly practices ethical values," that organizational leaders behave as good ethical models, and that "throughout the organization there are examples of individuals who act out their commitment to do the right thing." The commitment to assume responsibility for actions means that throughout the organization people feel free to admit their mistakes and people take responsibility for ethical decision making.

Habit: Sharing Organizational Purposes and Directions. The commitment to develop and implement an ethical organizational mission means that the organization clearly states and promotes its mission and ethical values and that the organization's ethical values are reflected in its mission and goals. The commitment to establish accountability requires communication and enforcement of organizational ground rules for ethical behavior, the holding of people accountable throughout the organization, the provision of an organizational structure that clearly indicates where ethical responsibility rests, the provision of a structure that facilitates adequate planning and participation, and organizational insistence on "compliance with laws and regulations."

Habit: Valuing Stakeholder Perspectives. The commitment to act as stewards means that the organization believes in "acting to protect the welfare of others"—in following the principle of stewardship. The commitment to consider and involve stakeholders requires that the viewpoints of all of those who have a stake in its decisions are considered by the organization, that "those affected by a decision are involved in the decision-making process," and that possible consequences of a decision are anticipated and prepared for.

Habit: Practicing Personal Integrity. The commitment to be consistent means that persons know the ethical thing to do and do it, that the values of individuals and the organization are consistent, and that members practice the organization's standards. At the same time, the commitment to act with courage demands that persons are "true to their own personal ethical values" and are willing to "pay the price" for acting ethically even if at odds with the organization.

Ethical Standards for Communication in Organizations

We now turn to additional sets of ethical criteria that specifically have been suggested for promoting ethical communication in organizations. In several writings, George Cheney and Phillip Tompkins have drawn upon Kenneth Burke's concept of "identification" as central to persuasion and explored its functioning in organizational communication settings.[20] Humans identify with other humans, groups, objects, institutions, and symbols to the degree that there are perceived to be substantial commonalities of values, beliefs, attitudes, goals, language, nonverbal symbols, images, even common enemies. Identifications can have both powerful positive potentials and potent negative pitfalls, not only for individuals but also for organizations.

Cheney and Tompkins turn to Henry W. Johnstone, Jr., for the ethical standards they advocate to guide organizational communication. Here you may want to read again the earlier discussion of Johnstone's view of humans as persuaders in chapter 3. They believe that Johnstone's ethical stance harmonizes with Burke's view of rhetoric and offers a sound set of ethical principles for organizational communication. They accept Johnstone's premise that a defining characteristic of human nature is the capacity to persuade and be persuaded. Also they accept Johnstone's Basic Imperative: "So act in each instance to encourage, rather than suppress, the capacity to persuade and be persuaded, whether the capacity in question is yours or another's." Johnstone's four ethical duties of resoluteness, openness, gentleness, and compassion are modified by Cheney and Tompkins for application in organizational communication contexts and become guardedness, accessibility, nonviolence, and empathy.

Guardedness. Communicators in organizations should use their own persuasive abilities to assess thoroughly overt and subtle messages from the organization and should avoid automatically and unthinkingly accepting the conventional "way things are" viewpoint. The often subtle use of the assumed "we" in organizational messages may or may not accurately reflect the degree of identification an employee really feels toward an idea, policy, or organization. Inappropriate self-identification may occur, for example, when an employee confuses his or her power or status with the power or status of the company.

Accessibility. Communicators in organizations should be open to the possibility of being changed by messages of others—of being persuaded. Our dogmatically held beliefs or narrowly focused viewpoints that blind us to useful information, a different view of a problem, or alternative solutions need to be offset or minimized. Guardedness and accessibility are ethical duties of organization members toward themselves. Ethical duties of members toward others are nonviolence and empathy.

Nonviolence. Certainly coercion, overt or subtle, of others is ethically undesirable. What are some subtle forms of coercion that may occur in an organizational context? Also, members should avoid using a persuasive stance that advocates one position as the one-and-only reasonable position. Such a "one best way" norm often guides an organization's policies and procedures.

Empathy. The empathic communicator genuinely listens to the arguments, opinions, values, and assumptions of others, is open to differing viewpoints, sets aside stereotypes triggered by labels or nonverbal cues, and respects the rights of all persons as persons to hold diverse views. In the organizational setting, notes Cheney, empathy involves the balancing of individual and organizational interests. Cheney and Tompkins believe that the ethic for organizational communication which they advocate facilitates celebration of individual values within the organizational context and minimizes "mindlessness" in performance of duties by forcing members to ask, "What are we doing?" The ethic promotes a sense of "community" that stresses cooperation, dignity, equality, and local involvement. Finally, the ethic encourages consideration of "purpose" so that overemphasis on means and techniques is minimized.

In chapter 2, Karl Wallace's "Four Moralities" approach was summarized in some detail. You are encouraged to review that discussion. Pamela Shockley-Zalabak believes that Wallace's approach provides appropriate ethical guidelines for evaluating communication in organizational situations.[21] After summarizing Wallace's *Habit of Search*, *Habit of Justice*, *Habit of Preferring Public to Private Motivation*, and *Habit of Respect for Dissent*, she overtly applies them to organizational communication:

> When applied to the organizational setting, the Wallace guidelines suggest that individuals and groups are engaging in ethical communication behaviors when they thoughtfully analyze problems and issues, are open to diverse types and sources of information, conduct their deliberations openly without hidden agendas, and not only respect differing viewpoints but encourage disagreement and dissent in order to produce superior ideas and solutions. From this perspective, unethical organizational communication behavior suppresses examining issues, withholds relevant information in order to pursue personal interests or motivations, and uses dissent to press for personal rather than organizational advantage.

Gary Kreps advocates what he terms "three broad covering principles" that he finds useful "to evaluate the relative ethics of internal and external organizational communication.[22] These covering principles are rooted in the ethical values of honesty, avoiding harm, and justice.

Organization members should not purposefully deceive one another. While generally "honesty is the best policy," the organizational context provides its own complexities. Some types of organizational information (such as reports on disciplinary actions and health or credit reports) are not for general dissemination. Does honesty mean saying all of what you believe to be true or only some of what you believe to be true? In addition, a person may be honest yet unintentionally fail to provide the factual truth about something, since they only know part of that truth. The fudging of records and withholding of relevant information from government regulatory agencies, says Kreps, exemplify dishonesty in organizational communication.

Organization members' communication should not purposely harm any other organization members or members of the organization's relevant environment. Determinations need to be made of the level of harm, its intentionality, and whether the effect should even be viewed as a "harm." Does a behavior that accidentally and unintentionally results in harm warrant ethical condemnation? In the normal course of organizational life some members are reprimanded or punished for inappropriate behavior. Is such a reprimand, asks Kreps, unethically harmful? What kinds of communication might be unethically harmful to organization members, to constituents and "stakeholders," to customers, and to other organizations?

Organization members should be treated justly. The maxim of "equal treatment for all" may not fit every situation. For example, employees who perform with excellence may merit greater rewards than those whose performance is mediocre. Fairness of treatment more than literal equality may be the issue. Bribery and coercion in lobbying, industrial espionage, stock manipulation, and employment discrimination, suggests Kreps, are examples of unethical external organizational communication. Kreps contends: "Justice, like the principles of honesty and avoiding harm, is a relative ethical principle that has to be evaluated within the specific organizational contexts."

A manager of communications for the Lockheed-California Company, Robert Batchelder, provides a detailed application of the ethical principle of honesty to an organizational setting.[23]

> The commitment to honesty, as understood by supervisors and managers, is multifaceted. It involves not only truthful reporting of facts and numbers, but also such dimensions of good communication as openly giving employees information about higher management decisions that affect their work; being open to hear the concerns of employees; letting employees "know where they stand" by being explicit about the standards and expectations by

which their performance is judged; giving frequent feedback to employees on both the strengths and weaknesses of their performance; encouraging the development of a relationship of credibility and trust with one's superior as well as with subordinates; and finally, the obligation of each manager to make explicit the expectation that employees are to report accurately on problems as they emerge, rather than tell the manager what they think he or she wants to hear.

Whistleblowing

Employees in organizations sometimes face the complex and painful issue of whether to become a "whistleblower"—to go outside normal internal communication and appeal channels in order to expose publicly a serious problem of safety, legality, or ethics not being adequately faced by the organization. Depending on a person's perspective or vested interests, people in our culture may view the whistleblower either as a hero/heroine or as a traitor. On the one hand, a whistleblower may be seen as a patriot or, in the words of Myron and Penina Glazer in their book, *The Whistleblowers*, as "ethical resisters." On the other hand, our culture also enforces strong negative sentiment against the informer, squealer, fink, snitch, or tattler.

What guidelines might we use, for ourselves or in assessing actions of others, to separate responsible from irresponsible whistleblowing? "Ethical Tension Points in Whistleblowing" are explored at length by J. Vernon Jensen, and his judicious analysis merits reading in its entirety.[24] Jensen's two concluding paragraphs capture the complexity of both the procedural and substantive tension points to be resolved by the responsible whistleblower.

> In summary, a conscientious whistleblower struggles with a number of ethical tension points. Many reside in procedural decisions which the whistleblower has to make. (1) Am I fairly and accurately depicting the seriousness of the problem? (2) Have I secured the information properly, analyzed it appropriately, and presented it fairly? (3) Do my motives spring from serving a public need more than from serving a personal desire? (4) Have I tried fully enough to have the problem corrected within the organization? (5) Should I blow the whistle while still a member of the organization or after having left it? (6) Should I reveal my identity or keep it secret? (7) Have I made my claims with proper intensity and with appropriate frequency? (8) How ethical have I been in selecting my audience? (9) How ethical is it for me, a participant

in the functioning of the group, to assume the role of a judge? (10) How ethical is it to set into motion an act which will likely be very costly to many people?

In addition, in trying to balance loyalties in many directions, the sensitive whistleblower encounters a number of substantive ethical dilemmas. (1) How fully am I living up to my moral obligations to the well being of my organization? (2) How fully am I living up to my moral obligations to my colleagues in the group? (3) Am I appropriately upholding the ethical standards of my profession? (4) How adversely will my action affect my family and other primary groups? (5) Am I being true to myself, to my own integrity and well being? (6) How will my action affect the health of such basic values as freedom of expression, independent judgment, courage, fairness, cooperativeness, and loyalty?

Ethics for Communication Consulting and Training

Organizations often use communication experts, whether employed within the organization or hired as external consultants, to diagnose communication problems, propose appropriate solutions, or to train employees in improved communication skills. Labels such as training, organizational development, or human systems development frequently identify these functions for an organization. Communication experts may offer programs in public speaking, presentation of proposals or reports, argumentation, persuasion, interpersonal communication, nonsexist/nonracist communication, nonverbal communication, small group decision making, interviewing, listening, leadership, horizontal and vertical communication systems, and external organizational communication.

Charles Redding suggests five minimal yet challenging ethical guidelines that he believes all communication trainers should follow.[25] (1) Respect the integrity of the individual trainee. Individual dignity is fostered by deemphasizing rote learning of tasks and prescriptive drills and by capitalizing on the contributions and views of the trainee. (2) Provide opportunity for self-actualization. To enhance each trainee's ability to achieve his or her true potential, blind obedience to routine task and role specifications or to narrow, highly programmed ways of learning are deemphasized. Encouraged are creativity and autonomy in job performance and innovative and participative modes of learning. (3) Encourage the exercise of critical faculties. While not sowing seeds of discord or undermining motivation to carry out tasks, the trainer should encourage trainees to keep an "attitude of open-minded inquiry toward the directives, the mission, and the rhetoric of the organization." Rather than blind, "rah-rah" loyalty, stress should be on realistic perception of the organizational system (including "corporate politics") and on freedom to express doubts and to question what is being done. (4) Devote explicit attention to ethical problems and issues. A simple mind-set solely of results-orientation or ends-always-justify-the-means is replaced with an application of complexity in ethical judgment and of multiple relevant ethical criteria. (5) Demonstrate concern for long-term development of trainees. The trainer will devote attention not only to the trainee's skills for his or her immediate job but also to insights and techniques relevant to future career opportunities.

The Applied Communication Committee of the Texas Speech Communication Association proposed the following ethical guidelines for communication consultants.[26] Academic qualifications and experience should be fully disclosed to clients and not overstated. Work proposals should include specified objectives, services, and products of the consultation and should not be overstated. Client confidentiality must be maintained. Sources of material presented in workshops or seminars should be cited. Consultants should refuse to work for unethical clients. Focus should be on the needs of the client rather than research interests of the consultant. Consultants should possess a solid grasp of communication theory and practice and should stay current with advances in their field. Consultants should strongly encourage and seriously take into account evaluative feedback from clients.

Ethics in Public Relations

Public Relations is a crucial communication function for most modern organizations, whether they be business, union, military, governmental, educational, religious, or social service organizations. This important function may be performed by a single person or a staff, by employees within the organization or an external public relations consultant. Increasingly the function may exist under such labels as public affairs, public information, or corporate communications. Audiences addressed through public relations include internal ones such as line employees, supervisors, managers, or volunteers and external ones such as customers, stockholders, news media, government agencies, donors, critics, competitors, and the public-at-large.

188 Chapter Nine

Today public relations encompasses not only the transmission of information to the public but also the advocacy of corporate positions on public issues. Public relations is included among a number of standard management functions typical in organizations. According to the Public Relations Society of America, the public relations management function encompasses the following tasks:[27] public opinion, attitudes and issues which might positively or negatively impact the organization's plans or operations are anticipated, analyzed, and interpreted to management. Management at all levels is counseled with regard to policy decisions, courses of action and communication, while at the same time taking into account public ramifications and the organization's societal responsibilities. On a continuing basis, programs of action and communication to achieve informed public understanding necessary to the success of the organization's aims are researched, conducted, and evaluated. Such programs may include marketing, fund-raising, employee relations, and community or governmental relations. The organization's efforts to influence or change public policy are planned and implemented. The staff and facilities necessary to accomplish all of the above must be managed.

Don Bates is president of his own New York Public relations firm and is administrator of the Foundation for Public Relations Research and Education. Based upon over 25 years of experience as a public relations practitioner in business, government, and nonprofit organizations, Bates is convinced that a significant public relations responsibility is "helping to build and maintain ethical behavior."[28] The public relations person should be "actively involved in wrestling with what's right or wrong with management decisions and actions affecting key constituencies such as customers and employees." Each practitioner should ask whether he or she would "compromise my personal life, the codes of professional standards in my field, and the law to avoid unpleasant complications or to save my skin or the skin of my employer?" Consider for a moment your answer to some of the following troubling ethical questions that a public relations practitioner might face.[29] Would I lie to my boss or staff? Would I lie on behalf of a client or employer? Would I help to conceal a dangerous situation, hazardous condition, or illegal act? Would I use deception to gain information about another practitioner's client? Would I attempt to bribe reporters or government officials with a gift, travel, or information? Would I present information that represents only part of the truth? Would I present true but misleading information in an interview or news conference that will mask some unpleasant fact? Would I hide or destroy evidence? Would I break a trust or confidence?

In their book, *Public Relations as Communication Management*, Richard Crable and Steven Vibbert describe the public relations process as composed of three phases: task identification (analysis of the organization's self-image, audit of its current efforts, assessment of public reactions); task analysis (targeting publics, setting goals, determining evaluation methods, proposing a public relations effort); task performance (implementation and evaluation of the public relations effort or campaign). Crable and Vibbert suggest ethical guidelines for each phase.[30]

The Ethics of Task Identification

1. Deal fairly with both the organization and the environment. Understand that an organization's perceived wants and needs may be selfish and undesirable for the environment generally.
2. Sometimes the public interest will dictate that you play the role of "boundary person," and attempt to change the goals of the organization.
3. Your access to the corporate records of any organization (their current efforts) should not be disclosed to others without permission.
4. Any analysis of the public reaction should be presented fairly and accurately to the organization seeking an evaluation.
5. The efforts of current public relations practitioners should not be minimized simply to create jobs for additional public relations practitioners.
6. When the organization's goals and desires seem at odds with the public interest and the ethics of the public relations manager, the relationship should be ended as soon as possible.

The Ethics of Task Analysis

1. Deal fairly with everyone involved and work toward the public interest. This may mean that the targeted public is not a public at all, but instead, the organization itself. The goals for change may need to include changes in the organization's operations.
2. Decide on fair and objective evaluative methods, instead of creating procedures that automatically result in a favorable evaluation of the public relations efforts.
3. Proposals for campaigns should not be based on inaccurate or misleading ideas, or ideas in violation of acceptable standards of good taste.
4. Proposals should not contain unrealistic assurances that a prescribed approach to a situation will be absolutely successful.

The Ethics of Task Performance

1. Public relations programs or campaigns should not be unnecessarily elaborate, simply to increase profits by the consultant or budgets by the in-house manager.
2. Programs should not be created that subvert or contradict the public interest.
3. Public relations efforts should involve only those appeals that are truthful, accurate, and in the public interest.
4. Any public relations effort should be free from any suspicion of conflict of interest.
5. Public relations efforts should be considered a confidence between the organization and the manager of public relations; no other organization should benefit from this effort.
6. No public relations effort should cast a doubt on the general accuracy and truthfulness of communication media.
7. No information in a public relations campaign should be false or misleading.
8. The public relations client or organization should be identified if a question arises about the sponsorship of messages.
9. Any message using a group or organization and its credibility should be able to justify that use.
10. The public relations manager should not accept fees or any other valuable considerations from any other party without the consent of the original employer.

Examples of Ethical Problems

A survey of typical problematic situations in organizational communication ethics should sensitize us to complex and less-than-ideal circumstances, help us identify relevant ethical issues, and encourage us to consider several rather than only one ethical standard.[31] Pamela Shockley-Zalabak provides excellent illustrations of varied ethical dilemmas in organizational communication. We will summarize and adapt only a few of them.[32] "Communication specialists interview, conduct surveys, facilitate meetings, advise and counsel individuals, review documents, and in a variety of other ways generate data important to their jobs." During both data collection and dissemination activities, "ethical decisions are made concerning what should remain confidential, who has a need to know, how accurate the information is, and what the criteria of interpretation are."

Assume that you are being interviewed for a job and tell the interviewer that you have a skill that you really do not possess. You are highly motivated to do excellent work if hired. What ethical criteria should apply? Does your motivation make your deception acceptable? When being interviewed or submitting an employment résumé, is it more unethical to include untrue material than to omit relevant but negative true material? In what circumstances, if any, would you argue that falsification of a job résumé is ethically justifiable? In what way might the nature or amount of falsification influence your ethical assessment? In your view, what is the difference, if any, between unethical falsification and ethically acceptable exaggeration?

In your work group, do you keep information about your mistakes hidden from your supervisor in order to appear more competent than you are? Do you blame others for problems even though you legitimately share some of the responsibility? In a supervisory or managerial role, you must give feedback to others about their performance. Are you hesitant to give negative feedback to a problem employee and thus provide him or her with a false sense of security? Does this decision involve an ethical issue, or are you simply being realistic that the worker would be demoralized if criticized?

A member of the night shift's manufacturing group comes to you as her personnel contact and expresses concern about drug use on the production line. She avoids giving you specific details for fear of persons involved discovering who exposed them. While she urges you to investigate immediately, she also asks you not to involve her in any way. Among your options are the following: (you may think of others): you can ask the worker to provide more concrete information before you will take action; you could ask your supervisor for advice on your next step; you could attempt to investigate on your own; at a general staff meeting, you could mention (without names) the drug problems the plant is experiencing and observe the reactions of your peers; without further evidence, you could ignore the situation. What would you do? What should you do?

Linda Klebe Trevino provides an additional complex example. As a middle-level manager you express concern for public safety to your supervisor, who has asked you to falsify data on reports.[33] The supervisor assures you that you are not responsible for any negative consequences of such falsification, since higher officials in the organization are aware of the situation and will take responsibility for the consequences. What are the ethical courses of action you might take? How ethical is the supervisor's response to you? Why?

In *Bureaucratic Propaganda*, David Altheid and John Johnson examine the nature of official reports.[34] In their view, bureaucratic propaganda is "any report produced by an organization for evaluation and other practical purposes that is targeted for individuals, committees, or publics who are unaware of its promotive character and the editing process that shaped the report." You are urged to examine the diverse examples and case studies presented in their book. For instance, what ethical issues and criteria might be relevant for assessing official reports that "promote organizational careers, assign responsibility for a particular act to an 'enemy,' and in general 'cover your ass' from revelation before a sanctioning body."

Consider the examples and arguments of Eric Eisenberg, who contends that intentional (strategic) ambiguity often is a necessary and ethical technique in organizational communication.[35] Strategic ambiguity promotes "unified diversity" in an organization by fostering "agreement on abstractions without limiting specific interpretations." Intentional ambiguity may foster creativity and lessen "acceptance of one standard way of viewing organizational reality." Organizational goals must be expressed ambiguously to satisfy multiple constituencies and to allow flexibility in adjusting to future conditions. Within an organization in interpersonal relationships, strategic ambiguity may be an appropriate alternative on the one hand to brutally frank honesty or on the other hand to secrecy or lying. Here you may want to review our earlier discussion of the ethics of intentional ambiguity and vagueness in chapter 7. Also you are urged to read Eisenberg's analysis in its entirety in order to identify more clearly the issues and standards you believe are most relevant for assessing specific strategic uses of ambiguity by and in organizations.

Finally, how would you respond to several examples presented by the chair of the Board of Ethics of the Public Relations Society of America?[36] A distributor of medicinal products arranges with your firm to put on a press conference for an independent British scientist, who has tested the products and written favorably about them. You also arrange speaking engagements for the visiting scientist. After the press conference, you learn the scientist was actually an employee of the research arm of the manufacturer of the products. What actions should you take? Or assume that your employer asks you to give a series of talks in communities served by your company regarding its new plant and the service it will provide. During a visit to the plant to acquaint yourself with its operation, you get clear evidence that the plant cannot fulfill the expectations outlined in the talk prepared by your company. Can you give the talks as originally prepared? What are some of your alternatives?

Cynicism and Relevance

"Teaching ethics to business students cannot alter the facts of business practice. In a capitalistic system, greed is the main fuel that drives the engine. Ethics works against greed. Business practice is not inherently immoral, but it is amoral. For virtually all decisions, ethics are irrelevant." Although the author of this cynical assessment is Herbert Rotfeld, a professor of advertising, it sounds similar to the sentiments voiced by the wheeler-dealer, raider-trader character played by Michael Douglas in the Hollywood film, *Wall Street*.[37] The issues, approaches, and guidelines presented in this chapter have attempted to demonstrate the *relevance* of ethical concerns in corporate (and all organizational) decisions concerning communication goals and techniques. Here, again, we see manifested the tension between *is* and *ought*, between what the situation is and what it ought to be.

"I am convinced that most of the unethical acts I have seen committed in business were performed by essentially honest people. But they were people who felt under great pressure to achieve. In their desire to make good—to 'win'—they compromised themselves." To what extent do you agree with this judgment from a consultant on human resources management, Gerald Ottoson?[38] One goal of this chapter has been to stress formation over time of sound ethical "character" in organization members individually, and in the ethical "climate" of the organization as a whole, so that such compromises in communication can be kept at a minimum or avoided.

Notes

[1] Charles Redding, "Professionalism in Training—Guidelines for a Code of Ethics," paper presented at meeting of the Speech Communication Association, Chicago, November 1984. For example, see William G. Scott and David K. Hart, *Organizational America* (Boston: Houghton Mifflin, 1979), John Sabini and Maury Silver, *The Moralities of Everyday Life* (New York: Oxford University Press, 1982); Charles D. Pringle and Justin G. Longenecker, "The Ethics of MBO," *Academy of Management Review*, 7 (1982): 305–12.

[2] Robert Jackall, "Moral Mazes: Bureaucracy and Managerial Work," *Harvard Business Review*, 61 (1983): 118–30; also see Jackall, *Moral Mazes: The World of Corporate Managers* (New York: Oxford University Press, 1988).

³ Alfred G. Smith, "The Ethic of the Relay Man," in *Communication: Ethical and Moral Issues*, Lee Thayer, ed. (New York: Gordon and Breach, 1973), pp. 313–24.

⁴ See, for example, Richard T. DeGeorge, *Business Ethics*, 2d ed. (New York: Macmillan, 1986), pp. 82–100; Barbara Toffler, *Tough Choices: Managers Talk Ethics* (New York: Wiley, 1986), pp. 35–38.

⁵ Dennis F. Thompson, *Political Ethics and Public Office* (Cambridge: Harvard University Press, 1987), pp. 40–65.

⁶ T. E. Deal and A. A. Kennedy, *Corporate Cultures: The Rites and Rituals of Corporate Life* (Reading, MA: Addison-Wesley, 1982); M. E. Pacanowsky and N. O'Donnell-Trujillo, "Communication and Organizational Cultures," *Western Journal of Speech Communication*, 46 (1982): 115–30.

⁷ DeGeorge, *Business Ethics*, 2d ed., pp. 96–97; also Pamela Shockley-Zalabak, *Fundamentals of Organizational Communication*, (New York: Longman, 1988), pp. 317–25; Kathryn C. Rents and Mary Beth Debs, "Language and Corporate Values: Teaching Ethics in Business Ethics Writing Courses," *Journal of Business Communication*, 24 (Summer 1987): 37–48.

⁸ Bart Victor and John B. Cullen, "The Organizational Bases of Ethical Work Climates," *Administrative Science Quarterly*, 33 (1988): 101–25.

⁹ Gerald Ottoson, "Essentials of an Ethical Corporate Climate," in *Doing Ethics in Business*, Donald G. Jones, ed. (Cambridge, MA: Oelgeschlager, Gunn & Hain, 1982), pp. 155–64; Michael R. Rion, "Training for Ethical Management at Cummins Engine," in *Doing Ethics in Business*, pp. 27–44; Toffler, *Tough Choices*, pp. 328–46; M. Cash Mathews, *Strategic Intervention in Organizations: Resolving Ethical Dilemmas* (Newbury Park, CA: Sage, 1988).

¹⁰ DeGeorge, *Business Ethics*, 2d ed., pp. 169–170; Douglas Sturm, "Assessing the Sun Company's Ethical Condition," in *Doing Ethics in Business*, p. 110; Philip Meyer, *Ethical Journalism* (New York: Longman, 1987), pp. 189–200.

¹¹ Redding, "Professionalism in Training"; J. Weber, "Institutionalizing Ethics into the Corporation." *MSU Business Topics*, 29 (1981): 47–52.

¹² Toffler, *Tough Choices*, pp. 337–38. Also see Ronald R. Sims, *Ethics and Organizational Decision Making* (Westport, CT: Quorum, 1994), pp. 189–211.

¹³ Philip G. Clampitt, *Communicating for Managerial Effectiveness* (Newbury Park, CA: Sage, 1991), pp. 292–95.

¹⁴ Oliver F. Williams and Patrick Murphy, "The Ethics of Virtue: A Moral Theory for Business," in *A Virtuous Life in Business*, Oliver F. Williams and John W. Houck, eds. (Lanham, MD: Rowman and Littlefield, 1992), pp. 9–27.

¹⁵ See, for example, Terry L. Cooper and N. Dale Wright, eds., *Exemplary Public Administrators: Character and Leadership in Government* (San Francisco: Jossey-Bass, 1992).

¹⁶ William F. May, "The Virtues in a Professional Setting," *Soundings: An Interdisciplinary Journal*, LXVII (Fall 1984): 245–66.

¹⁷ Robert C. Solomon, *Ethics and Excellence: Cooperation and Integrity in Business* (New York: Oxford University Press, 1992). Also see Solomon, *Ethics: A Short Introduction* (Dubuque, IA: Brown Benchmark, 1993), pp. 95–163.

¹⁸ Toffler, *Tough Choices*, pp. 10–38. For a framework of "Twelve Questions for Examining a Business Decision," see Laura L. Nash, "Ethics Without the Sermon," in Jones, ed., *Doing Ethics in Business*, pp. 117–36.

[19] Julie Belle White, "Model of Organizational Integrity: Habits, Commitments, and Practices Indicative of an Organization's Ethical Climate," in *Proceedings of the Second National Communication Ethics Conference*, James A. Jaksa, ed. (Annandale, VA: Speech Communication Association, 1992), pp. 64–81.

[20] George Cheney, "Coping With Bureaucracy: Ethics and Organizational Relationships," presented at the Speech Communication Association conference, Chicago, November 1986; George Cheney and Philip K. Tompkins, "Toward an Ethic of Identification," presented at the Burke Conference, Temple University, March 1984; George Cheney, "The Rhetoric of Identification and the Study of Organizational Communication," *Quarterly Journal of Speech*, 69 (1983): 143–58; George Cheney and Philip K. Tompkins, "Coming to Terms With Organizational Identification and Commitment," *Central States Speech Journal*, 38 (Spring 1987): 1–15.

[21] Shockley-Zalabak, *Fundamentals of Organizational Communication*, pp. 329–30.

[22] Gary L. Kreps, *Organizational Communication*, 2d ed. (New York: Longman, 1989), ch. 12.

[23] Robert C. Batchelder, "Applied Ethics Management Training at Lockheed-California Company," in *Doing Ethics in Business*, p. 53.

[24] J. Vernon Jensen, "Ethical Tension Points in Whistleblowing," *Journal of Business Ethics* (May, 1987): 321–28. Also see Richard T. DeGeorge, *Business Ethics*, 3rd ed. (New York: Macmillan, 1990), pp. 200–216.

[25] Redding, "Professionalism in Training"; also summarized in Gerald M. Goldhaber, Organizational Communication, 6th ed. (Dubuque, IA: Wm. C. Brown, 1993), 340–44.

[26] "Guidelines for Speech Communication Consultants," Report of the Applied Communication Committee of the Texas Speech Communication Association, September 29, 1983.

[27] Official Statement on Public Relations adopted by the Public Relations Society of America Assembly, November 6, 1982, and reprinted in Otis Baskin and Craig Aronoff, *Public Relations: The Profession and the Practice*, 2d ed. (Dubuque, IA: Wm. C. Brown, 1988), pp. 2–22. Also see Thomas H. Bivins, "Applying Ethical Theory to Public Relations," *Journal of Business Ethics*, 6 (April 1987): 195–200.

[28] Don Bates, "The Role of the Public Relations Practitioner in Ethical organizational Behavior," presented at Northern Illinois University, September 22, 1988.

[29] Adapted from Bates and from Baskin and Aronoff, *Public Relations*, 2d ed., pp. 85–86.

[30] Richard E. Crable and Steven L. Vibbert, *Public Relations as Communication Management* (Edina, MN: Bellwether Press, 1986), pp. 114–18; Crabel and Vibbert's guidelines are based on their interpretation of the 1983 Code of Professional Standards for the Practice of Public Relations adopted by the Public Relations Society of America. The 1988 PRSA Code of Professional Standards is reprinted and evaluated in our chapter 10, "Formal Codes of Ethics."

[31] Dennis F. Thompson, *Political Ethics and Public Office*, p. 9.

[32] Shockley-Zalabak, *Fundamentals of Organizational Communication*, pp. 330–39.

[33] Adapted from Linda Klebe Trevino, "Ethical Decision Making in Organizations: A Person-Situation Interactionist Model," *Academy of Management Review*, 11 (1986): 601–17.

[34] David L. Altheide and John M. Johnson, *Bureaucratic Propaganda* (Boston: Allyn and Bacon, 1980), pp. 1–43.

[35] Eric M. Eisenberg, "Ambiguity as Strategy in Organizational Communication," *Communication Monographs*, 51 (September 1984): 227–42.

[36] Donald B. McCammond, cited in Baskin and Aronoff, *Public Relations*, 2d ed., pp. 97–98.

[37] Herbert Rotfeld, "Ethics training or not, business will still be business," *Chicago Tribune*, February 29, 1988, sec. 1, p. 11.

[38] Ottoson, "Essentials of an Ethical Corporate Climate," in *Doing Ethics in Business*, p. 159.

Chapter 10

Formal Codes of Ethics

Formal codes of ethics have been adopted or proposed by various communication-oriented professional associations, business organizations, and citizen-action groups in such fields as commercial advertising, public relations, technical writing, organizational consulting, print and broadcast journalism, and political campaigning. For some people, formal codes are a necessary mark of a true profession. For others, codes are worthless exercises in vagueness, irrelevance, and slick public relations.*

Controversies surrounding computer communication on the Internet and World Wide Web illustrate not only the tension between freedom and responsibility but also pressures for legalistic approaches to ethics and for the formation of formal codes of ethics. Should you be free to say or depict anything you want, without restriction, on Internet, e-mail, or WWW? The freedom-responsibility tension is underscored by Frank Connolly, a professor of computer science at American University (*Washington Post National Weekly Edition*, Oct. 30–Nov. 5, 1995, p. 36): "With the Internet, we are in the situation where there are no controls, no cyber-cops, no speed limits. The other side of these freedoms is that individuals have to exercise responsibility for their actions." But there are pressures for controls and for formal rules of responsibility. In 1995 a bill providing for severe criminal penalties for anyone transmitting obscene or indecent material passed in the U.S. Senate but stalled in the House of Representatives. University officials debated whether to apply existing campus speech codes that prohibit "hate speech" and harassment to the

The early sections of this chapter are adapted (with permission of the editor) from Richard L. Johannesen, "What Should We Teach About Formal Codes of Communication Ethics?" *Journal of Mass Media Ethics*, 3, no. 1 (1988): 59–64.

Internet and e-mail activities of students or whether to formulate special codes of computer communication ethics to guide student use. Virginia Tech University, for example, instituted a student code that prohibited abusive conduct in words or actions that "demeans, intimidates, threatens, or otherwise interferes with another person's rightful action or comfort," *both on-line and elsewhere on campus.* The dean of students at Virginia Tech said the university's position was that "if you use our server, then you have some responsibility because you associate the name of the institution with what you say." (See, for example, *Washington Post National Weekly Edition*, Oct. 30–Nov. 5, 1995, p. 36; Nov. 6–12, 1995, p. 27; *Chicago Tribune*, Nov. 24, 1995, sec. 1, p. 30.) What is your view on how ethical responsibility for computer communication on Internet should be promoted?

We need to understand the range and complexity of pro and con arguments surrounding formal codes. I will summarize the major criticisms levied against codes. Then, standards for a sound ethical code will be presented. Next, a trend will be described toward more concrete and enforceable codes developed by specific communication organizations. Finally, a number of positive functions of codes will be examined, with special emphasis on two.

Objections to Formal Codes

What are some typical objections to formal codes of ethics?[1] First, frequently they are filled with meaningless language, "semantically foggy clichés," and thus are too abstract, vague, and ambiguous to be usefully applied. For example, outsiders may interpret the unclear terms broadly as involving stringent standards while persons governed by the code may interpret them narrowly as allowing lesser standards.[2] Second, their existence in the mass media, corporations, and political campaigning seems not to have promoted a significant improvement in ethicality of communication. Third, there is the danger that a code will be viewed as static, as settling matters once and for all. Fourth, standards in a code may appear universal when they are not. Contrary to face-value assumptions, the standards may not easily apply to cross-cultural communication or be flexibly applied in unique situations. Fifth, especially within journalism, some object that a formal code would inappropriately restrict the journalist's constitutional rights of free speech and free press. Sixth, many codes are castigated because they lack effective enforcement procedures to punish violators; they have no "teeth." Finally, many codes are dismissed as mere public relations ploys aimed just at enhancing the group's image of responsibility with the public.

Developing a Sound Formal Code

Many of these objections might be lessened or removed. Drawing upon suggestions made by Richard DeGeorge, John Kultgen, and others, we can describe guidelines for developing a sound formal code of ethics. First, the code should make clear which of its statements are *ideal goals* to be striven for but often not fully attained and which statements are *minimum conditions* that must be met to be considered ethical and to avoid punishment.[3] Second, under ordinary circumstances the code should not require heroic virtue, extreme sacrifice, or doing right no matter what the obstacles. Rather it should be aimed at persons of ordinary conscientiousness and persons willing to follow it on the condition that others do likewise.[4]

Third, language in the code should be clear and specific. Vagueness and ambiguity should be minimized. Key terms in code provisions, especially abstract value-laden terms, could be clarified through further explanation and concrete illustration. Among such terms might be distort, falsify, misrepresent, mislead, deceive, rational, reasonable, and public interest. Fourth, code provisions should be logically coherent. That is, relationships among provisions should be clear as to sequence, precedence, and scope.[5] For example, there could be some indication of the precedence among obligations to the client, the employer, the public, and the profession.

As a fifth guideline, the code should protect the general public interest and the interests of persons served by the group. The code should not be self-serving; it should not protect interests of the group at the expense of the public.[6] Kultgen goes so far as to urge the obligations of distributing the group's services more fairly in society, of providing full information to clients concerning viable options, their chances of success, costs and long-term consequences, and of avoiding paternalistic abuse of authority and expertise to pressure clients.[7] Sixth, code provisions should go beyond general admonitions against lying and cheating to focus on those facets of the group's functions "that pose particular and specialized temptations to its members."[8] Seventh, a code should stimulate continued discussion and reflection leading to possible modification or revision.[9] Eighth, a code for a profession or a business should provide ethical guidance for that profession as a whole not just for individual members. For example, what action should be taken and by whom when the group as a whole, as an institution, acts unethically?[10]

As a ninth guideline, the code should make clear the general moral principles on which it is founded, the basic ethical values from which its provisions flow, such as justice, fairness, respecting rights of others, and weighing the consequences of an act for all those affected by it. DeGeorge illustrates the point: "The injunction, found in one code, to act in such a way that you would not be ashamed to have your actions exposed to the public—for instance in the headlines of a local newspaper—is a step in the right direction."[11] It is important to know not only *what* is the ethical thing to do but also *why* it is right. Tenth, provisions in a code for a specific organization should be developed through participation of a wide range of members of that organization. This means substantial participation by both management and labor, employers and employees, corporations and unions, higher- and lower-level professionals.[12]

A final and obvious guideline is that the code should be enforceable and enforced. There should be procedures and mechanisms for bringing charges and applying penalties. An enforcement system would provide mechanisms for interpreting what a code means and what it requires. A committee, board, or high-level executive officer, supported by necessary funds and staff, should administer fair procedures for reporting violations, investigating allegations, and reaching decisions.[13] Possible punishment options might include an informal warning, a request to cease a practice, a formal reprimand that becomes part of a record, suspension without pay, and expulsion or firing, possibly with a public explanation that justifies the action and names names.[14]

Codes for Individual Organizations

Codes of national associations, while useful as general guidelines and to stimulate reflection on ethical issues, usually lack the practicality, detail, and comprehensiveness necessary for maximum effectiveness. However, there is a definite trend in various individual print and broadcast news organizations, and in some other types of companies, toward setting up their own more precise and enforceable ethical codes. CBS, NBC, ABC, the *Washington Post*, *Philadelphia Inquirer*, *Chicago Sun-Times*, *Des Moines Register*, *Louisville Courier-Journal*, and *Milwaukee Journal* all have done so.[15]

Crable and Vibbert, and also Kultgen, suggest that at the level of individual companies a "contractual" approach to codes of ethics might be utilized.[16] Through negotiation, employer and employees (or even company and client) would agree to a legally binding ethics contract that spells out mutual rights, obligations, objectives, and expectations. Such might be possible for companies in journalism, public relations, advertising, or communication consulting. Provisions of the ethics contract would be enforceable in court.

I want to focus now on some of the useful functions of precisely worded ethical codes.[17] First, codes can educate new persons in a profession or business by acquainting them with guidelines for ethical responsibility based on the experience of predecessors and by sensitizing them to ethical problems specific to their field. Second, codes can narrow the problematic areas with which a person has to struggle; of course the more complex or unusual ethical problems still remain for deliberation. Third, the very process of developing the formal code can be a healthy one that forces participants to reflect on their goals, on means allowable to achieve those goals, and on their obligations to peers, to clients or customers, to employees, and to the public at large. A fourth function, openly urged in some organizations, is that an appropriate and effective voluntary code may minimize the need for cumbersome and intrusive governmental regulations. I move now to two additional functions of codes that I believe merit serious consideration, an argumentative function and a character-depiction function.

Argumentative Function

By an argumentative function I mean that it can serve as a starting point to stimulate professional and public scrutiny of major ethical quandaries in a field.[18] It could be the basis from which to launch a public debate over a specific communication practice. Or the standards in a code could provide focus as a corporation, profession, or other organization debates the ethicality of a communication policy *prior to* adoption or approval of that policy. As another argumentative application, provisions in a code could be cited by a communicator as justification for saying "no" to a communication practice requested of them by peers or employers.[19]

Richard Crable believes that formal ethical codes provide a visible and impersonal standard to which both critics and defenders of a communication practice can appeal in arguing their judgment.[20] The codes provide a "comparative standard by which to examine and justify behavior." By synthesizing and adapting the separate analyses of Richard Crable and of Peter Brown, we can sketch a range of argumentative claims that critics or defenders of a communication practice might use to assess ethicality in light of a code.[21] It could be argued that a particular practice (1) clearly is contrary to a precise, relevant, well-justified code; (2) is ethically suspect even though it falls outside the boundaries of any established code; (3) is ethical because the code invoked is irrelevant or inappropriate; (4) is unethical because, while the strict "letter" of the code was honored, the "spirit" of the code was violated; (5) is ethical because key terms of the code are too vague and ambiguous for precise or meaningful application; (6) is ethically justified because one applicable code is superseded by another relevant code, or because "higher" values take precedence over the formal code; (7) is ethical because the facts of the situation, including intent and context, are unclear; and (8) should be judged primarily by legal statutes rather than by an ethical code.

Character-Depiction Function

In her book, *Professional Ethics*, Karen Lebacqz suggests that formal ethical codes, especially in the professions, should be seen as having a function quite different from the typical one, namely, as rules for specific behavior or as admonitions concerning specific instances.[22] In her view, we must look beyond the action-oriented language of most codes ("do this," "avoid that") to the "overall picture of the type of person who is to *embody* those actions." As reconceptualized by Lebacqz, a code embodies a picture of the moral "character" to be expected of a professional in a given field; it would depict an ethical communicator's "being" collectively and over time. She contends that "codes do not give specific guidance for action as much as they say something about the character traits necessary for someone to be a professional." "In short," she says, "codes are geared primarily toward establishing expectations for character." In this view, codes are "guideposts to understand where stresses and tensions have been felt within a profession and what image of the good professional is held up to assist professionals through those stresses and tensions."

According to Lebacqz a wide range of professional codes reflect a core of central character traits, ethical principles, or obvious duties: "justice, beneficence, non-maleficence, honesty, and fidelity." Often these are manifested in code provisions that collectively represent the ethical professional as fair, competent, honest, oriented toward the good of clients and society, and avoiding taking advantage of others by abusing knowledge or power.

Lebacqz believes that a "professional is called not simply to *do* something but to *be* something." At a fundamental level, codes depict a professional as "bound by certain ethical principles *and* as incorporating those principles *into his or her very character*." Ideally a code depicts the professional as "a person of integrity who not only does the 'right' thing, but is an *honorable person*." For example, a trustworthy person not only keeps a confidence but is "thoughtful about the impact" of decisions on others and is "sensitive to their needs and claims." An honest person "tries to avoid any kind of deception, not just explicit lies." Indeed, believes Lebacqz, "when we act, we not only *do* something, we also shape our own character. . . . And so each choice about what to *do* is also a choice about whom to *be*—or, more accurately, whom to become." This function of codes as embodying desirable character traits more than specific rules for specific actions is, I urge, a function overlooked and one meritorious of serious consideration.

Charles Levy examined the codes of ethics of eighty-nine organizations in various human service fields. His summary observation captures quite accurately the range and complexity of views on the functions and usefulness of formal codes.[23]

> Codes of ethics are at once the highest and lowest standards of practice expected of the practitioner, the awesome statement of rigid requirements, and the promotional material issued primarily for public relations purposes. They embody the gradually evolved essence of moral expectations, as well as the arbitrarily prepared shortcut to professional prestige and status. At the same time, they are handy guides to the legal enforcement of ethical conduct and to punishment for unethical conduct. They are also the unrealistic, unimpressive, and widely unknown and ignored guides to wishful thinking.

Advertising Association Codes

The American Association of Advertising Agencies code of ethics was last revised in 1990. As you read the following standards, consider their degree of adequacy and the extent to which they presently are followed by advertisers. Association members agree to avoid intentionally producing advertising that contains:

1. False or misleading statements or exaggerations, visual or verbal.
2. Testimonials that do not reflect the real choice of the individual(s) involved.
3. Price claims that are misleading.

4. Comparisons that unfairly disparage a competitive product or service.
5. Claims insufficiently supported or that distort the true meaning or practicable application of statements made by professional or scientific authority.
6. Statements, suggestions, or pictures offensive to public decency or to minority segments of the population.

The American Advertising Federation in 1984 adopted the following Advertising Principles of American Business.

1. Advertising shall tell the truth, and shall reveal significant facts, the omission of which would mislead the public.
2. Advertising claims shall be substantiated by evidence in possession of the advertiser and advertising agency, prior to making such claims.
3. Advertising shall refrain from making false, misleading, or unsubstantiated statements or claims about a competitor or his products or services.
4. Advertising shall not offer products or services for sale unless such offer constitutes a bona fide effort to sell the advertised products or services and is not a device to switch consumers to other goods or services, usually higher priced.
5. Advertising of guarantees and warranties shall be explicit, with sufficient information to apprise consumers of their principal terms and limitations, or, when space or time restrictions preclude such disclosures, the advertisement should clearly reveal where the full text of the guarantee or warranty can be examined before purchase.
6. Advertising shall avoid price claims which are false or misleading, or savings claims which do not offer provable savings.
7. Advertising containing testimonials shall be limited to those of competent witnesses who are reflecting a real and honest opinion or experience.
8. Advertising shall be free of statements, illustrations or implications which are offensive to good taste or public decency.

The Code of Advertising issued by the Better Business Bureau in 1985 is a guide for advertisers, advertising agencies, and advertising media. It is very comprehensive and detailed in its coverage and much too lengthy to reproduce here. Its guidelines encompass comparative pricing, claims of savings, credit offers, "bait and switch" offers, warranties and guarantees, layout and illustrations, comparative quality claims, contests, and results claims. Words and labels that frequently are abused get specific discussion: irregulars, seconds, factory to you, up to, sale, free, easy credit, as is, used, rebuilt, and discontinued. Superlative claims (the best, the most, etc.) are divided into objective (tangible quality and performance subject to measurement against accepted standards or tests) and subjective (puffery—expressions of opinion or personal evaluation of intangible qualities). Puffery that misleads should be avoided. Misleading or confusing testimonials and endorsements include those that do not represent the current opinion of the endorser, that are quoted out of context thus altering the meaning, that are literally true but create deceptive implications, and where the endorser is not competent or qualified to express a judgment of quality about the product or service. There are three basic principles that support the detailed ethical guidelines.

1. The primary responsibility for truthful and nondeceptive advertising rests with the advertiser. Advertisers should be prepared to substantiate any claims or offers before publication or broadcast and, upon request, present such substantiation promptly to the advertising medium or the Better Business Bureau.
2. Advertisements which are untrue, misleading, deceptive, fraudulent, falsely disparaging of competitors, or insincere offers to sell, shall not be used.
3. An advertisement as a whole may be misleading although every sentence separately considered is literally true. Misrepresenting may result not only from direct statements but by omitting or obscuring a material fact.

International Association of Business Communicators

The Code of Ethics of the International Association of Business Communicators (as revised in 1995) provides guidelines for IABC members and other communication professionals. The code covers communication and information dissemination, standards of conduct, confidentiality and disclosure, and professionalism.

1. Professional communicators uphold the credibility and dignity of their profession by practicing honest, candid and timely communication and by fostering the free flow of essential information in accord with the public interest.
2. Professional communicators disseminate accurate information and promptly correct any erroneous communication for which they may be responsible.
3. Professional communicators understand and support the principles of free speech, freedom of assembly, and access to an open marketplace of ideas; and, act accordingly.
4. Professional communicators are sensitive to cultural values and beliefs and engage in fair and balanced communication activities that foster and encourage mutual understanding.

5. Professional communicators refrain from taking part in any undertaking which the communicator considers to be unethical.
6. Professional communicators obey laws and public policies governing their professional activities and are sensitive to the spirit of all laws and regulations and, should any law or public policy be violated, for whatever reason, act promptly to correct the situation.
7. Professional communicators give credit for unique expressions borrowed from others and identify the sources and purposes of all information affecting the welfare of others.
8. Professional communicators protect confidential information and, at the same time, comply with all legal requirements for the disclosure of information affecting the welfare of others.
9. Professional communicators do not use confidential information gained as a result of professional activities for personal benefit and do not represent conflicting or competing interests without written consent of those involved.
10. Professional communicators do not accept undisclosed gifts or payments for professional services from anyone other than a client or employer.
11. Professional communicators do not guarantee results that are beyond the power of the practitioner to deliver.
12. Professional communicators are honest not only with others but also, and most importantly, with themselves as individuals; for a professional communicator seeks the truth and speaks that truth first to the self.

Public Relations Society of America Code

The Code of Professional Standards for the Practice of Public Relations (as adopted in 1988 and based on a 1983 code) rests on a declaration of foundational principles and embodies a set of 17 ethical standards. Those principles and standards are reprinted here. In addition, the PRSA provides members with official written interpretations of a number of those standards. Also provided are official interpretations of the code as it applies specifically to political and to financial public relations.

Declaration of Principles

Members of the Public Relations Society of America base their professional principles on the fundamental value and dignity of the individual, holding that the free exercise of human rights, especially freedom of speech, freedom of assembly, and freedom of the press, is essential to the practice of public relations.

In serving the interests of clients and employers, we dedicate ourselves to the goals of better communication, understanding, and cooperation among the diverse individuals, groups, and institutions of society, and of equal opportunity of employment in the public relations profession.

We pledge:

To conduct ourselves professionally, with truth, accuracy, fairness, and responsibility to the public;

To improve our individual competence and advance the knowledge and proficiency of the profession through continuing research and education;

And to adhere to the articles of the Code of Professional Standards for the Practice of Public Relations as adopted by the governing Assembly of the Society.

Code of Professional Standards for the Practice of Public Relations

These articles have been adopted by the Public Relations Society of America to promote and maintain high standards of public service and ethical conduct among its members.

1. A member shall conduct his or her professional life in accord with the **public interest**.
2. A member shall exemplify high standards of **honesty and integrity** while carrying out dual obligations to a client or employer and to the democratic process.
3. A member shall **deal fairly** with the public, with past or present clients or employers, and with fellow practitioners, giving due respect to the ideal of free inquiry and to the opinions of others.
4. A member shall adhere to the highest standards of **accuracy and truth**, avoiding extravagant claims or unfair comparisons and giving credit for ideas and words borrowed from others.
5. A member shall not knowingly disseminate **false or misleading information** and shall act promptly to correct erroneous communications for which he or she is responsible.
6. A member shall not engage in any practice which has the purpose of **corrupting** the integrity of channels of communications or the processes of government.
7. A member shall be prepared to **identify publicly** the name of the client or employer on whose behalf any public communication is made.
8. A member shall not use any individual or organization professing to serve or represent an announced cause, or professing to be inde-

pendent or unbiased, but actually serving another or **undisclosed interest**.

9. A member shall **not guarantee the achievement** of specified results beyond the member's direct control.
10. A member shall **not represent conflicting** or competing interests without the express consent of those concerned, given after a full disclosure of the facts.
11. A member shall not place himself or herself in a position where the member's **personal interest is or may be in conflict** with an obligation to an employer or client, or others, without full disclosure of such interests to all involved.
12. A member shall **not accept fees, commissions, gifts or any other consideration** from anyone except clients or employers for whom services are performed without their express consent, given after full disclosure of the facts.
13. A member shall scrupulously safeguard the **confidences and privacy rights** of present, former, and prospective clients or employers.
14. A member shall not intentionally **damage the professional reputation** or practice of another practitioner.
15. If a member has evidence that another member has been guilty of unethical, illegal, or unfair practices, including those in violation of this Code, the member is obligated to present the information promptly to the proper authorities of the Society for action in accordance with the procedure set forth in Article XII of the Bylaws.
16. A member called as a witness in a proceeding for enforcement of this Code is obligated to appear, unless excused for sufficient reason by the judicial panel.
17. A member shall, as soon as possible, sever relations with any organization of individual if such a relationship requires conduct contrary to the articles of this Code.

As with many formal codes of ethics, typical criticisms of the PRSA code focus on ambiguity and vagueness of key terms, on internal coherence, and on matters of enforcement. Analyses by Crable and Vibbert and by Olasky call attention to vagueness and ambiguity in such terms and phrases as: deal fairly; in accord with the public interest; truth; accuracy. Crable and Vibbert observe that "definitions of these concepts will vary among individuals; how these concepts should be applied in particular situations also will vary."[24] After interviewing 50 public relations practitioners at one of the top ten American corporations, Olasky reported that "serious mention of the Code was a surefire source of merriment among the practitioners interviewed. Words which make sense only if they have a clear and objective definition—truth, public interest, and so on—were twisted like wax noses."[25]

To some extent the official interpretations accompanying the code do attempt to reduce the vagueness and ambiguity of some terms. To what degree do you believe these attempts are successful? The official PRSA interpretation primarily defines "public interest" as "the rights guaranteed by the Constitution of the United States." Practices which tend to "corrupt the integrity of channels of communication or processes of government" are practices that "tend to place representatives of the media or government under any obligation to the member, or the member's employer or client, which is in conflict with their obligations to media or government." In declaring that a member "shall not guarantee the achievement of specified results beyond the member's direct control," the official interpretation explains that this does not prohibit "guarantees of quality or service," but it does prohibit, for example, "a guarantee that a news release would appear specifically in a particular publication."

Internal coherence of standards also is a potential issue. To what degree does there seem to be an inconsistency between, on the one hand, being "prepared to identify publicly the name of the client or employer on whose behalf any public communication is made" and, on the other hand, safeguarding "the confidences of present and former clients"? How might we determine which of two potentially conflicting standards takes precedence in a given instance?[26]

A study covering the 35-year period 1950–1985 found that 168 issues, complaints, and investigations had been initiated either with the PRSA national grievance board or with one of nine regional judicial panels. Of 32 decisions ultimately rendered by judicial panels, two persons were expelled, two suspended, three censured, and three reprimanded. Five persons resigned from the PRSA before action could be taken. Charges were dismissed in 17 other cases because of insufficient evidence or other reasons. The study concludes that on the whole, "members of the Public Relations Society of America have adhered to the ethical code. . . ."[27]

Olasky argues that the PRSA code enforcement must be much more severe or the result is hypocrisy and futility. While the PRSA Board of Directors must publicize the fact (but not details) of an expulsion, suspension, or censure, the findings of reprimand, warning or admonition may be published at its discretion. Olasky contends that the PRSA should "provide models of what not to do by publicly explaining the reasons for expulsion, with names named. PRSA would bring shame into play." But since "neither buyers or sellers of public relations services seem ready to publicize shameful activities," Olasky believes there is a need for numerous "public relations watchers"—persons, groups and media who monitor the ethicality of public relations practice and through exposure "help to restore a sense of shame."[28]

Baskin and Aronoff temper their criticism of inadequacy of the code's enforcement and punishment. "The investigation of charges independent of those who make them is an expensive process most organizations cannot afford. Moreover, the legal and ethical responsibility to avoid damage to someone's reputation and livelihood without cause requires that any group proceed cautiously in the enforcement of a code practice."[29]

Ethical Values and Principles in Public Service

The Josephson Institute for the Advancement of Ethics is a nonprofit organization established to "advance ethical awareness, commitment and behavior in both the public and private sectors of society." The Institute's various programs are designed "to engage individuals in serious, thoughtful discussions of realistic problems in the context of the practical and personal considerations that sometimes make it difficult to act according to one's conscience." While the Institute's initial programs focused on government and the legal profession, other programs encompass journalism, medicine, business, and education. "In difficult cases," the Institute recognizes, "ethically committed individuals may disagree; there is no uniform solution for every conscience. What *is* important is that ethical concerns and analysis are given weight in the decision-making process, and that decisions are reached that maximize benefits and minimize negative consequences."

The Josephson Institute publishes a suggested code of "Ethical Values and Principles in Public Service."[30] These principles incorporate "the characteristics and values that most people associate with ethical behavior." An ethical decision would consider systematically "which, if any," of the principles are involved. To what degree and in what respects do you agree that "most people" accept these guidelines as components of ethical behavior? Although the code does not specifically focus on communication ethics, many of its elements could be adapted appropriately for communication. Which principles most easily apply to communication ethics and which ones seem largely irrelevant? Why?

I. *Honesty.* Honest persons are truthful, sincere, forthright, straightforward, frank, candid; they do not cheat, steal, lie, deceive, or act deviously.
II. *Integrity.* Persons with integrity are principled, honorable and upright; they are courageous and act on convictions; they will fight for their beliefs and will not adopt an ends justifies the means philosophy that ignores principles or be expedient at the expense of principle, be two-faced, or unscrupulous.
III. *Promise-Keeping.* Persons worthy of trust keep promises, fulfill commitments, abide by the spirit as well as the letter of an agreement; they do not interpret agreements in an unreasonably technical or legalistic manner in order to rationalize noncompliance or create justifications for escaping their commitments.
IV. *Fidelity.* Persons worthy of trust demonstrate fidelity and loyalty to persons and institutions by friendship in adversity, support and devotion to duty; they do not use or disclose information learned in confidence for personal or political advantage. They safeguard the ability to make independent professional judgments by scrupulously avoiding undue influences and conflicts of interest.
V. *Fairness.* Fair persons manifest a commitment to justice, the equal treatment of individuals, tolerance for and acceptance of diversity, and they are open-minded; they are willing to admit they are wrong, and where appropriate, change their positions and beliefs; they do not overreach or take undue advantage of another's mistakes or difficulties.
VI. *Caring.* Concern for the well-being of others manifests itself in compassion, giving, kindness and serving; it requires one to attempt to help those in need and to avoid harming others.
VII. *Respect.* Ethical persons demonstrate respect for human dignity, privacy, and the right to self-determination of all competent adults; they are courteous, and decent; they provide others with the information they need to make informed decisions about their own lives.
VIII. *Citizenship.* In a democracy, responsible citizenship is an ethical obligation; it involves lawfulness (abiding by laws and rules of society), participation (by voting and expressing informed views), social consciousness and public service; public sector professionals have the additional responsibility of encouraging participation of others and a special obligation to respect and honor democratic processes of decision making and avoiding unnecessary secrecy or concealment of information, and assuring that the citizenry has all the information needed to exercise responsible citizenship.
IX. *Excellence.* Ethical persons are concerned with the quality of their work; they pursue excellence, they are diligent, reliable, industrious, and committed. A public sector professional must be well informed and well prepared to exercise public authority.

X. *Accountability*. Ethical persons accept responsibility for decisions, for the foreseeable consequences of their actions and inactions, and for setting an example for others.

XI. *Protection of Public Trust*. Persons in the public sector have special obligations to lead by example, to safeguard and advance the integrity and reputation of the legislative process, to avoid even the appearance of impropriety, and to take whatever actions are necessary to correct or prevent inappropriate conduct of others.

Codes for Political Campaign Communication

For the 1976 presidential campaign, Common Cause, a national citizen lobbying organization, proposed a set of standards that still might aid voters in assessing the ethics of any political candidate's campaign. According to their criteria, an ethical candidate exhibits the following communication behavior:

1. Engages in unrehearsed communication with voters, including participation in open hearings and forums with other candidates on the same platform, where the public is given opportunities to express their concerns, ask questions, and follow up on their questions
2. Holds press conferences at least monthly throughout the campaign, and in every state where contesting a primary, at which reporters and broadcasters are freely permitted to ask questions and follow-up questions
3. Discusses issues which are high on the list of the people's concerns, as evidenced, for example, by national public opinion polls; clarifies alternatives and tradeoffs in a way that sets forth the real choices involved for the nation; and makes clear to the American people what choices he or she would make if elected to office
4. Makes public all information relating to a given poll if releasing or leaking any part of a campaign poll (including when and where the poll was conducted, by whom, a description of the sample of the population polled, as well as all questions and responses)
5. Allows interviews by a broad spectrum of TV, radio and newspaper reporters, including single interviewer formats which provide maximum opportunity for in-depth questions
6. Takes full public responsibility for all aspects of his or her campaign, including responsibility for campaign finance activities, campaign practices of staff, and campaign statements of principal spokespersons
7. Makes public a statement of personal financial holdings. . . .
8. Does not use taxpayer-supported services of any public office now held—such as staff, transportation or free mailing privileges—for campaign purposes, except as required for personal security reasons

Formal Codes of Ethics 213

9. Uses only advertising which stresses the record and viewpoint on issues of the candidates

The following Code of Ethics for Political Campaign Advertising was revised by the American Association of Advertising Agencies in 1984.

1. The advertising agency should not represent any candidate who has not signed or who does not observe the Code of Fair Campaign Practices of the Fair Campaign Practices Committee, endorsed by the A.A.A.A.
2. The agency should not knowingly misrepresent the views or stated record of any candidates nor quote them out of proper context.
3. The agency should not prepare any material which unfairly or prejudicially exploits the race, creed, or national origin or gender of any candidate.
4. The agency should take care to avoid unsubstantiated charges and accusations, especially those deliberately made too late in the campaign for opposing candidates to answer.
5. The agency should stand as an independent judge of fair campaign practices, rather than automatically yield to the wishes of the candidate or his authorized representatives.
6. The agency should not indulge in any practices which might be deceptive or misleading in word, photographs, film, or sound.

The Committee on Decent Unbiased Campaign Tactics (CONDUCT) is a nonpartisan citizen watchdog group in Chicago. This organization believes that some campaign tactics are "morally wrong, undermine the community peace and subvert the political process." CONDUCT provides a forum for all candidates and political parties to present complaints. If a complaint is substantiated and the offensive remark, statement or action is not publicly repudiated by the offender, CONDUCT will publicize both the refusal and its findings on the complaint.[31] CONDUCT urges candidates to pledge themselves to observe the following Code of Fair Campaign Practice. Candidates:

1. should not suggest directly or indirectly through speeches or campaign literature, that their opponents ought to be defeated because of their race, religion, national origin or gender.
2. should campaign among *all* the voters in the community they seek to represent or serve, being careful not to systematically exclude neighborhoods or groups other than their own.
3. should not appeal to negative stereotypes or hostilities based on race, religion, ethnicity, gender or other irrelevant group identification.
4. should not seek to gain support by arousing or exploiting the fears of one group toward other, different groups.

5. should not use pamphlets, flyers, code words or advertising which appeal to bigotry or fear.
6. should publicly condemn bigoted literature, statements or actions in support of their candidacy or in opposition to their opponent.
7. should be accountable for the actions of their campaign staffs relative to this code.

Spero's Proposed Code for Televised Political Campaign Advertisements

In his book, *The Duping of the American Voter: Dishonesty and Deception in Presidential Television Advertising*, Robert Spero proposes a comprehensive program to "break the back" of political campaign advertisements, especially those on television.[32] Some elements of his program would alter significantly the nature of our election processes: abolish the Electoral College; limit presidents and senators to one (long) term of office; shorten the length of national political campaigns. Other elements relate to the role of the Federal Communications Commission. New FCC regulations would require that political television advertisements be five minutes or longer in length, that candidates actually appear in their advertisements, and that such advertisements "consist only of the candidate speaking directly to the viewer."

Free national television time offered equally to all qualified candidates but under specified guidelines also is part of Spero's program. Time blocks would range from 15 to 60 minutes. Varied formats would be utilized: candidates explaining their views and policies; direct-clash debates between candidates; unscreened questioning by journalists, political scientists, citizen representatives, etc. Neither film nor tape could be edited. Programs provided by the candidate depicting his or her biography and political accomplishments would be forbidden.

Spero proposes that state legislatures pass laws requiring the licensing of political media specialists and advisors, including rigorous standards for certification and provisions for review following each election. He also advocates use of interactive (two-way) cable television, such as the Qube system, to allow average citizens and interested experts to respond almost immediately to unethical advertising practices or to offer omitted viewpoints.

At the heart of Spero's program would be a new "tough public interest group" that would administer a new code of ethics and operate a Political Fact Bank. Such a code and group can be established without legislation.

The Political Fact Bank would, in computerized form, include facts on a candidate's education, work experience, public service, wealth, past and present accomplishments claimed, past promises broken, and past and present positions on major issues. Also the bank would contain statistics and facts, compiled by nonpartisan experts, on major national and international issues and problems; this would facilitate double-checking of factual claims made by candidates. Candidates would be requested to put facts concerning their policies and backgrounds on the bank file.

The administrative group implementing the new code of ethics would not wait to receive complaints, but would actively monitor key campaigns to seek out violations and quickly expose them. Broadcast and print journalists would be furnished on a regular basis (daily near the end of a campaign) with news of code violations. Additionally, the administrative group could publish its findings in the form of counter-advertisements, primarily in newspapers and weekly news magazines. Descriptions of code violations could be sent to various educational, religious, legal, business, labor, and citizen action organizations, such as Common Cause or the League of Women Voters, who could report the violations in their own publications. Here in detail is Spero's new proposed code of ethics.

A New Code of Political Campaign Ethics and Citizen Action[33]

The code that follows would apply to all forms of political advertising but would deal primarily with television. The code would provide a simple yet comprehensive test of the character, background, intent, policies, and promises of those people who would govern the country.

The code, while paying ample attention to what candidates say about each other, would concentrate on the claims and representations they make about themselves.

Politicians would *not* be allowed to sign the code and so attempt to make political capital from the act. The code functions not for the politician's benefit but for the public benefit; the code works whether or not politicians agree with it or like it.

Much of the code is modeled on the present codes of the television networks and the National Association of Broadcasters for product advertising, the codes used here as a standard to measure false and deceptive presidential campaign advertising. The code would apply to political advertising at any level. Although the television networks and stations are legally prohibited from enforcing violations of their codes by political advertising,

216 Chapter Ten

it would soon become clear to the public from the work of the political code's administrative group what those violations were, who was guilty, how, and why. Political smear, the bulwark of the old code of the Fair Campaign Practices Committee, would constitute but one of many possible violations of the new code.

Code Standards for Political Television Commercials

General Principles

The public accepts political advertising only after securing satisfactory evidence of:
1. Integrity of advertising and the candidate on whose behalf it has been purchased.
2. Availability of service or programs promised by the candidate.
3. Realistic chances of making good on promises.
4. Existence of support for claims made by candidate and authentication of demonstrations.
5. Acceptable taste of the presentation.

Unacceptable Presentations, Approaches, and Techniques

1. Claims or representations which have the capacity to deceive, mislead, or misrepresent.
2. Claims that unfairly attack opponents, political parties, or institutions.
3. Unqualified references to the safety of a political position, program, or claim if "normal" execution of the position, program, or claim is found to represent a hazard to the public. (Example: a candidate's claim of the safety of nuclear energy.)
4. "Bait and switch" tactics which feature campaign promises not intended to be carried out but are designed to lure the public into voting for the candidate or party making the promise.
5. The use of "subliminal perception" or other techniques attempting to convey information to the viewer by transmitting messages below the threshold of normal awareness.
6. Use of visual devices, effects, or juxtaposition which attempt to deceive.
7. Use of sound effects to deceive.
8. The misuse of distress signals. (Example: a politician's claim that the nation is in poor condition, as in John F. Kennedy's "missile gap" charge.)
9. Use of the flag, national emblems, anthems, and monuments to gain campaign advantage. (Example: an incumbent president using the White House as a setting for a commercial.)
10. Use of the Office of the President of the United States or any governmental body to gain campaign advantage.

11. Interpersonal acts of violence and antisocial behavior or other dramatic devices inconsistent with prevailing standards of taste and propriety. (Example: Nixon's use of Vietnamese civilian and American military suffering for his own benefit in his 1968 commercials.)
12. Damaging stereotyping, including deliberately staged stereotyping of his or her own image by the candidate. (Example: Carter's "peanut farmer" image.)
13. Unsupported or exaggerated promises to the public of employment or earnings.
14. Preemption of the truth. (Example: a candidate's claiming that a policy is his or hers alone when other candidates also favor it.)
15. Altering of opinion on an issue from market to market to cater to audiences with different views.
16. The use of "guilt by association."
17. Playing on the public's fears. (Example: a candidate's claim of the necessity for what are in fact redundant weapons systems.)
18. Creating fear in voters. (Example: a candidate describes an alleged flaw in an opponent without showing how he or she is different; a candidate blames an opponent for a condition for which the opponent is not responsible; a candidate alleges that an opponent cannot solve a problem without telling how he or she would solve it.)
19. Changing facts and conditions. (The facts and/or conditions stated in a candidate's commercial may change as the campaign progresses, thereby rendering a once valid commercial unfair or misleading.)

Comparative Advertising

Opponents identified in the advertising must actually be in competition with one another.

Research and Surveys

1. Reference may be made to the results of bona fide surveys or research relating to the candidate or campaign advertised, provided the results do not create an impression that the research does not support.
2. "Bandwagon" commercials shall be subject to careful scrutiny for misleading effect. (Example: from dozens of "people on the street" interviews a half dozen are edited to appear in rapid order, the individuals speaking in simplistic phrases of the candidate's alleged attributes: "He's honest," "She's truthful." This technique may create the illusion that vast numbers of voters share these beliefs.)

Testimonials

1. Testimonials used, in whole or in part, must honestly reflect, in spirit and content, the sentiments of the individuals represented.

2. All claims and statements, including subjective evaluations of testifiers, must be supportable by facts and free of misleading implications.
3. If presented in the candidate's own words, testimonials shall contain no statement that cannot be supported.

Last-Minute Campaign Charges

No campaign charges against an opponent are acceptable in commercial form, including claims which appear to be valid, unless equal time in the same prime time period is granted to the opponent. If the opponent cannot afford to pay for a last-minute commercial in rebuttal to the charges, then either the station must provide free time or the candidate making the charges must pay for the opponent's commercial.

Would this code of ethics, if instituted, be effective? You are encouraged to evaluate it in light of our previous discussion of weaknesses and use of formal codes. Predictably, Spero himself believes the code would be effective in the long run. The code functions, he contends, to "provide a public benchmark, a reasonable standard, by which to measure those who would wish to lead us." While no code can "end corruption, malfeasance, arrogance, and lies," such a code as this one would "force the offending politician into the light," there to "squirm, if only briefly." Then citizens would have to determine what to do about the politician.

Notes

[1] See Jay Black and Ralph Barney, "The Case Against Media Codes of Ethics," *Journal of Mass Media Ethics*, 1 (Fall/Winter 1985–1986): 27–36; Clifford Christians, "Enforcing Media Codes of Ethics," *Journal of Mass Media Ethics*, 1 (Fall/Winter 1985–1986): 14–21; John C. Merrill, *Existential Journalism* (New York: Hastings House, 1977), pp. 129–138; Merrill, "Professionalization: Danger to Press Freedom and Pluralism," *Journal of Mass Media Ethics*, 1 (Spring/Summer 1986): 56–60; M. Cash Mathews, *Strategic Intervention in Organizations: Resolving Ethical Dilemmas* (Newbury Park, CA: Sage, 1988), pp. 51–82; William S. Howell, *The Empathic Communicator* (1982; reissue, Prospect Heights, IL: Waveland Press, 1986, pp. 188, 197; John L. Hulteng, *The Messenger's Motives: Ethical Problems of the News Media*, 2d ed. (Englewood Cliffs, NJ: Prentice-Hall, 1985), pp. 205–7; Dan Nimmo, "Ethical Issues in Political Communication," *Communication* 6, no. 2 (1981): 193–212.

[2] John Kultgen, "Evaluating Professional Codes of Ethics," in *Profits and Professions: Essays on Business and Professional Ethics*, eds. Wade L. Robison, et al. (Clifton, NJ: Humana, 1983), pp. 225–64.

[3] Richard DeGeorge, *Business Ethics*, 2d ed. (New York: Macmillan, 1986), pp. 341–42; Deni Elliott-Boyle, "A Conceptual Analysis of Ethical Codes," *Journal of Mass Media Ethics*, 1 (Fall/Winter 1985–1986): 22–26.

[4] Kultgen, "Evaluating Professional Codes of Ethics," p. 251.

[5] Kultgen, "Evaluating," pp. 232–35; Philip Meyer, *Ethical Journalism* (New York: Longman, 1987), p. 22.

[6] DeGeorge, *Business Ethics*, 2d ed., p. 342.

[7] Kultgen, "Evaluating," pp. 257–60.

[8] DeGeorge, *Business Ethics*, 2d ed., p. 342.

[9] DeGeorge, *Business Ethics*, 2d ed., p. 346; Kultgen, "Evaluating," p. 239.

[10] DeGeorge, *Business Ethics*, 2d ed., pp. 343–44; Michael D. Bayles, *Professional Ethics* (Belmont, CA: Wadsworth, 1981), p. 24.

[11] DeGeorge, *Business Ethics*, 2d ed., p. 345.

[12] Lucinda D. Davenport and Ralph S. Izard, "Restrictive Policies of the Mass Media," *Journal of Mass Media Ethics*, 1 (Fall/Winter 1985–1986): 4–9; Kultgen, "Evaluating," pp. 247–50; Christians, "Enforcing Media Codes of Ethics," p. 19.

[13] DeGeorge, *Business Ethics*, 2d ed., p. 342; Kultgen, "Evaluating," pp. 250–53; Bayles, *Professional Ethics*, 139–43; Norman E. Bowie, "Business Codes of Ethics: Window Dressing or Legitimate Alternative to Government Regulation?" in *Ethical Theory and Business*, Tom L. Beauchamp and Norman E. Bowie, eds. (Englewood Cliffs, NJ: Prentice-Hall, 1979), pp. 236–38.

[14] Davenport and Izard, "Restrictive Policies of the Mass Media," p. 8; DeGeorge, *Business Ethics*, 2d ed., p. 347; Marvin N. Olasky, "Ministers or Panderers: Issues Raised by the Public Relations Society Code of Standards," *Journal of Mass Media Ethics*, 1 (Fall/Winter 1985–1986): p. 46.

[15] Christians, "Enforcing Media Codes of Ethics," pp. 18–19; DeGeorge, *Business Ethics*, 2d ed. p. 344; H. Eugene Goodwin, *Groping for Ethics in Journalism*, 2d ed. (Ames: Iowa State University Press, 1987), pp. 16–17, 158, 179–80, 229–33, 352–53; Bruce Swain, *Reporter's Ethics* (Ames: Iowa State University Press, 1978), pp. xi, 85, 114, 116–34; Donald G. Jones, ed., *Doing Ethics in Business: New Ventures in Management Development* (Cambridge, MA: Oelgeschlager, Gunn and Hain, 1982).

[16] Richard E. Crable and Steven L. Vibbert, *Public Relations as Communication Management* (Edina, MN: Bellwether, 1986), pp. 111–12, 120–24; Kultgen, "Evaluating," pp. 247–50.

[17] Sissela Bok, *Lying: Moral Choice in Public and Private Life* (New York: Vintage, 1979), p. 260; Thomas M. Garrett, *Ethics in Business* (New York: Sheed and Ward, 1963), pp. 166–68; Earl W. Kintner and Robert W. Green, "Opportunities for Self-Enforcement Codes of Conduct," in *Ethics, Free Enterprise, and Public Policy*, Richard T. DeGeorge and Joseph A. Pichler, eds. (New York: Oxford University Press, 1978), pp. 249–50; DeGeorge, *Business Ethics*, 2d ed., 345–46; Christians, "Enforcing Media Codes of Ethics," p. 25; Meyer, *Ethical Journalism*, p. 20.

[18] Meyer, *Ethical Journalism*, pp. 23–24.

[19] DeGeorge, *Business Ethics*, 2d ed., p. 346.

[20] Richard E. Crable, "Ethical Codes, Accountability, and Argumentation," *Quarterly Journal of Speech*, 64 (February 1978): 23–32.

[21] Peter Brown, "Assessing Public Officials," in *Public Duties*, Joel Fleishman, et al., eds. (Cambridge: Harvard University Press, 1981), pp. 291–94.

[22] Karen Lebacqz, *Professional Ethics: Power and Paradox* (Nashville: Abingdon, 1985), pp. 63–91.

[23] Charles S. Levy, "On the Development of a Code of Ethics," *Social Work*, 19 (March 1974): 207–16.

[24] Crable and Vibbert, *Public Relations as Communication Management*, p. 116.

[25] Olasky, "Ministers or Panderers," pp. 44–45.

[26] This possible inconsistency was suggested by the analysis of John Llewellyn, "Spinning Flacks into Gold: The Rhetorical Effect of the National Association of Government Communicators' Statement of Ethics," presented at the Southern Speech Communication Convention, Houston, April 1986. The NAGC code is very similar to the PRSA code.

[27] "PRSA Code of Professional Standards for the Practice of Public Relations: History of Enforcement 1952–1985," funded by the Foundation for Public Relations Research and Education (1987). Also see Otis W. Baskin and Craig E. Aronoff, *Public Relations*, 3rd ed. (Dubuque, IA: Wm. C. Brown, 1992), pp. 97–99.

[28] Olasky, "Ministers or Panderers," pp. 45–47. Also see Robert Kaus, "There's No Shame Anymore," *Harper's* (August 1982).

[29] Baskin and Aronoff, *Public Relations*, 3rd ed., p. 99.

[30] The Josephson Institute programs and code are presented in its quarterly journal, *Ethics: Easier Said Than Done*, 1 (Spring/Summer 1988). This entire issue focuses on ethics in government. The code is reprinted by permission of the Institute. A longer analysis and proposal is W. J. Michael Cody and Richardson R. Lynn, *Honest Government: An Ethics Guide for Public Service* (Westport, CT: Praeger, 1992).

[31] For example, see the *Chicago Tribune*, February 25, 1989, pp. A1, A6.

[32] Robert Spero, *The Duping of the American Voter: Dishonesty and Deception in Presidential Television Advertising* (New York: Lippincott and Crowell, 1980), especially ch. 10 and the concluding "Last Notes on the Next Election."

[33] From pp. 204–7 in *The Duping of the American Voter* by Robert Spero (Lippincott-Crowell). Copyright 1980 by Robert Spero. Reprinted by permission of Harper & Row, Publishers.

Chapter 11

Feminist Contributions

Feminism is not a concept with a single, universally accepted definition. For our purposes, elements of definitions provided by Barbara Bate and by Julia Wood are helpful.[1] Feminism holds that both women and men are complete and important human beings and that societal barriers (typically constructed through language processes) have prevented women from being perceived and treated as valued persons of equal worth with men. Feminism involves commitment to equality and respect for life. Feminism rejects oppression and domination as desirable values and believes that difference need not be equated with inferiority or undesirability. And the feminist movement is not a monolithic, unitary social movement. Indeed, Wood describes a number of branches of the feminist movement: radical feminism; middle-class liberal feminism; separatism; structural feminists; lesbian feminists; and womanists.[2]

So, too, with feminist ethics. Alison Jaggar concludes her survey of issues in feminist ethics by noting that "feminist ethics, far from being a rigid orthodoxy, instead is a ferment of ideas and controversy. . . ."[3] In general, however, feminist ethicists offer critiques of male-dominated ethical traditions with special focus on ways in which traditional ethics have functioned to subordinate or trivialize women's ethical experience; rather, the moral experiences of women are worthy of equal respect. Among other things, feminist ethicists question the privileging of rationality over emotion, of universalizability and detachment over particularity and engagement, of the public sphere of discourse over the private sphere, and of individualism over relationships. Feminist scholars argue the case against sexist language, and some argue for the necessity to slant the truth in order to survive in a male-dominated world.[4]

Feminist ethicists, along with postmodern social critics and some other contemporary ethicists, challenge the standard image of the moral agent in traditional masculine-dominated Western philosophy—the autonomous, unencumbered, individual self deciding ethical questions objectively about abstract others apart from the social, economic, and institutional contexts in which that self is imbedded and constructed. Rather, feminist ethicists envision a situated or contextualized self imbedded in a web of relationships, roles, and responsibilities, making decisions about concrete, particular persons.[5] Some feminists remind us that gender is only one of a number of important interrelated situational variables, including ethnicity/race, economic/social class, age, marital status, and sexual orientation that must be considered in building adequate ethical theory and making sensitive ethical decisions.[6]

Traditional male-oriented European-American ethical theories generally have ignored a significant realm of ethical activity—the realm of interpersonal ethics. Traditional ethics has paid scant attention to the moral significance of family and friendship relationships and of emotions such as sympathy, compassion, care, and concern for individual others. Manning reminds us that these are "issues that arise in what is called the private sphere, a sphere that has been seen, in the Western tradition, as the province of women. Men were identified with the public sphere." And Jaggar argues that a key requirement for an adequate feminist ethic is that "it should be equipped to handle moral issues in both the so-called public and private domains."[7]

An Ethic of Care: Gilligan, Noddings, Manning, Tronto, and Wood

While acknowledging the diversity and ferment within contemporary feminist ethics, Virginia Held believes that "the ethic of care" is the "phrase which is gathering most support as a way of designating an alternative feminist moral outlook. While no label seems adequate yet, 'care' seems to come closest, and to contrast well with traditional approaches based on rationality, rules, and the conceptualization of morality in terms of such public or political concerns as justice, liberty, or equality."[8] We will examine now some of the different versions of an ethic of care that feminists have developed and touch on some of the issues raised by such conceptions.

The first version to be developed, and the one which generated considerable scholarly response that supported or criticized, elaborated or modified that version, is by developmental psychologist Carol Gilligan. In her book, *In a Different Voice*, Gilligan critiques the work of others and presents her own research on the sequence or stages of individual human moral development. Gilligan contends that many studies of human moral development, such as the work of Lawrence Kohlberg, generalized the experiences and views of men as adequate to describe moral development for both men and women. With male standards taken as universal, moral judgments made by women frequently are viewed as deficient. In contrast, Gilligan argues that in contemporary American culture there are two different but valuable and potentially complementary moral "voices" of full adulthood. These male and female voices, while typically manifested in men and women respectively, are modes of thought and themes that could be found either in men or women.[9]

An *ethic of justice*, according to Gilligan, characterizes the male moral voice. Rooted in a desire for individual autonomy and independence, the ethic of justice centers on the balance of competing rights and claims of one's self and others. This male moral voice is rule-centered and embodies a logic of equality and fairness. Everyone should be treated the same. In contrast, an *ethic of care* characterizes the female moral voice. Rooted in the primacy of relationships and the interdependence of self and others, compassion and nurturance are standards that help resolve conflicting responsibilities to all concerned, including self. The female moral voice considers the needs both of self and others, not just the survival of one's self and not just avoidance of hurting others. Ideally, no one should be hurt. While justice and fairness are important, moral decisions should make allowances for differences in needs.[10]

A number of controversies exist over research on human moral development. You can examine some of the evidence and argument on the issues in Lawrence Kohlberg's book, *The Psychology of Moral Development: The Nature and Validity of Moral Stages*, and in a published symposium, "On *In a Different Voice*: An Interdisciplinary Forum."[11] My purpose here is not to debate or resolve the controversies, but an awareness of some of them should stimulate your thoughtful examination of communication ethics generally and of versions of an ethic of care specifically. To what degree does an ethic of justice characterize American men and an ethic of care characterize American women? In what ways do the ethics of justice and care typify men and women in other cultures? How frequently does a man (or woman) combine *both* justice and care as standards for deciding the moral thing to do in a particular situation? Does the specific nature of a situation seem to determine whether justice or care is the ethical framework primarily to be applied? Are people in certain occupations, such as law or counseling, more prone to use one rather than the other of these moral stances? If the two characteristic moral voices exist, are they primarily due to biological differences or to divergent cultural training?

Another version appears in *Caring: A Feminine Approach to Ethics and Moral Education* by Nel Noddings. Noddings grounds her ethic of caring in a kind of human nature ethical perspective. Her bedrock assumption is that "relation"—human encounter and emotional response—is a "basic fact of human existence." Natural caring is a relation which humans innately long and strive for and which they recognize as desirable. We "respond as one-caring out of love or natural inclination." Natural caring motivates ethical caring. "We want to be *moral* in order to remain in the caring relation and to enhance the ideal of ourselves as one-caring."[12]

Although Noddings intentionally avoids formal definition of a care ethic, she does at various points underscore what clearly are central dimensions of a caring relation.[13] *Engrossment*, the one-caring being engrossed in the needs of the one cared-for, permeates to some degree all caring. The one-caring is fully disposed and attentive toward the cared-for, has regard for the other, desires the other's well-being, and is responsive and receptive to the other. Noddings echoes Buber's concept of "being present" in describing engrossment. Through *motivational displacement* the one-caring retains but moves beyond her or his own interests to an empathy for or "feeling with" the experiences and views of the cared-for. Noddings draws upon Martin Buber's concept of "inclusion" to describe motivational displacement. The one-caring does strive to accurately and nonselectively understand both emotionally and intellectually the position of the cared-for. The one-caring accepts the motives and intentions and freedom of choice of the cared-for as long as they do not require abandonment of the one-caring's own ethical ideal. *Reciprocity* is required by the cared-for in order to complete the caring relationship. Here, again, Noddings has employed Martin Buber's concepts to elaborate her view. Reciprocity is not a contractual arrangement, nor does it demand one-to-one exchange of equal contributions. In Noddings's words: "The freedom, creativity, and spontaneous disclosure of the cared-for that manifest themselves under the nurture of the one-caring complete the relation. . . . What the cared-for gives to the relation either in direct response to the one-caring or in personal delight or in happy growth before her eyes is genuine reciprocity."

Noddings rejects "principles and rules as the major guide to ethical behavior." They are, she believes, too "ambiguous and unstable" because they always imply exceptions and foster divisiveness and denigration toward persons who hold "different" principles. The one-caring should not depend entirely or even primarily on rules—upon "a prior determination of what is fair and equitable." The one-caring is suspicious of rules and principles, "formulates and holds them loosely, tentatively," and persists in focusing on particular concrete persons and relations. At the same time, the one-caring is willing to develop principles rooted in concrete experience. Noddings also rejects the traditional ethical requirement of universalizability—the requirement that an ethical rule or principle that applies to me in my circumstances must also apply equally and universally to all other persons in similar circumstances. But Noddings does describe aspects of her ethic of caring as having universality. "The caring attitude," she argues, "that attitude which expressed our earliest memories of being cared for and our growing store of memories of both caring and being cared for, is universally accessible." Noddings contends that while caring stems most naturally from the experiences of women (childbirth and child-rearing), the ethic of caring is available universally to both women and men. She believes that we have a primary, ongoing, and universal "obligation to meet the other as one-caring."[14]

Although Noddings rejects the primacy of rules and principles in ethics, she does describe a guide for our conduct, namely, the "ethical ideal."[15] The ethical ideal is "our best picture of ourselves caring and being cared for." It is our remembered image of the way we have been in genuine caring relationships and situations both as one-caring and as cared-for. That image changes as our caring experiences multiply. It also may be influenced by our insights gained from a person who is superior to us in caring. "It is limited by what we already have done and by what we are capable of, and it does not idealize the impossible so that we may escape into ideal abstraction." As the three most significant means of nurturing the ethical ideal, Noddings describes processes of practice, dialogue, and confirmation. Again, the latter two reflect in part Buber's philosophy of dialogic communication.

Noddings limits the realm of her ethic primarily if not wholly to that of the private sphere of family, friendship, education, and intimate relationships. She offers little insight concerning whether or how an ethic of caring might apply in public arenas such as business and politics, organizations and institutions, and economic and social policy both nationally and internationally. Linda Bell criticizes Noddings's ethic of caring as "too limited, too personal, and ultimately apolitical." In a relationship of ethical caring in the private sphere, Noddings believes: "We are not out to transform the world, but we are allowing ourselves to be transformed." Bell's criticism is that Noddings's "focus on individual relationships obscures and allows her not to worry about responsibility for and obligations to do something about complicity in systems of oppression . . . throughout the world."[16]

Rita Manning presents her version of an ethic of care in her book, *Speaking from the Heart: A Feminist Perspective on Ethics*. On some points she holds views similar to Noddings, but on others she differs. Like Noddings, Manning grounds her ethic of care in a type of human nature perspective. Manning believes that "we need not reject conceptions of human nature as providing a foundation for morality" and that "an ethic of care requires a new conception of human nature" which involves "a picture of humans as essentially involved with relationships with other humans." The moral bedrock of the "obligation to care . . . rests on our human capacity for caring interaction." In addition, Manning sees the ethic of care as appropriate for all humans, both women and men, and does not link it to sex and gender.[17]

At some length Manning describes her version:

> An ethic of care involves morality grounded in relationships and response. When we are committed to an ethic of care, we see ourselves as part of a network of care and our obligation as requiring a caring response to those who share those networks and to those whose need creates an obligation to respond. In responding we do not appeal to abstract principles though we may appeal to rules of thumb; rather, we pay attention to the concrete other in his or her real situation. We also pay attention to the effect of our response on the networks of care that sustain us both.

In the care ethic the "importance of intimacy and connection to others is assumed." No one is expendable or simply a vehicle for utility. "Ties of affection, trust, and loyalty matter." Compromise and accommodation are valued in the search for solutions that try to accommodate everyone. Manning argues that "one need not respond to every need." We must consider carefully how and when to respond, the seriousness of the other's need, the benefit of our response to the one needing care, our capacity to respond to a particular need, and the competing needs of others (including oneself) affected by responding to the need. With attention focused on particular persons in an ethic of care, there must be recognition of all relevant facts of a situation and sensitive understanding of potential outcomes. Further, we must be willing to relate to the other on an emotional level.[18]

There are situations and contexts where rules and rights and an ethic of justice are most appropriate, notes Manning, and other occasions where relationship and response and an ethic of care are most relevant. Manning does not agree with Noddings's rejection of rules as moral guides. There are situations, perhaps in guiding our actions toward strangers, where tentative moral rules of thumb and principles based on our experiences with intimates are appropriate guides. For Manning, rules and rights could serve three purposes: (1) To persuade others who only will see a situation in terms of rules and rights; (2) to set a minimum standard of morality and provide some protection for the marginalized and helpless; and (3) to be used in deliberating about the needs of those persons to be cared for with whom we are not in direct relationship. Although Manning does not discuss the point at great length, she does emphasize that an adequate care ethic must have relevance to both the public and private spheres. Caring persons must work for changes in institutions, organizations, policies, and programs that would facilitate a caring world where all persons are able to "respond to his/her demands of care for self and other."[19]

In her book, *Moral Boundaries: A Political Argument for an Ethic of Care*, Joan Tronto develops her version of a care ethic primarily in the context of the public sphere of politics and power relationships. While an ethic of care clearly is relevant to private situations and intimate relationships, Tronto argues that such an ethic should have significant application in the public political and social contexts. She explores at length the ways in which care is valued and devalued, facilitated and undermined, strengthened and weakened by cultural norms, institutional structures, political policies, and power imbalances. She contends that if we "look at questions of race, class, and gender, we notice that those who are least well off in society are disproportionately those who do the work of caring and that the best-off members of society often use their positions of superiority to pass off caring work to others." She believes that the "world will look different if we move care from its current peripheral location to a place near the center of human life."[20] Tronto also argues that an ethic of care and an ethic of justice both are needed to address the significant issues in current moral theory. She does not view the ethic of care as unique or limited to women and that of justice to men. She stresses that an ethic of care "is incomplete unless imbedded in a theory of justice," that "justice without a notion of care is incomplete," and that an "ethic of care remains incomplete without a political theory of care."[21]

In a very general sense, Tronto views caring as all activities that we do "*to maintain, continue, and repair our 'world' so that we can live in it as well as possible.* That world includes our bodies, ourselves, and our environment, all of which we seek to interweave in a complex, life-sustaining web." She suggests four phases of caring as an ongoing process. First, *caring about* involves recognition that a need exists, recognition that caring is necessary, and understanding of the position of the person or group in need. Second, *taking care of* involves "assuming some responsibility for the identified need" and deciding concretely how to respond to it. Third, *care-giving* involves actually caring through direct contact and physical work. The giving of money is more properly categorized as taking care of rather than care-giving. Fourth, *care-receiving* involves the actual responses of the cared-for and allows assessment of the adequacy of our care efforts. From these four phases derive four "ethical elements of care." *Attentiveness*, in a sense, means "to suspend one's own goals, ambitions, plans of life, and concerns, in order to recognize and to be attentive to others." *Responsibility* differs, Tronto contends, from obligation. In matters of obligation we look to formal relationships, formal agreements, explicit promises, formal rules, and agreed-upon duties. Responsibility looks beyond obligation, for example, to what our direct and indirect role may have been in contributing to the circumstances that give rise to the need for care and to whether we are somehow uniquely the most capable of giving the needed care. *Competence* demands that the caring work is performed competently thus demonstrating that one truly cares. Except when adequate resources are lacking, competence is a necessary "part of the moral quality of care." And in a broader context, those in authority who should provide adequate resources for the care-giver should be held accountable. *Responsiveness* of the care-receiver to the care is the fourth moral element in an ethic of care. Responsiveness as a moral precept should alert us to potential abuses that may arise from inequality or vulnerability of the care-receiver. We must exercise caution in presuming to know accurately the needs of the care-receiver. Rather than projecting ourself into the other's position as a way of understanding the other's needs, we should "consider the other's position as the other expressed it." In sum, Tronto believes that an ethic of care in society necessitates "an assessment of needs in a social and political, as well as a personal, context."[22]

Who Cares? Women, Care, and Culture is the book that presents Julia Wood's version of an ethic of care, although she does not overtly label it as an ethic. She identifies three qualities that our culture values in care givers: (1) *Partiality* involves focusing with feeling directly on the context and the "concrete perspectives, needs, concerns, and the like of particular others"; (2) *empathy* involves having "insight into the others' perspectives, feelings, and needs"; and (3) *willingness to serve or nurture others*. In Wood's view, the care giver should develop a flexible sense of individual autonomy in which value is given both to the relationships with others and to one's own needs and interests. Later Wood moves from these general orientations that mark caring to "more concrete activities and mental proclivities that comprise caring." *Responsiveness to others* involves "deciding to focus on another, responding to others as a means of affirming their presence and value, and listening and observing carefully in order to discern what it is that another means by her or his behaviors." *Sensitivity to others* involves listening to others on their own terms (not yours), "learning to recognize and interpret patterns in their thoughts, feelings, and activities, and figuring out what their ways of indicating various things are." *Acceptance of others* involves an openness and nonjudgmentalism toward others that encourages them to express their beliefs, feelings, and needs. *Patience* requires a willingness to proceed at the other's pace, "to lay aside one's own schedule in order to accommodate others without making them seem burdensome or slow." *Dynamic autonomy* involves an interdependent sense of self and an ability to appropriately choose when to emphasize one's own desires, plans, and viewpoints and when to emphasize those of others in cooperation or relationship with them.[23]

Wood especially criticizes Noddings for limiting an ethic of care primarily to the private, interpersonal sphere. Wood criticizes Gilligan's view of the care ethic on a number of grounds, but she especially faults Gilligan for using language and examples (despite Gilligan's opening disclaimers to the contrary) that force a dichotomy between the natures and abilities of women and men and force the association of the care ethic with women and the justice ethic with men. Wood emphasizes that care is a capacity that can and should be nurtured in both women and men (just as justice should be).[24]

Wood examines at length how in Western culture care has been structured to be seen as primarily applicable in the private, personal realm, has been designated the primary responsibility of women and subordinates, and has been devalued as of less societal worth than work (usually by men) in the public realm. She also investigates the ways in which discourse (both individual language habits and institutional communication practices) have structured this view of care. Finally Wood describes sites where changes in public discourse may influence changes in institutions and policies related to public perception and practice regarding care: governmental actions; business and industrial innovations; educational institutional change; local community efforts. Wood concludes: "Liberated from its historical situatedness in the private sphere and women's domain, we can now recover the idea of caring as a responsibility and privilege of us all and as a central concern of public life."[25]

"Telling It Slant": Women and Lying

"Telling it slant" is a phrase from a poem by Emily Dickinson that some feminists have adopted to describe a way of speaking that they believe is forced upon women by a male-dominated society. According to Shirley Ardener, public discourse has been encoded by men; women need to monitor or transform their meanings to conform to male requirements. Muted group theory explains that the language of a culture does not serve all its speakers equally. Women are "muted" because the words for speaking are not generated from or descriptive of *women's* experiences; the language women use is derivative because it developed from a male perception of reality. There is a block between experience and the verbal expression of those feelings. Shirley Ardener refers to this block as a necessary indirectness rather than spontaneity. Tillie Olsen refers to it as telling it slant. Gillian Michell defines this phrase as a "way of speaking that conveys a message by distorting the truth somehow, so that what is conveyed is not the whole truth." Such a statement distorts the truth or withholds it in some way without actually being completely false.[26]

Michell gives the example of a woman who "tells it slant" when stating "Joan and Bob don't always agree with one another" rather than precisely describing the situation as "Joan and Bob fight constantly with one another." While telling it slant might be viewed as falling somewhere between being truthful and lying, Michell notes that usually it would be categorized as a lie according to Sissela Bok's conception in her book, *Lying*. You may want to review Bok's conception as summarized earlier in chapter 7, "Some Basic Issues." Usually, telling it slant would be an intentionally deceptive message meant to make others believe what we personally do not believe.

Earlier in the chapter entitled "Interpersonal Communication and Small Group Discussion" I explored a possible ethic for everyday conversation extended from the work of philosopher H. P. Grice. Recall that Grice assumes that contributions by participants will be appropriate for the purpose and stage of conversation. To guide adequate conversation, Grice presents the maxims of *quantity*, *quality*, *relation*, and *manner*. Gillian Michell argues that Grice's rules are applicable most probably for white, male, middle-class conversation. Michell contends that the constraints of a sexist society frequently require that women tell it slant, and thus they could be judged as violating one or more of Grice's rules.

Michell sees telling it slant as ethically excusable and justifiable. First, telling it slant often is the most effective way for a woman to exchange information in a sexist setting—the best way to get her point across in a workable manner. Constraints on women's rights and options in male-dominated conversations are so potent in our patriarchal society that women are forced to tell it slant in order to survive or be successful. Second, concern for not hurting her hearer often motivates a woman to tell it slant. Recall here the "ethic of care" earlier analyzed in this chapter as the characteristic moral voice of women. Michell speculates that women also may sometimes tell it slant to "protect" men from views of reality with which men could not cope. An unfortunate consequence of telling it slant is that women may "lose the habit of telling it straight, even with those who have no real power over us, such as our female peers." Telling it slant, believes Michell, denies to both women and men the adequate information about life's complexities that they may need for sound decisions.

Carefully consider Michell's conclusion. "We see women are faced with a dilemma. If we tell it straight, our truth is not communicated effectively; if we tell it slant, what is communicated effectively is not really our truth. This dilemma complicates moral choices about truth telling for women in the most ordinary circumstances. It may be that for a woman to tell the truth requires more courage and requires it more often than we had thought."

Now what is your own personal viewpoint on telling it slant? Is it most accurately labeled as lying or as something else? Is it morally justifiable? Why? In your own experience, is telling it slant more characteristic of women than men in contemporary American culture? To what extent do you agree with Gillian Michell's analysis?

Rhetoric, Persuasion, Communication, and Mass Communication

"My indictment of our discipline of rhetoric springs from my belief that any intent to persuade is an act of violence." Thus Sally Miller Gearhart opens her attack on rhetoric-as-persuasion because it reflects a masculine-oriented, "conquest/conversion mentality."[27] Traditional views of rhetoric have assumed that "it is a proper and even a necessary function to attempt to change others." The conquest/conversion model for persuasion is subtle and insidious, says Gearhart, "because it gives the illusion of integrity.... In the conversion model we work very hard not simply to conquer but to give every assurance that our conquest of the victim is really giving her what she wants." Gearhart contends that the rational discourse of traditional rhetoric actually is a "subtle form of Might Makes Right." Teachers of rhetoric, she argues, "have been training a competent breed of weapons specialists who are skilled in emotional maneuvers, experts in intellectual logistics...."

Based upon feminist assumptions, Gearhart offers a particular view of "communication" as a more desirable and ethical alternative. This view of communication involves "deliberate creation or co-creation of an atmosphere in which people and things, if and only if they have the internal basis for change, may change themselves; it can be a milieu in which those who are ready to be persuaded persuade themselves, may choose to hear or choose to learn." Participants entering into this kind of interaction would try to develop an atmosphere where change for all participants can take place, would recognize that participants may differ in knowledge of subject matter and in basic beliefs, would look beyond these differences to attempt to create a sense of equal power for all, would be committed to working hard to achieve communication, and would be willing at a fundamental level to "yield her/his position entirely to the other(s)." This view of communication, believes Gearhart, moves away from a male-dominated model that assumes that all power was in the speaker/conqueror. Instead, the "womanization of rhetoric" focuses on atmosphere, listening, receiving, and a "collective rather than a competitive mode."

You are urged to compare and contrast Gearhart's view with several views of rhetoric examined in earlier chapters. For example, do Henry W. Johnstone's view of "humans as persuaders" (in chapter 3) and suggestions "toward an ethic for rhetoric" (presented at the end of chapter 4) tend more toward the conquest/conversion, speaker-centered conception of persuasion or more toward the view of communication or "womanized" rhetoric presented by Gearhart?

While they accept much of Gearhart's critique of a speaker-centered rhetoric of conquest, conversion, domination, and control, Sonja Foss and Cindy Griffin believe that such persuasion should remain one among several rhetorics available to humans for selection in varying contexts. They do not want to characterize such a view of rhetoric as inaccurate or misguided. But as one alternative, Foss and Griffin develop an "invitational rhetoric" rooted in the feminist assumptions that relationships of equality are usually more desirable than ones of domination and elitism, that every human being has value because she or he is unique and is an integral part of the pattern of the universe, and that individuals have a right to self-determination concerning the conditions of their lives (they are expert about their lives).[28]

"Invitational rhetoric," say Foss and Griffin, invites "the audience to enter the rhetor's world and to see it as the rhetor does." The invitational rhetor "does not judge or denigrate others' perspectives but is open to and tries to appreciate and validate those perspectives, even if they differ dramatically from the rhetor's own." The goal is to establish a "nonhierarchical, nonjudgmental, nonadversarial framework" for the interaction and to develop toward the audience "a relationship of equality, respect, and appreciation." Invitational rhetors make no assumption that their "experiences or perspectives are superior to those of audience members and refuse to impose their perspectives on them." While change is not the intent of invitational rhetoric, change may be a result. Change may occur in the "audience or rhetor or both as a result of new understandings and insights gained in the exchange of ideas."

In the process of invitational rhetoric, contend Foss and Griffin, the rhetoric "offers" perspectives without advocating their support or seeking their acceptance. In invitational rhetoric, individual perspectives are expressed "as carefully, completely, and passionately as possible" to invite their full consideration. In offering perspectives, "rhetors tell what they currently know or understand; they present their vision of the world and how it works for them." Rhetors in invitational rhetoric "communicate a willingness to call into question the beliefs they consider most inviolate and to relax a grip on these beliefs." Invitational rhetors strive to create the conditions of safety, value, and freedom in interaction with audience members. *Safety* involves "the creation of a feeling of security and freedom from danger for the audience." Participants do not "fear rebuttal of or retribution for their most fundamental beliefs." *Value* involves acknowledging the intrinsic worth of audience members as human beings. In interaction, attitudes that are "distancing, depersonalizing, or paternalistic" are avoided. In invitational rhetoric, "listeners do not interrupt, comfort, or insert anything of their own as others tell of their experiences." *Freedom* involves the power to choose or decide. Restrictions are not placed on the interaction. Participants may introduce for consideration any and all matters; "no subject matter is off limits, and all presuppositions can be challenged." Furthermore, in invitational rhetoric the "rhetor's ideas are not privileged over those of the audience. . . ."

In concluding their explication of an invitational rhetoric, Foss and Griffin suggest that this rhetoric requires "a new scheme of ethics to fit interactional goals other than inducement of others to adherence to the rhetor's own beliefs." What might be some appropriate ethical guidelines for invitational rhetoric? What ethical standards seem already implied by the dimensions or constituents of such rhetoric described by them?

From her stance as a feminist teacher and scholar of communication, Lana Rakow spoke to an audience of students and teachers of communication at The Ohio State University.[29] She employed the norms of "trust, mutuality, justice, and reciprocity" as touchstones for communication relationships. As a part of a wide-ranging address on the "mission" of the field of communication study, Rakow contends that we must develop a communication ethic to guide our "relations between individuals, between cultures, between organizations, between countries." She asks, "What kind of 'ground-rules' would work across multiple contexts to achieve relationships that are healthy and egalitarian, and respectful?" She suggests three:

1. *Inclusiveness* means openness to multiple perspectives on truth, an encouragement of them, and a willingness to listen. Persons are not dehumanized because of their gender, race, ethnicity, sexual orientation, country, or culture.
2. *Participation* means ensuring that all persons must have the "means and ability to participate, to be heard, to speak, to have voice, to have their opinions count in public decision making."

All persons "have a right to participate in naming the world, to be part of the discussion in naming and speaking our truths."

3. *Reciprocity* assumes that participants be considered equal partners in a communication transaction. There should be a "reciprocity of speaking and listening, of knowing and being known as you wish to be known."

In her article, "Feminist Theorizing and Communication Ethics," Linda Steiner explores particular applications to mass communication.[30] While acknowledging that (as of 1989) there was no single, fully developed, generally accepted feminist ethic, she argues that an adequate feminist ethic should confront "questions of systematic imbalances, including those that are mass mediated. It should address questions about whose interests are regarded as worthy of debate, who gets to talk, and who is regarded as an effective communicator to whom others must listen." Feminist ethics, believes Steiner, allows wide variation in ethical theories as individuals and systems reflect differences in gender, race, class, and historical circumstances. Also it focuses on *degrees* of rightness and wrongness of human actions. Feminist ethics rejects the conception of "the moral agent as the rational autonomous individual, and of moral actions as short-term, discrete acts unaffected by history." Instead, feminist ethics envisions "the moral self as embedded in a web of family and communal relationships" and regards "caring and empathy as morally significant and legitimate virtues." Steiner rejects a sharp dichotomy between care and justice orientations. She contends that virtues such as empathy, caring, and nurturance can function in conjunction with integrity, respect for others, and fairness.

A feminist ethic for mass communication, in Steiner's view, assumes the significance of "who the communicators are, who is allowed to communicate and who is excluded, in part because this controls what is communicated, how, and to whom." A feminist ethic would "require mass media institutions to redefine communication in terms of process, rather than commodity; and to invent means of extending and broadening who gets to communicate." "Feminism," argues Steiner, "calls into question the very definition of news, as well as of entertainment, assumed by the dominant mass media." Media institutions would be challenged to define as news "communications by, for, and about peoples who are ignored, suppressed, or oppressed." Views of those who are outside of or who resist conventional authority structures should actively be sought. Lower profits and alienation of those in power are risks that mass media institutions should take. News,

Steiner urges, should serve some larger transformatory good rather than simply present information for and about people in authority and thus "legitimate and reinforce existing institutional structures and values."

Finally, according to Steiner, a feminist ethic challenges the treatment of mass media subjects as objects—challenges the objectification of both mass media sources as well as audiences. "The goal would be to respect others' dignity and integrity, to make the process more collaborative and egalitarian, less authoritarian and coercive." Journalists, for example, could allow sources to raise issues as they see them, to ask questions, or to redirect questions. Or journalists might "share information and/or interpretations with sources before publication" and thus secure the sources' sense of accuracy and completeness of a story. You are encouraged to compare Steiner's suggested feminist ethic for mass communication with Clifford Christians's ethical norms for new mass media technologies presented as a case study in the appendix of this book.

Additional Communication Issues

As we saw in chapter 3 on human nature perspectives, there are some human nature perspectives in the Western male-dominated cultural tradition that privilege rationality as an ethical standard for communication. These perspectives often have a built-in bias that automatically casts suspicion on communication by women. In the Western tradition, women have been assumed to be, by nature (rather than culture), less capable of rationality and more inclined toward irrational emotionality than men. Marilyn Pearsall vividly depicts the circumstances.[31]

> Women's nature has been held to be not only different from men's but also lesser, especially in regard to rationality. Men's nature is taken to be the standard for human nature, and women, presumably, fall short of that standard. Women have been described as emotional rather than rational, intuitive rather than logical, passive rather than active, and so on. This view, in turn, justified the confinement of women to the private/domestic sphere. And because women were held to be unfit for the public (political) sphere, where rationality is supposedly required, they were denied literacy and education and were kept from participating in political, legal, economic, and religious institutions.

Nel Noddings emphatically reminds us:

> It is not the case that women cannot arrange principles hierarchically and derive conclusions logically. It is more likely that we see this process as peripheral to, or even alien to, many problems of moral action. . . . Moral decisions are, after all, made in real situations; they are qualitatively different from the solution of geometry problems. Women can and do give reasons for their acts, but the reasons often point to feelings, needs, impressions, and a sense of personal ideal rather than to universal principles and their application."[32]

Certainly pornography as a type of contemporary communication generates heated debates concerning exactly what it is, whether it should be allowed, on what grounds it might be condemned or defended, and how First Amendment protections of freedom of speech should (or should not) apply to it.[33] Feminist ethicists do pinpoint some ethical grounds for condemning pornography. Helen Longino defines immoral behavior as that which "causes injury to or violation of another person or people. Such injury may be physical or psychological. To cause pain to another, to lie to another, to hinder another in the exercise of his or her rights, to exploit another, to degrade another, to misrepresent and slander another are instances of immoral behavior."[34] Beyond pornography's degrading and dehumanizing depiction of women, to accomplish its purposes pornography must lie about women. Longino contends that pornography lies by saying women's sexual life is or ought to be subordinate to that of men, that women are depraved, that women's pleasure consists of pleasure for men not themselves, and that women are appropriate victims for rape, torture, bondage, or murder. "Pornography lies explicitly about women's sexuality," stresses Longino, "and through such lies fosters more lies about our humanity, our dignity, and our personhood." Jacqueline MacGregor Davies takes a post-liberal feminist position that condemns pornography as both politically and ethically objectionable. The assault, coercion, exploitation, sexual objectification, and dehumanization fostered by pornography "threaten the consensual process of articulating what it is to be human." In pornography "women are no longer present as human subjects who can generate signs. . . . They are spoken through." Pornography, in Davies's view, functions to deny women their status as members "of the community of subjects."[35]

In chapter 7, "Some Basic Issues," the ethical implications of nonverbal communication were explored. Silence, it was stressed, may carry ethical implications. Feminist theory can aid us in considering ethical implications of the silence and the silencing of women.[36] In American culture, in many situations, women are expected to bear the primary responsibility for keeping talk going while men (by nature?) are not expected to be talkative. In these situations silence on the part of women is open to generally negative interpretations. In other situations, because they are viewed as inferior to men by nature, women must keep silent and let the men do the talking. Because the public sphere of politics and business has, until recently, been seen as the realm of male expertise and action, women effectively have been silenced by exclusion. Women are silenced when certain topics, communication roles, media of communication, and arenas of deliberation are assumed to be "off-limits" to them. In interpersonal communication, women are silenced when men feel quite free routinely to interrupt them but feel they have the right not to be interrupted. On the one hand, women may be silenced (denied their own personal voice) when routinely they are expected to communicate "like a man" in order to be taken seriously and to be successful. On the other hand, women may be silenced when routinely they are expected to communicate "like a woman" in certain stereotyped ways.

Finally, Adrienne Rich vividly probes the matters of lying and trust in personal relationships between women.[37] Rich describes a woman as feeling "a little crazy" when she discovers that another woman has lied to her. "We take so much of the universe on trust," Rich believes, so that when that bond of trust is broken we are "forced to reexamine the universe, to question the whole instinct and concept of trust." In Rich's imagery: "For awhile, we are thrust back onto some bleak, jutting ledge, in a dark pierced by sheets of fire, swept by sheets of rain, in a world before kinship, or naming, or tenderness exist; we are brought close to formlessness." In addition, Rich argues that "women have been forced to lie, for survival, to men"—to lovers, bosses, and any men who have power over them. With what effects? Lying to others (men or women) involves a woman in lying to herself by denying the truth or significance of something; thus she removes a part of her life and lessens her confidence in her own life. Furthermore, when women lie so routinely that they forget they are lying or when they routinely use lying as a weapon of power, they run the great risk that lying will "carry over into relationships with people who do not have power over us," such as close friends and lovers.

Robert Solomon provides a fitting summary for our exploration of feminist contributions to communication ethics:[38]

Feminist ethics has become one of the most important influences in ethics today. . . . The feminist argument reminds us of the important role of the moral sentiments and close and intimate relationships in happiness and the good life. It suggests that dispassionate reason . . . need not be seen as the highest virtue and insists that an admirable person will also be a passionate person who is concerned with other people and cares deeply about his or her family and loved ones.

What makes us moral, first of all, is our personal concern for those closest to us. Secondarily we learn to have similar concerns, even if based on principles rather than personal attachments, for the many people we never have met and for humanity in general.

Notes

[1] Barbara Bate, *Communication and the Sexes* (1988; reissue, Prospect Heights, IL: Waveland Press, 1992), p. 227; Julia T. Wood, *Gendered Lives: Communication, Gender, and Culture* (Belmont, CA: Wadsworth, 1994), p. 4.

[2] Wood, *Gendered Lives*, pp. 97–106.

[3] Alison Jaggar, "Feminist Ethics: Some Issues for the Nineties," *Journal of Social Philosophy*, 20 (Spring/Fall 1988): 91–107.

[4] For example, see Rita C. Manning, *Speaking from the Heart: A Feminist Perspective on Ethics* (Lanham, MD: Rowman & Littlefield, 1992), pp. 15, 28–29; Mary C. Raugust, "Feminist Ethics and Workplace Ethics," in *Explorations in Feminist Ethics*, Eve Browning Cole and Susan Coultrap-McQuin, eds. (Bloomington: Indiana University Press, 1992), pp. 127–28.

[5] Manning *Speaking from the Heart*, pp. 2–5; Michael Sandel, *Liberalism and Its Critics* (New York: New York University Press, 1984), pp. 5–6; Seyla Benhabib, *Situating the Self: Gender, Community and Postmodernism in Contemporary Ethics* (New York: Routledge, 1992), pp. 148–77.

[6] Jaggar "Feminist Ethics," p. 94; Eve Browning Cole and Susan Coultrap-Quin, "Toward a Feminist Conception of Moral Life," in *Explorations in Feminist Ethics*, p. 9.

[7] Manning, *Speaking from the Heart*, p. 14; Jaggar, "Feminist Ethics," p. 92; Virginia Held, *Feminist Morality: Transforming Culture, Society, and Politics* (Chicago: University of Chicago Press, 1993), pp. 57, 73.

[8] Held, *Feminist Morality*, p. 169.

[9] Carol Gilligan, *In a Different Voice: Psychological Theory and Women's Development* (Cambridge: Harvard University Press, 1982), pp. 2, 14, 18, 155–56, 173–74.

[10] *In a Different Voice*, pp. 19, 73–74, 127, 143, 156–65, 174.

[11] Lawrence Kohlberg, *The Psychology of Moral Development: The Nature and Validity of Moral Stages* (San Francisco: Harper and Row, 1984). "On *In a Different Voice*: An Interdisciplinary Forum," *Signs: A Journal of Women in Culture and Society* 11, no. 2 (1986): 304–33. In considering these issues, the author also gained valuable insight from Barbara Dickey, Becky Swanson Kroll,

and Lynn Jenkins, "Gilligan Revisited: Methodological Issues in the Study of Gender and Moral Development," paper presented at the Speech Communication Association national conference, Boston, November 1987.

[12] Nel Noddings, *Caring: A Feminine Approach to Ethics and Moral Education* (Berkeley: University of California Press, 1984), pp. 4–5, 27–28, 49, 83, 130, 175.

[13] *Caring*, pp. 17–19, 33, 69–75, 170, 176–77, 182–97.

[14] On rules, principles, universalizability, and universality, see *Caring*, pp. 5, 13, 17, 55, 85.

[15] *Caring*, pp. 49, 80, 104–31, 182–97.

[16] Linda A, Bell, *Rethinking Ethics in the Midst of Violence: A Feminist Approach to Freedom* (Lanham, MD: Rowman & Littlefield, 1993), pp. 35–45; Noddings, *Caring*, p. 34. But see Nel Noddings, *Women and Evil* (Berkeley: University of California Press, 1989) for her expansion of a relationship ethic beyond the private sphere.

[17] *Speaking*, pp. 49, 56, 65–69, 139, 152.

[18] *Speaking*, pp. xiv, 48, 64, 149, 161.

[19] *Speaking*, 29, 62, 69, 73–82, 147–49, 156, 160.

[20] Joan C. Tronto, *Moral Boundaries: A Political Argument for an Ethics of Care* (New York: Routledge, 1993), pp. 13, 102–80.

[21] *Moral Boundaries*, pp. 61–97, 151–69.

[22] *Moral Boundaries*, pp. 102–8, 126–37.

[23] Julia T. Wood, *Who Cares? Women. Care, and Culture* (Carbondale: Southern Illinois University Press, 1994), pp. 41–49; 106–10.

[24] *Who Cares?*, pp. 40, 62–85, 143–44. Also see Julia T. Wood, "Gender and Moral Voice: Moving from Women's Nature to Standpoint Theory," *Women's Studies in Communication*, 15 (Spring 1992): 1–24.

[25] *Who Cares?*, pp. 10–13, 56, 113–61. An ethic of care (from a non-feminist perspective) for organizational management is Hyler Bracey, et al., *Managing from the Heart* (New York: Delacorte, 1990).

[26] Gillian Michell, "Women and Lying: A Pragmatic and Semantic Analysis of 'Telling it Slant'," *Women's Studies International Forum*, 7 (1984): 375–83. Also See Shirley Ardener, ed., *Perceiving Women* (Malaby Press, 1987); Cheris Kramarae, *Women and Men Speaking* (Newbury House Publishers, 1981); Tillie Olsen, *Silences* (Delacorte, 1978); Adrienne Rich, *Lies, Secrets and Silence* (Norton, 1979) and Dale Spender, *Man Made Language* (Routledge & Kegan Paul, 1980).

[27] Sally Miller Gearhart, "The Womanization of Rhetoric," *Women's Studies International Quarterly*, 2 (1979): 195–201.

[28] Sonja K. Foss and Cindy L. Griffin, "Beyond Persuasion: A Proposal for an Invitational Rhetoric," *Communication Monographs*, 62 (March 1995): 2–18. Also see Sonja K. Foss and Karen A. Foss, *Inviting Transformation: Presentational Speaking for a Changing World* (Prospect Heights, IL: Waveland Press, 1994).

[29] Lana Rakow, "The Future of the Field: Finding Our Mission," address presented at The Ohio State University, May 13, 1994.

[30] Linda Steiner, "Feminist Theorizing and Communication Ethics," *Communication*, 12 (1989): 157–73.

[31] Marilyn Pearsall, ed., *Women and Values: Readings in Recent Feminist Philosophy* (Belmont: CA: Wadsworth, 1986), p. 33.

[32] Noddings, *Caring*, pp. 2–3, 96.

[33] For a survey of the controversy, see Daniel Linz and Neil Malamuth, *Pornography* (Newbury Park, CA: Sage, 1993).

[34] Helen E. Longino, "Pornography, Oppression, and Freedom: A Closer Look," in Pearsall, ed., *Women and Values*, espec. pp. 168–72.

[35] Jacqueline MacGregor Davies, "Pornographic Harms," in Lorraine Code, Sheila Mullett, and Christine Overall, eds., *Feminist Perspectives: Philosophical Essays on Method and Morals* (Toronto: University of Toronto Press, 1988), espec. pp. 137–38, 142–43.

[36] Many of the following points are raised in Adam Jaworski, *The Power of Silence: Social and Pragmatic Perspectives* (Newbury Park, CA: Sage, 1993), pp. 118–22; Tillie Olsen, *Silences* (New York: Delacorte, 1978).

[37] Adrienne Rich, *On Lies, Secrets, and Silence* (New York: Norton, 1979), pp. 185–94.

[38] Robert C. Solomon, *Ethics: A Short Introduction* (Dubuque, IA: Brown & Benchmark, 1993), pp. 132–33.

Chapter 12

Intercultural and Multicultural Communication

"North Americans . . . too often assume that people elsewhere hold comparable values, or would, at least if they were given the opportunity." Thus John Condon underscores the fact that standards for ethical communication rooted in an American value system, such as the political perspectives discussed in chapter 2, are not widely shared throughout the world. Criteria of linear logic, empirical observation, and objective truth are not used to assess communication ethicality in various other cultures, religions, and political systems.[1]

Some scholars advocate development of an overarching, transcendent, "metaethic" to guide communication between people of different cultures. Dean Barnlund argues: "Until a metaethic . . . can be articulated in ways that gain wide allegiance, or until a common one emerges from the thousands of daily confrontations, confusions, and antagonisms that characterize such encounters, we shall continue to conduct intercultural affairs in a moral vacuum." Such a metaethic, he believes, should be created or be synthesized from codes in existing cultures, to state the "minimum consensus required to discourage the grossest forms of destructive interaction while promoting the widest variations of behavior within cultures."[2] In contrast, other scholars argue that such a search for an intercultural communication metaethic may be a "fool's errand," and impossible task.[3]

Thomas Cooper analyzed numerous national and international codes of journalistic ethics in a search for a common ground of "global universals." He explores the concepts of truth, responsibility, and freedom as potential universals. You are encouraged to read his lengthy analysis in his book, *Communication Ethics and Global Change*.[4] In that same book, John Merrill asked whether global commonalities for journalistic ethics were an "idle dream or realistic goal?" On the one hand, Merrill argues that a formal code of international journalistic ethics is best characterized as unreasonable, impossible, unrealistic, and fruitless. "Such a code will be either a politically propagandistic document," Merrill believes, "or it will be a collection of generalized aphorisms and abstract maxims, so devoid of substance and specificity as to make them meaningless and useless." On the other hand, Merrill suggests that there may be some "broad ethical principles that transcend any particular culture or nation—in other words, that there are universals." Merrill personally believes that two broad principles are appropriate. One is an adaptation of the Golden Rule: "Communicate only unto *willing* others those things and employing only those techniques which you would be willing for others to use in communicating with you." The second is an adaptation of Kant's Categorical Imperative: "Communicate only such things and in such a way that you would be willing to make what you do universal."[5]

Consider for yourself whether you believe there should be an ethic especially for intercultural or cross-cultural communication. What might a communication ethic that transcends cultures look like? In chapter 6 of this book, we described at some length William Howell's "social utility" approach. You are urged to review that discussion. Howell explicitly sees this approach as capable of yielding "ethical judgments universally, at all times and places." It can be applied meaningfully "in any culture, anywhere, at any time." Howell recommends that intercultural communicators always "show respect for values, morals, and normative practices of the other culture" and that they also "refrain from evaluation."[6]

One standard often suggested as a principle to guide intercultural communication ethics is some version of the Golden Rule: "Do unto others as you would have them do unto you." But Milton Bennett argues convincingly that the Golden Rule best applies *within* a culture that has wide consensus on fundamental values, goals, structures, and customs. In other words, the Golden Rule assumes that all people are alike, that other people *want* to be treated like you do. Such an assumption is not applicable in intercultural communication. As an alternative, Bennett offers the "Platinum Rule": "Do unto others as they themselves would have done unto them." As an essential communication skill to implement this rule, he urges development of empathy, of the "imaginative intellectual and emotional participation in another person's experience."[7]

Sitaram and Cogdell's Ethic

In *Foundations of Intercultural Communication*, K. S. Sitaram and Roy Cogdell present a detailed and extensive "code of ethics for all intercultural communicators." They believe that their proposed code covers "almost the entire area of intercultural communication." Here for your evaluation we reprint the first 24 of their 35 ethical standards.[8] The intercultural communicator shall:

1. Recognize that he does not set world standards
2. Treat the audience culture with the same respect he would his own
3. Not judge the values, beliefs and customs of other cultures according to his own values
4. At all times be mindful of the need to understand cultural bases of other's values
5. Never assume superiority of his own religion over that of the other person
6. In dealing with members of a different religion, try to understand and respect that religion.
7. Endeavor to understand the food habits of other peoples which were developed on the basis of their particular needs and resources
8. Respect the way people dress in other cultures
9. Not treat with contempt the unfamiliar odors which may be considered pleasant by people of other cultures
10. Not use the color of a person's skin as a basis for the nature of his relationship with that person
11. Not look down at another person because he speaks with an accent different from one's own
12. Recognize that each culture, however small, has something to offer the world and no one culture has a monopoly in every aspect
13. Not take undue advantage of one's superior position in the hierarchy of his culture to sway the actions of members of his own culture
14. Always remember there is no scientific evidence to prove that one ethnic group is superior or inferior to others
15. Not manipulate his communicative techniques to bring about change in the behaviors of peoples in another culture to suit his own needs
16. Not create an atmosphere to reinforce stereotypes of another people
17. Not employ preconceived notions of others in attempting to communicate with them
18. Make honest attempts to learn the language of his audience in preparing to interact with them
19. Make honest attempts to learn, respect and adapt the customs of his audience of another culture in preparing to interact with them

20. Recognize that the primary values of one's own culture are different from those of other cultures, and not communicate in such a way as to impose one's own values on them
21. Be aware that the nonverbal symbols used in one's culture, if used in another culture might be insulting to members of that culture
22. Refrain from speaking one's language with another of one's culture in the company of those who cannot understand that language
23. In using mass media of another culture, use communication techniques to suit their media system and format
24. When using mass media, not create false, inaccurate, insulting images of another people in order to suit one's own interests, necessities and conveniences

Now consider what difficulties there might be in interpreting and applying this code.[9] For example, standard 15 seems to be another way of describing the process of persuasion, a process having varying degrees of ethicality. Perhaps the real issue here is not as much the negatively loaded word, "manipulate," as it is whether our own needs take primary importance to the detriment of the needs of others. If standard 22 were literally interpreted, an international diplomat at a conference might be judged unethical for speaking her or his native language in the presence of nonspeakers of that language, even though the comments were being translated into other languages. Standard 12 might be viewed as lacking necessary clarity of meaning. And consider the word "respect" whenever it occurs in the code (2, 6, 8, 19). Does the word seem to have a consistent meaning, or is it used in several senses? Should "respect" as used in this code have the primary meaning of agreement or approval, or of tolerance, or of being considerate, or of holding in esteem?

Kale's Human Nature Ethic

The grounding of David Kale's proposed ethic for intercultural communication is his view of human nature. While acknowledging that different cultures develop different value systems and "thus must have different ethical codes," he also assumes that all people "share a human spirit that is the same regardless of cultural background."[10] This fundamental human spirit generates our capacities to hold values and make value judgments, to make ethical decisions about degrees of right and wrong, and to envision dimensions of a worthwhile life. Kale believes that "the guiding principle of any universal code of intercultural communication should be to protect the worth and dignity of the human spirit." Kale also grounds his ethic, not in freedom of choice as a fundamental human value, but rather in world cultures living at peace with each other. Such a goal represents a continuum ranging from minimal peace (absence of conflict) through moderate peace ("conflicting parties are willing to compromise on goals they want to achieve") to optimal peace ("parties consider each others' goals as seriously as they do their own").

Based on these groundings, Kale proposes four principles as a universal code of ethics for intercultural communication. *Principle 1*: "Ethical communicators address people of other cultures with the same respect that they would like to receive themselves." In light of this principle, verbal or nonverbal communication that demeans or belittles others' cultural identity is unethical. *Principle 2*: "Ethical communicators seek to describe the world as they perceive it as accurately as possible." Because deception undermines the ability of people of different cultures to trust each other, ethical communicators avoid intentionally deceiving or misleading. *Principle 3*: "Ethical communicators encourage people of other cultures to express themselves in their uniqueness." No matter the degree of popularity or unpopularity of their political or social views, it is both ethnocentric and unethical to grant peoples of other cultures equal status in international debate and dialogue "only if they choose to express themselves in the same way we do." *Principle 4*: "Ethical communicators strive for identification with people of other cultures." The goal is mutual understanding and unity of spirit while allowing for uniqueness of cultural identities. Communication that stirs racial hatred or heightens ethnic divisions is ethically suspect because it probably will promote conflict rather than peace.

Plagiarism as Culturally Variable

In order to illustrate how an ethical standard may be assumed to be universal by persons of one cultural heritage but not to be an ethical standard at all by persons of other cultural heritages, I will focus on the ethics of plagiarism.[11] In contemporary North American (indeed Euro-American) culture, plagiarism uniformly is condemned as an unethical communication practice. Politicians, journalists, and academicians are criticized for acts of plagiarism. Students, including those in composition and communication classes, are warned that plagiarism is dishonest and unethical, especially in the context where ultimate individual responsibility for improvement of skills and insights is assumed.

Two fundamental judgments undergird our contemporary view of plagiarism as unethical. First, plagiarism is condemned as theft of an idea, the stealing of property, that belongs to another person. Second, plagiarism is condemned as fraud or deception. A communicator misrepresents the words or ideas of others as his or her own. Standard explanations of plagiarism say that it involves stealing another person's words or ideas by not properly acknowledging their source and presenting those words or ideas as one's own. Plagiarism is assumed to violate some universal, culture-free, ethical principle.

However, plagiarism as a concept is deeply imbedded in the Euro-American tradition of print orientation, individual originality, and capitalistic commodification of ideas. The conventional view sees a person's words and ideas as private property or commodities to be owned and sold. In fact, however, concern for the ethicality (and legality) of plagiarism developed with the increasing emphasis in Western culture on writing and print, on individual originality, and on capitalism. The ethical offense of plagiarism developed in the shift from orality to writing to print. The development of print typography fostered the view of words as commodities and private property. Throughout the sixteenth and seventeenth centuries, ever more value was placed on individual uniqueness, originality, and creativity. During the eighteenth and nineteenth centuries when the first English copyright laws were enacted, the ethical condemnation of plagiarism grew ever louder. The commodification of ideas—the view that words and ideas are private property and original commodities to be owned and sold—is a significant feature of capitalism in the United States.

In contrast, other cultures may view words and ideas not as individually created, privately owned commodities, but as communal intellectual resources to be shared and adapted. Such is true for primarily oral cultures. Although in ancient Greece and Rome public speakers believed that imitation and borrowing should be openly and proudly admitted rather than concealed or hidden, they also believed that ideas and subject matter were common property, public material, belonging to all. During the Middle Ages our current concepts of plagiarism, copyright, and authorship did not exist. Quoting without identifying the source or borrowing ideas and language without attribution caused little or no worry for speakers and writers. Most African cultures can be viewed as recent primarily oral cultures and the creative power of the word is central to such cultures. The primarily oral rather than print tradition of Africa was transferred to the black folk-preaching tradition in America. The process of composition of folk sermons in the black folk-preaching tradition did not assume that sources or ideas were the exclusive property of one person. Communal invention of discourse was the norm in the black folk-preaching tradition. Black folk preachers freely borrowed without acknowledgement from other black preachers and from standard sermons that had been in circulation for decades. The black folk-preaching tradition assumed that language and ideas were communal resources to be shared and adapted rather than commodities, personal possessions, or private property.

The ethics of plagiarism now can be reconsidered in a light different than the traditional Euro-American view. Plagiarism as unethical is not a universal, invariable, culture-free principle on the order of a Kantian Categorical Imperative. Instead plagiarism is a communication norm derived from the Euro-American tradition of print orientation, individual originality, and capitalistic commodification. In contrast, for example, in the African-American oral culture and folk-preaching tradition, oratorical "plagiarism" might be seen as natural, accepted, and ethical.

What might be some avenues for the reconsideration of the ethics of plagiarism? There can be additional research on the extent and ways which the norm against plagiarism has evolved out of Euro-American cultural perspectives and assumptions. We might explore the possibility of an alternative term for acceptable unacknowledged uses—perhaps "borrowing"—and reserve "plagiarism" for the instances of clear unethical violation of applicable norms. We can explore implications for both the conventional and reconsidered views of plagiarism in light of the growing body of scholarship on intertextuality (the influence of multiple "texts" on a particular text), on "collaborative" writing, and on discourse as a "social" more than an individual process.[12]

Multicultural Communication

Multicultural communication is a concept much discussed today and often defined in quite varied ways. For the purposes of this chapter, the definition offered by Lawrence Blum will suffice.[13]

> Multiculturalism involves an understanding, appreciation, and valuing of one's own culture, and an informed respect and curiosity about the ethnic cultures of others. It involves a valuing of other

cultures, not in the sense of approving all aspects of those cultures, but of attempting to see how a given culture can express value to its own members.

As used in this chapter, multicultural communication will focus on communication between sub-cultural groups within the larger American national culture and between members of sub-cultural groups and the dominant white heterosexual male culture. Instead of multicultural communication, Marquita Byrd employs the term "intracultural communication" for communication "among people who are citizens of the same geopolitical system, and also hold membership in one or more tributary groups." Tributary groups are "distinguishable from the power dominant/general population on the basis of racial characteristics, ethnic heritage, religious beliefs, gender identification, sexual orientation, socioeconomic level, age, and/or ableness." As examples of intracultural (multicultural) communication, Byrd mentions women with men, disabled with abled, homosexuals with heterosexuals, blacks with whites, and Hispanic Americans with Asian Americans.[14] We need to remember that multiculturalism may apply to an individual. "For many people . . . not one but several cultures contribute to a single identity. . . . Not only societies, but people are multicultural."[15] Bear in mind that some of the issues and principles discussed in the first half of the this chapter also may apply here.

Ethnic Ethics

In his book, *Ethnic Ethics: The Restructuring of Moral Theory*, Anthony Cortese argues at length that "morality must be bound to a particular cultural or sociocultural context."[16] "Morality," he contends, "contains no intrinsic laws of development. Its validity has no ultimate basis. Instead, moral systems prosper or fail within specific cultural and historical settings." From Cortese's perspective, traditional "moral principles that are allegedly universal are viewed as the highest good." But he takes the position "that people are more important than principles, that relationships are more crucial than conceptions of justice, and that subcultural moral systems are more relevant than universal standards of ethics."

"The key to morality is in social relations," argues Cortese, "not in abstract rational principles." "Ethnic background, gender, role demands, and socioeconomic status" are key factors. And yet "the structures of moral reasoning used by Western middle-to-upper-middle-class white males appear to be taken to be everyone's ideal type by many researchers. Similarly the norms of the dominant culture are taken as the model for the entire society." Cortese takes seriously "the possibility that ethnic groups have different moral structures, each adequate to the reproduction of the social life-world found in each ethnic group." "One must also consider," he believes, "the possibility that the 'scientific findings' on moral development are more appropriately viewed as ideology that sets the Western European social life-world as the model for all people in all places."

Modified Universalism

The moral pluralism view developed by Cortese need not necessarily lead to a radical cultural relativism wherein whatever ethical standards "work" for an ethnic group or culture uniformly ought to be acceptable. Rather what Emmet terms "soft" moral relativism, what Gutmann calls "deliberative universalism," and what Benhabib labels "interactive universalism" open up for examination the possibility that cultural variation in certain moral principles between cultures or within a culture does not preclude moral judgments of better or worse between or within those cultures.[17] Lack of commitment solely to a complete set of invariable or universalizable principles does not mean impossibility of a minimum set of ethical norms that are or should be transcultural. I would suggest for consideration such potential transcultural ethical standards as humaneness, truthfulness, trust, promise keeping, nonviolence, and caring relationships. Other ethical standards within a culture or subculture properly may be more relative to specific cultural, ethnic, class, or gender factors; some of these more relativistic standards might be critiqued in light of the transcultural norms. The Josephson Institute of Ethics, for instance, proposes six "core consensus ethical values that transcend cultural, ethnic, and socioeconomic differences": trustworthiness; respect; responsibility; justice and fairness; caring; and civic virtue and citizenship. Yet, the Institute also recognizes that there are additional ethical values that properly vary among cultures, ethnic groups, religions, and political philosophies.[18] As universal ethical standards/moral values for social justice, Gutmann urges life, liberty, opportunity, truth telling by governments, impartial law enforcement, freedom from enslavement, torture, and poverty, and a robust and fair system of debate and deliberation to reach some tentative agreements concerning other ethical norms that are more culture-bound.[19]

Moral Exclusion

Moral exclusion, in Susan Opotow's description, "occurs when individuals or groups are perceived as *outside the boundary in which moral values, rules, and considerations of fairness apply*. Those who are morally excluded are perceived as nonentities, expendable, or undeserving; consequently, harming them appears acceptable, appropriate, or just." Persons morally excluded are denied their rights, dignity, and autonomy.[20]

Opotow isolates for analysis and discussion over two dozen symptoms or manifestations of moral exclusion. For our purposes a noteworthy fact is that many of them directly involve communication behavior. While all of the symptoms she presents are significant for a full understanding of the mind-set that characterizes a person who engages in moral exclusion, here I will paraphrase only those that clearly involve communication.

1. Showing the superiority of you or your group by making unflattering comparisons to others or another group
2. Denigrating and disparaging others by characterizing them as lower life forms (vermin) or inferior beings (barbarians, aliens)
3. Denying that others possess humanity, dignity, ability to feel, or the right to compassion
4. Redefining as an increasingly larger category the category of "legitimate victims"
5. Blaming the victim; placing the blame for any harm on the victim not the doer
6. Justifying harmful acts by claiming that the morally condemnable acts committed by the adversary are significantly worse
7. Misrepresenting cruelty and harm by masking, sanitizing, and conferring respectability on them through use of neutral, positive, technical, or euphemistic terms to describe them
8. Justifying harmful behavior by claiming it is widely accepted (everyone is doing it) or that it was isolated and uncharacteristic behavior (just this once)

In the following section we will see how moral exclusion functions through racist and sexist language and through "hate speech" on college campuses.

Racist/Sexist Language and Hate Speech

In *The Language of Oppression*, Haig Bosmajian demonstrates how names, labels, definitions, and stereotypes have been employed to degrade, dehumanize, and suppress Jews, blacks, Native Americans, and women. His goal is to expose the "decadence in our language, the inhumane uses of language," that have been used "to justify the unjustifiable, to make palatable the unpalatable, to make reasonable the unreasonable, to make decent the indecent." Bosmajian reminds us: "Our identities, who and what we are, how others see us, are greatly affected by the names we are called and the words with which we are labelled. The names, labels, and phrases employed to 'identify' a people may in the end determine their survival."[21]

"Every language reflects the prejudices of the society in which it evolved. Since English, through most of its history, evolved in a white, Anglo-Saxon, patriarchal society, no one should be surprised that its vocabulary and grammar frequently reflect attitudes that exclude or demean minorities and women." Such is the fundamental position of Casey Miller and Kate Swift, authors of *The Handbook of Nonsexist Writing*. Conventional English usage, they believe, "often obscures the actions, the contributions, and sometimes the very presence of women." Because such language usage is misleading and inaccurate, they see ethical implication in it. "In this respect, continuing to use English in ways that have become misleading is no different from misusing data, whether the misuse is inadvertent or planned."[22]

To what degree is use of racist/sexist language unethical and by what standards? At the least, racist/sexist terms place people in artificial and irrelevant categories. At worst, such terms intentionally demean and "put down" other people through embodying unfair negative value judgments concerning traits, capacities, and accomplishments. What are the ethical implications, for instance, of calling a Jewish person a "kike," a black person a "nigger" or "boy," an Italian person a "wop," an Asiatic person a "gook" or "slant-eye," or a thirty-year-old woman a "girl" or "chick"? Here is one possible answer: "In the war in Southeast Asia, our military fostered a linguistic environment in which Vietnamese people were called such names as *slope, dink, slant, gook,* and *zip*; those names made it much easier to despise, to fear, and to kill them. When we call women in our society by such names as *gash*, *slut*, *dyke*, *bitch*, or *girl*, we—men and women alike—have put ourselves in a position to demean and abuse them."[23]

The issue of "hate speech" on college and university campuses illustrates the tension between the right of freedom of speech and ethically responsible exercise of that right.[24] For our purposes in this section, however, the focus will be on ethical issues and standards. Hate speech is a very broad label that has come to designate verbal attacks (spoken or written) on persons because of their race, religion, ethnicity, sex, or sexual orientation.

Examples of hate speech on college campuses from the late 1980s and the 1990s typify the kinds of communication at issue.[25] Eight Asian-American students on their way to a dance at the University of Connecticut were harassed for almost an hour by a group of football players who called them "Oriental faggots," spat on them, and challenged them to a fight. At the University of Arizona at Tempe, a fight broke out and police were called to restore order after some white fraternity members harassed a black student by chanting "coon," "nigger," and "porchmonkey." A fraternity at the University of Wisconsin held a mock slave auction. Two white freshmen at Stanford put obviously Negroid features on a picture of Beethoven and posted it in a black studies dormitory. "African Nigger do you want some bananas? Go back to the jungle" was the message that an African woman at Smith College found under her dormitory door. "A mind is a terrible thing to waste—especially on a nigger" was written anonymously on a blackboard at the University of Michigan.

By 1992 over 100 American colleges and universities had instituted speech codes to prohibit such hateful and offensive messages. Among the varied forms of expression punishable under these speech codes were: use of derogatory names, inappropriately directed laughter, inconsiderate jokes, and conspicuous exclusion of another person from conversation; language that stigmatizes or victimizes individuals or that creates in intimidating or offensive environment; face-to-face use of epithets, obscenities, and other forms of expression that by accepted community standards degrade, victimize, stigmatize, or pejoratively depict persons based on their personal, intellectual, or cultural diversity; extensive or outrageous acts or communications intended to harass, intimidate, or humiliate a student on the basis of race, color, or national origin thus reasonably causing him or her severe emotional distress.[26] When the constitutionality of some of the campus speech codes has been tested in court, typically the codes have been ruled unconstitutional as violations of First Amendment protections of freedom of speech.

Several scholars of the First Amendment rest their cases for control of hate speech through law or codes primarily on ethical grounds. R. George Wright advocates the adoption of tort laws or criminal laws both because of the psychological harms he believes stem from hate speech and, more importantly, because of community agreement that the "use of racial epithets involves a clear and fundamental moral wrong." Wright rests his view firmly on the "sheer moral disvalue of racist speech." Hate speech fundamentally is a "deontic moral wrong."[27] In other words, hate speech is, in his view, by its very nature unethical; it is unethical in and of itself; it never is ethically justifiable. Wright seeks use of legal enforcement of a primarily ethical judgment.

Andrew Altman favors narrowly worded regulations against hate speech because it is a type of illocutionary "speech act" that by its very utterance treats someone as a moral subordinate—as having inferior moral status. "Treating persons as moral subordinates," argues Altman, "means treating them in a way that takes their interests to be intrinsically less important, and their lives inherently less valuable" than those of others. Epithets such as "kike," "faggot," "spic," or "nigger" are "verbal instruments of subordination" and degradation that not only express hatred and contempt for persons but also "put them in their place" as having inferior moral standing. Altman roots his ethical judgment in a version of a political perspective—the belief that "wrongs of subordination based on such characteristics as race, gender, and sexual preference . . . are among the principle wrongs that have prevented—and continue to prevent—Western liberal democracies from living up to their ideals and principles."[28] In contrast, Franklyn Haiman objects to "speech act" theory as a sound basis for free speech because it blurs necessary distinctions between speech and action.[29]

Regardless how issues of First Amendment constitutionality are decided concerning campus hate speech, clearly such communication, and racist/sexist language generally, should be condemned on ethical grounds that previously we have discussed as representative democracy political perspectives, human nature perspectives, dialogical perspectives, and feminist viewpoints. Hate speech in the form of racist, sexist, and homophobic communication dehumanizes—makes a person less than human—by demeaning other people through embodying unfair negative value judgments concerning traits, capacities, or accomplishments. Communication that dehumanizes reinforces stereotypes, conveys inaccurate depictions of people, dismisses taking serious account of people, dismisses people as citizens worthy of participating in public discourse on public issues, and even makes people invisible for purposes of decision or policy. Communication that dehumanizes undermines or subverts the human capacities for symbol-use and reasonableness. Communication that dehumanizes reflects a superior, exploitative, inhumane attitude of one person toward another, thus hindering equal opportunity for self-fulfillment. Communication that dehumanizes views others not as persons inherently worthy of minimal respect as humans but as things or objects to be manipulated for the communicator's pleasure or selfish gain.

Ethical Guidelines for Intracultural Communication

Marquita Byrd proposes standards for ethical communication between racial and ethnic groups, subcultures, and what she terms "tributary groups" within the larger national American culture. Ethical communication between members of such groups, she believes, should facilitate informed choice making, enhance opportunities for persons to maximize their potential, reinforce justice and fairness, be motivated by worthy intent, utilize ethical communicative means, and avoid destructive consequences. To clarify her view of ethical intracultural communication, Byrd suggests the following guidelines:[30]

Language

1. Treat the language and dialects of others with respect.
2. Do not assume your language is superior to another.
3. Recognize the right of tributary groups to speak their own languages/dialects.
4. Refrain from using racist, sexist, and ageist language.

Uniqueness/Stereotyping

5. Do not perpetuate stereotypes in public or private communication.
6. Recognize the uniqueness of each individual regardless of the tributary group from which he/she originates.
7. Tailor messages for the unique individual, and do not assume you can talk to everyone the same way.

Interpersonal/Group Interactions

8. Discourage the use of humor that degrades, devalues, or dehumanizes others on the basis of race, religion, gender, sexual orientation, etc.
9. In interpersonal and small group settings do not exclude or ignore others because they look or sound different.
10. Do not interrupt people simply because they look or talk in a manner that is different from your own or the group's.
11. Respect the right of others for interpersonal and sexual interactions among consenting adults (regardless of gender, or race).
12. Allow others to define themselves.
13. Practice active listening regardless of who you are listening to.

Keep in Mind That

14. Similarity or difference from self does not determine the worth of another.
15. Potential is not determined by membership in any tributary or power dominant group and cannot be determined by "looking at" someone.
16. Foods and odors are part of the cultural experience; that they vary from tributary to tributary group; and that what is unfamiliar to one may be pleasant to another.

Do Not

17. Ridicule others because they do not dress as you do.
18. Allow injustice to be perpetuated through silence.
19. Perpetuate notions of religious superiority.
20. Usurp the right of others to make choices simply because they are different from self.
21. Speak as though your perspective on reality is the only one.
22. Use the power inherent in your position in the hierarchy to reduce, restrict, or destroy the potential of others.
23. Ignore the cultural conventions of other groups in regard to titles of address, amount and type of eye contact, appropriate touching, and the use of interpersonal space.

Do

24. Recognize that values and traditions vary among the tributary groups and that they all deserve to be taken seriously.
25. Acknowledge the contribution of each tributary group to the general American culture.
26. Refrain from judging the values, traditions, and language of others against the absolute standards of your own.
27. Make sure that your intent or motive towards another is honorable regardless of how different they are from you.

28. Practice religious tolerance by refraining from denigrating the religious beliefs and traditions of others.
29. Judge the values, traditions and practices of others on the basis of whether or not they facilitate or restrict human potential, not on the basis of their similarity or differences from your own.
30. Present information in an accurate and undistorted fashion to all people in as far as they are of an age and mental capacity to understand.
31. Speak to others in a manner that facilitates the development of your and their potential regardless of their similarity to or difference from self.

Are any of these guidelines impractical? Why? Are any of them inappropriate? Why? In what ways are any of these guidelines vague or unclear? Which of these guidelines might routinely be followed for communication within a particular ethnic group but often violated in communication between that group and other ethnic groups?

Discarding Rigidity

As for the chapter on feminist contributions, Robert Solomon offers a fitting summary of many of the issues and themes discussed in this chapter on intercultural and multicultural communication ethics.[31]

> We try too hard, and impossibly, to be above any particular society and culture and so, in the name of universalism, find ourselves nowhere at all. . . . But ethics need not take the form of a rigid set of moral principles backed by an ironclad theory of justification. Rather it is a shared way of life in which certain practices and rules of morality play an accepted role but are flexible and always open to question. To question everything is to be left with nothing, but to refuse to question at all, or to insist on an ultimate justification, relegates morality to the realm of stubborn habits and condemns multicultural society to bitter political and endless battles.

Solomon advocates a new ethics of pluralism especially suited to contemporary American society rather than to ancient Greek society or to Kant's eighteenth-century Germany. America, he contends, is a society with values and one capable of making ethical judgments among better and worse actions. "But we are a society with a multiplicity of values, in which it therefore becomes all the more urgent for each of us to clarify, understand, and within modest limits, justify our values and our views." In his view, the complex ethos or national "character" that "constitutes American society is still in the making, and it is by doing ethics that we can assist in its formation."

Notes

[1] John Condon, "Values and Ethics in Communication Across Cultures: Notes on the North American Case," *Communication* 6, no. 2 (1981): 255–66; John Condon and Fathi Yousef, *An Introduction to Intercultural Communication* (Indianapolis: Bobbs-Merrill, 1975), chs. 4, 5, 10, 11.

[2] Dean C. Barnlund, "The Cross-Cultural Arena: An Ethical Void," in *Ethical Perspectives and Critical Issues in Intercultural Communication*, Nobleza Asuncion-Lande, ed. (Falls Church, VA: Speech Communication Association, 1980), pp. 8–13. Also see Nobleza Asuncion-Lande, "Ethics in Intercultural Communication: An Introduction," in *Ibid.*, pp. 3–7.

[3] William B. Gudykunst, "Communication, Ethics, and Relativism: The Implications of Ethical Relativity Theory for Intercultural Communication," paper presented at the Speech Communication Association convention, New York City, November 1980. Also see William B. Gudykunst and Young Yum Kim, *Communicating With Strangers: An Approach to Intercultural Communication* (Reading, MA: Addison-Wesley, 1984), pp. 199–204.

[4] Thomas W. Cooper, et al., eds., *Communication Ethics and Global Change* (New York: Longman, 1989), pp. 20–39, 227–41, 251–69.

[5] John C. Merrill, "Global Commonalities for Journalistic Ethics: Idle Dream or Realistic Goal?" in *Communication Ethics and Global Change*, pp. 284–290.

[6] William S. Howell, "Ethics of Intercultural Communication," paper presented at the Speech Communication Association convention, Anaheim, CA, November 1981; Howell, "Foreword," in *Ethical Perspectives and Critical Issues in Intercultural Communication*, Nobleza Asuncion-Lande, ed., pp. viii–x; Howell, *The Empathic Communicator* (1982; reissued, Prospect Heights, IL: Waveland Press, 1986), ch. 8.

[7] Milton J. Bennett, "Overcoming the Golden Rule: Sympathy and Empathy," in *Communication Yearbook 3*, Dan Nimmo, ed. (New Brunswick, NJ: Transaction Books, 1979), pp. 407–22. For some interpretations critical of the Golden Rule and the Platinum Rule, see James A. Jaksa and Michael S. Pritchard, *Communication Ethics: Methods of Analysis*, 2d ed. (Belmont, CA: Wadsworth, 1994), pp. 101–5.

[8] Reprinted with permission from K. S. Sitaram and Roy T. Cogdell, *Foundations of Intercultural Communication* (Columbus, OH: Charles E. Merrill Co., 1976), pp. 236–40.

[9] Several of these difficulties are discussed in Gudykunst, "Communication, Ethics, and Relativism."

[10] "David W. Kale, "Peace as an Ethic for Intercultural Communication," in *Intercultural Communication: A Reader*, 7th ed., Larry A. Samovar and Richard E. Porter, eds. (Belmont, CA: Wadsworth, 1994), pp. 435–40.

[11] Documentation of the sources for the following discussion of plagiarism is in Richard L. Johannesen, "The Ethics of Plagiarism Reconsidered: The Oratory of Martin Luther King, Jr.," *Southern Communication Journal*, 60 (Spring 1995): 185–94.

[12] For example, see James E. Porter, "Intertextuality and the Discourse Community," *Rhetoric Review*, 5 (Fall 1986): 34–47; Lisa Ede and Andrea Lunsford, *Singular Texts/Plural Authors: Perspectives on Collaborative Writing* (Carbon-

dale: Southern Illinois University Press, 1990); Karen Burke LeFevre, *Invention as a Social Act* (Carbondale: Southern Illinois University Press, 1987).

[13] Lawrence Blum, cited in Larry and Shari Collins Sharratt, eds., *Applied Ethics: A Multicultural Approach* (Englewood Cliffs, NJ: Prentice Hall, 1994), p. 2.

[14] Marquita L. Byrd, *The Intracultural Communication Book* (New York: McGraw-Hill, 1993), pp. 1, 10.

[15] Amy Gutmann, "The Challenge of Multiculturalism in Political Ethics," *Philosophy and Public Affairs*, 22 (Summer 1993): 171–206.

[16] Anthony Cortese, *Ethnic Ethics: The Restructuring of Moral Theory* (Albany: State University of New York Press, 1990), pp. 1–6, 41, 91–94, 107. For one brief critique of Cortese's moral pluralism view, see Joan C. Tronto, *Moral Boundaries: A Political Argument for an Ethic of Care* (New York: Routledge, 1993), p. 94.

[17] Dorothy Emmet, *Rules, Roles, and Relations* (London: Macmillan, 1966), pp. 89–109; Gutmann, "The Challenge of Multiculturalism in Political Ethics," pp. 171–206; Seyla Benhabib, *Situating the Self: Gender, Community and Postmodernism in Contemporary Society* (New York: Routledge, 1992), pp. 1–19, 153.

[18] Michael Josephson, *Making Ethical Decisions*, 2d ed. (Marina del Rey, CA: The Josephson Institute of Ethics, 1993), pp. 1–10.

[19] Gutmann, "The Challenge of Multiculturalism in Political Ethics."

[20] Susan Opotow, "Moral Exclusion and Injustice: An Introduction," *Journal of Social Issues*, 46 (1990): 1–20. (italics in original).

[21] Haig Bosmajian, *The Language of Oppression* (Washington, DC: Public Affairs Press, 1974), pp. 1–10. Also see J. Dan Rothwell, *Telling It Like It Isn't* (Englewood Cliffs, NJ: Prentice-Hall, 1982), chs. 5 and 6.

[22] Casey Miller and Kate Swift, *The Handbook of Nonsexist Writing* (New York: Barnes and Noble paperback, 1981), pp. 3–8. Second Edition, Harper & Row, 1988.

[23] Richard W. Baily, "George Orwell and the English Language," in *The Future of Nineteen Eighty-Four*, Ejner J. Jensen, ed. (Ann Arbor: University of Michigan Press, 1984), pp. 42–43. Also see two essays in *Philosophy and Sex*, Robert Baker and Frederick Elliston, eds. (Buffalo, NY: Prometheus Books, 1975): Barbara Lawrence, "Four Letter Words Can Hurt You," pp. 31–33; Robert Baker, "'Pricks' and 'Chicks': A Plea for 'Persons'," pp. 45–64.

[24] For extensive analysis of ethical issues and free speech issues in the areas of hate speech, pornography, and obscene rock and rap music lyrics, see Richard L. Johannesen, "Diversity, Freedom, and Responsibility in Tension," in *Communication Ethics in an Age of Diversity*, Josina M. Makau and Ronald C. Arnett, eds. (Champaign: University of Illinois Press, 1997), ch. 8.

[25] The following examples are cited in Thomas L. Tedford, *Freedom of Speech in the United States*, 2d ed. (New York: McGraw-Hill, 1993), p. 183; Samuel Walker, *Hate Speech: The History of an American Controversy* (Lincoln: University of Nebraska Press, 1994), pp. 129–30.

[26] Tedford, pp. 183–84; Walker, pp. 127–58.

[27] R. George Wright, *The Future of Free Speech Law* (New York: Quorum, 1990), pp. 58–59, 69, 73–76.

[28] Andrew Altman, "Liberalism and Campus Hate Speech: A Philosophical Examination," *Ethics*, 103 (January 1993): 302–17.

[29] Franklyn S. Haiman *"Speech Acts" and the First Amendment* (Carbondale: Southern Illinois University Press, 1992), pp. 10–20. Also see Barry M. Bracken, *Freedom of Speech: Words Are not Deeds* (Westport, CT: Praeger, 1994.)

[30] Byrd, *The Intracultural Communication Book* (1993), pp. 116–23. These guidelines are reprinted by permission of the publisher, McGraw-Hill, from pages 121–23.

[31] Robert C. Solomon, *Ethics: A Short Introduction* (Dubuque, IA: Brown Benchmark, 1993), pp. 159–63.

Appendix

Case Studies of Theory and Practice

Each of the case studies reprinted in this Appendix reflects one or more of the ethical "perspectives" discussed in this book. Where ethical standards are applied to specific instances of communication, you are encouraged to render your own ethical judgments of the instances examined. Does the critic show that the standards he or she employs are reasonable and relevant for the techniques being evaluated? Does the critic indicate in what ways the techniques examined measure up or fail to measure up to clearly explained standards? To what extent, and why, do you agree or differ with the critic's ethical assessment?

In *The Abuse of Casuistry* (Berkeley: University of California Press, 1988), Albert Jonsen and Stephen Toulmin detail the historical development and potential current applications of casuistry [kazh´ ö i strē] as a method of moral reasoning about paradigm ethical cases or "cases of conscience." They formally define casuistry as "the analysis of moral issues, using procedures of reasoning based on paradigms and analogies, leading to the formulation of expert opinion about the existence and stringency of particular moral obligations, framed in terms of rules or maxims that are general but not universal or invariable. . . ." (257). In "Stories, Values, and Health Care Decisions," David H. Smith explores the use of the casuistic method for the communication ethics of medical doctors (in *The Ethical Nexus*, Charles Conrad, ed., Norwood, NJ: Ablex, 1993, pp. 123–48). David Boeynik, "Casuistry: A Case Bound Method for Journalists," *Journal of Mass Media Ethics* 7, no. 2 (1992): 107–20), modifies the casuistic method for application to situations involving journalistic ethics. Read these sources to determine in what ways casuistry might be used in doing case studies of communication ethics.

Preview to "An Ethical Assessment of the Regan Rhetoric." *In addition to employing ethical standards derived from values essential to the functioning of representative democracy as a system of governing, at the outset this essay suggests two other possible ethical stances for analysis. As you read the essay, consider to what extent you could apply either Henry W. Johnstone's "humans as persuaders" view discussed earlier in the chapter, "Human Nature Perspectives," or the concept of projected speaker attitude toward audience discussed earlier in the chapter, "Dialogical Perspectives." In the next essay reprinted in this appendix, another possible approach is sketched—a "narrative paradigm" that emphasizes rhetoric-as-story-telling. The ethical framework and standards selected to carry out an ethical assessment definitely influence the range, severity, and relevance of the ethical judgments reached. In what ways? Also, as you read this essay, especially consider how adequately the following concepts and issues are discussed and applied: conscious intent; sincerity; intentional ambiguity and vagueness; ethical responsibilities stemming from formal roles.*

President Reagan's habit of playing fast and loose with the facts was not limited to the time frame 1981–1982. His misstatement of fact, statistics, and situations and his use of dubious stories and anecdotes continued throughout both of his terms in office. While the print and broadcast media less and less reported these communication problems (perhaps because they were so routine as to no longer be "news"), nevertheless the misstatements and misuses persisted. An intensive case study of Reagan Administration rhetoric that employs a "representative democracy" political perspective is Ralph E. Dowling and Gabrielle Marraro, "Grenada and the Great Communicator: A Study of Democratic Ethics," Western Journal of Speech Communication, 50 (Fall 1986): 350-67. Probably the most exhaustive compendium and analysis of Reagan's erroneous statements and stories is Mark Green and Gail MacColl, Reagan's Reign of Error: The Instant Nostalgia Edition, *expanded and updated (New York: Pantheon Books, 1987).*

The glaring misuse of facts and anecdotes in ethically suspect ways continues in recent national political discourse. For example, syndicated columnist Joseph Spear takes to task House Speaker Newt Gingrich for this habit ("Third-wave Newt comes unglued," DeKalb, IL Daily Chronicle, March 17, 1995, p. 4). Spear observes: "We know that Newt doesn't care that his facts are often not factual. He spoke about a ten-year-old student in St. Louis who was suspended for asking God's blessings on his cafeteria meals. It was not true. He told how the FDA refused to approve an innovative heart pump. It was not true. He rattled on and on about a 'federal shelter' in Denver that was outperformed by a private facility down the street. It was not true." Spear's judgment is that "Newt is a prattler, a careless accuser, an irresponsible teller of tales." An editorial in the Washington Post National Weekly Edition *(March 13–19, 1995, p. 27)* contends that trying "to get the story straight, whether you're in our business or Speaker Gingrich's, is not a luxury, but a responsibility."

An Ethical Assessment of the Reagan Rhetoric: 1981–1982*
Richard L. Johannesen

In keeping with the American political tradition of evaluating the performance of presidents at the midpoint in their term of office, it seems fitting to assess the ethicality of President Reagan's rhetoric during the first two years of his administration.[1] What ethical criteria, what standards for ethical responsibility, might be appropriate for such judgment? We might apply an ethic embedded in the nature of the rhetorical process itself, such as outlined by Henry W. Johnstone, Jr. (Johannesen, 1983, pp. 36–37; Johnstone, 1981). Or we could explore the ethicality of Reagan's projected attitude or stance toward voters, legislators, and foreign officials as either conducive or detrimental to public political dialogue (Johannesen, 1983, chap. 4).

---

*Reprinted with permission of the publisher from Richard L. Johannesen, "An Ethical Assessment of the Reagan Rhetoric: 1981-1982," in *Political Communication Yearbook 1984*, Keith R. Sanders, Lynda Lee Kaid, and Dan Nimmo, eds. (Carbondale: Southern Illinois University Press, 1985), pp. 226–41.

Political Perspective

However, I believe it is especially reasonable to examine the ethics of the Reagan rhetoric from what has been termed a "political" perspective (Johannesen, 1983, chap. 2). Any system of governing usually contains within its ideology an implicit and explicit set of values and procedures accepted as crucial to the health and growth of that political system. Once these essential political values are identified for a political system, they can generate criteria for evaluating the ethics of communicative means and ends within that particular system. The assumption is that communication should foster realization of these values and that communication tactics and techniques which retard, subvert, or circumvent these fundamental political values should be condemned as unethical.

Naturally each different political/governmental system could embody differing values leading to differing ethical judgments. Within the context of American representative democracy, for instance, various analysts pinpoint values and procedures traditionally viewed as fundamental to optimum functioning of our political system. Such values can guide ethical scrutiny of communication therein. Among such fundamental values and procedures would be: enhancement of citizen capacity to reach rational decisions; access to channels of public communication; access to relevant and accurate information on public issues; maximization of freedom of choice; toleration of dissent; honesty in presenting motivations and consequences; and thoroughness, accuracy, and fairness in presenting evidence and alternatives (Fleishman, Liebman, & Moore, 1981, chaps. 1, 3, 4, 8, 12; Nilsen, 1974, chaps. 1-4; Redford, 1969, chap. 1).

Responsibility, Intent, and Sincerity

Before proceeding to scrutinize Reagan's rhetoric, I believe that three concepts merit brief discussion—responsibility, intent, and sincerity (Johannesen, 1983, pp. 6-7). As communicators, our ethical responsibilities may stem from a status or position we have earned or been granted, from commitments (promises, pledges, agreements) we have made, or from subsequent consequences of our communication on others. Responsibility includes the elements of fulfilling duties and obligations, of being accountable to other individuals and groups, and of being accountable as evaluated by agreed upon standards. Responsible communication reflects the exercise of thoughtful and deliberate judgment; that is, the responsible communicator would carefully analyze claims, soundly assess probable consequences, and conscientiously weigh relevant values. In a sense, responsible communicators are *response-able*; they respond to the needs and communication of others in sensitive, thoughtful, and fitting ways (Freund, 1960; Neibuhr, 1963, pp. 47–89, 151–54; Pennock, 1960; Pincoffs, 1975).

Whether communicators seem intentionally and knowingly to use particular content or techniques is a factor most of us take into account in judging degree of communication ethicality. If a dubious communication behavior seems to stem more from accident, from an unintentional slip of the tongue, or even from ignorance, often we are less harsh in our ethical assessment. For most of us, it is the intentional use of ethically questionable techniques that merits our harshest condemnation. In contrast, it might be contended that communicators have an ethical obligation to double-check the soundness of their information, evidence, and reasoning before they present it to others. Superficial preparation would not be an adequate excuse to lessen the severity of our ethical judgment. A similar view might be advanced concerning elected or appointed government officials. If they use obscure or jargon-laden language that clouds the accurate and clear representation of ideas, even if that use is not intended to deceive or hide, they are ethically irresponsible. Such officials, according to this view, should be obligated to communicate clearly and accurately with citizens in fulfillment of their governmental duties.

As a related question we can ask, does sincerity of intent release a communicator from ethical responsibility concerning means and effects? Could we say that *if* Adolf Hitler's contemporary Germans judged him to be sincere, they should not assess the ethics of his persuasion? In such cases, evaluations probably are best carried out it we appraise sincerity and ethicality separately. For example, a communicator sincere in intent nevertheless may be found to utilize unethical strategies. Wayne Booth (1974, p. 157) reminds us that "sincerity is more difficult to check and easier to fake than logicality or consistency, and its presence does not, after all, guarantee very much about the speaker's case."

The Claims

In assessing the ethics of the Reagan rhetoric, I will examine two broad issues or areas of concern, both with several subissues. First, I will examine the claim that the Reagan rhetoric plays fast and loose with the facts, and thus warrants ethical condemnation. Second, I will probe the claim that the Reagan rhetoric intentionally employs ambiguity and vagueness, and thus warrants ethical condemnation. In evaluating these claims, I have sampled Reagan's major and minor speeches for the two-year period, primarily those addressed to American citizens, his news conferences and interviews, and selected additional statements. (See *Weekly Compilation of Presidential Documents*; hereafter cited as *WCPD*.)

Misstatement of Facts

First, then, I turn to the claim that the Reagan rhetoric plays fast and loose with the facts. The charge is that, in his news conferences, informal comments, and sometimes in speeches, Reagan misstates facts, statistics, and situations and misuses factual illustrations and stories as proof. He does this, not just on rare occasions, but with dismaying, almost routine, frequency. Such disparate sources as the *Christian Century*, the *Nation*, *Time*, and the *Washington Post* concur in this judgment. (See Barone and Allen, 1982; Johnson, 1982a; Leahy, 1982; "Pool Reports," 1982; "Presidential Fatigue," 1983; Rowan, 1982; Rowley, 1983; Von Hoffman, 1982; Wagman, 1982; Wall, 1982.) In fact the *Nation* monitored Reagan's alleged "stream of documented whoppers, bloopers, and deceptions" through a periodic column by Mark Green, run under the continuing title of "There He Goes Again" (Green, 1982a, 1982b, 1982c, 1983).

We can look briefly at a cross section of examples before examining one message in detail. In a December 25, 1981, interview aired on the Public Broadcasting System, Reagan repeated a charge he had made on other occasions. According to Reagan, many members of Franklin D. Roosevelt's New Deal Brain Trust advocated a Mussolini-style fascism and the secretary of the interior, Harold Ickes, espoused a modified form of communism. However, Reagan never has produced specific references to verify his assertions, and acknowledged experts on Ickes and on the New Deal views toward Mussolini have failed to uncover such proof (Green, 1982a; Lescaze, 1981). *Newsweek* identified four erroneous descriptions of American involvement in Vietnam in Reagan's February 18, 1982, news conference ("Lyndon B. Reagan on Vietnam," 1982; *WCPD*, 1982, *18*, 191–92). At his March 31, 1982, news conference, Reagan misstated the particulars of anywhere from three to five separate governmental programs (Green, 1982b; *WCPD*, 1982, *18*, 414–16).

On April 15, 1982, Reagan was asked his views on gun control by a group of elementary school students. As part of his reply, he alluded to a British law under which "a criminal with a gun, even if he was arrested for burglary, was tried for first degree murder and hanged if found guilty." A *New York Times* search failed to uncover such a law (Green, 1982b). White House Deputy Press Secretary Larry Speakes defended Reagan's use of the example by saying, "It made the point, didn't it?" To which an editorial in the *Washington Post* responded ("Facts About," 1982), "That's not a good enough standard for public discourse." During a speech in Houston, Texas, on June 15, 1982, the president (*WCPD*, 1982, *18*, 804) quoted Justice Oliver Wendell Holmes as saying, "Keep the government poor and remain free." An acknowledged scholar on Holmes was unaware of anything in Holmes' writings that resembled the quotation. Later an official in the White House speechwriting office was quoted as explaining that "Holmes never said anything point-blank exactly like that . . . we're still trying to track it down" (Green, 1982c).

In a speech to the National Black Republican Council on September 15, 1982, Reagan (*WCPD*, 1982, *18*, 1152–57) claimed that his administration had enforced civil rights laws just as actively as previous administrations. This assertion is directly contradicted in numerous specifics by internal records of the Equal Employment Opportunity Commission and by a report of the Washington Council of Lawyers, a bipartisan association of attorneys from private firms, government, and public interests groups ("Reagan's Claims," 1982). Newspaper editorials, including ones in the *Atlanta Constitution*, *Des Moines Tribune*, and *Roanoke Times and World News*, challenged Reagan's interpretation of his administration's civil rights record (*Editorials on File*, 1982b). In this same September 15 speech, Reagan depicted Lyndon Johnson's Great Society effort as more of a detriment than an aid to the progress of blacks. A *Washington Post* editorial ("Revisionism," 1982) challenged Reagan's interpretation of the Great Society programs and concluded, "At best, it's a joke, at worst a travesty." Syndicated political columnist Colman McCarthy (1982) judged Reagan's claim as "deceitful in its ignoring of the evidence" (also see Denton, 1982b; Johnson, 1982b).[2]

Political reporter Martin Schram (1982) judges a fall 1982 Republican party television advertisement to be a "shameless political deception." Viewers see a white-haired postman delivering a July Social Security check that includes the automatic cost-of-living benefit increase. Viewers are told that President Reagan "kept his promise to the American people." In fact the increase was mandated by law, and Reagan even had proposed cutting it. This advertisement was given the first place 1982 Doublespeak Award by the Committee on Public

Doublespeak of the National Council of Teachers of English. The award goes to communication that is "grossly unfactual, deceptive, evasive, euphemistic, confusing, or self-contradictory" (*Quarterly Review*, 1983). Also in the fall of 1982, a 75-page book, titled *Fairness Issues: An Executive Briefing Book*, was issued to aid the president and his cabinet officers in presenting accurate descriptions of problems and solutions. Schram (1982) examined this "blend of statistics and rationales" to assess its own accuracy and fairness. He describes three major instances where the statistics stated are accurate as far as they go, but because relevant additional facts are omitted the impression created is quite misleading.

In an early October 1982 speech to a gathering of veterans in Ohio (*WCPD*, 1982, *18*, 1259–60), Reagan alleged that the current nuclear weapons freeze movement is being manipulated by people who "want the weakening of America." Later the president admitted that he "did not have any Americans in mind" as particular subversives. Senate Majority Leader Howard Baker excused Reagan's allegations as "broad brush comments on the campaign trail." But the *Chicago Tribune* ("A Freeze," 1982) editorially denounced Reagan's assertion as "false and slanderous," condemned the implication that Soviet agents may be manipulating the movement, and defended most of the movement's activists as having "loyalty and integrity" beyond question. Numerous newspaper editorials condemned this charge of Soviet manipulation as, among other things, unfounded, demogogic, gutter-level, poisonous, and hogwash. Included among such editorials are those in the *Des Moines Register*, *St. Louis Post-Dispatch*, *Detroit Free Press*, *Boston Globe*, and *Philadelphia Inquirer* (see *Editorials on File*, 1982c).

When asked at his November 11, 1982, news conference (*WCPD*, 1982, *18*, 1462–63) if he had any evidence that the nuclear weapons freeze movement in America was being "manipulated" by the Soviets, Reagan replied, "Yes, there is plenty of evidence." He contended that Soviet agents helped organize the summer 1982 peace march in New York City and that such agents helped instigate and perpetuate the peace/freeze movement. When invited to provide more explicit evidence of Soviet manipulation, he said he could not because that would involve "intelligence matters." The White House press office, when asked to produce evidence to substantiate Reagan's charges, mentioned articles in the *American Spectator*, *Commentary*, and *Readers Digest*. The author of the *Digest* article, a former intelligence officer named Frank Barron, reportedly used information from three "intelligence and/or security services" which he was not free to name ("Court Journalism," 1982).[3] In a question-and-answer session with reporters on national radio and television on December 10, 1982, Reagan alluded to these articles again as documenting Soviet "participation" in the peace/freeze movement. But he sidestepped a question asking whether he accepted the House Intelligence Committee report that concluded that the nuclear freeze proponents were not being manipulated by Soviet agents (WCPD, 1982, 18, 1602–5).

A Case Study

The news conference of January 19, 1982, can serve as an extended illustration of Reagan's difficulties (WCPD, 1982, 18, 39–46). In a performance that Newsweek described as "shot through with errors of fact," Reagan several times used inaccurate and misleading statistics on unemployment. (Sources documenting the errors discussed in this and the next two paragraphs are: "The Hard Times," 1982; Lescaze, 1982; "More Reagan Remarks," 1982; "To Tell the Truth," 1982; "There He Goes Again," 1982.) Reagan gave a dubious interpretation to a letter he had received from Pope John Paul II concerning American actions toward Poland, an interpretation quickly questioned by the Vatican. The president defended his decision to revoke the Internal Revenue Service rule prohibiting tax-exempt status for racially segregated schools. He claimed that he was correcting a procedure he thought "had no basis in law." Actually, in 1971 the Supreme Court upheld a lower court decision that the IRS was within its legal authority in such prohibition. When questioned about the high unemployment rate of blacks, Reagan mentioned over twenty pages of job advertisements in the prior Sunday's *Washington Post*. Argued Reagan, "What we need to do is make more people qualified to go and apply for those jobs." Actually the Reagan administration budget cuts in 1981 eliminated about one-third of the federal job-training programs.[4] Concerning his recently instituted policy of "volunteer" lie-detector tests for administration employees as a means of plugging leaks of Defense Department information, Reagan explained he was simply "abiding by the existing law" on security leaks. Actually, employees "volunteered" in order to save their jobs, and there is no such "existing law" that includes lie-detector tests.

Also at this January 19 news conference, Reagan mentioned in sad retrospect a 1967 abortion law he had signed as California governor, a law that he asserted "literally led to abortion on demand on the plea of rape." Actually, the rape provision in the law accounted for only a small proportion of abortions; most of the abortions were performed under a provision that protected the mother's mental and physical health. Both in this news conference and in a January 14 speech to the New York City Partnership Luncheon (*WCPD*, 1982, *18*, 30–31), Reagan described a program to aid the elderly in Pima, Arizona. The president praised the Arizona program of food for the elderly for cutting costs by using volunteers while significantly increasing the number of persons aided. *Time* directly questioned his statistics on the program. The *Washington Post* contended that costs were cut only temporarily because some workers continued as volunteers while waiting for a lapsed federal grant to be restored. And more elderly were served, said the *Post*, because other government sponsored facilities formerly aiding the elderly had been closed. In a later news conference (*WCPD*, 1982, *18*, 195–96), Reagan claimed that his account of the Arizona program had been reconfirmed by Pima officials as accurate "word for word." But Reagan did not refute the *Post*'s description of the circumstances explaining those statistics.

In addition to the speculation that Reagan simply is something of a "klutz," what explanations did Reagan's staff offer for his difficulties at the January 19 news conference in presenting facts and statistics? White House Communications Director David Gergen argued that a "good faith" effort to check the facts of the Arizona program had been made just prior to Reagan's New York Speech. Deputy White House Press Secretary Larry Speakes offered no explanation on how Reagan got the inaccurate unemployment statistics and concluded, "I don't think we can assess any blame here."

Misuse of Anecdotes

Another aspect of playing fast and loose with the facts is Reagan's misuse of factual illustrations and stories for proof. This long-standing habit has been characterized satirically as Reagan's "anecdotage" problem. He likes to use vivid and dramatic, real-life stories to prove this point or that. Unfortunately, these anecdotes, even if not misstated, frequently are found to be misleading or unrepresentative. In this regard, William Safire (1982), a former speech writer for President Nixon, chastises Reagan for taking a "simplistic approach to complex matters." Syndicated political columnists Jack Germond and Jules Witcover (1982) describe Reagan's proclivity for "generalizing from the simplistic particular," for overgeneralizing individual abuses into proof of a major problem. A *Christian Century* editorial (Wall, 1982) objects that Reagan's illustrations too often do not inform or provide evidence for an argument; rather they "exacerbate feelings" by arousing "latent hostility among true believers." James David Barber (1982) condemns Reagan for having "contempt for the facts" and issuing "spurious specifics with cavalier abandon." More precisely, Barber depicts Reagan as the "Aesop of the Oval Office, tossing off parables instead of arguments." Such stories are not easily judged by tests of evidence, notes Barber, and he urges that we must "rely on public discourse in which the proposals meet facts in a test clear enough for reason to grasp."

Reagan has, for example, used such questionable anecdotes as a kind of proof of alleged widespread abuses in the federal welfare program, the food stamp program, and the school lunch program. In this latter case, Reagan recounted a story of wealthy children taking advantage of a school lunch program in upstate New York. When asked for more details at his February 18, 1982, news conference (*WCPD*, 1982, *18*, 195-196; also Horowitz, 1982), the president was at a loss to identify the source of the information and to verify its validity. Reagan lamely explained, "I simply recounted it as having been told to me by someone." "I know that it was up in New York someplace."

In a kind of "you're another" response, Reagan criticizes the news media for themselves overplaying unrepresentative or erroneous negative stories. He gave an example of such a story in a March 16, 1982, interview (*WCPD*, 1982, *18*, 314–15) and also complained, "Is it news that some fellow out in South Succotash someplace has been laid off, that he should be interviewed nationwide?" Reagan also objects that some critics of his budget overstress unrepresentative, emotion-charged cases of hardship when he believes that his program actually isn't hurting anyone truly in need (Germond and Witcover, 1982; "More on the Anecdote Front," 1982; "News," 1982).

Ethical Assessment

Now in order is my assessment of Reagan's degree of ethicality in playing fast and loose with the facts. Does Reagan intentionally misstate facts, statistics, and situations and intentionally use dubious anecdotes? There seems to be scant hard evidence of such outright deception. Haynes Johnson (1982a), the respected political reporter for the *Washington Post*, seems to acknowledge Reagan's basic honesty and sincerity: "You don't think he's trying to put one over on you"; "he sincerely believes what he says."

Nevertheless, suspicions as to Reagan's motives and intentions persist. Mark Green (1982a) contends that Reagan has "a long history of inaccuracies that suspiciously and invariably favor his positions." Michael Barone and Jodie Allen (1982), of the *Washington Post* editorial staff, provide an illustration of this contention from Reagan's news conference on September 28, 1982 (*WCPD*, 1982, *18*, 1219–27). With reference to three instances where the president used inaccurate statistics, they observe a "selectivity in the slips" and note that in each case the "accurate statistic would have less impact than the inaccurate one." Aside from faulty memory, Green (1982a) attributes Reagan's "pattern of errors" to his tendency to shade the truth "in the service of ideology," to alter the facts rather than his ideology. Furthermore, believes Green, Reagan is so optimistically self-delusional that he transforms "bad news into good." Finally, Green notes that Reagan often "wings it" in his presentations rather than basing them on "long hours of study of complex issues."[5]

Lou Cannon, the White House correspondent for the *Washington Post*, published an evenhanded biography of Reagan that supports Green's analysis in several respects. (Cannon, 1982, pp. 19–20, 271–73, 322, 328, 372–74, 409, 414.) Cannon describes Reagan's "unwillingness to make himself conversant with the complex issues of nuclear weaponry." Additionally, when Reagan "finds an idea that serves his purposes, he rarely bothers with details that get in the way of its promotion." Cannon clearly is uneasy about Reagan's frequent unconcern for accuracy.[6] Analysts for both *Newsweek* and *Time* underscore the view that Reagan's selective perception in decision making borders on distortion and self-deception (Watson, et al., 1982; Church, 1982). His optimism so blinds him to disagreeable facts that he only hears what he wants to hear. Reagan seizes on one item of good news, magnifies it into an encompassing truth, and blocks out most unpleasant evidence.

An editorial in the *Nation* ("The Gaffer," 1982) recites a long list of major Reagan policy pronouncements where there seems to be an "inverse relationship between his word and his deed," where he says "one thing while doing the opposite" (also see Reston, 1982). At his February 18, 1982, press conference (*WCPD*, 1982, *18*, 195–96), Reagan's response to critics of his anecdotes was to wave alleged "documentation" of his stories, and then refuse to release the documentation ("Disappointing Performance," 1982; Germond and Witcover, 1982). Such a tactic, reminiscent of Joseph R. McCarthy's "briefcase" of evidence ploy, does not inspire confidence in Reagan's motives (Baskerville, 1954; Luthin, 1954).

Perhaps the rhetorical context and circumstances in which Reagan employs anecdotes that are of doubtful proof-value should influence our judgment of his ethicality. Several political columnists (Germond and Witcover, 1982; Safire, 1982) imply such a viewpoint. According to this view, anecdotes as pseudoproof may be ethically acceptable in stump oratory on the campaign trail. But such anecdotes are ethically questionable when used to justify policies in news conferences and in conversations with legislators. Unfortunately, these columnists do not specify the exact characteristics of the differing rhetorical contexts that might justify such a differential ethical judgment. Their belief may be that standards and expectations for what is ethically acceptable in campaign oratory are, or should be, lower than those for presidential communication in fulfillment of the duties of office.

Should Reagan's sincere belief in what he says, even if what he says is inaccurate, misleading, or unrepresentative, soften our ethical judgment of his rhetoric? David Gergen, White House director of communications, would seem to believe so. Gergen told reporters that what is important is not "making sure we have every single fact straight," but rather "whether the larger points are right." Gergen also defended Reagan's storytelling as a "folk art" wherein the anecdotes have a "parable-like quality to them" and are used simply to illustrate "how society works" (Barber, 1982; Denton, 1982a; Wagman, 1982). However, as I urged earlier, sincerity of intent and ethicality of rhetorical techniques most appropriately should be judged separately. In Reagan's case, whether he is sincere or not, the ethicality of his rhetorical tactics must be independently assessed.

Regardless of whether Reagan intends to play fast and loose with the facts, I believe he is ethically irresponsible in rather regularly employing erroneous, misleading, or atypical information. Reagan has a duty to present to citizens the relevant and accurate data they need to make reasonable decisions on public issues. Meg Greenfield (1982b), the *Newsweek* political columnist, contends that Reagan is obliged in justifying his policies to use "arguments and real evidence" rather than "episodes or isolated case studies."

Intentional Ambiguity and Vagueness

The second major claim I will examine is that the Reagan rhetoric intentionally employs ambiguity and vagueness. Textbooks on oral and written communication typically warn against ambiguity and vagueness; often they directly or indirectly contend that intentional ambiguity is an unethical communication tactic. Most people probably would agree that intentional ambiguity is unethical in situations where accurate instruction or efficient transmission of precise information is the acknowledged purpose. Even in most persuasive communication situations, intentional ambiguity would be ethically suspect.

In some situations, however, communicators may feel that the intentional creation of ambiguity or vagueness is necessary, accepted, expected as normal, and even ethically justified. Such might be the case, for example, in some instances of religious discourse, legal discourse, advertising, political campaigning, labor-management negotiations, or international diplomatic negotiations. Among the purposes for which communicators might feel that intentional ambiguity is justified ethically would be to use ambiguity on one controversial issue to allow for understanding and possible agreement on other basic issues. Another purpose might be to promote maximum latitude for revision of a position by avoiding being "locked-in" to a single absolute or dogmatic stance. (For extended discussion, see Johannesen, 1983, pp. 106–8.)

A Diplomatic Communiqué

I will focus on only several areas where ambiguity and vagueness have been apparent. Of course others might suggest additional dimensions of the Reagan rhetoric that warrant examination for vagueness or ambiguity. On August 17, 1982, the United States and China issued a joint communiqué (*WCPD*, 1982, *18*, 1039–41), dubbed by the press as Shanghai II, which described American and Chinese positions toward the future of Taiwan. Among other items, China pledged use of only "peaceful" means for eventual reunification with Taiwan, while the United States agreed to limit its military arms sales to Taiwan to a level not exceeding that of recent years and to gradually reduce such sales leading to a "final resolution" (Knickerbocker, 1982).

Some critics condemned these portions of the communiqué for irresponsible use of language. Senator Barry Goldwater severely denounced Shanghai II as full of "double-talk and false statements." *Newsweek* political columnist George Will (1982) questioned the ethics of Reagan's assertion that American policy had not changed while at the same time committing us in the communiqué to eventual termination of arms sales. Concluded Will, "The Taiwan debacle suggests that Reagan thinks he can use words any which way, with impunity."

Other sources ("Papering Over," 1982) argued that the "calculated diplomatic ambiguity" of the communiqué was valuable and appropriate. Washington correspondent Lee Roderick (1982) felt that Reagan got "the best of both worlds" by leaving the language vague: "He has not committed the U.S. to an arms cutoff by a specific date—giving Washington time to assess China's promise to unify the country by 'peaceful' means—yet has underscored U.S. recognition of China's claim to Taiwan." Editorials in the *Christian Science Monitor, St. Louis Post Dispatch, Boston Herald American,* and *Chicago Tribune* praised Reagan's realism and sound judgment in approving Shanghai II, including its vague language (*Editorials on File,* 1982a; "Mr. Reagan and China," 1982). Said the *Tribune* ("When Doubletalk," 1982): "If the U.S. and Chinese negotiators had to confine themselves to straight talk, there never could be any agreement at all. A communiqué full of doubletalk has the marvelous quality of enabling both sides to claim victory."

In this case of the intentionally vague and ambiguous language of the Shanghai II communiqué, I would not be harsh on the ethics of the Reagan administration rhetoric. The values and ethical standards basic to communication within American representative democracy need not apply uniformly to international diplomatic messages and agreements among nations with differing cultures and political systems. Given the norms and expectations of international diplomatic negotiation, where some points are left vague to facilitate agreement on more concrete points, and where flexibility of interpretation on present disputes may avoid crises while facilitating future negotiations, the language here would seem to be used ethically.

Appeals to Values

What can be said of the ethics of the appeals to values made in Reagan's rhetoric during his first two years in office? Reagan has expressed his belief that America "longs to see traditional values reflected in public policies again." What are the primary and subsidiary values invoked by Reagan in his major and minor addresses? The central "traditional values itemized by Reagan in his speech to the Alabama state legislature, March 15, 1982 (*WCPD,* 1982, *18,* 302–7), are the same ones repeated in a number of presidential addresses, in his nomination acceptance speech, in campaign speeches, and even a speech to Republicans in 1978 (Evans and Novak, 1981, p. 10): patriotism, freedom, family, work, and neighborhood. Scattered in his presidential addresses are other values he believes necessary for a restored America: individualism, free enterprise, risk-taking, peace, sacrifice, volunteerism, government accountability, national security, equality of opportunity, and optimism.[7]

In recent but separate analyses, both Walter Fisher (1982) and Charles Kauffman (1982) describe the Reagan rhetoric, especially on domestic issues, as one in which present problems are depicted as results of the immediate past. The solution to ensure a good future is a return or reversion to basic values and principles supposedly characteristic of America's long past of the eighteenth and nineteenth centuries. Fisher and Kauffman both identify values central to Reagan's image of America's heroic, romantic past: family, work, neighborhood, peace, freedom, individualism, and competition. In these value appeals to America's long past, note Fisher and Kauffman, the values remain vague and general in meaning so that citizens are invited to fill in their own meanings. Fisher (1982, pp. 305–6) attempts to decode or decipher some of these central values as follows: "'family' means the nuclear family—dad, mom, son, and daughter; the 'neighborhood' means no busing; 'work' means no welfare; 'peace' means the United States must be the biggest, strongest country in the world in order that we not only preserve the peace, but also fulfill our manifest destiny to spread our way of life everywhere; and 'freedom' means freedom from governmental interference in the 'free enterprise' system."

In *The New Rhetoric*, Perelman and Olbrechts-Tyteca (1969, pp. 76–77) contend that effective persuasion intertwines appeals to abstract, universal values, such as truth and justice, with appeals to somewhat more concrete values, such as fidelity, loyalty, nation, solidarity, and discipline. They argue that the rhetorical potency of more abstract values stems from the vagueness and lack of specificity of their content. The more details and examples we provide for such values, the more controversial and more questioned they become. Nevertheless, Perelman and Olbrechts-Tyteca believe that such an interweaving of abstract and concrete values is normal and acceptable as a part of human nature.

Ethical Assessment

In my opinion, Reagan's use of value appeals that are vague in content should not be condemned as unethical solely and automatically because of their vagueness. Rather, in any specific instance in a specific rhetorical context, a more intensive analysis than undertaken here would be needed. To assess the degree of ethicality, such an analysis would attempt to cover the following points that are rooted in the standards central to ethical communication within our political/governmental system: honesty, relevance, accuracy, fairness, and reasonableness. To what degree do the value appeals serve as relevant motivational reinforcement for a point or proposal that has an independent basis in reasonable evidence? To what degree do the value appeals serve a legitimate function of promoting social cohesion, of reinforcing audience commitment to ideas they already believe? With what degree of appropriateness are the consequences of commitment to the values clarified? To what degree do the value appeals serve as substitutes, as pseudoproof, for the factuality of an assertion? To what degree do the value appeals divert attention from more fundamental, pressing, or controversial matters? To what degree do the value appeals seem to promote, intentionally or not, unreflective stimulus-response reactions when the occasion demands reflective judgment? (For one analytic framework, see Fisher, 1978, 1980.)

Conclusions

What can be said in summary concerning the ethicality of Ronald Reagan's rhetoric during the first two years of his presidency? In the instance of the Shanghai II communiqué, I would judge the vague and ambiguous language approved by Reagan to be ethically acceptable. As for appeals to value concepts with vague and ambiguous meanings, I do not view them by definition as unethical. To determine ethicality, specific usages would need to be examined as to purpose, function, and effects.

As to the claim that President Reagan plays fast and loose with the facts and thus warrants ethical condemnation, I would agree that he is ethically irresponsible. I believe that this judgment is not overly severe for two reasons. First, Reagan's misstatements of facts and misuse of anecdotes are not rare, occasional, or on minor matters. The standard is not perfect accuracy. Occasional slips on minor details may be expected. The obligation is not to ultimate truth in some absolute and invariable sense. But given the major resources at his command for verifying information, a president does have an obligation to present regularly highly probable conclusions and data that are as accurate and as fair as possible (Barone and Allen, 1982; Johannesen, 1983, pp. 17–18, 24). In Reagan's case of misstatement and misuse, no matter whether intentional, the effect still is deception on significant matters of public concern. A *New York Times* editorial concluded: "Whether jobs are going up or down is not just a flub. To state social facts wrong in a way that makes his Administration look good is not just a flub and not just a fudge, but a deception. . . . When he tosses facts around so loosely, does he think no one will notice?" ("The Quiz Kid," 1982; also see Wall, 1982).

A second reason why the judgment of ethical irresponsibility is not too harsh is that a president has an obligation to reinforce rather than undermine the trust between government and the citizenry so vital to functioning of our representative democracy (Johannesen, 1983, pp. 24–26). To answer the question posed in the *New York Times* editorial, citizens are taking notice (for example, Gelman, 1982). In a significant part because of the mounting pattern of playing fast and loose with the facts ("Presidential Fatigue," 1983) and of saying one thing and doing the opposite, Reagan's once large reservoir of trust and credibility with the American public seems to be shrinking. What is at stake, in the view of Meg Greenfield (1982a), is Reagan's "overall authority and plausibility" as president, his "power to awe, move, frighten, guide and persuade." She succinctly describes the increasing spiral of lack of trust and growing suspicion. "You cease to credit one thing, then you begin to suppose the worst about another. . . . Less is accepted; more becomes suspect." The eventual consequences of such spiraling suspicion must be faced. The ominous warning of David Wise (1973, pp. 18, 342, 345) in his book, *The Politics of Lying*, still merits repeating. "The American system is based not only upon formal checks and balances among the three branches of government; it depends also, perhaps most importantly, on a delicate balance of confidence between the people and the government. . . . If the governed are misled, if they are not told the truth, or if through official secrecy and deception they lack information on which to base intelligent decisions, the system may go on—but not as a democracy."

Notes

[1] This essay is based on a paper presented at the annual meeting of the Speech Communication Association, Louisville, KY, November 7, 1982.

[2] Also see Reagan's speech to black college and university presidents, Sept. 22, 1982 (*WCPD*, 1982, *18*, 1190).

[3] For journalistic analyses which undercut Reagan's charge of manipulation, see Donner (1982), Graves (1983), and Radash (1983). Donner replies to his critics in the letters columns, *Nation*, Dec. 4, 1982, pp. 578–79, and Dec. 25, 1982, p. 674.

⁴ On October 13, 1982, Reagan signed a bill to retrain one million unemployed workers for different jobs, but this bill has disputed authorship. Democrats in Congress, and some Republicans, note that the bill originated there and that only in the preceding several weeks did Reagan drop his earlier opposition and embrace the bill (Hoffman, 1982).

⁵ Green has published further analyses since this manuscript was prepared. See Green and MacColl, *Reagan's Reign of Error* (1987).

⁶ For a discussion of Reagan's "penchant for the alarming claim, the inaccurate fact, the impolitic remark" in informal speaking situations during the 1980 campaign, see Stacks (1981, pp. 232–35). By the end of 1982, however, Cannon and Hoffman (1982) report on their December 16 interview in which Reagan "demonstrated a more secure grasp of issues, especially in foreign policy, and a greater appreciation of subtleties" than he had in many prior interviews and statements.

⁷ In addition to the Alabama speech, other representative value appeals can be found in: speech to Oklahoma state legislature, Mar. 16, 1982 (*WCPD*, 1982, *18*, 316–21); inaugural address, Jan. 20, 1981 (*WCPD*, 1981, *17*, 1–5); televised speech on the economy, Feb. 5, 1981 (*WCPD*, 1981, *17*, 93–98); address to Congress on the economy, Feb. 18, 1981 (*WCPD*, 1981, *17*, 130–37); state of the Union address, Jan. 26, 1982 (*WCPD*, 1982, *18*, 76–83); speech to Republican party rally in Omaha, Nebraska, Oct. 21, 1982 (*WCPD*, 1982, *18*, 1368–72).

References

Barber, J. D. (1982, November 7). The oval office Aesop. *New York Times*, p. E17.
Barone, M., and Allen, J. (1982, October 10). The "great communicator" or the "great prevaricator"? *Washington Post*, p. C8.
Baskerville, B. (1954). Joe McCarthy: Brief-case demagogue. *Today's Speech*, 2 (September), 8–15.
Booth, W. M. (1974). *Modern dogma and the rhetoric of assent*. Notre Dame: University of Notre Dame Press.
Cannon, L. (1982). *Reagan*. New York: Putnam.
Cannon L., and Hoffman, D. (1982, December 19). At midterm in Reagan presidency, the problem seems less simple. *Washington Post*, pp. A1, A6–A8.
Church, G. J. (1982, December 13). How Reagan decides. *Time*, pp. 12–17.
Court journalism. (1982, November 27). *The Nation*, p. 548.
Denton, H. H. (1982a, March 19). Regan declares faith in press, but Gergen boils over. *Washington Post*, p. A6.
Denton, H. H. (1982b, September 27). Reagan's reproach of the great society overlooks a few facts. *Washington Post*, p. A6.
Disappointing performance. (1982, March 1). *Newsweek*, pp. 28–29.
Donner, F. (1982, November 16). But will they come? The campaign to smear the nuclear freeze movement. *The Nation*, pp. 456–465.
Editorials on File. (1982a). 13, 949, 952.
Editorials on File. (1982b). 13, 1118–1121.
Editorials on File. (1982c). 13, 1204–1209.
Evans, R., and Novak, R. (1981). *The Reagan revolution*. New York: Dutton.
The facts about "us people." (1982. April 26). *Washington Post*, p. A16.
Fisher, W. R. (1978). Toward a logic of good reasons. *Quarterly Journal of Speech*, 64, 376–384.
Fisher, W. R. (1980). Rationality and the logic of good reasons. *Philosophy and Rhetoric*, 13, 121–130.

Fisher, W. R. (1982). Romantic democracy, Ronald Reagan, and presidential heroes. *Western Journal of Speech Communication*, 46, 299–310.
Fleishman, J. L., Liebman, L., and Moore, M. H. (eds.). (1981). *Public duties: The moral obligations of public officials.* Cambridge: Harvard University Press.
A freeze in understanding. (1982, October 7). *Chicago Tribune*, Sec. 1, p. 10.
Freund, L. (1960). Responsibility—definitions, distinctions, and applications in various contexts. In C. J. Friedrich (ed.), *Nomos III: Responsibility* (pp. 28–42). New York: Liberal Arts Press.
The gaffer. (1982. February 13). *The Nation*, p. 164.
Gelman, R. (1982, October 9). Why let him get by with that? [Letter to the editor]. *Washington Post*, p. A17.
Germond, J., and Witcover, J. (1982, March 9). Complicating the simple. *Chicago Tribune*, Sec. 1. p. 11.
Graves, F. (1983, January/February). Are these men Soviet dupes? *Common Cause*, pp. 26–31.
Green, M. (1982a, March 6). The president (mis)speaks: There he goes again. *The Nation*, pp. 273–274.
Green, M. (1982b, May 29). There he goes again. *The Nation*, p. 648.
Green, M. (1982c, August 7–14). Reagan's reign of error: There he goes again. *The Nation*, pp. 103–104.
Green, M. (1983. March 5). Reagan's reign of error: There he goes again. *The Nation*, pp. 263–264.
Green, M. (1983, October 29). Method to his badness? Presidential truth and consequences. *The Nation*, pp. 399–403.
Greenfield. M. (1982a, March 22). The challenge to the president. *Newsweek*, p. 92.
Greenfield, M. (1982b, April 5). Assignment for the president. *Newsweek*, p. 84.
Hard times of Ronald Reagan. (1982, February 1). *Newsweek*, p. 16.
Hoffman, D. (1982, October 13). Job bill to be signed, minus sponsors. *Washington Post*, pp. A1, A9.
Horowitz, R. (1982, April 16). Material for the president. *Chicago Tribune*, Sec. 1, p. 27.
Johannesen, R. L. (1983). *Ethics in human communication* (2d ed.). Prospect Heights, IL: Waveland Press.
Johnson, H. (1982a, January 24). Reagan presidency: Make-or-break year for him and the nation. *Washington Post*, p. A3.
Johnson. H. (1982b, September 19). The president's revisionist accounting of poverty in America. *Washington Post*, p. A3.
Johnstone, H. W., Jr. (1981). Toward an ethics for rhetoric. *Communication*, 6, 305–314.
Kauffman, C. (1982). The failure of the "great communicator." *Exetasis*. 7 (April), 20–37.
Knickerbocker, B. (1982. August 18). Impact from Reagan's decision to choose Peking over Taiwan. *Christian Science Monitor*, pp. 1, 9.
Leahy, P. J. (1982, November 28). Reality—or a caricature? *Washington Post*, p. C8.
Lescaze, L. (1981, December 24). Reagan still sure some in new deal espoused fascism. *Washington Post*, p. A7.
Lescaze, L. (1982, January 21). President fumbles figures. *Washington Post*, p. A2.
Luthin, R. (1954). *American demagogues.* Boston: Beacon Press.
Lyndon B. Reagan on Vietnam. (1982, March 1). *Newsweek*, p. 30.
McCarthy, C. (1982, September 25). Blaming LBJ. *Washington Post*, p. A25.
More on the anecdote front. (1982, March 19). *Washington Post*, p. A22.
More Reagan remarks held in dispute. (1982, January 22). *Washington Post*, p. A3.
Mr. Reagan and China. (1982, August 19). *Christian Science Monitor*, p. 24.
News from South Succotash. (1982, April 3). *America*, pp. 252–253.
Niebuhr, H. R. (1963). *The Responsible Self.* New York: Harper & Row.
Nilsen. T. R. (1974). *Ethics of speech communication* (2d ed.). Indianapolis: Bobbs-Merrill.

Papering over the cracks. (1982, August 30). *Newsweek*, p. 42.
Pennock, J. R. (1960). The problem of responsibility. In C. I. Friedrich (ed.), *Nomos III: Responsibility* (pp. 3–27). New York: Liberal Arts Press.
Perelman, C., and Olbrechts-Tyteca, L. (1969). *The new rhetoric* (J. Wilkinson and P. Weaver, Trans.). Notre Dame, IN: University of Notre Dame Press.
Pincoffs, E. L. (1975, December). On being responsible for what one says. Paper presented at convention of Speech Communication, Houston, Texas.
Pool reports: TRB from Washington. (1982. October 4). *New Republic*, p. 6.
Presidential fatigue? (1983, May 16). *Newsweek*, p. 30. *Quarterly Review of Doublespeak* (1983), IX (January), 1–2.
The quiz kid. (1982, February 23). *New York Times*, p. A22.
Radosh, R. (1983, January 31). The "peace council" and peace. *New Republic*, pp. 14–18.
Reagan's claims on civil rights disputed. (1982, September 28). *Chicago Tribune*, pp. 1, 8.
Redford, E. S. (1969). *Democracy in the administrative state*. New York: Oxford University Press.
Reston, J. (1982, October 10). Let the voter beware. *New York Times*, p. E17. Revisionism: LBJ and blacks. (1982, September 20). *Washington Post*, p. A14.
Roderick, L. (1982, August 25). Reality forces Reagan to bow to China. *DeKalb* (Illinois) *Daily Chronicle*, p. 4.
Rowan, H. (1982, September 30). November chill at the White House. *Washington Post*, p. A23.
Rowley, S. (1983, January 7). White House denies Reagan bent the numbers in TV talk. *Chicago Tribune*, Sec. 1, p. 4.
Safire, W. (1982, March 11). The purpose of a chin-fly. *Chicago Tribune*, Sec. 1, p. 11.
Schram, M. (1982, October 3). A "fair" president's foul means. *Washington Post*, p. B5.
Stacks, J. F. (1981). *Watershed: The campaign for the presidency, 1980*. New York: Times Books.
There he goes again. . . . (1982, February 2). *Time*, p. 13.
To tell the truth, (1982. February 6). *The Nation*, p. 132.
Von Hoffman, N. (1982, September 6). The White House news hole. *New Republic*, p. 23.
Wagman, R. J. (1982, April 8). President plays fast and loose with the facts. *DeKalb* (Illinois) *Daily Chronicle*, p. 4.
Wall, J. M. (1982, April 14). Embarrassing White House errors. *Christian Century*, p. 435.
Watson, R., et al. (1982, November 15). Reagan and the art of compromise. *Newsweek*, p. 40.
Weekly compilation of presidential documents. (1982). Washington, DC: United States Government Printing Office. Cited as *WCPD*.
When doubletalk is useful. (1982, August 18). *Chicago Tribune*, Sec. 1, p. 10.
Wicker, T. (1982, October 3). The pot and the kettle. *New York Times*, p. E17.
Will, G. (1982, August 30). Slow motion sellout. *Newsweek*, p. 76.
Wise, D. (1983). *The politics of lying: Government deception, secrecy, and power*. New York: Random House.

Preview to: "A Rational World Ethic Versus a Narrative Ethic for Political Communication." One way to view the "narrative paradigm" of communication is to see it as a version of the human nature perspective on communication ethics. In other words, the narrative paradigm identifies the human capacity for narration—for storytelling—as the characteristic that gives humans their humanness. Note that in the opening of this essay, philosopher Alasdair MacIntyre is quoted as contending that "man is in his actions and practices . . . essentially a story-telling animal. . . . " In his book, Human Communication as Narration (pp. 62–63), Walter Fisher argues that "the essential nature of human beings" is best captured by the root metaphor of homo narrans—"human beings as storytellers."

This essay suggests that a critic's choice of ethical perspective or selection of specific ethical standards to assess a communication event constrains the ethical judgments possible or appropriate. Different initial ethical assumptions or frameworks may lead to quite different ethical judgments of the communication. Consider how adequately the essay illustrates the claim that "our judgments of ethicality for any particular communication might be rather different depending upon whether we employed a rational world paradigm or a narrative paradigm."

This essay also summarizes two attacks on the adequacy of Fisher's conception of the narrative paradigm—those by Barbara Warnick and by Robert Rowland. More recently Rowland has attempted to sharpen his criticisms in a journal article, "On Limiting the Narrative Paradigm," and Fisher has offered an indirect reply to his critics by "Clarifying the Narrative Paradigm" (both in Communication Monographs, 6, March 1989, pp. 39–58). You are urged to read both of these articles. Also see Rowland, "The Value of the Rational World and Narrative Paradigms," Central States Speech Journal, 39 (Fall-Winter 1988): 204–17.

A Rational World Ethic Versus a Narrative Ethic for Political Communication*

Richard L. Johannesen

In their essay, "Toward a New Political Narrative," Lance Bennett and Murray Edelman argue: "Stories are among the most universal means of representing human events. In addition to suggesting an interpretation for a social happening, a well-crafted narrative can motivate the belief and action of outsiders toward the actors and events caught up in its plot" (1985, p. 156). A central thesis presented by philosopher Alasdair MacIntyre in *After Virtue* (1984, p. 216) is that "man is in his actions and practices, as well as in his fictions, essentially a story-telling animal . . . , a teller of stories that aspire to truth. . . . I can only answer the question 'What am I to do?' if I can answer the prior question 'Of what story do I find myself a part?'"

Scholars in such disciplines as anthropology, sociology, law, history, literary criticism, and rhetoric are exploring the centrality of narrative to human belief and action. Some specifically are suggesting standards for assessing the rationality and/or ethicality of narrative in public discourse. Political communication would seem one obvious arena on which to focus such exploration. By political communication I mean not just the communication of presidents, politicians, political campaigns, or a particular party. I would include communication by appointed governmental officials. I would include any public communication by citizens on public issues and policy broadly defined, whether military, economic, social, or governmental, whether national, state, or local.

My intent is to compare what Walter Fisher describes as the "rational world paradigm" for the rhetoric of public issues with what he proposes as the "narrative paradigm." First, I will explore the premises, values, procedures, and ethical standards that seem basic to this rational, or traditional, paradigm as those norms typically are espoused for American political communication. Second, I will examine

---

*This essay originally was presented at the annual national conference of the Speech Communication Association, Boston, November 6, 1987.

the standards for an ethic of narrative in political communication suggested by Fisher. Third, using Ronald Reagan's rhetoric as an illustrative case, I show how rather different ethical judgments can be reached depending upon which paradigm is employed. Finally, I note some of the modifications and criticisms that have been made of Fisher's view.

For almost a decade in articles and essays, and synthesized in his 1987 book, *Human Communication as Narration*, Walter Fisher has developed his view of the traditional "rational world paradigm" for sound and ethical rhetoric as contrasted with the more encompassing and adequate "narrative paradigm." In a public lecture in 1986 at Marquette University on "Ethics, Rationality, and Narrativity," Fisher declared that "conceptions of rationality are intertwined with ethics" (1986, p. 3).

According to Fisher, the fundamental presuppositions of the rational world paradigm are (1987b, pp. 59–60):

> (1) humans are essentially rational beings; (2) the paradigmatic mode of human decision making and communications is argument—discourse that features clear-cut inferential and implicative structures; (3) the conduct of argument is ruled by the dictates of situations—legal, scientific, legislative, public, and so on; (4) rationality is determined by subject-matter knowledge, argumentative ability, and skill in employing the rules of advocacy in given fields; and (5) the world is a set of logical puzzles that can be solved through appropriate analysis and application of reason conceived as an argumentative construct. In short, argument as product and process is the means of being human, the agency of all that humans can know and realize in achieving their *telos*.

The logicality of reasons is judged by the traditional tests of sound evidence and reasoning (Fisher, 1987b, pp. 108–109; 1986, pp. 13–14). First, determine whether the statements in a message that purport to be "facts" are actually facts, "that is, are confirmed by consensus or reliable, competent witnesses." Second, "determine whether relevant facts have been omitted or misrepresented." Third, "using mainly the standards from informal logic," assess the soundness of patterns of reasoning, such as sign, cause, classification, analogy, and example. Fourth, assess the individual arguments for relevance, distortion, and omission. Fifth, "determine whether the key issues have been addressed: the questions on which the matter should turn." Fisher believes that Douglas Ehninger and Wayne Brockriede's

Decision by Debate (1st ed. 1963; 2d ed. 1979) "is the best representative available" of the rational world paradigm (1987b, pp. 46–47).

Within our culture I would contend that the rational world paradigm typically is reflected in values and procedures central to the health and growth of our system of governing, namely, representative democracy. These values guide ethical scrutiny of political communication within our system. Scholars have identified a number of such fundamental values and procedures (Burke, 64, 67, 235; Margolis; Moore; Nilsen, 1958; Nilsen, 1974, Chs. 1–4; Redford, 6–9; Wallace; Warwick, 115–124). Among them are: the intrinsic dignity and worth of all persons; equal opportunity for fulfillment of individual potential; enhancement of citizen capacity to reach rational decisions; access to channels of public communication; access to relevant and accurate information on public issues; maximization of freedom of choice; toleration of dissent; honesty and clarity in presenting values relevant to problems and policies; honesty in presenting motivations and consequences; thoroughness, accuracy, and fairness in presenting evidence and alternatives; and recognition that the societal worth of an end seldom should be the sole justification of the ethics of the means to achieve that end.

Typical textbook discussions of the ethics of communication, persuasion, and argument often include lists of ethical standards. Such criteria frequently are rooted, implicitly if not explicitly, in the values and procedures central to American representative democracy. I have attempted elsewhere to synthesize a number of such traditional lists (1983, pp. 21–22).

1. Do not use false, fabricated, misrepresented, distorted, or irrelevant evidence to support arguments or claims.
2. Do not intentionally use unsupported, misleading, or illogical reasoning.
3. Do not represent yourself as informed or as an "expert" on a subject when you are not.
4. Do not use irrelevant appeals to divert attention or scrutiny from the issue at hand. Among the appeals that commonly serve such a purpose are: "Smear" attacks on an opponent's character; appeals to hatred and bigotry; derogatory insinuations—innuendos; God and Devil terms that cause intense but unreflective positive or negative reactions.
5. Do not ask your audience to link your idea or proposal to emotion-laden values, motives, or goals to which it actually is not related.
6. Do not deceive your audience by concealing your real purpose, by concealing self-interest, by concealing the group you represent, by concealing your position as an advocate of a viewpoint.

7. Do not distort, hide, or misrepresent the number, scope, intensity, or undesirable features of consequences or effects.
8. Do not use "emotional appeals" that lack a supporting basis of evidence or reasoning, or that would not be accepted if the audience had time and opportunity to examine the subject themselves.
9. Do not over-simplify complex, gradation-laden situations into simplistic, two-valued, either-or, polar views or choices.
10. Do not pretend certainty where tentativeness and degrees of probability would be more accurate.
11. Do not advocate something in which you do not believe yourself.

Now, I turn to Fisher's description of the narrative paradigm for rhetoric, which he believes overarches and subsumes the rational world paradigm (1987b, xi, pp. 64–65; 1986, pp. 8–9). (1) Humankind should be reconceptualized as storytellers, as *homo narrans*. (2) The distinctive mode of human decision making and communication is "good reasons"—values or value-laden warrants for believing or acting. These vary in form among communication situations, genre, and media. (3) Presentation of good reasons is governed by history, culture, character, and the constraints of specific circumstances. (4) All humans have a natural capacity for narrative logic and naturally use the principles of probability/coherence and of fidelity for assessing narration. (5) The world is a set of stories from which we must choose if we are to live our lives in a continual process of re-creation.

As standards for narrative rationality and ethicality, Fisher suggests the dual touchstones of probability (coherence) and fidelity (truthfulness and reliability). *Probability*, whether a story "hangs together," is tested first by internal argumentative and structural coherence; second by material coherence, by comparison and contrast with stories in other discourses; and third by characterological coherence, the harmony of character and action, the dependability of characters both as narrators and actors (1987b, p. 47; 1986, p. 12).

Fidelity addresses the "truth" qualities of the story, the truth both of reasoning and of value judgment (1987b, pp. 47–48,108–109; 1986, pp. 13–14). The logic of reasons within the story is assessed by the traditional standards for evidence and reasoning previously itemized. The values imbedded in the story are tested according to the standards of fact, relevance, consequence, consistency, and transcendental issues. "What are the explicit and implicit values? Are the values appropriate to the nature of the decision that the message bears upon? What would be the effects of adhering to the values in regard to one's concept of oneself, to one's behavior, to one's relationship with others and society, and to the process of rhetorical transaction? Are the values confirmed or validated in one's personal experience, in the lives and statements of others whom one admires or respects, and/or in a conception of the best audience that one can conceive? And even if a *prima facie* case exists or a burden of proof has been established, are the values the message offers those that would constitute an ideal basis for human conduct?" (1986, p. 14; 1987b, p. 109).

We will now turn to the consideration that our judgments of ethicality for any particular political communication might be rather different depending upon whether we employed a rational world paradigm or a narrative paradigm. Depending on the paradigm used, for example, ethical assessments might vary of President Reagan's habitual use of stories and anecdotes and his identification with powerful narrative or mythic structures in American culture, such as the hero, the jeremiad tradition, or the American Dream.

In 1984 I published a detailed evaluation of the ethics of President Reagan's rhetoric for the 1981–1982 period. I operated primarily from a rational worldview within the context of values and procedures central to American representative democracy. After examining representative news conferences, interviews, speeches, and informal comments, I concluded that President Reagan warranted ethical condemnation for rather routinely misstating facts, statistics: and situations and for misusing factual illustrations and anecdotes as proofs. I shall quote several of my conclusions at length.

> This long-standing habit has been characterized satirically as Reagan's "anecdotage" problem. He likes to use vivid and dramatic real-life stories to prove this point or that. Unfortunately, these anecdotes, even if not misstated, frequently are found to be misleading or unrepresentative. In this regard, William Safire, a former speech writer for President Nixon, chastises Reagan for taking a "simplistic approach to complex matters." Syndicated political columnists Jack Germond and Jules Witcover describe Reagan's proclivity for "generalizing from the simplistic particular," for overgeneralizing individual abuses into proof of a major problem. A *Christian Century* editorial objects that Reagan's illustrations too often do not inform or provide evidence for an argument; rather they "exacerbate feelings" by arousing "latent hostility among true believers." James David Barber condemns Reagan for having "contempt for the facts" and issuing "spurious specifics with cavalier abandon." More precisely, Barber depicts Reagan as the "Aesop of the Oval Office, tossing off parables instead of arguments." Such stories are not easily judged by tests of evidence, notes Barber, and he urges that we must "rely on public discourse in which the proposals meet facts in a test clear enough for reason to grasp." (p. 233)

> Should Reagan's sincere belief in what he says, even if what he says is inaccurate, misleading, or unrepresentative, soften our ethical judgment of his rhetoric? David Gergen, White House director of communications, would seem to believe so. Gergen told reporters that what is important is not "making sure we have every single fact straight," but rather "whether the larger points are right." Gergen also defended Reagan's story-telling as a "folk art" wherein the anecdotes have a "parable-like quality to them" and are used simply to illustrate "how society works." However, as I urged earlier, sincerity of intent and ethicality of rhetorical techniques most appropriately should be judged separately. In Reagan's case, whether he is sincere or not, the ethicality of his rhetorical tactics must be independently assessed. . . . I believe he is ethically irresponsible in rather regularly employing erroneous, misleading, or atypical information. Reagan has a duty to present to citizens the relevant and accurate data they need to make reasonable decisions on public issues. Meg Greenfield, the *Newsweek* political columnist, contends that Reagan is obliged in justifying his policies to use "arguments and real evidence" rather than "episodes or isolated case studies." (p. 236)

In contrast we turn to William Lewis' narrative interpretation of Reagan's rhetoric. He contends that Reagan's primary vehicle for communication is the story, both individual anecdotes and a larger tapestry of mythic structures that are potent in American culture. Lewis modifies Fisher's standards for narrative rationality. Lewis excludes the traditional tests for soundness of evidence and reasoning. He proposes scrutinizing the internal coherence and consistency of the rhetorical narrative, examining the implicit and explicit morals and values promoted, and assessing consistency with "common sense," the knowledge shared by the community as opposed to elitist, technical, or scientific knowledge.

Even from the narrative viewpoint, Lewis does fault Reagan for overextending the applicability of a "single, unquestioned narrative structure" and for assuming that this dominant narrative is permanent and insulated from contrary events and criticism (1987, pp. 295–296). Nevertheless, the tone of Lewis' interpretation is much more generous and less hostile than mine. In part Lewis argues (pp. 288–290):

> If the story is not true, it must be true-to-life; if it did not actually happen, it must be evident that it could happen or that, given the way things are, it should have happened. When narrative dominates, epistemological standards move away from empiricism. . . . Events become meaningful in stories and meaning depends upon the significance of the events within the context of the story. As a

> consequence, the perception of truth depends upon the story as a whole rather than upon the accuracy of its independent statements.
>
> Because his story is so dominant, so explicit, and so consistent, political claims are likely to be measured against the standard of Reagan's mythic American history rather than against other possible standards such as technical competence or ideological dogma. In this way, the story's dominance has diminished the significance of claims about factual inaccuracies. . . . Those most successful in confronting Reagan, such as Mario Cuomo, have been those few politicians who offer alternative stories.
>
> Reagan's stories are not completely self-contained . . . but this is a special kind of reality. The basis for accepting the referential value of Reagan's stories is not empirical justification, but consistency with the moral standards and common sense of his audience.

In these extremely brief excerpts from my and Lewis' analyses, we glimpse the possibility of quite different ethical assessments of Reagan's rhetoric stemming from the rational mind and narrative paradigms. For similar contrasts, we could turn to Fisher's own evaluation of Reagan's rhetoric in his book (1987b, pp. 143–157), to the article by Dowling and Marraro in the *Western Journal of Speech Communication* (1986), and to my own article on "Ronald Reagan's Economic Jeremiad" (1986).

Now I will discuss some of the reactions generated, directly or indirectly, by Fisher's work. Several scholars have offered alternative or supplementary tests for narrative rationality or ethicality. I already have mentioned Lewis' modifications. Within the context of conversation and rhetoric, Farrell offers a series of questions as a start toward an "ethic of narrative" (1985, pp. 124–125):

> What public character is implied by the course we have taken? What forms of social learning are yet available to us? What legacy of experience do we wish our story to yield to future generations? Which episodes in our unfinished and unbounded narrative of collective action are irretrievable or lost? Which need to be ended altogether, which prolonged, which begun anew? Which audiences, thus far neglected, need to have their own stories articulated?

Bennett and Edelman contrast undesirable "stock political narratives" with a desirable "new political narrative" that promotes creativity and critical insight. Evaluative criteria can be inferred from their analysis. The distortions and contradictions characteristic of stock political narratives should be avoided: (1) they rest "on claims of dubious historical standing" and "rationalize such claims in tautological fashion"; (2) they "will overlook features of a situation that would change the narrative if taken into account"; and (3) the "significance will be changed, often into an ideologically opposing view, when documenting details are moved from central to peripheral positions in the narrative structure" (1985, p. 170). A new political narrative would meet the tests "descriptive adequacy, testability, and openness to change based on challenge and feedback." Such a narrative would introduce "new information in terms of unfamiliar dilemmas, puzzles, and contradictions of the sort that promote critical thought and a self-consciousness of problem-solving behavior" (pp. 162, 164, 168).

Lucaites and Condit argue that tests of narrative adequacy differ for its three pure functions, poetic (to delight), dialectical (to instruct), and rhetorical (to move). Rhetorical discourse, they contend, aims at the enactment of an interest or the wielding of power and the tests of rhetorical narrative flow from the demands of audience adaptation, context, and material gain. In their view a sound rhetorical narrative is internally consistent with itself as well as the larger discourse of which it is a part and is externally consistent with the audience's logical and sociological expectations. It is brief enough to avoid audience weariness and disinterest through digressions or unnecessary detail. It is univocal, having a unity of direction and purpose, thus reinforcing proof of a single interpretation of a fact, value, or policy claim. Finally, using an extended example of British Prime Minister Margaret Thatcher, they contend that a sound rhetorical narrative rests on credibility, on "inherent, formal unity of narrator, author, and speaker" (1985, pp. 101–102).

Other scholars have gone beyond modification to direct attack. It is important to note that the critics mentioned here did not have the benefit of Fisher's most recent version of his position as found in his book or in two published essays incorporated into it. Lewis rejects "Fisher's assertion of the moral superiority of the narrative paradigm" and his belief, along with Aristotle, that "the 'people' have a natural tendency to prefer the true and the just" (Lewis, 1987, pp. 296–297). While Fisher sees the rational and narrative paradigms as different yet essentially compatible, Lewis contends that they "can be distinctive and incommensurable" (pp. 294–295, 297).

McGee and Nelson conceive of narration as the "*techne* of translation," with a function similar to the syllogism in scientific demonstration, and they believe that narrative rationality in public argument should be rooted in an "epistemology of myth," a move not developed by Fisher (McGee and Nelson, 1985, pp. 146, 149–152). They reject Fisher's claim that "experts" have dominated public discourse and decisions with technical reasoning, and they reject his dichotomy between technical/traditional rationality and narrative rationality (pp. 140, 144).

Warnick has mounted a massive attack, adding her own to the "small chorus of voices expressing reservations about the paradigm as originally articulated" (1987, p. 172). First, Fisher is unclear, across his various works, whether traditional rationality is less desirable than narrative rationality and whether it is compatible with but subsumed by narrative. Second, the "people" do not necessarily prefer the "true and just" view, and Fisher fails to demonstrate "how we can assume that the public will not choose bad stories based on self-delusion or rationalization" (pp. 176–177, 181). Third, the concept of "good reasons" is circular, and Fisher is equivocal in wanting to include the standards of "the best audience one can conceive" and the "ideal basis for human conduct" while admitting that "values are context-dependent and particular to the rhetorical situation giving rise to discourse" (pp. 178–179, 181). Finally, without traditional rationality, the ideal audience, or audience judgment as reliable standards, we are left with the "arbitrary and personal" judgment of the critic, which "in the applications demonstrated by Fisher as critic, is unsupported by data on public values, the effects of value adoption, or rational analysis" (pp. 179–181). In sum, Warnick finds that the "narrative rationality concept in his paradigm itself lacks narrative probability or coherence" (pp. 181).

A second frontal assault on Fisher's position comes from Rowland. While preserving a major role for narrative argument in human decision making, Rowland questions the clarity and generalizability of the proposed narrative paradigm. He argues, first, "that the narrative has been defined so broadly that the term loses much of its explanatory power" (1987, pp. 265–268). Second, the narrative paradigm offers inadequate standards of rationality as an alternative to the informal logic tests of the rational world paradigm. Indeed Rowland believes that, as developed so far, the narrative tests of probability and fidelity are not significantly different from "traditional tests of evidence and reasoning" (pp. 268–271). Finally, Rowland contends that Fisher's fear of "elite domination of the public sphere" through technical reason is a fear overstated and a fear not adequately solved, to the degree it exists, through the narrative paradigm (pp. 271–273). Rowland concludes that, "despite its potential, narrative theory has not yet reached the point that it makes sense to treat narrative as a paradigm rather than a mode of discourse" (p. 274).

The conclusion reached by Lucaites and Condit in 1985 still seems true today: ". . . if there is a unified narrative paradigm of human communication, or a universal narrative metacode, they have not yet been discovered." But they also believe that the search should continue and that, even if not productive of a paradigm or metacode, "it should at least illuminate the full range of practices in which narrative participates" (pp. 105–106). Clearly, political communication is a major arena of narrative practice. In his recently published book, *Tales of a New America*, Robert Reich notes that on the surface we take political discourse about public issues to be editorials, political candidates' programs, economists' analyses, Congressional committee hearings, television documentaries, and specialists' disagreements. "But in the background—disguised and unarticulated—are the myth-based morality tales that determine when we declare a fact to be a problem, how policy choices are characterized, how the debate is framed. These are the unchallenged subtexts of political discourse" (1987, p. 6).

References

Ackerman, Bruce A. *Social Justice and the Liberal State*. New Haven: Yale University Press, 1980.

Bennett, W. Lance, and Murray Edelman. "Toward a New Political Narrative." *Journal of Communication*, 35 (Autumn 1985): 156–171.

Burke, John P. *Bureaucratic Responsibility*. Baltimore. MD: Johns Hopkins University Press. 1986.

Dowling, Ralph E., and Gabrielle Marraro. "Grenada and the Great Communicator: A Study in Democratic Ethics." *Western Journal of Speech Communication*, 50 (Fall 1986): 350–367.

Farrell, Thomas B. "Narrative in Natural Discourse: On Conversation and Rhetoric." *Journal of Communication*, 35 (Autumn 1985): 109–127.

Fisher, Walter R. "Ethics, Rationality, and Narrativity." Unpublished lecture, Marquette University, Milwaukee, November 11, 1986.

Fisher, Walter R. "Technical Logic, Rhetorical Logic, and Narrative Rationality." *Argumentation*, 1 (1987a): 3–21.

Fisher, Walter R. *Human Communication as Narration: Toward a Philosophy of Reason, Value, and Action*. Columbia: University of South Carolina Press, 1987b.

Johannesen, Richard L. *Ethics in Human Communication*, 2d ed. Prospect Heights. IL: Waveland Press,1983.

Johannesen, Richard L. "An Ethical Assessment of the Reagan Rhetoric: 1981–1982." In *Political Communication Yearbook 1984*, Keith R. Sanders, Lynda Lee Kaid,

and Dan Nimmo, eds. Carbondale: Southern Illinois University Press, 1985, pp. 226–241.
Johannesen, Richard L. "Ronald Reagan's Economic Jeremiad." *Central States Speech Journal*, 37 (Summer 1986): 79–89.
Lewis, William F. "Telling America's Story: Narrative Form and the Reagan Presidency." *Quarterly Journal of Speech*, 73 (August 1987): 280–302.
Lucaites, John Lewis, and Celeste Michelle Condit. "Reconstructing Narrative Theory: A Functional Perspective." *Journal of Communication*, 35 (Autumn 1985): 90–108.
MacIntyre, Alasdair. *After Virtue*, 2d ed. Notre Dame: University of Notre Dame Press, 1984.
Margolis, Joseph. "Democracy and the Responsibility to Inform the Public." In *Ethical Issues in Government*, Norman E. Bowie, ed. Philadelphia: Temple University Press, 1981, pp. 237–248.
McGee, Michael Calvin, and John S. Nelson. "Narrative Reason in Public Argument." *Journal of Communication*, 35 (Autumn 1985): 139–155.
Moore, Mark H. "Realms of Obligation and Virtue." In *Public Duties: The Moral Obligations of Government Officials*, Joel L. Fleishman, Lance Liebman, and Mark H. Moore, eds. Cambridge: Harvard University Press, 1981, pp. 3–31.
Nilsen, Thomas R. "Democratic Ethics and the Hidden Persuaders." *Quarterly Journal of Speech* XLIV (December 1958): 385–392.
Nilsen, Thomas R. *Ethics of Speech Communication*, 2d ed. Indianapolis: Bobbs-Merrill, 1974.
Redford, Emmette S. *Democracy in the Administrative State*. New York: Oxford University Press. 1969.
Reich, Robert B. *Tales of a New America*. New York: Times Books, 1987.
Rowland, Robert C. "Narrative: Mode of Discourse or Paradigm?" *Communication Monographs*, 54 (September 1987): 264–275.
Wallace, Karl R. "An Ethical Basis of Communication." *Speech Teacher*, IV (January 1955): 1–9.
Warnick, Barbara. "The Narrative Paradigm: Another Story." *Quarterly Journal of Speech*, 73 (May 1987): 172–182.
Warwick, Donald P. "The Ethics of Administrative Discretion." In *Public Duties: The Moral Obligations of Government Officials*, Joel L. Fleishman, Lance Liebman, and Mark H. Moore, eds. Cambridge: Harvard University Press, 1981, pp. 93–127.

Preview to: "Virtue Ethics, Character, and Political Communication." *This essay first explores the tradition of virtue ethics or character ethics as a complement to the current dominant deontological (duty-based) theories, such as Kant's Categorical Imperative, and to teleological (consequentialist) theories, such as utilitarianism. The essay probes the applications and implications of character ethics for the practice of political communication, whether by candidate or office-holder. Recall that the general role of character in communication ethics was introduced in chapter 1, and the implications of character ethics for organizational communication was explored in that chapter. As you read this essay, consider possible relevances of virtue ethics for interpersonal and mass communication.*

In what ways does the issue of "ethical character" apply to the 1992 presidential campaign of Bill Clinton and subsequently to his presidency? How would you relate the arguments and issues raised in the following essay to Bill Clinton as candidate and president? For example, see the following sources: Jonathan Alter, "The Real Character Issues," Newsweek, March 30, 1992, p. 33; Joan Beck, "Voters are Right to Weigh Rumors of Infidelity," Chicago Tribune, January 30, 1992, Sec. 1, p. 23; Meg Greenfield, "The Real 'Character Issue,'" Newsweek, May 23, 1994, p. 70; Harrison Rainie, "But Do They Believe?" U.S. News and World Report, March 14, 1994, pp. 10–11.

A number of sources on virtue ethics that are not mentioned in the essay are listed in the appropriate section of Sources for Further Reading at the end of this book. But several general sources merit mention as excellent introductions: Nancy Sherman, The Fabric of Character: Aristotle's Theory of Virtue *(New York: Oxford University Press, 1989); Robert B. Kruschwitz and Robert C. Roberts, eds.,* The Virtues: Contemporary Essays on Moral Character *(Belmont, CA: Wadsworth, 1987); Joel Kupperman,* Character *(New York: Oxford University Press, 1991); Stephen Hudson,* Human Character and Morality *(Boston: Routledge, 1986).*

Virtue Ethics, Character, and Political Communication*
Richard L. Johannesen

The contemporary philosophy of ethics has been dominated by an emphasis on duties, obligations, rules, rights, principles, and the resolution of complex ethical dilemmas, quandaries, or borderline cases (Jonsen and Toulmin 1988; Kupperman 1988; Pincoffs 1986). This dominant emphasis has been true whether as variations on Immanuel Kant's categorical imperative, on John Rawls's depersonalized veil of ignorance to determine justice, on statements of intrinsic ultimate goods, or on Jeremey Bentham's or John Stuart Mill's utilitarian/consequentialist views. The past several decades, however, have seen a growing interest among ethicists in a largely ignored tradition that goes back at least as far as Plato's and Aristotle's philosophies of ethics (Adler 1970, 235–65; Geatch 1977; MacIntyre 1984, 146–64; Mayo 1958, 200, 209–12; Palmour 1987; Rorty 1980, 106). This largely bypassed tradition typically is called virtue ethics or character ethics. Indeed, Alderman argues that "Aristotle's moral philosophy is *properly* to be construed as the first important virtue theory" (1982, 128).

Most ethicists of virtue or character see that stance as a crucial complement to the current dominant ethical theories (Becker 1975, 1986; Brandt 1981; Frankena 1970; Kupperman 1988, 123; Meilaender 1984, 4–5; Pincoffs 1986, 5, 35; Sichel 1988, 82; Wallace 1978; Walton 1988, 7). A few elevate character ethics to the position of "primary moral category" and argue that "character is a more adequate final court of appeal in moral philosophy than either rights, goods, or rules" (Alderman 1982). But Hudson (1981) contends that a complete moral theory should encompass *both* rules and principles "which specify a person's moral obligations and duties" *and* the significant role of the virtues of character in guiding moral action. The strengths and weaknesses of a character or virtue ethics approach are explored in an anthology edited by French, Uehling, and Wettstein (1988).

*Reprinted by permission of the publisher from Richard L. Johannesen, "Virtue Ethics, Character, and Political Communication," in *Ethical Dimensions of Political Communication*, Robert E. Denton, Jr., ed. (New York: Praeger, 1991), pp. 69–90. Praeger is an imprint of Greenwood Publishing Group, Inc., Westport, CT.

Some philosophers draw distinctions between ethics and morals as concepts. Ethics denotes the general and systematic study of what ought to be the grounds and principles for right and wrong human behavior. Morals (or morality) denotes the practical, specific, generally agreed-upon, culturally transmitted standards of right and wrong. Other philosophers, however, use the terms ethics and morals more or less interchangeably, as will be the case here.

The Nature of Ethical Character

In *After Virtue*, MacIntyre views moral character as "the arena of the virtues and vices" (1984, 168). Ethicists describe virtues variously as deep-rooted dispositions, habits, skills, or traits of character that incline us to see, feel, and act in ethically right and sensitive ways. Virtues also are described variously as learned, acquired, cultivated, reinforced, capable of modification, capable of conflicting, and ideally coalesced into a harmonious cluster (see Hauerwas 1981a, 115; Hauerwas 1981b, 49; MacIntyre 1984, 149, 154, 205, 219; Mayo 1958, 101-2, 214; Meilaender 1984, 6-11; Pinckaers 1962; Pincoffs 1986, 73-100; Sichel 1988, 75, 83; Slote 1983).

Consider the nature of moral character as described at some length by three ethicists and a theorist of rhetoric. According to Richard DeGeorge,

> As human beings develop, they tend to adopt patterns of actions, and dispositions to act in certain ways. These dispositions, when viewed collectively, are sometimes called character. A person who habitually tends to act as he morally should has a good character. If he resists strong temptation, he has a strong character. If he habitually acts immorally, he has a morally bad character. If despite good intentions he frequently succumbs to temptation, he has a weak character. Because character is formed by conscious actions, in general people are morally responsible for their characters as well as for their individual actions. (1986, 89)

Karen Lebacqz believes that

> indeed, when we act, we not only *do* something, we also shape our own character. Our choices about what to do are also choices about whom to be. A single lie does not necessarily make us a liar; but a series of lies may. And so each choice about what to *do* is also a choice about whom to *be*—or, more accurately, whom to become. (1985, 83)

In line with this view, Joseph Kupfer (1982; also see Michell 1984; Minnick 1985) contends that the "moral presumption against lying" rests on two lines of argument that demonstrate ultimate negative effects on the "character" *of the liar*. First, lying causes immediate restriction of the freedom of the deceived. Lying inclines the liar toward a general disrespect for persons—toward abuse of the uniquely human capacity for language as necessary for understanding and reflective choice. Second, lying involves the self-contradiction of "repudiating in speech what we believe." Liars disguise their "real self" from others by contradicting their real beliefs and, thus, who they really are. This self-opposition threatens the integration or coherence of the liar's personality. By disguising the self, the liar rejects the opportunity for self-knowledge; reactions of others useful for self-definition are possible only in response to truthful self-disclosure of beliefs.

Both of the negative effects on the liar—an attitude of disrespect for persons and threat to coherence of personality—weaken his or her moral character. Walter Fisher considers character to be an "organized set of actional tendencies" (1987, 47) and observes: "If these tendencies contradict one another, change significantly, or alter in 'strange' ways, the result is a questioning of character. . . . Without this kind of predictability, there is no trust, no community, no rational human order" (1987, 147–48).

Significant in many discussions of character ethics is the concept of "vision" (Birkhead 1989; Palmour 1987, 20–22). Moral character involves a spectrum of moral excellences or a range of reasons for our actions that provide moral vision (Hauerwas 1981b, 59; Sichel 1988, 256–258). To live morally, believes Hauerwas, "we must not only adhere to public and generalizable rules but also see and interpret the nature of the world in a moral way. The moral life is as much a matter of vision as it is a matter of doing" (1981b, 66). Meilaender describes "*vision* as a central theme of any ethic of virtue" (1984, ix). "Our virtues do not simply fit us for life; they help shape life. They shape not only our character but the world we see and inhabit" (1984, 5). He concludes: "*Being* not *doing* takes center stage; for what we ought to do may depend on the sort of person we are. What duties we perceive may depend upon what virtues shape our vision of the world" (1984, 10).

Some Functions of Ethical Character

In living the ethical life, what functions may be served by the virtues of character? Our formed ethical character does influence our choices and actions (Adler, 1970, 162, 253; Adler 1988, 247, 253–55, 266; Cunningham 1970; Hauerwas 1981b, 62). "Character surrounds action" and often is "a set of limitations restraining or shaping actions in certain ways. . . . Action occurs within the context of character" (Wilbur 1984, 176). In urging us to take virtues seriously, Hudson maintains that "an ethic of virtues can require both that we be of a certain character and that we perform certain kinds of acts. Human good *consists* (in part) both in virtuous action and in being a person of a certain character" (1981, 198–99). He explains that while a coward occasionally may do a courageous thing, this "does not make him a courageous" person, for the courageous person acts courageously as a matter of course or "second nature." Mayo says that according to character ethics, "there is another way of answering the fundamental question 'What ought I to do?' Instead of quoting a rule, we quote a quality of character, a virtue: we say 'Be brave,' or 'Be patient' or 'Be lenient'" (1958, 213). Sommers explains that the virtue-based theorist, by "concentrating attention on character rather than action, tacitly assumes that a virtuous person's actions generally fall within the range of what is right and fair" (1985, xii-xiii).

Our ethical character sensitizes us to ethically difficult or problematic situations, motivates our concern so that the situation matters to us, and undergirds our commitment—our long-term loyalty—to necessary values and actions (Kupperman 1988, 115–21). Hauerwas believes that only "if we have a morally significant character can we be relied upon to face morally serious questions rather than simply trying to avoid them" (1981b, 64). Also, however, as Meilaender argues, in redressing the overemphasis in current ethical theory on "troubling moral dilemmas" and on "borderline cases":

> An ethic of virtue seeks to focus not only on such moments of great anxiety and uncertainty in life but also on the continuities, the habits of behavior which make us the persons we are. Not whether we should frame one innocent man to save five—but on the virtue of justice, with its steady, habitual determination to make space in life for the needs and claims of others. Not whether to lie to the secret police—but on that steady regard for others which uses language truthfully and thereby makes a common life possible. (1984,-5)

Ethical character influences what *roles* we play in life and how we play them. The roles that we choose should be appropriate to and reflective of our character, not supplant that character (Cochran 1982, 17–21). The ethical virtues and commitments that comprise our moral character "control which roles can be accepted" and "influence how any role is actually lived" (Sichel 1988, 229–30; also see MacIntyre, 1984, 204–8). Ethical character also is related to the *rules* and abstract principles specified by various ethical theories. MacIntyre (1984, 150, 232–35, 257, 268) traces some of these relationships throughout the history of ethical theory. But particularly important is the way in which ethical character can humanize the application of abstract rules and principles. According to Sichel, the virtues of character "interject concern for concrete persons and foster more humane and sensitive feelings, compassion and sympathy, concern for moral ideals and qualities that abstract principles often seem to ignore" (1988, 266; see also Williams 1981, 1–19).

Ethical Character and Communication

A virtue is not a "habit" in the sense of dictating a "weary repetition of identical acts" (Cunningham 1970, 98) or in the sense of automatic, mechanistic repetition (Simon 1986). Rather, Pinckaers (1962) argues at length that moral virtues are formed by the repeated exercise of "interior acts" of practical reason and will that "insure their mastery" over exterior actions. Varied exterior acts in various circumstances may reflect the same internal disposition of virtue. Moral virtues reflect creativity and inventiveness in both their formation and their application, and they dispose a person to produce the maximum of what he or she "is able to do on a moral plane." Although a virtue does not involve "a series of identical material acts tirelessly reproduced," it is characteristic of a moral virtue "to permit an action to be performed without further need for lengthy reflection, without hesitation, and without interior conflict" (Pinckaers 1962, 65, 81).

Ethical communication is not simply a series of careful and reflective decisions, instance by instance, to communicate in ethically responsible ways (Cochran 1982, 32–33; Hauerwas 1977, 20, 29; Klaidman and Beauchamp 1987, 17–20; Lebacqz 1985, 77–91; Sichel 1988, 26, 33–37). Deliberate application of ethical rules sometimes is not possible. Pressure may be so great or a deadline so near for a decision that there is not adequate time for careful deliberation. We may be unsure what ethical criteria are relevant or how they apply. The situation may seem unique, and thus applicable criteria do not readily come to mind. In such times of crisis or uncertainty, our decision concerning ethical communication stems less from deliberation than from our "character." Furthermore, our ethical character influences the terms with which we describe a situation and whether we believe the situation contains ethical implications.

In Judeo-Christian or Western cultures, good moral character usually is associated with the habitual embodiment of such virtues as courage, temperance, prudence (or practical wisdom), justice, fairness, generosity, patience, truthfulness, and trustworthiness. Contemporary feminist scholars would interject additional vital virtues: caring for self and others, compassion, nurturance of relationships, responsiveness to growth and appreciation for change, resilient good humor and clear-sighted cheerfulness, attentive and realistic love, and a humble "sense of the limits of one's actions and of the unpredictability of the consequences of one's work" (Ruddick 1980; Gilligan 1982; Gilligan et al. 1988; Noddings 1984). Martin Buber's dimensions of true dialogue could be viewed as virtues of ethical character: authenticity, inclusion, confirmation, and presentness (Johannesen 1990, 57–77). Other cultures may praise additional or different virtues that they believe constitute good ethical character. Instilled in us as habitual dispositions to feel, see, and act, such virtues guide the ethics of our communication when careful or clear deliberation is not possible.

Codes of Ethics and the Character-Depiction Function

We turn to the possible connection between formal codes of ethics and the concept of character ethics. Formal codes of ethics have been proposed by various communication-oriented professional associations, corporations, and citizen-action groups in such fields as commercial advertising, public relations, technical writing, organizational consulting, print and broadcast journalism, and political communication. While varied objections have been raised concerning the usefulness of formal codes, and while a number of significant functions for formal codes of ethics have been identified (Johannesen 1990, 169–91), I will concentrate on one important and largely ignored function of such codes.

In her book, *Professional Ethics* (1985, 63–91), Karen Lebacqz suggests that formal ethical codes, especially in the professions, should be seen as having a function quite different from the typical one, namely, as rules for specific behavior or as admonitions concerning specific instances. In her view, we must look beyond the action-oriented language of most codes ("do this," "avoid that") to the "overall picture of the type of person who is to *embody* those actions." As reconceptualized by Lebacqz, a code embodies a picture of the moral "character" to be expected of a professional in a given field; it would depict, for example, an ethical communicator's "being" collectively and over time. She contends that "codes do not give specific guidance for action as much as they say something about the character traits necessary for someone to be a professional." "In short," she says, "codes are geared primarily toward establishing expectations for character." On this view, codes are "guideposts to understand where stresses and tensions have been felt within a profession and what image of the good professional is held up to assist professionals through those stresses and tensions."

According to Lebacqz, a wide range of professional codes reflect a core of central character traits, ethical principles, or obvious duties: "justice, beneficence, non-maleficence, honesty, and fidelity." She believes that a "professional is called not simply to *do* something but to *be* something." At a fundamental level codes depict a professional as "bound by certain ethical principles *and* as incorporating those principles *into his or her very character*." Ideally a code depicts the professional as "a person of integrity who not only does the 'right' thing, but is an *honorable person*." As illustration Lebacqz says that a trustworthy person not only keeps a confidence but is "thoughtful about the impact" of decisions on others and is "sensitive to their needs and claims." An honest person "tries to avoid any kind of deception, not just explicit lies." As noted earlier, Lebacqz contends that "when we act, we not only *do* something, we also shape our own character.... And so each choice about what to *do* is also a choice about whom to *be*—or, more accurately, whom to become."

This function of ethical codes as depicting desirable virtues of character more than (or at least as much as) specific rules for specific actions is exemplified by a code urged by the Josephson Institute for the Advancement of Ethics. The institute is a nonprofit organization established to "advance ethical awareness, commitment and behavior in both the public and private sectors of society." In its journal, *Ethics: Easier Said Than Done*, the Josephson Institute published a code of "Ethical Values and Principles in Public Service" (Spring/Summer 1988, 153). The institute believes that these are the "characteristics and values that most people associate with ethical behavior." Although the code does not specifically focus on communication ethics, many of its elements appropriately could be adapted for communication. Each of the eleven values presented in the Josephson code might be viewed as a character virtue for persons in public service—whether elected public official, political campaigner, or appointed bureaucrat: honesty, integrity, promise keeping, fidelity, fairness, caring, respect, good citizenship, excellence, accountability, and public trust (Johannesen 1990, 182–84). Each of the values or virtues is briefly explained in the code by describing obligations stemming from it. For example, promise keeping: "Persons worthy of trust keep promises, fulfill commitments, abide by the spirit as well as the letter of an agreement; they do not interpret agreements in an unreasonably technical or legalistic manner in order to rationalize noncompliance or create justifications for escaping commitments." Or consider caring: "Concern for the well-being of others manifests itself in compassion, giving, kindness and serving; it requires one to attempt to help those in need and to avoid harming others." The Josephson code does, I believe, serve a character-depiction function.

Ethical Character and Political Communication

A social/institutional ethic for assessing political communication can be rooted in the values and procedures central to the health and growth of our system of governing, representative democracy. Among them are the intrinsic dignity and worth of all persons; equal opportunity for fulfillment of individual potential; enhancement of citizen capacity to reach rational decisions; access to channels of public communication; access to relevant and accurate information on public issues; maximization of freedom of choice; toleration of dissent; honesty and clarity in presenting values relevant to problems and policies; honesty in presenting motivations and consequences; thoroughness, accuracy, and fairness in presenting evidence and alternatives; and recognition that the societal worth of an end seldom should be the sole justification of the ethics of the means to achieve that end (Johannesen 1990, 21–37, 236–37, 255). Often informal standards and formal codes of ethics for various types of political communication are founded implicitly or explicitly on such fundamental values (Johannesen 1990, 31–34, 184–91).

In contrast, a number of scholars are suggesting that virtue ethics or character must have a significant place in political ethics. Such books as *Character, Community, and Politics* (Cochran 1982) and *Character: An Individualistic Theory of Politics* (Homer 1983) represent attempts to situate character ethics at the center of the philosophy of political ethics. In ancient Greece, according to MacIntyre (1984, 135, 138, 219), whether the ethical views of the older sophists, Plato, or Aristotle are considered, all took "it for granted that the milieu in which the virtues are to be exercised and in terms of which they are to be defined is the *polis.*" Today ethical character is no less important for politics and public service.

> Today's leaders have neglected the whole issue of moral character in both theory and practice and no longer encourage informed public reflection on the kind of people we are becoming and on our responsibilities to one another now and in the future. . . .The reality of moral character is unavoidable . . . in the so-called "character" issue of the public's trust in politicians. (Palmour 1987, 14–15)

If the concept of ethical character were given a preeminent place in political philosophy, contends Homer, the result would be "a profound change in the way we think about politics. . . . Character would force us to reexamine the way we bring up our children to think about politics, the way we should know political institutions, and the way we should act in the world." Emphasis on character would "refocus the debate in political theory on the enduring question of how to live well in the proximity of others" (1986, 166–67). Lilla laments the overemphasis in the education of students preparing for public service on ethical rules for application and on the study of ethical dilemmas and catastrophic cases. The moral life of the public official primarily consists, Lilla believes, of "a set of virtues which the official has acquired through his education and it reveals itself in the attitudes and habits he displays to the political process and the public in his day-to-day work" (1981, 5). And what Gilligan (1982; et al. 1988) describes as the male moral voice of rights, rules, justice, and fairness and the female moral voice of care, compassion, relationships, and responsiveness both must be legitimized as encompassing virtues necessary for the moral conduct of politics broadly defined (Ruddick 1980, 345, 361; Sichel 1988, 218–24).

Cynical Views

Humbuggery and Manipulation is F. G. Bailey's analysis of the art of leadership—primarily political leadership. One of his main arguments is that "no leader can survive as a leader without deceiving others (followers no less than opponents) and without deliberately doing to others what he would prefer not having done to himself" (1988, ix). Bailey summarizes his view:

> Leaders are not the virtuous people they claim to be: they put politics before statesmanship; they distort facts and oversimplify issues; they promise what no one can deliver; and they are liars. But I have also insisted that leaders, if they are to be effective, have

no choice in the matter. They could not be virtuous (in the sense of morally excellent) and be leaders at the same time. I do not mean that a leader should necessarily behave immorally. . . . I mean only that he must have the imagination (and—a paradox—the moral courage) to set himself above and beyond established values and beliefs if it is necessary to do so to attain his ends. (1988, 174–75)

To what degree should we accept Bailey's viewpoint? Does he believe that leaders must lie and deceive routinely or only occasionally? Do political leaders really have no "choice," as he argues? From his perspective, Bailey seems to describe not only what *is* the case but also what *ought to be* the case. I would contend that while we might agree with the former, we should reject the latter view.

Although scholars continue to debate the meaning of Niccolo Machiavelli's conception of virtue (Garver 1987; Hannaford 1972; Plamenatz 1972; Wood 1967), arguably Machiavelli saw prudence and practical wisdom as intellectual virtues more than as moral virtues; described other traditional moral virtues, such as honesty and courage, simply as means to be used strategically (even violated) to preserve the state; and urged that a leader must exercise the practical virtue of self-control. Machiavelli also believed that private moral virtues were inappropriate and ineffective for public political life and that at best a leader need only pretend to possess these moralities (Hariman 1989; O'Leary 1989).

During his presidential campaign and his administration, Jimmy Carter "offered a vision of authority based entirely on character" and "argued that virtue was the sole criterion for leadership" (O'Leary 1989, 123). Carter explicitly offered the virtues of honesty, efficiency, competence, compassion, and love. He assumed that essentially private virtues also appropriately operate in the conduct of public duties. In the long run, however, Carter was unable to translate these virtues into effective public policies and into sufficient public support. Indeed, contends O'Leary, Carter's reliance on a classical conception of virtue was "ultimately bound to fail in a world that has accepted the assumptions of the Machiavellian ethic" (1989, 123). Furthermore, he argues, "To a public that has accepted the assumption that it is not only permissible, but necessary, for a politician to lie in the performance of his duties, Carter's promise of honesty (to the extent that it was believed) could only serve as direct evidence of his incompetence" (1989, 126).

Presidents Johnson and Reagan

In her book, *Character*, Gail Sheehy describes the "habit of deceit" that had developed throughout Lyndon Johnson's lifetime; it was the "aspect of his character most deeply engraved and evident as a pattern throughout his youth and adulthood" (1988, 16). His public duplicity on the Vietnam war as candidate and as president "played a crucial role in the disillusionment of a political generation." The legacy of the "credibility gap" and a "long-term mistrust of the president . . . can be laid directly at the door of one man's character" (1988, 17).

Throughout his two terms as president, Ronald Reagan continued a long-standing habit of playing fast and loose with the facts (Barber 1985, 491–96; Green and MacColl 1987; Johannesen 1990, 235–52; Sheehy 1988, 257–303). In his news conferences, informal comments, and speeches, Reagan routinely misstated facts, statistics, and situations. Another aspect of playing fast and loose with the facts was Reagan's misuse of factual illustrations and stories for proof, characterized satirically by the press as his "anecdotage" problem. Reagan frequently used vivid and dramatic real-life stories to prove this point or that. Unfortunately, these anecdotes, even when not misstated, often were found to be misleading or unrepresentative. Reagan's misstatements of facts and misuse of anecdotes were not rare, occasional, or on minor matters. Rather, they were routine, sometimes repeated even after exposure, and often on matters of important public policy. The standard is not perfect accuracy. Occasional slips on minor details may be expected. The obligation is not to ultimate truth in some absolute and invariable sense. But given the major resources at his or her command for verifying information, a president does have an obligation regularly to present highly probable conclusions and data that are as accurate and fair as possible.

Is what James David Barber terms Reagan's attitude of "contempt for the facts" an ethical character flaw, a vice? Reagan was "literally shameless when it came to the question of factuality" (Barber 1985, 493; Green and MacColl 1987, 11). His unconcern for accuracy was, in view of Green and MacColl, "a habit he apparently cannot unlearn." Indeed, they characterize Reagan as "incorrigible" on this matter. "He is simply incapable of entertaining information that conflicts with his ideology. When facts differ from his beliefs, he changes the facts, not his beliefs. He has sunk to a point where he can't make a major statement without making a major misstatement" (Green and MacColl 1987, 18).

The 1988 Presidential Candidates

During 1987 and 1988 intense news media scrutiny of presidential primary candidates focused on the "character issue" and the search for significant "character flaws." Democratic candidate Gary Hart temporarily withdrew from the race after allegations of a pattern of sexual indiscretion in his private life. If nothing else, the virtues of temperance, fidelity, and prudence were at issue. Republican television evangelist Marion "Pat" Robertson denied any pattern of deception in the numerous exaggerated, misleading, or erroneous statements about himself in his résumé, speeches, and books (see Alter 1987b; Reid 1987; Wills 1987).

The withdrawal of Senator Joseph Biden from the Democratic presidential primary race clearly illustrates the relation of moral character and communication ethics. A pattern of plagiarism was a major issue of communication ethics in Biden's case. *Plagiarism* stems from the Latin word for kidnapper. It involves a communicator who steals another person's words and ideas without properly acknowledging their source and who presents those words or ideas as his or her own. Plagiarism may take such varied forms as repeating almost word for word another's sentences, "repeating someone else's particularly apt phrase without appropriate acknowledgment, paraphrasing another person's argument as your own, and presenting another's line of thinking in the development of an idea as though it were your own" (Gibaldi and Achtert 1988, 21).

Previously the press had characterized Biden positively as the most eloquent of the Democratic contenders or negatively as glib and shallow-minded. Now the press revealed that in campaign speeches Biden often presented as his own, without acknowledgment, various phrases, sentences, and long passages from speeches by John F. Kennedy, Robert Kennedy, and Hubert Humphrey. On two occasions Biden plagiarized a lengthy segment from a speech by British Labour Party leader Neil Kinnock. In this case, however, Biden also inaccurately presented parts of Kinnock's life history as his own. Biden falsely claimed that his ancestors were coal miners and that he was the first in his family to attend college. In addition, evidence surfaced that while a first-year law student, Biden had plagiarized, word for word, five pages from a law journal article. Although not a matter of plagiarism, a final element in Biden's flawed character emphasized by the news media involved his false claims in an informal interview with a small group of New Hampshire voters. Biden claimed that he graduated with three degrees and was given an award as the outstanding political science student. Further, he claimed that he attended law school on a full academic scholarship and won an international moot court competition. In fact, none of these claims were true ("Biden's Borrowings" 1987; "Biden Was Eloquent" 1987; Kaus 1987; Margolis 1987a, 1987c).

What defenses and excuses were offered by Biden and his staff? Staff members pointed out that on some occasions Biden had credited Kinnock and Robert Kennedy as sources. Biden contended that the episodes of plagiarism stemmed from ignorance, stupidity, or inattention to detail rather than from intentional deceptiveness. Concerning the plagiarism from Kinnock's speech by Biden at the Iowa State Fair, an aide explained: "He's under a huge amount of pressure. He didn't even know what he said. He was just on automatic pilot" (Coffey 1987; Margolis 1987b).

To what degree, if at all, should any of these defenses justify Biden's communication or soften our ethical judgment? In what ways should inattention to detail or lack of conscious intent to deceive influence our ethical assessment (Johannesen 1990, 10–11)? Biden's case illustrates patterns or habits of communication that the news media interpreted as serious character flaws. Lack of judgment to restrain impulses, falsification of facts, and inflation of his intellectual and communication abilities became the elements of Biden's doubtful character. At issue were such ethical virtues as humility, prudence, temperance, fairness, truthfulness, and trustworthiness (Broder 1987; Kaus 1987).

Character, Image, and Issues in Campaigns

Praise of an issue-oriented campaign as responsible and condemnation of an image-oriented campaign as superficial, even as unethical, has become a conventional judgment in political commentary (Bennett 1989). However, some political and rhetorical scholars do not share this automatic preference for issues over image in political campaigns. These scholars argue that issues and stands on issues are too transitory and too complex for voters to make dependable judgments. For example, an issue vital today often soon fades, to be replaced by one unforeseen during the campaign. Or issues may have to be created if none loom large in the public mind at the inflexible time when the campaign must occur. Instead, suggest some scholars, the basic dimensions of a candidate's image, largely defined as character, are as important as, if not more important than, particular stands on particular issues for citizen evaluation of political candidates during campaigns (Sheehy 1988, 21). One view describes images and issues as inextricably intertwined through the values espoused and contested by a candidate (Fish 1989; Weiss 1981; Werling et al. 1987).

Granted, image stereotypically is viewed as intentionally deceptive and misleading—as largely unrelated to the candidate's actual nature. But image also may be conceived of as a composite audience perception of the candidate's actual personal qualities and abilities as reflected in her or his record of choices. With image defined in this manner, the key questions in the long run become the following: Does the candidate's past record demonstrate strength of moral character, decisiveness of action, openness to relevant information and alternative viewpoints, thoroughness in studying a problem, respect for the intelligence of other persons, and ability to lead through public and private communication (Barber 1985, 1–11; Hahn and Gonchar 1972; Gonchar and Hahn 1973)?

Rhetorician Lloyd Bitzer contends that "the stuff of ordinary campaigns consists of arguments, position statements, testimonials, commercials, and other materials relating to the prudence, good character, and right intentions of the candidate—to the image" (1981, 242–43). He argues

> The public forms fairly reliable judgments about the candidates by observing their mistakes—especially their flaws in reasoning, character, and prudence. Most voters are not well educated about details of issues and legislation, although they should be; consequently, most are not good judges of a candidate's pronouncements on complicated issues. But most voters do have sound views on the constituents of logical reasoning, good character, and prudence. Thus when a candidate makes a mistake of reasoning, or of practical wisdom, or a mistake resulting from a flaw in character, the public is quick to recognize and, by and large, competent to judge it. (1981, 242)

Michael McGee, from the viewpoint of a rhetorician, argues that the conventional wisdom of preferring "issues" over "images" actually may be "ultimately unjustifiable and dangerous." Citizens generally

> do not have the necessary information to judge measures; such information could not be communicated to them in the context of an election campaign because the decisions to be made are too complicated for the limited time available; and, finally, the information needed for decision seems so technical and esoteric that most of "the people" could not judge it properly if it were available. (1978, 53)

Indeed, contends McGee, the only "issue" that the citizen is competent to judge is "the general character and trustworthiness displayed by candidates for office." Even when we believe that our choice stems from our evaluation of "the issues, we are in fact judging the character and the general trustworthiness of those who tell us what 'the issues' are" (1978, 154).

In her book, *Eloquence in an Electronic Age*, Kathleen Jamieson describes the current era as one in which

> voters are searching behind the promises for clues about whether a candidate is honest, knowledgeable, high principled, and temperamentally suited to lead the nation. In voter decisions, the candidate's character is now more central than his or her stands on issues and party identification. (1988, vii-viii)

However, in contrast with eras with fewer filters of communication mediation interposed between candidate and citizen, Jamieson views the present era as a time in which assessment of ethos—of practical wisdom, goodwill, and worthy moral character—is increasingly difficult. She concludes:

> With the advent of an electorate of millions and a country spanning oceans, direct experience of the character of a speaker is unattainable for most called on to judge public discourse. When we see a potential leader through the filter provided by pseudo-events, news bites, or nuggetized ads and then can know for certain only that most politicians do not speak their own words, ethos is a less reliable anchor for belief. (1988, 240)

In a synthesis of political theory and empirical survey research, Miller, Wattenberg, and Malanchuk argue that

> Evaluating candidates on the basis of personal qualities has for years been regarded as emotional, irrational, and lacking in political relevance. . . . The evidence now suggests that a reinterpretation is clearly needed. Rather than representing a concern with appearance, previously labeled "personality," the candidate assessments actually concentrate on the manner in which a candidate would conduct the affairs of office. (1985, 210)

Such assessments indeed may be "reasonable and intelligible performance evaluations." Miller et al. (1985) believe that voters primarily assess candidates along four dimensions of personal qualities: (1) competence—political experience and statesmanship, comprehension of political issues, realism, and intelligence; (2) integrity—trustworthiness, honesty, and sincerity; (3) reliability—dependable, strong, hardworking, decisive, and aggressive; and (4) charisma—leadership, dignity, humbleness, patriotism, and ability to communicate with people and inspire them.

"Of course issues are important. . . . But can any issue be more important in a presidential election than character?" Marshall Manley, chief executive officer of an insurance company, elaborates this position in a "My Turn" citizen editorial in *Newsweek*. He contends that

> No matter how much we know about a candidate's views on specific issues, we can't really predict how he, or she, will react to the shifting demands and crises of an actual term in office. . . . Most voters wisely look beyond a candidate's stand on the issues to something more important: qualities of mind and character. (1988, 8)

Manley suggests five qualities of character essential for a president: (1) trustworthiness and integrity; (2) toughness in the sense of courage, stamina, and determination; (3) gregariousness, including ability to build coalitions, shape consensus, and work with peers; (4) a grasp of the lessons of history, both problems and solutions; and (5) a capacity for "love of country, love of family, and love of the rough and tumble of politics" (1988, 8).

As guidelines for assessing the character of a political candidate, we can reflect on the adequacy of the four dimensions described by Miller et al. and the five qualities suggested by Manley. Are there additional dimensions or qualities that should be significant for evaluating a candidate's character? Which of the dimensions or qualities seem to focus primarily on ethical characteristics? For example, to what degree should competence, determination, a grasp of the lessons of history, or love of the rough and tumble of politics be viewed as matters of ethics generally or more specifically as ethical virtues?

Conclusions

Political columnist Stephen Chapman (1987) offers three reasons why media scrutiny of character was so intense on the 1988 presidential candidates. First, voters are imposing increasingly higher ethical standards. Second,

> Personal integrity is one of the few matters that lend themselves to firsthand judgments by the voters. Most voters may feel unable to judge whether a politician is right about the defense appropriations bill. But they are able to consider evidence about a politician's ethics and reach a verdict, since they make similar evaluations about people every day. (1987, 3)

Third, voters "tend to vote for general themes, trusting candidates to apply them in specific cases. A politician who creates doubt about his personal honesty . . . creates doubt that his concrete policies will match his applause lines" (1987, 3).

In greater depth, Gail Sheehy probes three reasons why it is essential that "we examine the character of those who ask us to put our country in their hands" (1988, 20). Primarily, "it is to protect ourselves from electing a person whose character flaws, once subjected to the pressures of leading a superpower through the nuclear age, can weaken or endanger the course of our future" (1988, 21). With issues a less sure guide than we once thought, we "are left to search out those we can believe in as strong and sincere, fair and compassionate: real leaders to whom we can leave the responsibility to use good judgment when crises catch us unaware" (1988, 29).

Second, "We need the cold slap of insight to wake us up from the smoothly contrived images projected by highly paid professional media experts who market the candidates like perfumed soap" (1988, 29). Of course, candidates and their managers can exploit the "character issue" to their own advantage. But reporters, editorialists, commentators, and investigative journalists could assist citizens in major ways by providing information about a candidate's character development—about past and present relevant virtues and vice—about significant contexts and influences through which the moral character was formed, so that the manufactured pseudo character can be penetrated to judge character more realistically. "In judging character," Sheehy reminds us, "one can never be sure the judgment is 100 percent accurate." But to that reminder I would add that it is crucial that we continue to make the most informed judgment that we can.

A final reason that we should examine the moral character of our leaders and potential leaders is to learn about ourselves. In Sheehy's view, the case histories of the characters of political leaders

> instruct us in how, and how not, to conduct ourselves to win at life. We can use these characters as mirrors of our own character reflecting both our flaws and strengths. Seeing how their various attempts to change and adapt have played out from earliest childhood through public life can be a catalyst for taking steps to change ourselves. (1988, 29)

In *The Virtuous Journalist*, Klaidman and Beauchamp argue that citizens "should expect good character in our national leaders, and the same expectations are justified for anyone in whom we regularly place trust" (1987, 17). The *Wall Street Journal* ("Oliver North" 1987) surveyed dozens of top executives of American companies to see if they would hire Lt. Col. Oliver North (of the Iran-Contra scandal) if he applied for a job. Many executives enthusiastically said they would hire him, but some would restrict his responsibilities. Among those who would refuse to hire him, one especially pinpointed the matter of character, saying, "It is a real character flaw when someone is willing to lie, cheat, and steal to accomplish the end of his superiors. That flaw will ultimately hurt the company. It's a character flaw that I would find unacceptable despite the strengths of his loyalty. The integrity flaw outweighs any other" ("Oliver North" 1987, 35). Here we see the virtue of fidelity in conflict with the virtues of truthfulness and trustworthiness. An emphasis on virtue ethics or character ethics as a viable approach to ethics in organizations, both business and governmental, is reflected in such essays and books as Des Jardins's "Virtues and Corporate Responsibility" (1984); Kolenda's *Organizations and Ethical Individualism* (1988); Scott and Mitchell's "The Problem or Mystery of Evil and Virtue in Organizations" (1988); Walton's *The Moral Manager* (1988); and Wilbur's "Corporate Character" (1984).

Admittedly, the news media (or anyone) may at times be overzealous and focus on trivial or irrelevant character traits. But in general the emphasis on moral character in evaluating presidential candidates is central "to what the electorate seems to value most in its presidents—authenticity and honesty" (Taylor 1987, 23; Broder 1987, 7). To aid in assessing the ethical character of any person who is in a position of responsibility or who seeks a position of trust, we can modify guidelines suggested by journalists (Alter 1987a). Will the recent or current ethically suspect communication probably continue? Does it seem habitual? Even if a particular incident seems minor in itself, does it "fit into a familiar pattern that illuminates more serious shortcomings?" If the person does something inconsistent with his or her public image, "is it a small miscue or a sign of hypocrisy?"

"At this point in our political history," Sheehy emphasizes, "the concentration on character issues is unparalleled in its intensity" (1988, 11). The reason, she says, "is simple and stark." "By the time they become national leaders, the candidates' characters are sown. And if the character is destiny, the destiny they reap will be our own. . . . We must therefore know our would-be leaders in a deeper way than ever before" (1988, 21).

Communication ethics should encompass both individual ethics and social ethics. What are the ethical virtues of character and the central ethical standards that should guide individual choices? What are the ethical standards and responsibilities that should guide the communication practices of organizations and institutions—public and private, corporate, governmental, or professional? For an ethically suspect communication practice, where should individual and collective responsibility be placed? The study of communication ethics should suggest standards both for individual daily and context-bound communication choices and also for institutional/systemic policies and practices.

In her provocative essay, "Ethics Without Virtue," Christina Hoff Sommers (1984) warns that the present "system of moral education is silent about virtue." She condemns moral education as presented in most American universities today for addressing itself "not to the vices and virtues of individuals, but to the moral character of our nation's institutions." She argues:

> Inevitably the student forms the idea that applying ethics to modern life is mainly a question of learning how to be for or against social and institutional policies. . . . In that sort of ethical climate, a student soon loses sight of himself as a moral agent and begins to see himself as a moral spectator or protojurist. . . . The result of identifying normative ethics with public policy is justification for and reinforcement of moral passivity in the student. (1984, 388)

A curriculum of ethics without virtue, Sommers concludes, "is a cause for concern."

References

Adler, Mortimer J. 1970. *The time of our lives: The ethics of common sense*. New York: Holt, Rinehart and Winston.
——— 1988. *Reforming education: The opening of the American mind*. New York: Macmillan.
Alderman, Harold. 1982. By virtue of a virtue. *Review of Metaphysics* 36 (September): 127–53.
Alter, Jonathan. 1987a. The search for personal flaws. *Newsweek* 19 October, 79.
——— 1987b. A change of Hart. *Newsweek* 28 December, 12–16.
Bailey, F. G. 1988. *Humbuggery and manipulation: The art of leadership*. Ithaca, NY: Cornell University Press.
Barber, James David. 1985. *The presidential character: Predicting performance in the White House*, 3rd ed. Englewood Cliffs, NJ: Prentice-Hall.
Becker, Lawrence C. 1975. The neglect of virtue. *Ethics* 85 (January): 110–22.
——— 1986. *Reciprocity*. London: Routledge and Kegan Paul.
Bennett, W. Lance. 1989. Where have all the issues gone? Explaining the rhetorical limits in American elections. In *Spheres of argument*, ed. Bruce E. Gronbeck, 128–35. Annandale, VA: Speech Communication Association.
Biden was eloquent—if not original. 1987. *Chicago Tribune* 12 September, sec. 1, 1–2.

Biden's borrowings become an issue. 1987. *Chicago Tribune* 16 September, sec. 1, 4.
Birkhead, Douglas. 1989. An ethics of vision for journalism. *Critical Studies in Mass Communication* 6 (September): 283–94.
Bitzer, Lloyd F. 1981. Political rhetoric. In *Handbook of political communication*, ed. Dan D. Nimmo and Keith R. Sanders, 225–48. Beverly Hills: Sage.
Booth, Wayne C. 1988. *The company we keep: An ethics of fiction.* Berkeley: University of California Press.
Brandt, R. B. 1981. W. K. Frankena and the ethics of virtue. *Monist* 64 (July): 271–92.
Broder, David S. 1987. The latest departed candidate. *Indianapolis News* 25 September, A–7.
Chapman, Stephen. 1987. How seriously has Joe Biden hurt his presidential effort? *Chicago Tribune* 20 September, sec. 4, 3.
Cochran, Clarke E. 1982. *Character, community, and politics.* University: University of Alabama Press.
Coffey, Raymond. 1987. Biden's borrowed eloquence beats the real thing. *Chicago Tribune* 18 September, sec. 1, 23.
Cunningham, Stanley B. 1970. Does "does moral philosophy rest upon a mistake?" make an even greater mistake? *Monist* 54 (January): 86–99.
DeGeorge, Richard T. 1986. *Business ethics*, 2d ed. New York: Macmillan.
Des Jardins, Joseph. 1984. Virtues and corporate responsibility. In *Corporate governance and institutionalizing ethics*, ed. W. Michael Hoffman, Jennifer Mills Moore, and David A. Fedo, 135–42. Lexington, MA: D. C. Heath.
Fish, Duane R. 1989. Image and issue in the second Bush-Dukakis debate: The mediating role of values. In *Spheres of argument*, ed. Bruce E. Gronbeck, 151–57. Annandale, VA: Speech Communication Association.
Fisher, Walter R. 1987. *Human communication as narration: Toward a philosophy of reason, value, and action.* Columbia: University of South Carolina Press.
Foot, Phillipa. 1978. *Virtues and vices and other essays in moral philosophy.* Oxford: Basil Blackwell.
Frankena, William K. 1970. Pritchard and the ethics of virtue. *Monist* 54 January): 1–17.
French, Peter A., Theodore Uehling, Jr., and Howard K. Wettstein, eds. 1988. *Midwest studies in philosophy*, Vol. XIII, *Ethical theory—character and virtue.* Notre Dame, IN: University of Notre Dame Press.
Garver, Eugene. 1987. *Machiavelli and the history of prudence.* Madison: University of Wisconsin Press.
Geatch, Peter. 1977. *The virtues.* Cambridge: Cambridge University Press.
Gibaldi, Joseph, and Walter S. Achtert. 1988. *MLA handbook for writers of research papers*, 3rd ed. New York: Modern Language Association.
Gilligan, Carol. 1982. *In a different voice: Psychological theory and women's development.* Cambridge: Harvard University Press.
Gilligan, Carol, et al. 1988. *Mapping the moral domain: A contribution of women's thinking to psychological theory and education.* Cambridge: Harvard University Graduate School of Education.
Gonchar, Ruth, and Dan Hahn. 1973. Rhetorical biography: A methodology for the citizen-critic. *Speech Teacher* 22 January): 48–53.

Green, Mark, and Gail MacColl. 1987. *Reagan's reign of error*, Rev. and enl. ed. New York: Pantheon Books.

Hahn, Dan, and Ruth Gonchar. 1972. Political myth: The image and the issue. *Today's Speech* 20 (Summer): 57–65.

Hannaford, I. 1972. Machiavelli's concept of virtù in *The Prince* and *The Discourses* reconsidered. *Political Studies* 20 (June): 185–89.

Hariman, Robert. 1989. Before prudence: Strategy and the rhetorical tradition. In *Spheres of Argument*, ed. Bruce E. Gronbeck, 108–16. Annandale, VA: Speech Communication Association.

Hauerwas, Stanley. 1977. *Truthfulness and tragedy*. Notre Dame: University of Notre Dame Press.

——— 1981a. *A Community of character: Toward a constructive Christian social ethic*. Notre Dame: University of Notre Dame Press.

——— 1981b. *Vision and virtue*. Notre Dame: University of Notre Dame Press.

Homer, Frederic D. 1983. *Character: An individualistic theory of politics*. Lanham, MD: University Press of America.

Hudson, Stephen. 1981. Taking virtues seriously. *Australasian Journal of Philosophy* 59 (June): 189–202.

Jamieson, Kathleen Hall. 1988. *Eloquence in an electronic age: The transformation of political speechmaking*. New York: Oxford University Press.

Johannesen, Richard L. 1990. *Ethics in human communication*, 3rd ed. Prospect Heights, IL: Waveland Press.

Jonsen, Albert R., and Stephen Toulmin. 1988. *The abuse of casuistry: A history of moral reasoning*. Berkeley: University of California Press.

Josephson Institute. 1988. Ethical values and principles in public service. *Ethics: Easier Said Than Done* 1 (Spring/Summer): 153.

Kaus, Mickey. 1987. Biden's belly flop. *Newsweek* 28 September, 23-24.

Klaidman, Stephen, and Tom L. Beauchamp. 1987. *The virtuous journalist*. New York: Oxford University Press.

Kolenda, Konstantin, ed. 1988. *Organizations and ethical individualism*. New York: Praeger.

Kupfer, Joseph. 1982. The moral presumption against lying. *Review of Metaphysics* 36 (September): 103–26.

Kupperman, Joel. 1988. Character and ethical theory. *Midwest studies in philosophy*, Vol. XIII, *Ethical theory: Character and virtue*, ed. Peter A. French, Theodore E. Uehling, Jr., and Howard K. Wettstein, 115–25. Notre Dame: University of Notre Dame Press.

Lebacqz, Karen. 1985. *Professional ethics*. Nashville, TN: Abingdon Press.

Lilla, Mark T. 1981. Ethos, "ethics," and public service. *The Public Interest* 63 (Spring): 3–17.

MacIntyre, Alasdair. 1984. *After virtue*, 2d ed. Notre Dame: University of Notre Dame Press.

Manley, Marshall. 1988. Going beyond "the issues." *Newsweek* 18 January, 8.

Margolis, Jon. 1987a. Biden threatened by accusations of plagiarism in his speeches. *Chicago Tribune* 17 September, sec. 1, 3.

——— 1987b. Biden on quote furor: I've done some dumb things. *Chicago Tribune* 18 September, sec. 1, 3.

——— 1987c. For Biden, as for Hart, it's the stupidity that hurts. *Chicago Tribune* 22 September, sec. 1, 15.

Mayo, Bernard. 1958. *Ethics and the moral life*. London: Macmillan.

McGee, Michael. 1978. "Not men, but measures": The origins and import of an ideological principle. *Quarterly Journal of Speech* 64 (April): 141–54.
Meilaender, Gilbert C. 1984. *The theory and practice of virtue.* Notre Dame: University of Notre Dame Press.
Michell, Gillian. 1984. Women and lying: A pragmatic and semantic analysis of "telling it slant." *Women's Studies International Forum* 7: 375–83.
Miller, Arthur H., Martin P. Wattenberg, and Oksana Malanchuk. 1985. Cognitive representations of candidate assessments. *Political communication yearbook 1984*, ed. Keith R. Sanders, Lynda Lee Kaid, and Dan Nimmo, 183–210. Carbondale: Southern Illinois University Press.
Minnick, Elizabeth. 1985. Why not lie? *Soundings* 68 (Winter): 493–509.
Noddings, Nel. 1984. *Caring: A feminine approach to ethics and moral education.* Berkeley: University of California Press.
O'Leary, Stephen D. 1989. Machiavelli and the paradox of political hypocrisy: The fragmentation of virtue in the public and private spheres. In *Spheres of argument*, ed. Bruce E. Gronbeck, 117–27. Annandale, VA: Speech Communication Association.
Oliver North, businessman? Many bosses say that he's their kind of employee. 1987. *Wall Street Journal* eastern ed. 14 July, sec. 2, 35.
Palmour, Jody. 1987. *On moral character: A practical guide to Aristotle's virtues and vices.* Washington, DC: Archon Institute for Leadership Development.
Pinckaers, Servais. 1962. Virtue is not a habit. *Cross Currents* 12 (Winter): 65–81.
Pincoffs, Edmund L. 1986. *Quandaries and virtues: Against reductivism in ethics.* Lawrence: University of Kansas Press.
Plamenatz, John. 1972. In search of Machiavellian "virtù." In *The political calculus: Essays on Machiavelli's philosophy*, ed. Anthony Parel, 157–78. Toronto: University of Toronto Press.
Reid, T. R. 1987. Rewriting the book on Pat Robertson. *Washington Post National Weekly Edition* 15 October, 15.
Rorty, Amelie Oksenberg, ed. 1980. *Essays on Aristotle's ethics.* Berkeley: University of California Press.
Ruddick, Sara. 1980. Maternal thinking. *Feminist Studies* 6 (Summer): 342–67.
Scott, William G., and Terence R. Mitchell. 1988. The problem or mystery of evil and virtue in organizations. In *Organizations and ethical individualism*, ed. Konstantin Kolenda, 47–72. New York: Praeger.
Sheehy, Gail. 1988. *Character: America's search for leadership.* New York: William Morrow.
Sichel, Betty A. 1988. *Moral education: Character, community, and ideals.* Philadelphia: Temple University Press.
Simon, Yves R. 1986. *The definition of moral virtue.* New York: Fordham University Press.
Slote, Michael. 1983. *Goods and virtues.* New York: Oxford University Press.
Sommers, Christina Hoff. 1984. Ethics without virtue. *The American Scholar* 53 (Summer): 381–89.
―――, ed. 1985. *Vice and virtue in everyday life.* New York: Harcourt Brace Jovanovich.
Taylor, Paul. 1987. Our people-magazined race for the presidency. *Washington Post National Weekly Edition* 2 November, 23.
Wallace, James D. 1978. *Virtues and vices.* Ithaca, NY: Cornell University Press.
Walton, Clarence C. 1988. *The moral manager.* Cambridge, MA: Ballinger.

Weiss, Robert. 1981. The presidential campaign debates in their political context: The image-issue interface in the 1980 campaign. *Speaker and Gavel* 18: 22–27.
Werling, David S. 1987. Presidential debates: Epideictic merger of images and issues in values. In *Argument and critical practices*, ed. Joseph W. Wenzel, 229–38. Annandale, VA: Speech Communication Association.
Wilbur, James B., III. 1984. Corporate character. In *Corporate governance and institutionalizing ethics*, ed. W. Michael Hoffman, Jennifer Mills Moore, and David A. Fedo, 173–84. Lexington, MA: D. C. Heath.
Williams, Bernard. 1981. *Moral luck*. Cambridge: Cambridge University Press.
Wills, Gary. 1987. Hart's guilt trick. *Newsweek* 28 December, 17–18.
Wood, Neal. 1967. Machiavelli's concept of virtù reconsidered. *Political Studies* 15 (June): 159–72.

320   Clifford G. Christians

Preview to "Social Responsiblity." *Clifford Christians offers for consideration a clearly structured theoretical framework, justifications of his judgmental principles, and immensely illustrative applications of those principles. He presents a particular set of ethical norms as an essential part of institutional policy formation for new communication technologies. Christians argues for a flexibly defined "cultural continuity" that junctions as an over-arching metanorm to be implemented through the ethical standards of justice, openness, harmony, stewardship, and discovery. He sees Ivan Illich's concept of "convivial" technologies as a crystallizing synthesis of his own ethical stance. For a view of the norms that should guide ethical journalism, see Clifford G. Christians, John P. Ferré, and P. Mark Fackler,* Good News: Social Ethics and the Press *(New York: Oxford University Press, 1993), pp. 175–85.*

You may wish to compare several points made by Christians with somewhat parallel points discussed earlier in this book. First, consider Christians's fundamental argument that technology is not ethically neutral—that "valuing penetrates all technological activity." Recall that two contemporary theorists of rhetoric, Kenneth Burke and Richard M. Weaver (chapter 1), share the conviction that, to varying degrees, all intentional use of language is "sermonic." To them the idea that language can be used in a completely neutral and objective manner is unsound. Second, you might compare and contrast Christians's normative framework with the view of John Phelan in his book, Disenchantment: Meaning and Morality in the Media. *The public interest philosophy envisioned by Phelan includes the social values of justice, equality, and democratic rule and the mass media values of diversity, regionalism, access, and high quality.*

In some applications of his ethical standards for new communication technologies, Christians advocates "people-based development from below" and a "bottom-up" participatory ethic. You are urged to compare Christians's view with that developed by Larry Gross, who argues that "the critical test of ethical guidelines applied to mass media practice will be to examine the treatment of those outside the mainstream: minorities and deviants of all kinds." Gross's first ethical criterion is that "groups should be allowed to speak for themselves." The mass media should "permit a diversity of voices and perspectives to be represented." His second ethical criterion applies "when speaking for others." "The power of the media should be used to equalize and not to skew further the radically unequal distribution of material and symbolic resources in our society." Gross prefers small-scale to large-scale communication systems because they have the "potential to permit and possibly even ensure communal interaction and even accountability. . . . (See Larry Gross, John Stuart Katz, and Jay Ruby, eds., Image Ethics, *New York: Oxford University Press, 1988, pp. 188–202.)*

Social Responsibility: Ethics and New Technologies*
Clifford G. Christians

In Jacques Ellul's perspective, ethics and the new technologies are a contradiction in terms. The modern technological process is governed by a technicized Geist fundamentally impervious to all moral considerations. *La technique* acts tyrannically as a spiritual guillotine, decapitating other values. A civilization engrossed in means obviates all genuine concern for ends, "as in ancient days men put out the eyes of nightingales in order to make them sing better" (*Presence of the Kingdom*, 1967, p. 67). Ellul foresaw already in 1948 that as the world of technics expands, ethical imperatives will be replaced by cost and time effectiveness, by administrative niceties, faster transmission, and ephemeral politics.

Ellul's philosophy of technology deserves a hearing and exhibits a prophetic prescience; such voices of resistance have been scandalously underplayed until very recently. However, he operates in the *sociological* arena of morality and amorality; his observations, therefore, do not preclude the academic enterprise we know as ethics. I wish to demonstrate that ethics as a scholarly domain—first established in the Pythagorean academy—opens important windows on new media technologies. I do not discredit political, historical, psychological, or economic appraisals, but I find it profoundly unsettling that ethical questions have not shaped sufficiently the current debates.

---

*Christians's analysis reprinted here originally was presented at the annual national conference of the Speech Communication Association, New Orleans, November 4, 1988. It is printed with the permission of the author.

While not capitulating to Ellul's problematic, I consider the naivete on the opposite end of the spectrum inexcusable. Even if the technological gods have failed us before, we catch ourselves thinking, perhaps this time salvation is at hand. The doxologies are much too uncritical, our enthusiasm often cut loose from sober-minded history, and our intellectual efforts too consumed by a value-free scientific naturalism. In Heidegger's terms, modem technology is *herausforderend*; that is, its demanding character presses itself upon us.

I am keenly aware that ethicists themselves have largely frittered away their birthright. We have a penchant for an individualistic, relativistic, quandary ethics which fails to encompass social structures, institutions, and cultural forms. Thus I accept Hans Jonas' challenge in *The Imperative of Responsibility* (1984) that our ethics be sophisticated enough to confront the complications of a technological age capable on the one hand of annihilating humanity while at the same time involving the entire globe in one another's business through the communications media.

The Problematic

Before we can meaningfully articulate an ethical framework for any particular media technology, we need a more sophisticated understanding of technology itself. I want to argue in this paper against the commonplace that technology is neutral—that only uses involve human valuing (Monsma, 1984, Ch. 3). Once the value-ladenness of technology is established, it becomes self-evident that we need an ethical framework by which to orient the technological process responsibly.

We too readily assume that technology is merely a tool which can be used rightly or wrongly. As in Arnold Pacey's illustration, in Swedish Lapland snowmobiles are used for reindeer herding, among Canada's Eskimos for trapping, and in Wisconsin for leisure. Technological products are independent, we are told; they can be used to support completely different cultures and lifestyles. A knife in the surgeon's hands saves a life and takes it away when used by a murderer. The same projector shows pornography and National Geographic Specials.

The prevailing opinion that technology is neutral typically focuses on hardware, on tools and mechanical artifacts. I find that definition deficient in scope and view technology instead as a human process, value-laden throughout. Technology in my view is the distinct cultural activity in which human beings form and transform natural reality for practical ends. On this view, I would argue that valuing penetrates all technological activity, from the analytical framework used to understand technological issues, through the processes of design and fabrication, to the resulting tools and products. Although valuing is surely involved in the uses to which people put these technological objects, valuing saturates every phase prior to usage as well.

There can be no isolated, neutral understandings of technology as though it exists in a presuppositionless vacuum. Instead, technology proceeds out of our whole human experience and is directed by our ultimate commitments. Technology is value laden, the product of the primordial valuing activities of human beings. It not only arises as technology interacts with political and social factors, but emerges from the basic fact that technological objects are unique, not universal.

Any technological instrument embodies particular values which by definition give to this artifact properties that other artifacts do not possess. Harold Innis and Marshall McLuhan recognized that fact regarding communication technologies, for example. Innis argued that each medium is biased toward space and time in particular ways—print having proclivities toward space, oral communication toward time, television toward immediacy, and cinema toward visual realism.

The technological process carries within it the values that people have inevitably—even if unconsciously—placed there. Obscuring this fact with presumed neutrality has been very costly. For one thing, it typically allows scientists and engineers to escape responsibility. And in its heaviest form, it promotes a version of technological determinism in which technology's own inner logic appears to drive its development. Moreover, it leads to an exaggerated, unbalanced emphasis on magnitude, control, uniformity, and integration—what Arnold Pacey calls the virtuosity values (*Culture of Technology*, 1983, p. 102). The narrow view fosters the working rule that "If it can be done, it should be done," pushing out other significant dimensions in our decision making.

But the claim that technology is a value-loaded enterprise is only a first-level approximation. The only valid option finally, it seems to me, concerns our choice of the supremely valued—that is, the norms by which our value judgments are ordered. Otherwise I have only presented the innocuous argument that valuing is expressed preference and nothing more. Known as an emotive view of values, this perspective makes the minimalist claim that to value something says I like it. In contrast, I would contend that the values which infuse the technological process must simultaneously be considered process transcendent.

These are debatable matters to be sure, but at least they provide a general indication why the only legitimate alternative to neutral technology is normative technology. Human beings, peculiar among living organisms, act upon a structural whole—a universum—rather than in terms of natural surroundings or immediate experience only. Therefore, the theoretical model itself must be normative and not merely descriptive. Ethics is not an independent entity which periodically invades the technological domain like a kamikaze pilot. Given technology's value-ladenness, our perspective on technology in general and new media technologies in particular must be integrated pervasively into all phases of this cultural activity.

Without a brawny, comprehensive ethics for technology, its alienating capacity tends to allow it an independent existence apart from human values. Heidegger made it clear that the technological order driven by necessity is fundamentally at odds with human freedom. As noted at the beginning, Jacques Ellul has developed this insight into a wide-ranging critique of the technological imperative, in which technologies take on a life of their own, driven by self-augmenting, internal dynamics.

Ellul portrays the communication system as spreading the technicized animus throughout public life. And in the face of those perilous trends—so obvious to those who know history—where is the resistance? Moral purpose has been sacrificed to technical excellence. Thus, once the printing press was invented, a process was set in motion for constantly increasing its capacity, speeding its production, and refining it organizationally. Obeying the same autonomous development, electronics are expanded from Atlantic cable to communication satellites, from seven TV channels to forty, from specialized companies to multinational conglomerates. As the *Christian Science Monitor* has complained: "Television is widely pictured as a runaway, money-driven machine without a heart—pumping out lowest-common-denominator programming at the behest of the highest bidder." And Norman Lear recently charged that television is inspired only by the cult of large audiences: "Television's moral North Star is quite simply, 'How do I win Tuesday night at 8?'" They speak of the technological imperative out of control.

On Wall Street's Black Monday (17 October 1987), computer technology played the material role in the market's free fall toward oblivion. While such dramatic collapses are complicated phenomena, Wall Street's computer-driven system at crucial points was no longer subject to human direction. The technology took its own direction, impervious to all frenzied attempts to redirect or stop it. That serves as an analog of my concern for the technological imperative in the mass media. When we define news as whatever reporters do, the imperative is driving us forward. Whenever new technologies are assessed and implemented according to efficiency criteria, we see the stage for media capabilities determining what happens independent of ethical principles.

The neutrality view feeds technology's alienating propensity. Only with the normative theoretical model outlined below do we have the possibility of retaining human mastery over the design, fabrication, and use of new technologies that have recently emerged or are currently envisioned. I consider this normative theory to answer the question of how new media technologies can become socially responsible.

Cultural Continuity

The theory of normative technology I consider defensible is controlled by the master norm of cultural continuity. Cultures I take to be those patterns of belief and behavior which orient life and provide it significance. They constitute the human kingdom by organizing reality and indicating what we ought to do and avoid. Cultures are humankind's distinctive and immediate environment built from the material order by women and men's creative effort. Cultures are those webs we stitch together to direct societal practice, the embodiments of our living as persons-in-community. Max Weber called them the "webs of significance," within which the human species uniquely lives.

Therefore, to place this controlling norm in more technical language, I establish a formal criterion: New technological products are legitimate if and only if they maintain cultural continuity. This value-laden enterprise we call technology, to be set in a normative direction, must comport well with cultural continuity. We ought to consider the viability of historically and geographically constituted peoples to be nonnegotiable. Given culture's centrality in our humanness, its continuity warrants the primary focus.

I am suggesting that our technological activities must "comport well" with the controlling norm of cultural continuity. "Comport well" carries with it a creative ambiguity. On the one hand, it asks for a strong relationship, one rooted in cultural continuity. On the other hand, it does not specify this relationship precisely. This does not suggest that all technological activities are detailed in that first principle or that they can be deduced directly from it.

I thereby insist on humility about human knowledge. No one should expect to find a complete system of normative standards for technological activities that results by simple deduction. All human effort—including theorizing—is done by beings whose knowledge is incomplete, whose insights are imperfect, and whose understanding is often blinded by tentativeness.

And, of course, I speak of historical continuity. I am not proposing a static view of continuity without discontinuity; that, at best, represents an ancient Greek cyclical view of history. But I choose to emphasize continuity so as to contradict notions of blind evolutionary progress that undervalue continuity altogether. Also, continuity undercuts the modernization schemes devised by transnational companies or colonial powers to strengthen their hegemony. Perhaps oscillation conveys the appropriate image, a dialectic between continuity and discontinuity—with the overall pattern one of cultural formation rather than rejection.

Clearly, opposites are at work here—differentiation and integration, centralization and decentralization, large scale and small scale, uniformity and pluriformity. And difficult choices must often be made between those opposites. But the prevailing direction is always toward differentials, decentralization, small scale, and pluriformity. Sometimes that results in a break with past practices (discontinuity), but such disruptions are made more gradually and by smaller steps when controlled by continuity as the first principle. The point is to place the final decision about the mix in the hands of the users who know best which technological innovations most appropriately serve their local cultures.

Arnold Pacey gives an example of historical continuity (1983, pp. 70–77). The state of Kerala in south India follows a basic-needs approach rather than rapid-growth. In medical care, for instance, rather than a sophisticated centralized hospital, one of Kerala's notable features has been a well-staffed network of primary health clinics established throughout the state. Largely accessible by walking, the clinics concentrate on childbirth, public hygiene, and basic medical care. In the process, operating costs are manageable locally; surgeons and specialized equipment need not be imported from technologically advanced countries. This exemplifies a commitment to continuity, with an element of progress or discontinuity (a drop in infant mortality rates, for instance, to the point of favorable comparison at present with England).

Operating Principles

With the controlling norm established, one can derive a set of normative principles in terms of the major components in historical-cultural formation, operating principles which are technology specific: in politics, justice; for users, openness; with nature, harmony; in industry, stewardship; for education, discovery (Monsma, 1984, pp. 170–177).

I mean these normative principles to operate simultaneously and not sequentially. While primary responsibility in the educational-scientific community, for example, is discovery, the norms of justice, openness, harmony, and stewardship ought to simultaneously shape the decision-making process. Thus we have expanded our theory to argue that the controlling aim of responsible technology is cultural continuity and its operating principles are justice, openness, harmony, stewardship, and discovery. And, given the overview character of this essay, it is sufficient at this stage to define these terms in the briefest possible manner.

Regarding justice, I refer to distributive justice, to the allocation of resources which respects right relationships in that all participants receive their proper due. Therefore, introducing tools which make work easier while maintaining cultural continuity is objectionable if workers are still exploited and subjugated. In the user domain, open communication is essential if decision makers are to fulfill their own responsibility regarding economic value, safety, appropriateness, and dependability. Regarding nature, only those technological products which do not violate physical reality and protect nonrenewable resources are morally legitimate. Industry, in the fabrication process, ought to operate by the stewardship principle, using human, physical, and financial resources in a nonexploitative manner. On this view, scientists and engineers in particular—and educators in general—are expected to invent, explore and create unencumbered by the needs of profit or political power.

In thus establishing a controlling norm and operating principles, we have established a normative theory of two interconnected and irreducible tiers. This theory insists on a straightforward realism which emphasizes rules (what I have called operating principles). Rules guide actions on the psychological and social levels, and outlining them in detail prevents us from operating in a vacuum or toward ends determined by others. However, the theory recognizes the need to ground our rules, and to use law formulas (what I have called the "controlling norm") as the basis for effective technological rules. Given this two-dimensional approach, one seeks in law statements that they be more or less true and in rules that they be more or less effective.

In developing my theoretical model, I have established a proto-norm (continuity) and introduced the relevant operating principles while insisting on their simultaneity. These elements of the theory are best summarized, I believe, with Ivan Illich's conviviality. Given culture building as a universal and fundamental human practice, I prefer to think of socially responsible technology in terms of his *Tools for Conviviality*—explicating that notion in terms of the master norm and operating principles outlined above.

"Convivial" is Illich's "technical term to designate a modern society of responsibly limited tools . . . [in which they] serve politically interrelated individuals rather than managers" (1973, pp. xii–xiii). I choose the term "conviviality," he writes,

> to designate the opposite of industrial productivity. I intend it to mean autonomous and creative intercourse among persons . . . and with their environment; this is in contrast with the conditioned response of persons to the demands made upon them . . . by a man-made environment. I consider conviviality to be individual freedom realized in personal independence and, as such, an intrinsic ethical value. (p. 11)

Convivial technology, by integrating the master norm and operating principles, respects the dignity of human work, needs little specialized training to operate, is generally accessible to the public, and emphasizes personal satisfaction and ingenuity in its use. Such convivial tools would be feasible, Illich says, if we simply placed limits on the extent, scale and power of industrial tools—on the speed of vehicles, the size of engines, the right to extraordinary amounts of packaged medical care or education, and the requirements for professional certification. Convivial tools are dialogical: they maintain a kind of open-ended conversation with their users. Convivial tools require far less capital investment per tool, so they are widely available and accessible. Convivial tools are also more self-explanatory; they do not require the user to submit to expert pedagogy; they encourage experimentation, disassembly and repair. Finally, convivial tools, because of the simplicity and openness of their design, cannot be mystified, so they do not give rise to professional monopolies of knowledge.

For Illich, a society in which true dialogue could occur must inevitably be a society of convivial tools. Because convivial tools conform to the desires and purposes of their users, rather than transform human desires to fit the shape of the tools, they can become true extensions of human subjects. Women and men can use convivial tools to act directly in the world, rather than letting industrial technologies dictate their way of life (cf. John Pauly, 1983, pp. 259–280).

Three Examples

1. As one illustration of how my normative model operates vis-a-vis new technologies, note that the current U.S. policy regarding media satellites is anti-normative. Satellite technology currently in place is a nonconvivial instrument.

While there are more than 4,000 satellites in space at present, only 35 orbital slots are available in fixed, geostationary position. The issue is whether orbital positions should be allocated on a first-come, first-served basis or whether they ought to be distributed according to the country-by-country principle. The World Administrative Radio Conference (1979) argued that only by reserving orbital spaces for every country can we guarantee equal access to information in the future. The country-by-country principle is also recommended by UNESCO through their MacBride commission that originated from the 1976 Nairobi conference. In contrast, the United States has continued to advocate a first-come, first-served policy on the grounds that satellite technology will continue to improve and thereby meet the information needs of the future as more countries demand greater use of satellites.

The debate here is over cultural imperialism. The smaller nations since World War II have sought political independence from colonial powers and economic independence from transnational corporations. In the 1980s they were demanding cultural independence. I mean cultural imperialism in the sense of control over a country's information, the dominance by an industrial country over the films, television and news—the popular culture—of developing countries. This form of colonialism prevents smaller nations from achieving their own identity, from maintaining cultural continuity. When we employ our formal criterion regarding cultural continuity and the normative principle of justice in the political arena, we can only support a master plan which guarantees access country-by-country, reserving positions for future use, rather than the principle of first-come, first-served favorable to the United States, Western Europe and Russia.

Injustice here is obvious in that developed countries have almost total technological hegemony over the satellite network—setting advantageous prices, facilities, and service for themselves. Injustice is also seen in the flagrant imbalance of media content. Eighty percent of news received in Third World countries originates from developed nations. The majority of television shows are produced by developed countries and ill-suited to other nations. In addition, the inaccurate and unrepresentative depiction of nondeveloped countries—without sufficient means to correct distorted information—is unjust. No international code of ethics, for example, describes a policy for redressing grievances.

Therefore, we must conclude that a new technology such as satellites cannot merely be viewed as technologically neutral, as an efficient machine transmitting global messages faster at less cost. New technologies such as satellites, for all their benefits, do not automatically result in the global unity and greater human understanding suggested by Marshall McLuhan. And clearly Buckminster Fuller's engineering criterion is patently unacceptable—arguing as he does the virtue of satellite communication because the same volume of information can be transmitted by a technological instrument 1/700 thousandth the weight of the transatlantic cable.

2. A second application of the normative model can be made to third-generation cable systems. If we envision a home information utility built from fiber optics, capable of 200 interactive channels, and providing a complete range of cultural services, how ought this technological system be ordered ethically? My purpose is not blue-sky prognostications but, at this early stage of the informatic society, to formulate ethical guidelines by which further developments ought to unfold—if they unfold at all—and by which false versions are resisted.

The important ethical question is whether one can develop and use this resource in terms of the master norm and five operating principles. To make the issue more specific: Can we assume comprehensive information to every person regardless of income or geographic location? Given the realities of marketplace economics, I wish to ask, will a third-generation cable system merely provide an added convenience for those already information rich? I contend we are morally bound to initiate only those information structures marked by cultural continuity, justice, openness, stewardship, discovery, and harmony.

Citizens, politicians, and company officials tend to operate with a vague notion of equal distribution, of fairness. But these values rarely get fully clarified and are easily subverted by political realities and marketplace economics. In spite of its prominence as a standard for media practice, the appeal to a neutral technology subject to the open market fails to provide a sound ethical framework. Ability to pay fails to recognize the levelling involved in emergencies. Should police, fire, medical, and disaster protection only be made available to the prosperous? And as cable increasingly serves in opinion polling, referenda, and the political process, is not everyone by citizenship entitled to participate?

If the standard conception is unaccepted—that is, to each according to ability to pay in the open marketplace of supply and demand—I wish to argue that to each according to her essential needs is particularly relevant to a home information utility. A need conception of justice covers more appropriately the issues raised by a third-generation cable system and expresses most precisely the ideal of conviviality. Given the economics of monthly costs in urban poverty areas and the high expenditures to wire rural areas, for example, complete saturation will not be automatic in a system established on profitability. A need principle of social justice, in effect, endorses only that institution which accords equal access to all. As third-generation cable emerges, therefore, it becomes imperative to either establish it on a comprehensive basis or forego its pace of deployment until a full-scale structure becomes feasible.

I do not contend that individual whims or frivolous wants ought to be met, but that basic human needs must be satisfied equally. Needs related to consideration of survival or existence can be distinguishable from felt needs or wants. Essential needs are typically assumed to be given rather than acquired. Agreement is rather uniform on most fundamental issues such as food, housing, safety, and medical care. People as persons share genetic endowments which define them as human. Everyone is entitled—without regard for individual success—to that which permits them to live humanely.

The normative model of technology envisions the third-generation system as a social necessity. By virtue of its qualification as an essential need without which an industrial economy could not exist, this necessity of life ought to be distributed impartially, regardless of income or geographic location. Unless such impartiality occurs, cable will be anti-cultural for all except the information rich, and to the degree a society is unresponsive regarding its disenfranchised, it is not being socially responsible.

The most obvious institutional implication regards ownership. For those committed to a two-way information system, disseminated equally to all, the free market is insufficient. In this light, rather than promoting the status quo I would advocate experiments with public ownership. If we are genuinely concerned about the necessity of equal access, local community ownership might well make this possible. Municipal ownership is worth pursuing now during cable's second generation. I do not suggest it because I believe it is paradise, nor am I motivated by ideology toward this alternative.

Our information on public ownership is embarrassingly scanty in the United States; we have virtually ignored it since the days of the influential Sloan Commission, which did not even mention public ownership as an option. At present, more than 4,200 cable systems exist in the United States and 33 of them are municipally owned. They vary in population size from Copper Canyon, Colorado with 250 people to a municipal system in San Bruno, California with a population of 50,000. Such experiments with city ownership can aid in resolving the pertinent issues about third-generation cable based on the equal access principle.

Perhaps city officials are too petty and benighted to run cable systems effectively. But several variations of public control and planning are theoretically possible: governance by the city council itself, a city-sponsored public corporation, and a special regional authority. Building up case studies from different countries should help trigger ideas also.

In the same manner we have determined our schools ought to be run by the public domain, I call for more research and aggressive experiments with public ownership of cable. The neutrality model determines the growth of a home information utility by engineering and profitability criteria. My normative model orients the development of hardware and software according to a need-conception of distributive justice.

3. A third example involves democratized media, not necessarily new inventions per se but media organized in different structures and used for nontraditional purposes. Consistent with a normative theory of technology is the worldwide movement at present toward participatory media as an alternative to monologic, centralized oligopolies which characterize most mass media systems presently. As Robert

White concludes: "Research on the democratization of communication is presently increasing. . . . There are a large number of case studies of democratization now in progress and the theoretical focus on participatory communication is clearer" (1984, p. 32). Some of the cases internationally are: 1) The Shah of Iran, though controlling the mass media, was "brought down by an alternative 'mass' media based on audio cassettes, photocopies and local small-group meeting places." 2) Dissident peasant agrarian movements and national liberation movements have developed new models of political and economic organization. 3) In Latin America there have been a "flourishing multiplication of forms of popular communication—various types of revolutionary or alternative radio, networks of group communication and popular theatre, documentation centers and varieties of underground press." 4) The popular music movement in Sweden began to establish cooperatives and small independent commercial facilities for record production in the early 1970s (White, 1984, pp. 8–24).

TV Globo has a virtual monopoly in Brazil. It follows the political and economic interests of the State and is congruent with the expectations of the government. Videocassettes have provided an alternative communication system from below, allowing the users themselves to devise their own production and distribution strategies (Festa and Santoro, 1987, pp. 27–30). Those involved with video in Brazil testify to the usefulness of video as a tool for social change:

> Social movements need their own channels for expression and distribution of information which, in many European and North American countries, is guaranteed by the existing structure. Those guarantees do not exist in Latin America, where successive authoritarian regimes have silenced opposition and reduced the majority of the population to absolute poverty. In these situations which are in urgent need of transformation, groups interested in the communication aspect of the question produce programmes, information and even videos with grassroot groups, according to their needs and interests. (p. 28)

Video has been involved in all the important working-class events in Brazil since 1983. Labor unions have found video particularly helpful in sharing ideas and strategies from one local to another, and the Metalworkers' Union of Sao Bernardo has organized a training and documentation project called Workers' TV. Since political repression has closed the door to democratic opposition, the diffusion of video helps organize audiences outside government control. In Brazil today, according to Festa and Santoro,

> . . . there are about a hundred groups active in video, spread throughout the country, in both rural and urban areas. They are linked to unions, neighborhood and cultural associations, organizations that support the grassroots movements, the Church, or they are independent. The total volume of finished productions by these groups is estimated at 400. (p. 28)

Harry Boyte's major work, *The Backyard Revolution: Understanding the New Citizen Movement* (1981), provides a synopsis of actual grassroots organizing in North America. The main social movements on which he draws are populism in the 1880s and 1890s, trade union organizing in the 1930s, Saul Alinsky in the thirties and forties, the Civil Rights movement, the 1960s, and then every sign of backyard activism that he can find today. In staking out this history, Boyte is particularly concerned with the relationship between the protest movements of the sixties and current efforts at community building. Regarding this point, he concludes:

> Contemporary citizen organizing is more down to earth, more practical, above all more enduring and rooted in the social fabric. It seeks to build ongoing organizations through which people can wield power. It is accompanied by a sense of the richness, creativity and vitality in people's traditions, folkways and culture that sixties radicals were prone to scorn or dismiss. (p. 208)

The animating impulse in all these evidences of democratization is the threat posed by powerful bureaucracies and technologies. Emphasis in all these communication forms is placed on an empowering process which gives people strength to create a space for themselves and within these provinces to build up all the assets necessary to support their own self-realization. This philosophy of people-based development from below assumes that participatory technologies are not merely an end in themselves but also a fundamental precondition for any successful social transformation.

Conclusion

An ethical framework for technology can be summarized in the word conviviality. Its constituent elements are the proto-norm of cultural continuity, integrated with the simultaneous realization of justice, openness, harmony, stewardship, and discovery. Such an ethic enables technologies to serve healing and beneficent change. Entrenched media technologies may be largely impervious to this normative framework and operate instead by the technological imperative. However, as new media technologies are designed, fabricated, and distributed, they provide us an unusual opportunity to orient their direction and shape their structure consistent with conviviality.

References

Boyte, Harry. *The Backyard Revolution: Understanding the New Citizen Movement.* Philadelphia: Temple University Press. 1981.

Buchanan, R. A. *Technology and Social Progress.* Oxford: Pergamon Press, 1965. p. 163.

Christians, Clifford. "A Theory of Normative Technology." In E. H. Byrne and J. C. Pitt, eds., *Technological Transformation: Contextual and Conceptual Implications.* Dordrecht: Kluwer Academic Publishers, 1989, pp. 123–139.

Christians, Clifford, and Leon Hammond. "Social Justice and a Community Information Utility." *Communication*, 9, 2 (1986): 127–149.

Ellul, Jacques. *The Presence of the Kingdom*, New York: Seabury Press, 1967.

Festa, Regina, and Luiz Santoro. "Policies from Below—Alternative Video in Brazil," *Media Development*, Vol. 1, 1987, pp. 27–30.

Heidegger, Martin. *The Question Concerning Technology and Other Essays*, trans. William Lovitt. New York: Harper Torchbooks, 1977. p. 14 ff.

Illich, Ivan. *Tools for Conviviality.* New York: Harper & Row, 1973.

Jonas, Hans. *The Imperative of Responsibility.* Chicago: University of Chicago Press, 1984, p. 6.

Lear, Norman. "Does Television Have the Courage to Pioneer a New Commercial Ethics?" *Television Quarterly* 21, No. 1 (1985): 8.

Monsma, Stephen, ed. *Responsible Technology.* Grand Rapids, MI: Eerdmans, 1984.

Pacey, Arnold. *The Culture of Technology.* Cambridge: The MIT Press, 1983, pp. 1–3.

Pauly, John. "Ivan Illich and Mass Communication Studies," *Communication Research*, 10, 2 (April 1983): 259–280.

White, Robert. "Democratization of Communication: The Need for New Research Strategies," unpublished paper, Center for the Study of Communication and Culture, May 1984.

Sources for Further Reading

General Sources

Aarons, Victoria, and Willis A. Salomon, eds. *Rhetoric and Ethics: Historical and Theoretical Perspectives.* Lewiston, NY: Edwin Mellen Press, 1991.

Andersen, Kenneth. *Persuasion: Theory and Practice,* 2nd ed. Boston: Allyn and Bacon, 1978. Chapters 15 and 16.

Arnett, Ronald. "The Status of Communication Ethics Scholarship in Speech Communication Journals from 1915 to 1985." *Central States Speech Journal* 38 (Spring 1987): 44-61.

Bauman, Zygmunt. *Postmodern Ethics.* Oxford, UK: Blackwell, 1993.

Bayles, Michael D. *Professional Ethics.* Belmont, CA: Wadsworth, 1981.

Becker, Lawrence C., and Charlotte B. Becker, eds. *Encyclopedia of Ethics,* 2 vols. New York: Garland Publishing, 1992.

Benjamin, Martin. *Splitting the Difference: Compromise and Integrity in Ethics and Politics.* Lawrence: University Press of Kansas, 1990.

Bennett, W. Lance. "Communication and Social Responsibility." *Quarterly Journal of Speech* 71 (August 1985): 259-88.

Bierstedt, Robert. "The Ethics of Cognitive Communication." *Journal of Communication* 13 (September 1963): 199-203.

Bowie, Norman E., ed. *Making Ethical Decisions.* New York: McGraw-Hill, 1985.

Brembeck, Winston L., and William S. Howell. *Persuasion: A Means of Social Influence,* 2d ed. Englewood Cliffs, NJ: Prentice-Hall, 1976. Chapter 10.

Caputo, John D. *Against Ethics: Contributions to a Politics of Obligation with Constant Reference to Deconstruction.* Bloomington: Indiana University Press, 1993.

Chesebro, James. "A Construct for Assessing Ethics in Communication." *Central States Speech Journal* 20 (Summer 1969): 104-14.

Chisholm, Roderick M., and Thomas D. Feehan. "The Intent to Deceive." *Journal of Philosophy* LXXIV (March 1977): 143-59.

Communication, 12, no. 3 (1991). Entire issue on "Communication Ethics and Contemporary Theory."

Communication Quarterly 38 (Summer 1990). Special issue on communication ethics.

Cooper, Martha. *Analyzing Public Discourse,* Prospect Heights, IL: Waveland Press, 1989. Chapters 7, 8, and 9.

Crable, Richard E. *Argumentation as Communication: Reasoning with Receivers.* Columbus, OH: Chas. E. Merrill, 1976. Chapter 8.

Garver, J. N. "On the Rationality of Persuading." *Mind* 69, n.s., 274 (April 1960): 163-74.

Gert, Bernard. *Morality: A New Justification of the Moral Rules.* New York: Oxford University Press, 1988.

Greenberg, Karen Joy, ed. *Conversations on Communication Ethics.* Norwood, NJ: Ablex, 1991.

Hampshire, Stuart, ed. *Public and Private Morality*. Cambridge: Cambridge University Press, 1978.
Hashimoto, I. "Persuasion as Ethical Argument." *Rhetoric Review* 4 (September 1985): 46-53.
Hillbruner, Anthony. "The Moral Imperative of Criticism." *Southern Speech Communication Journal* 40 (Spring 1975): 228-47.
Jaksa, James A., and Michael S. Pritchard. *Communication Ethics: Methods of Analysis*, 2d ed. Belmont, CA: Wadsworth, 1994.
Jensen, J. Vernon. *Argumentation: Reasoning in Communication*. New York: Van Nostrand, 1981. Chapter 2.
———. "Teaching Ethics in Speech Communication." *Communication Education* 34 (October 1985): 324-30.
Johannesen, Richard L., "Ethics of Persuasion: Some Perspectives," delivered at the 1968 Fall Conference of the American Marketing Association, printed in *Marketing and the New Science of Planning*, Robert L. King, ed., Chicago: American Marketing Association, 1969, pp. 541–46.
———. "Issue Editor's Introduction: Some Ethical Questions in Human Communication," *Communication* 6, no. 2 (1981): 145–58.
———. "Perspectives on Ethics in Persuasion." In *Persuasion: Reception and Responsibility*, 7th ed. Charles U. Larson, ed. Belmont, CA: Wadsworth Publishing Co., 1995.
———. "Teaching Ethical Standards for Discourse." *Journal of Education* 162 (Spring 1980): 5–20.
Jonas, Hans. *The Imperative of Responsibility: In Search of an Ethics for the Technological Age*. Chicago: University of Chicago Press, 1984.
Jonsen, Albert R., and Stephen Toulmin. *The Abuse of Casuistry: A History of Moral Reasoning*. Berkeley: University of California Press, 1988.
Kohlberg, Lawrence. *The Psychology of Moral Development: The Nature and Validity of Moral Stages*. San Francisco: Harper & Row, 1984.
Lebacqz, Karen. *Professional Ethics: Power and Paradox*. Nashville: Abingdon Press, 1985.
Lower, Frank J. "Kohlberg's Moral Stages as a Critical Tool." *Southern Speech Communication Journal* 47 (Winter 1982): 178-91.
Lucas, J. R. *Responsibility*. New York: Oxford University Press, 1993.
McCroskey, James C. *An Introduction to Rhetorical Communication*, 5th ed. Englewood Cliffs, NJ: Prentice-Hall, 1986. Chapter 14.
Makau, Josina M. *Reasoning and Communication: Thinking Critically About Arguments*. Belmont, CA: Wadsworth, 1990. Chapter 6.
Makau, Josina M., and Ronald Arnett, eds. *Communication Ethics in an Age of Diversity*. Urbana: University of Illinois Press, 1996.
Minnick, Wayne C. *The Art of Persuasion*, 2d ed. Boston: Houghton Mifflin, 1968. Chapter 11.
———. "A New Look at the Ethics of Persuasion." *Southern Speech Communication Journal* 45 (Summer 1980): 352-62.
Murphy, Richard. "Preface to an Ethic of Rhetoric." In *The Rhetorical Idiom*, Donald Bryant, ed. Ithaca, NY: Cornell University Press, 1958, pp. 125-43.
Olbricht, Thomas H. *Informative Speaking*. Glenview, IL: Scott, Foresman, 1968. Chapter 8.
Oliver, Robert T. "Ethics and Efficiency in Persuasion." *Southern Speech Journal* 26 (Fall 1960): 10-15.

Oliver, Robert T. *The Psychology of Persuasive Speech*, 2d ed. Revised Impression. New York: McKay, 1968. Chapter 2.
Parker, Douglas H. "Rhetoric, Ethics, and Manipulation." *Philosophy and Rhetoric* 5 (Spring 1982): 69-87.
Perry, William G., Jr. *Forms of Intellectual and Ethical Development in the College Years*. New York: Holt, Rinehart and Winston, 1970.
Pojman, Louis P. *Ethics: Discovering Right and Wrong*, 2d ed. Belmont, CA: Wadsworth, 1995.
Pols, Edward. *Acts of Our Being: A Reflection on Agency and Responsibility*. Amherst: University of Massachusetts Press, 1982.
Rives, Stanley G. "Ethical Argumentation." In *Readings in Argumentation*, Jerry M. Andersen and Paul J. Dovre, eds. Boston: Allyn and Bacon, 1968, pp. 12-21.
Rubin, Rebecca B., and Jess Yoder. "Ethical Issues in the Evaluation of Communication Behavior." *Communication Education* 34 (January 1985): 13-18.
Sabini, John, and Maury Silver. *Moralities of Everyday Life*. New York: Oxford University Press, 1982.
Smith, Craig R. *Orientations to Speech Criticism*. Chicago: Science Research Associates, 1976. Chapter 4.
Sproule, J. Michael. *Argument: Language and Its Influence*. New York: McGraw-Hill, 1980, pp. 82-84, 272-304.
Taylor, Gabriele. *Pride, Shame, and Guilt: Emotions of Self-Assessment*. Oxford: Clarendon Press, 1985.
Thayer, Lee, ed. *Communication: Ethical and Moral Issues*. New York: Gordon and Breach, 1973.
Thompson, Wayne N. *The Process of Persuasion*. New York: Harper & Row, 1975. Chapter 12.
Toulmin, Stephen. "The Recovery of Practical Philosophy." *American Scholar* 57 (Summer 1988): 337-52.
Toulmin, Stephen, Richard Rieke, and Alan Janik. *An Introduction to Reasoning*, 2d ed. New York: Macmillan, 1984. Chapter 30.
Wellman, Carl. *Morals and Ethics*, 2d ed. Englewood Cliffs, NJ: Prentice-Hall, 1988.
Yoos, George E. "Licit and Illicit in Rhetorical Appeals." *Western Journal of Speech Communication* 42 (Fall 1978): 222-30.
———. "A Revision of the Concept of Ethical Appeal." *Philosophy and Rhetoric* 12 (Winter 1979): 41-58.
———. "Rational Appeal and the Ethics of Advocacy." In *Essays on Classical Rhetoric and Modern Discourse*, Robert Connors, Lisa Ede, and Andrea Lunsford, eds. Carbondale: Southern Illinois University Press, 1984, pp. 82-97.

Political Perspectives

Ackerman, Bruce A. *Social Justice in the Liberal State*. New Haven: Yale University Press, 1980, pp. 3-30, 177-80, 349-78.
Altman, Andrew. "Liberalism and Campus Hate Speech: A Philosophical Examination." *Ethics* 103 (January 1993): 302-17.
Arendt, Hannah. "Truth and Politics." In *Between Past and Future*, 2d ed., Hannah Arendt, ed. New York: Viking Press, 1968, pp. 227-64.

Arendt, Hannah. "Lying in Politics: Reflections on the Pentagon Papers." In *Crises of the Republic*, Hannah Arendt, ed. New York: Harcourt Brace Jovanovich, 1969, pp. 1-47.

Bloch, Maurice, ed. *Political Language and Oratory in Traditional Society*. New York: Academic Press, 1975. Chapters 1, 3, 6 and 9.

Bourke, Vernon. "Moral Problems Related to Censoring the Media of Mass Communication." In *Problems of Communication in a Pluralistic Society*. Milwaukee: Marquette University Press, 1956, pp. 113-37.

Bowie, Norman E., ed. *Ethical Issues in Government*. Philadelphia: Temple University Press, 1981.

Chase, Stuart. *Power of Words*. New York: Harcourt, Brace, 1953. Chapters 20 and 21.

Day, Dennis G. "The Ethics of Democratic Debate." *Central States Speech Journal* 17 (February 1966): 5-14.

Denton, Robert E., Jr., ed. *Ethical Dimensions of Political Communication*. New York: Praeger, 1991.

Denton, Robert E., Jr., and Gary C. Woodward. *Political Communication in America*. New York: Praeger, 1985, pp. 263-70, 327-56.

Eubanks, Ralph T., and Virgil Baker. "Toward an Axiology of Rhetoric." *Quarterly Journal of Speech* 48 (April 1962): 157-68.

Fleishman, Joel L., Lance Lieberman, and Mark H. Moore, eds. *Public Duties: Moral Obligations of Government Officials*. Cambridge: Harvard University Press, 1981.

Funk, Alfred A. "Logical and Emotional Proofs: A Counter-view." *Speech Teacher* 17 (September 1968): 210-17.

Gouran, Dennis. "Guidelines for the Analysis of Responsibility in Governmental Communication." In *Teaching about Doublespeak*, Daniel Dieterich, ed. Urbana, IL: National Council of Teachers of English, 1976, pp. 20-31.

Haiman, Franklyn S. "A Re-examination of the Ethics of Persuasion." *Central States Speech Journal* 3 (March 1952): 4-9.

———. "Democratic Ethics and the Hidden Persuaders." *Quarterly Journal of Speech* 44 (December 1958): 385-92.

Hook, Sidney. "The Ethics of Controversy." *The New Leader*, February 1, 1954, pp. 12-14.

———. "The Tactics of Controversy." *The New Leader*, March 1, 1954.

———. "The Ethics of Political Controversy." In *The Ethics of Controversy: Politics and Protest*, Donn W. Parson and Wil Linkugel, eds. Lawrence, KS: The House of Usher, 1968, pp. 50-71.

Huxley, Aldous. *Brave New World Revisited*. New York: Harper & Row, 1958. Chapter 6.

Jamieson, Kathleen Hall. *Dirty Politics: Deception, Distraction, and Democracy*. New York: Oxford University Press, 1992.

Johannesen, Richard L. "Haigspeak, Secretary of State Haig, and Communication Ethics." In *The Orwellian Moment*, Robert L. Savage, James Combs, and Dan Nimmo, eds. Fayetteville: University of Arkansas Press, 1989, pp. 109-18.

Johnstone, Christopher Lyle. "Reagan, Rhetoric, and the Public Philosophy: Ethics and Politics in the 1994 Campaign." *Southern Communication Journal* 60 (Winter 1995): 93-108.

Kruger, Arthur N. "The Ethics of Persuasion: A Re-examination." *Speech Teacher* 16 (November 1967): 295-305.

Kruger, Arthur N. "Debate and Speech Communication." *Southern Speech Communication Journal* 39 (Spring 1974): 233-40.
Ladd, Bruce. *Crisis in Credibility*. New York: New American Library, 1968.
Lake, Anthony. "Lying Around Washington." *Foreign Policy* (Spring 1971), pp. 91-113.
McGaffin, William, and Erwin Knoll. *Anything But the Truth: The Credibility Gap—How News Is Managed in Washington*. New York: Putnams, 1968.
McKeon, Richard. "Communication, Truth, and Society." *Ethics* 67 (January 1957): 89-99.
Mead, Margaret. "The Problem of Responsibility in Communications." In *The Communication of Ideas*, Lyman Bryson, ed. New York: Harper, 1948, pp. 17-26.
Nilsen, Thomas R. "Free Speech, Persuasion, and the Democratic Process." *Quarterly Journal of Speech* 44 (October 1958): 235-43.
———. "Ethics and Argument." In *Perspectives on Argument*, Gerald R. Miller and Thomas R. Nilsen, eds. Chicago: Scott, Foresman, 1966. Chapter 8.
———. "Ethics of Persuasion and the Marketplace of Ideas Concept." In *The Ethics of Controversy: Politics and Protest*, Donn W. Parson and Wil Linkugel, eds. Lawrence, KS: House of Usher, 1968, pp. 7-49.
———. *Ethics of Speech Communication*, 2d ed. Indianapolis: Bobbs-Merrill, 1974.
Nimmo, Dan. "Ethical Issues in Political Communication." *Communication* 6, no. 2 (1981): 193-212.
Novak, Michael. *Choosing Our King: Powerful Symbols in Presidential Politics*. New York: Macmillan, 1974. Chapters 29 and 33.
Redford, Emmette S. *Democracy in the Administrative State*. New York: Oxford University Press, 1969. Chapter 1.
Ryn, Claes G. *Democracy and the Ethical Life: A Philosophy of Politics and Community*, 2d ed. Washington, DC: Catholic University Press of America, 1990.
Schrier, William. "The Ethics of Persuasion." *Quarterly Journal of Speech* 16 (November 1930): 476-86.
Thompson, Dennis F. *Political Ethics and Public Office*. Cambridge: Harvard University Press, 1987.
Voegelin, Eric. "Necessary Moral Bases for Communicating in a Democracy." In *Problems of Communication in a Pluralistic Society*. Milwaukee: Marquette University Press, 1956, pp. 53-68.
Wallace, Karl R. "An Ethical Basis of Communication." *Speech Teacher* 4 (January 1955): 1-9.
Wilkie, Richard W. "The Marxian Rhetoric of Angelica Balabanoff." *Quarterly Journal of Speech* 60 (December 1974): 450-59.
Wise, David. *The Politics of Lying: Government Deception, Secrecy, and Power*. New York: Random House, 1973.

Human Nature Perspectives

Anderson, Raymond E. "Kierkegaard's Theory of Communication." *Speech Monographs* 30 (March 1963): 1-14.

Botan, Carl. "A Human Nature Approach to Image and Ethics in International Public Relations." *Journal of Public Relations Research* 5, no. 2 (1993): 71–81.

Brummett, Barry. "Some Implications of 'Process' and 'Intersubjectivity': Postmodern Rhetoric." *Philosophy and Rhetoric* 9 (Winter 1976): 21-51.

———. "A Defense of Ethical Relativism as Rhetorically Grounded." *Western Journal of Speech Communication* 45 (Fall 1981): 286-98.

Bugenthal, James F. T. "The Humanistic Ethic—The Individual in Psychotherapy as a Social Change Agent." In *Human Communication: The Process of Relating*, George A. Borden and John D. Stone, eds. Menlo Park, CA: Cummings Publishing, 1976, pp. 121-32.

Campbell, Karlyn Kohrs. "The Ontological Foundations of Rhetorical Theory." *Philosophy and Rhetoric* 3 (Spring 1970): 97-108.

———. "The Rhetorical Implications of the Axiology of Jean-Paul Sartre." *Western Speech* 35 (Summer 1971): 155-61.

Campbell, Paul N. *Rhetoric-Ritual*. Belmont, CA: Dickenson, 1972, pp. 6-7, 226-38.

Christians, Clifford G. "Can the Public Be Held Accountable?" *Journal of Mass Media Ethics* 3, no. 1 (1988): 50-58.

Degler, Carl N. *In Search of Human Nature*. New York: Oxford University Press, 1991.

Eubanks. Ralph T. "Nihilism and the Problem of a Worthy Rhetoric." *Southern Speech Journal* 33 (Spring 1968): 187-99.

———. "Reflections on the Moral Dimension of Communication." *Southern Speech Communication Journal* 45 (Spring 1980): 297-312.

Ferre, John P. "Grounding an Ethics of Journalism." *Journal of Mass Media Ethics* 3, no. 1 (1988): 18-29.

Flynn, Lawrence J., S.J. "The Aristotelian Basis for the Ethics of Speaking." *Speech Teacher* 6 (September 1957): 179-87.

Garrett, Thomas, S.J. *An Introduction to Some Ethical Problems of Modern American Advertising*. Rome: The Gregorian University Press, 1961, pp. 39-47.

Guignon, Charles. "Existentialist Ethics." In *New Directions in Ethics: The Challenge of Applied Ethics*. Joseph P. DeMarco and Richard M. Fox, eds. New York: Routledge & Kegan Paul, 1986, pp. 73–91.

Jaggar, Alison. *Feminist Politics and Human Nature*. Totowa, NJ: Rowman and Allanheld, 1983.

Johannesen, Richard L. "Richard M. Weaver on Standards for Ethical Rhetoric." *Central States Speech Journal* 29 (Summer 1978): 127-37.

Johnstone, Christopher Lyle. "Ethics, Wisdom, and the Mission of Contemporary Rhetoric." *Central States Speech Journal* 32 (Fall 1981): 177-88.

Johnstone, Henry W., Jr. "Toward an Ethics of Rhetoric." *Communication*, 6, no. 2 (1981): 305-14.

McGuire, Michael. "The Ethics of Rhetoric: The Morality of Knowledge." *Southern Speech Communication Journal* 45 (Winter 1980): 133-48.

Opitz, Edmund A. "Instinct and Ethics." In *Ethics and the Press*, John C. Merrill and Ralph D. Barney, eds. New York: Hastings House, 1975, pp. 17-24.

McShea, Robert J. *Morality and Human Nature: A New Route to Ethical Theory*. Philadelphia: Temple University Press, 1990.

Philipsen, Gary. "Navajo World View and Culture Patterns of Speech: A Case Study in Ethnorhetoric." *Speech Monographs* 39 (June 1972): 132-39.

Rappoport, Anatol. "Man, The Symbol User." In *Communication: Ethical and Moral Issues*, Lee Thayer, ed. New York: Gordon and Breach, 1973, pp. 21-48.

Rosenstock-Heussy, Eugene. *Speech and Reality*. Norwich, VT: Argo Books, 1970. Chapter 7.

Rowland, Robert C., and Deanna F. Womack. "Aristotle's View of Ethical Rhetoric." *Rhetoric Society Quarterly* XV (Winter-Spring, 1985): 13-32.

Rusk, Tom. *The Power of Ethical Persuasion*. New York: Penguin Books, 1993.

Scott, Robert L. "On Viewing Rhetoric as Epistemic." *Central States Speech Journal* 18 (February 1967): 9-17.

———. "On Viewing Rhetoric as Epistemic: Ten Years Later." *Central States Speech Journal* 27 (Winter 1976): 258-66.

Stevenson, Leslie. *Seven Theories of Human Nature*, 2d ed. New York: Oxford University Press, 1987.

Torrence, Donald L. "A Philosophy for Rhetoric from Bertrand Russell." *Quarterly Journal of Speech* 45 (April 1959): 153-65.

Walton, Clarence C. "Ethical Theory, Societal Expectations, and Marketing Practices." In *Speaking of Advertising*, John S. Wright and Daniel S. Warner, eds. New York: McGraw-Hill, 1963, pp. 359-73.

Wieman, Henry N., and Otis M. Walter. "Towards an Analysis of Ethics for Rhetoric." *Quarterly Journal of Speech* 43 (October 1957): 266-70.

Wilson, James Q. *The Moral Sense*. New York: Free Press, 1993.

Wright, Robert. *The Moral Animal: The New Science of Evolutionary Psychology*. New York: Pantheon, 1994.

Dialogical Perspectives

Anderson, Rob. "Phenomenological Dialogue, Humanistic Psychology and Pseudo-Walls: A Response and Extension." *Western Journal of Speech Communication* 46 (Fall 1982): 344-57.

Anderson, Rob, Kenneth N. Cissna, and Ronald C. Arnett, eds. *The Reach of Dialogue: Confirmation, Voice, and Community*. Cresskill, NJ: Hampton Press, 1994.

Arnett, Ronald C. "Toward a Phenomenological Dialogue." *Western Journal of Speech Communication* 45 (Summer 1981): 201-12.

———. "Rogers and Buber: Similarities, Yet Fundamental Differences." *Western Journal of Speech Communication* 46 (Fall 1982): 358-72.

———. *Communication and Community: Implications of Martin Buber's Dialogue*. Carbondale: Southern Illinois University Press, 1986.

———. "What is Dialogic Communication? Friedman's Contribution and Clarification." *Person-Centered Review* 4 (February 1989): 42–60.

Ayres, Joe. "Four Approaches to Interpersonal Communication: Review, Observation, Prognosis." *Western Journal of Speech Communication* 48 (Fall 1984): 408-40.

Beatty, Michael J. *Romantic Dialogue: Communication in Dating and Marriage*. Englewood, CO: Morton Publishing Co., 1986.

Berry, Donald L. *Mutuality: The Vision of Martin Buber*. Albany: State University of New York Press, 1983.

Sources for Further Reading

Brown, Charles T., and Paul W. Keller. *Monologue to Dialogue: An Exploration of Interpersonal Communication*, 2d ed. Englewood Cliffs, NJ: Prentice-Hall, 1979. Chapters 1, 11, and 12.

Buber, Martin. *I and Thou*, 2d ed., trans. Ronald Gregor Smith. New York: Scribners, 1958; trans. Walter Kaufmann. New York: Scribners, 1970.

———. Between Man and Man, trans. Ronald Gregor Smith. New York: Macmillan paperback edition, 1965, pp. 1-39, 83-103.

———. *The Knowledge of Man*, ed. with introduction by Maurice Friedman, trans. Maurice Friedman and Ronald Gregor Smith. New York: Harper & Row, 1965, pp. 72-88, 110-20, 166-84.

Byrne, Edmund F., and Edward A. Maziarz. *Human Being and Being Human*. New York: Appleton-Century-Crofts, 1969, pp. 262-94.

Cissna, Kenneth N., and Rob Anderson. "The 1957 Martin Buber-Carl Rogers Dialogue, As Dialogue." *Journal of Humanistic Psychology*, 33 (1993).

Clark, Allen. "Martin Buber, Dialogue and the Philosophy of Rhetoric." In *Philosophers on Rhetoric*, Donald G. Douglas, ed. Skokie, IL: National Textbook, 1973, pp. 225-42.

Darnell, Donald K., and Wayne Brockriede. *Persons Communicating*. Englewood Cliffs, NJ: Prentice-Hall, 1976. Chapters 1, 2, 11, and 12.

Downie, R. S., and Elizabeth Telfer. *Respect for Persons*. New York: Schocken Books, 1970. Chapters 1-3.

Evans, Richard L. *Carl Rogers: The Man and His Ideas*. New York: E. P. Dutton, 1975.

Friedman, Maurice S. *Martin Buber: The Life of Dialogue*. New York: Harper Torchbooks, 1960. Chapters 10-14, 22.

———. *The Confirmation of Otherness in Family, Community, and Society*. New York: Pilgrim Press, 1983.

———. "Carl Rogers and Martin Buber: Self-Actualization and Dialogue." *Person-Centered Review* 1 (November 1986): 409-35.

———. *Dialogue and the Human Image: Beyond Humanistic Psychology*. Newbury Park, CA: Sage, 1992.

Gusdorf, Georges. *Speaking (La Parole)*, trans. Paul T. Brockelman. Evanston: Northwestern University Press, 1965. Chapter 12.

Johannesen, Richard L. "The Emerging Concept of Communication as Dialogue." *Quarterly Journal of Speech* 57 (December 1971): 373-82.

Keller, Paul W. "Interpersonal Dissent and the Ethics of Dialogue." *Communication*, 6, no. 2 (1981): 287-304.

Kohanski, Alexander S. *An Analytical Interpretation of Martin Buber's I and Thou*. Woodbury, NY: Barron's Educational Series, 1975.

———. *Martin Buber's Philosophy of Interhuman Relation*. East Brunswick, NJ: Associated University Presses, 1982.

Levinas, Emmanuel. *Ethics and Infinity*, trans. Richard Cohen. Pittsburgh: Duquesne University Press, 1985.

Makay, John J., and Beverly A. Gaw. *Personal and Interpersonal Communication: Dialogue with the Self and with Others*. Columbus, OH: Chas. E. Merrill, 1975. Chapters 7-9.

Maslow, Abraham. *The Farther Reaches of Human Nature*. New York: Viking Press, 1971, pp. 17-18, 41-71, 260-68, 347.

Mayeroff, Milton. *On Caring*. New York: Harper & Row, 1971.

Sources for Further Reading   345

Moustakas, Clark E. "Honesty, Idiocy, and Manipulation." *Journal of Humanistic Psychology* 2 (Fall 1962): 1-15.
Nilsen, Thomas R. *Ethics of Speech Communication*, 2d ed. Indianapolis: Bobbs-Merrill, 1974. Chapter 5.
Poulakos, John. "The Components of Dialogue." *Western Speech* 38 (Summer 1974): 199-212.
Powell, John, S.J. *Why Am I Afraid to Tell You Who I Am?* Chicago: Argus Communications, 1969.
Rogers, Carl. *On Becoming a Person*. Boston: Houghton Mifflin, 1961.
———. *A Way of Being*. Boston: Houghton Mifflin, 1980. Chapters 1, 6 and 7.
Shostrom, Everett L. *Man, the Manipulator*. New York: Bantam Books, 1968.
Sillars, Alan L. "Expression and Control in Human Interaction: Perspective on Humanistic Psychology." *Western Speech* 38 (Fall 1974): 269-77.
Stewart, John. "Foundations of Dialogic Communication." *Quarterly Journal of Speech* 64 (April 1978): 183-201.
———. "Martin Buber's Central Insight: Implications for His Philosophy of Dialogue." In *Dialogue: An Interdisciplinary Approach*, Marcelo Dascal, ed. Amsterdam: John Benjamins B.V., 1985, pp. 321-35.
———, ed. *Bridges Not Walls: A Book About Interpersonal Communication*, 6th ed. New York: McGraw-Hill, 1995.
———. "Speech and Human Being: A Complement to Semiotics." *Quarterly Journal of Speech* 72 (February 1986): 55-73.
Stewart, John, and Carol Logan. *Together: Communicating Interpersonally*, 4th ed. New York: McGraw-Hill, 1993.
Strasser, Stephan. *The Idea of Dialogal Phenomenology*. Pittsburgh: Duquesne University Press, 1969.
Theunissen, Michael. *The Other: Studies in the Social Ontology of Husserl, Heidegger, Sartre, and Buber*, trans. Christopher Macann. Cambridge, MA: MIT Press, 1984, pp. 1-10, 258-344, 353-84.
Thomlison, T. Dean. *Toward Interpersonal Dialogue*. New York: Longman, 1982.

Situational Perspectives

Alinsky, Saul D. *Reveille for Radicals*, Rev. ed. New York: Vintage Books, 1969.
———. *Rules for Radicals*. New York: Random House, 1971.
Burgess, Parke G. "Crisis Rhetoric: Coercion vs. Force." *Quarterly Journal of Speech* 59 (February 1973): 61-73.
Cox, Harvey, ed. *The Situation Ethics Debate*. Philadelphia: Westminster Press, 1968.
Diggs, B. J. "Persuasion and Ethics." *Quarterly Journal of Speech* 50 (December 1964): 359-73.
Edelman, Samuel M. "The Rhetorical Situation and Situational Ethics in the Symbol of the 'Refugee' in the Israeli-Palestinian Arab Conflict." In *Conversations on Communication Ethics*, Karen Joy Greenberg, ed. Norwood, NJ: Ablex, 1991, pp. 167–77.
Fletcher, Joseph. *Situation Ethics: The New Morality*. Philadelphia: Westminster Press, 1966.
———. *Moral Responsibility: Situation Ethics at Work*. Philadelphia: Westminster Press, 1967.

Hoffman, Eleanor M. "Toward an Idealistic Rhetoric." In *Rhetoric 78: Proceedings of Theory of Rhetoric, An Interdisciplinary Conference*, Robert L Brown and Martin Steinmann, Jr., eds. Minneapolis: University of Minnesota Center for Advanced Studies in Language, Style, and Literary Theory, 1979, pp. 179-89.
Nelson, Harold A. "How Shall the Advocate Advocate? A Fictional Case Study in Role Conflict." *Ethics* 76 (July 1966): 239-52.
Rogge, Edward. "Evaluating the Ethics of a Speaker in a Democracy." *Quarterly Journal of Speech* 45 (December 1959): 419-25.
Simons, Herbert W. "Persuasion in Social Conflicts: A Critique of Prevailing Conceptions and a Framework for Future Research." *Speech Monographs* 29 (November 1972): 227-47, especially 238-40.
Stevenson, Charles L. *Ethics and Language.* New Haven: Yale University Press, 1944, pp. 163-64.

Religious, Utilitarian, and Legal Perspectives

Brembeck, Winston L., and William S. Howell. *Persuasion: A Means of Social Influence*, 2d ed. Englewood Cliffs, NJ: Prentice-Hall, 1976. Chapter 10.
Brockriede, Wayne. "Bentham's Philosophy of Rhetoric." *Speech Monographs* 23 (November 1956): 235-46.
Christians, Clifford G. "A Cultural View of Mass Communication: Some Explorations for Christians." *Christian Scholar's Review* 7 (1977): 3-22.
Christians, Clifford G., and Robert S. Fortner. "The Media Gospel." *Journal of Communication* 31 (Spring 1981): 190-99.
Griffin, Emory A. *The Mind Changers: The Art of Christian Persuasion.* Wheaton, IL: Tyndale House, 1976. Chapters 3 and 11.
Haselden, Kyle. *Morality and the Mass Media.* Nashville: Broadman Press, 1968.
Hearn, Thomas K., Jr., ed. *Studies in Utilitarianism.* New York: Appleton-Century-Crofts, 1971.
Hileman, Donald G., et al. "Ethics in Advertising." In *Advertising's Role in Society*, John S. Wright and John E. Mertes, eds. St. Paul, MN: West Publishing, 1974, pp. 259-64.
Howell, William S. *The Empathic Communicator.* 1981. Reissued Prospect Heights, IL: Waveland Press, 1986. Chapter 8.
———. "Foreward." In *Ethical Perspectives and Critical Issues in Intercultural Communication*, Nobleza Asuncion-Lande, ed. Falls Church, VA: Speech Communication Association, n.d., pp. viii-x.
Hunt, Arnold D., Marie T. Crotty, and Robert B. Crotty, eds. *Ethics of World Religions*, Rev. ed. San Diego: Greenhaven Press, 1991.
J. Vernon Jensen. "Ancient Eastern and Western Religions as Guides for Contemporary Communication Ethics." In *Proceedings of the Second National Communication Ethics Conference, June 11–14, 1992*, James A. Jaksa, ed. Annandale, VA: Speech Communication Association, 1993, pp. 58–67.
McLaughlin, Raymond W. *The Ethics of Persuasive Preaching.* Grand Rapids, MI: Baker Book House, 1979.
Nichols, J. Randall. "Notes Toward a Theological View of Responsibility in Communication." *Communication* 3, no. 1 (1978): 113-33.
Nielsen, Richard P. "Legal-Ethical Interactions in Journalism." In *Questioning Media Ethics*, Bernard Rubin, ed. New York: Praeger, 1978, pp. 180-206.

Phelan, John M. *Disenchantment: Meaning and Morality in the Media*. New York: Hastings House, 1980. Chapters 3 and 4.
Preston, Ivan. *The Great American Blow-up: Puffery in Advertising and Selling*. Madison: University of Wisconsin Press, 1975.
Spero, Robert. *The Duping of the American Voter: Dishonesty and Deception in Presidential Television Advertising*. New York: Lippincott and Crowell, 1980. Chapter 9.
Thayer, Lee. "Ethics, Morality, and the Media: Notes on American Culture." In *Ethics, Morality and the Media*, Lee Thayer, ed. New York: Hastings House, 1980, pp. 3-46.
Veenstra, Charles D., and Daryl Vander Kooi. "Ethical Foundations for 'Religious' Persuasion: A Biblical View." *Religious Communication Today* 1 (September 1979): 43-48.
Wellman, Carl. *Morals and Ethics*, 2d ed. Englewood Cliffs, NJ: Prentice-Hall, 1988.

Some Basic Issues

Black, Edwin. "Secrecy and Disclosure as Rhetorical Forms." *Quarterly Journal of Speech* 74 (May 1988): 133-50.
Bok, Sissela. *Lying: Moral Choice in Public and Private Life*. New York: Vintage paperback, 1979.
———. *Secrets: On the Ethics of Concealment and Revelation*. New York: Pantheon, 1983.
Bovee, Warren. "The End Can Justify the Means—But Rarely." *Journal of Mass Media Ethics* 6, no. 3 (1991): 135-45.
Combs, James E., and Dan Nimmo. *The New Propaganda: The Dictatorship of Palaver in Contemporary Politics*. New York: Longman, 1993.
Cunningham, Stanley B. "Sorting Out the Ethics of Propaganda." *Communication Studies* 43 (Winter 1992): 333-45.
Ekman, Paul. *Telling Lies: An Analysis of Lies, Liars, and Lie Catchers*. New York: Norton, 1985.
———. *Why Kids Lie: How Parents Can Encourage Truthfulness*. New York: Scribners, 1989.
Goldzwig, Steven R. "A Social Movement Perspective on Demagoguery: Achieving Symbolic Realignment." *Communication Studies* 40 (Fall 1989): 202-28.
Isenberg, Arnold M. "Deontology and the Ethics of Lying." *Philosophy and Phenomenological Research*, XXIV (June 1964): 463-80.
Johannesen, Richard L., "The Crisis in Public Confidence in Public Communication." In Thomas Tedford, ed., *Free Speech Yearbook*, Falls Church, VA: Speech Communication Association, 1971, pp. 43-49.
Johnson, Lawrence E. *Focusing on Truth*. London: Routledge, 1992.
Lester, Paul. *Photojournalism: An Ethical Approach*. Hillsdale, NJ: Erlbaum, 1991.
Ludwig, Arnold M. *The Importance of Lying*. Springfield, IL: Charles C. Thomas, 1965.
Marlin, R. R. A. "Propaganda and the Ethics of Persuasion." *International Journal of Moral and Social Studies* 4 (1989): 37-72.

Miller, Gerald R., and James B. Stiff. *Deceptive Communication*. Newbury Park, CA: Sage, 1993.
Nyberg, David. *The Varnished Truth: Truth Telling and Deceiving in Ordinary Life*. Chicago: University of Chicago Press, 1993.
Shibles, Warren H. *Lying: A Critical Analysis*. Whitewater, WI: Language Press, 1985.
Siegler, Frederick. "Lying." *American Philosophical Quarterly* III (April 1966): 128–36.
Smith III, Ted J., ed. *Propaganda: A Pluralistic Perspective*. New York: Praeger, 1989.
Wolk, Robert L., and Arthur Henley. *The Right to Lie: A Psychological Guide to the Uses of Deceit in Everyday Life*. New York: Wyden, 1970.

Interpersonal Communication and Small Group Discussion

Apel, Karl-Otto. *Towards a Transformation of Philosophy*, trans. Glyn Adey and David Frisby, eds. London: Routledge and Kegan Paul, 1980. Chapter 7.
Blum, Larry. "Deceiving, Hurting, and Using." In *Philosophy and Personal Relations*, Alan Monetiore, ed. London: Routledge and Kegan Paul, 1973, pp. 34-61.
Bormann, Ernest G. *Small Group Communication: Theory and Practice*, 3rd ed. New York: Harper and Row, 1990. Chapter 11.
———. "Ethical Standards in Interpersonal/Small Group Communication." *Communication* 6, no. 2 (1981): 267-86.
———. "Ethics and Small Group Communication." *Speech Association of Minnesota Journal* XII (1985): 225.
Brilhart, John K., and Gloria J. Galanes. *Effective Group Discussion*, 8th ed. Dubuque, IA: Brown Benchmark, 1995, pp. 15–16, 70, 74, 107, 121, 199–200, 222, 273, 314–15.
Condon, John C. *Interpersonal Communication*. New York: Macmillan, 1977. Chapter 8.
Carr, Jacquelyn B. *Communicating and Relating*, 3rd. ed. Dubuque, IA: Wm. C. Brown, 1991. Chapter 12.
Cialdini, R. B. "Interpersonal Influence: Being Ethical and Effective," In *Interpersonal Processes: The Claremont Symposium on Applied Social Psychology*, S. Oskamp and S. Spacapan, eds. Newbury Park, CA: Sage, 1987, pp. 148–65.
Cupach, William R., and Brian H. Spitzberg, eds. *The Dark Side of Interpersonal Communication*. Hillsdale, NJ: Erlbaum, 1994.
Deetz, Stanley. "Reclaiming the Subject Matter as a Guide to Mutual Understanding: Effectiveness and Ethics in Interpersonal Interaction." *Communication Quarterly* 38 (Summer 1990): 226–43.
———. "Keeping the Conversation Going: The Principle of Dialectic Ethics." *Communication*, no. 2 (1983): 263-88.
DeVito, Joseph A. *The Interpersonal Communication Book*, 6th ed. New York: HarperCollins, 1992. Chapter 5.
Fulkerson, Gerald. "The Ethics of Interpersonal Influence: A Critique of the Rhetorical Sensitivity Construct." *Journal of Communication and Religion* 13 (1990): 1–14.

Gudykunst, William B., Stella Ting-Toomey, Sandra Sudweeks, and Lea P. Stewart. *Building Bridges: Interpersonal Skills for a Changing World.* Boston: Houghton Mifflin, 1995, pp. 89–100, 290–93.

Harral, Harriet Briscoe. "An Interpersonal Ethic: Basis for Behavior." *Religious Communication Today* 2 (September 1979): 42-45.

Kale, David. "An Ethic for Interpersonal Communication." *Religious Communication Today* 2 (September 1979): 16-20.

Lumsden, Gay, and Donald Lumsden. *Communicating in Groups and Teams.* Belmont, CA: Wadsworth, 1993, pp. 34–40, 127–31, 199, 264–65, 314–17.

Miller, Gerald R., and Mark Steinberg. *Between People: A New Analysis of Interpersonal Communication,* Chicago: Science Research Associates, 1975, pp. 27-28, 134, 309-25, 344-47.

Rawlins, William K. "Individual Responsibility in Relational Communication." In *Communications in Transition,* Mary S. Mander, ed. New York: Praeger, 1983. Chapter 10.

———. "Openness as Problematic in Ongoing Friendships: Two Conversational Dilemmas." *Communication Monographs* 50 (March 1983): 1-13.

Ross, Raymond S., and Mark G. Ross. *Relating and Interacting.* Englewood Cliffs, NJ: Prentice-Hall, 1982, pp. 73-77, 138-41.

Wilson, Gerald L., and H. Lloyd Goodall, Jr. *Interviewing in Context.* New York: McGraw-Hill, 1991, pp. 19–20, 131, 166, 201–2, 235–36, 265, 291, 318.

Wilson, Gerald L., Alan M. Hantz, and Michael S. Hanna. *Interpersonal Growth Through Communication,* 4th ed. Dubuque, IA: Brown Benchmark, 1995, pp. 282–92.

Communication in Organizations

Andrews, Kenneth R., ed. *Ethics in Practice: Managing the Moral Corporation.* Boston: Harvard Business School Press, 1989.

Andrews, Patricia Hayes, and John E. Baird, Jr. *Communication for Business and the Professions,* 4th ed. Dubuque, IA: Wm. C. Brown, 1989. Chapter 4.

Arnett, Ronald C. "A Choice-Making Ethic for Organizational Communication: The Work of Ian I. Mitroff." *Journal of Business Ethics* 7 (1988): 151-61.

Blanchard, Kenneth, and Norman Vincent Peale. *The Power of Ethical Management.* New York: Morrow, 1988.

Baskin, Otis, and Craig Arnonoff. *Public Relations: The Profession and the Practice,* 3rd ed. Dubuque. IA: Wm. C. Brown, 1992. Chapter 5.

Bivins, Thomas H. "Applying Ethical Theory to Public Relations." *Journal of Business Ethics* 6 (1987): 195-200.

Bracey, Hyler, Jack Rosenblum, Aubrey Sanford, and Roy Trueblood. *Managing from the Heart.* New York: Delacorte, 1990.

Brown, Marvin T. *Working Ethics: Strategies for Decision Making and Organizational Responsibility.* San Francisco: Jossey-Bass, 1990.

Browning, Larry Davis. "The Ethics of Intervention: A Communication Consultant's Apology." *Journal of Applied Communication Research* 10 (Fall 1982): 101-16.

Burger, Chester. "Ethics and the Real World." *Public Relations Journal* 38, no. 12 (1982): 13, 16-17.

Burke, John P. *Bureaucratic Responsibility*. Baltimore: Johns Hopkins University Press, 1986.
Chonko, Lawrence B. *Ethical Decision Making in Marketing*. Thousand Oaks, CA: Sage, 1995.
Clampitt, Phillip G. *Communicating for Managerial Effectiveness*. Newbury Park, CA: Sage, 1991. Chapter 10.
Cooper, Terry L. *The Responsible Administrator*. Port Washington: Associated Faculty Press, 1982.
Conrad, Charles, ed. *The Ethical Nexus*. Norwood, NJ: Ablex, 1993.
Crable, Richard E., and Steven L. Vibbert. *Public Relations as Communication Management*. Edina, MN: Bellwether Press, 1986. Chapter 5.
DeGeorge, Richard T. *Business Ethics*, 3rd ed. New York: Macmillan, 1990. Especially Chapters 5, 8, 10, 11, 18.
Denhardt, Kathryn G. *The Ethics of Public Service: Resolving Moral Dilemmas in Public Organizations*. New York: Greenwood Press, 1988.
Drucker, Peter F. *The Changing World of the Executive*. New York: Truman Talley Books/Times Books, 1982, pp. 234-56.
Eisenberg, Eric M. "Ambiguity as Strategy in Organizational Communication." *Communication Monographs* 51 (September 1984): 227-42.
Elliston, Frederick A., et al. *Whistleblowing: Managing Dissent in the Workplace*. New York: Praeger, 1985.
Frankel, Mark S., ed. *Values and Ethics in Organizational and Human Development: An Annotated Bibliography*. Washington, DC: American Association for the Advancement of Science, 1987.
Freeman, Edward R., and Daniel R. Gilbert, Jr. *Corporate Strategy and the Search for Ethics*. Englewood Cliffs, NJ: Prentice-Hall, 1988.
Gallessich, J. *The Profession and Practice of Consultation*. San Francisco: Jossey-Bass, 1982, pp. 397-405.
Glaser, E. M. "Ethical Issues in Consultation Practice with Organizations." *Consultation* 1 (1981): 12-16.
Guy, Mary E. *Ethical Decision Making in Everyday Work Situations*. Westport, CT: Quorum Books, 1990.
Hackman, Michael Z., and Craig E. Johnson. *Leadership: A Communication Perspective*. Prospect Heights, IL: Waveland Press, 1991, pp. 204–11.
Hall, William D. *Making the Right Decision: Ethics for Managers*. New York: Wiley, 1993.
Harrison, Teresa M. "Toward an Ethical Framework for Communication Consulting." *Journal of Applied Communication Research* 10 (Fall 1982): 87-100.
Hodgson, Kent. *A Rock and a Hard Place: How to Make Ethical Business Decisions When the Choices are Tough*. New York: American Management Association, 1992. Chapters 6, 7, 10.
Hoffman, W. Michael, Jennifer Mills Moore, and David A. Fedo, eds. *Corporate Governance and Institutionalizing Ethics*. Lexington, MA: Lexington Books/D.C. Heath, 1984.
Howard, Carole, and Wilma Mathews. *On Deadline: Managing Media Relations*, 2d ed. Prospect Heights. IL: Waveland Press, 1994. Chapter 6.
Jackall, Robert. *Moral Mazes: The World of Corporate Managers*. New York: Oxford University Press, 1988.

Jaksa, James A., and Michael S. Pritchard, eds. *Responsible Communication: Ethical Issues in Business, Industry, and the Professions.* Cresskill, NJ: Hampton, 1995.

Jensen, J. Vernon. "Ethical Tension Points in Whistleblowing." *Journal of Business Ethics* 6 (May 1987): 321-28.

Jones, Donald G., ed. *Doing Ethics in Business: New Ventures in Management Development.* Cambridge, MA: Oelgeschlager, Gunn, and Hain, 1982.

Journal of Business Communication 27 (Summer 1990). Entire issue on ethics.

Journal of Mass Media Ethics 4, no. 1 (1989), entire issue on public relations ethics.

Kallendorf, C., and C. Kallendorf. "Aristotle and the Ethics of Business Communication." *Journal of Business and Technical Communication* 3 (1989): 55–69.

Kelley, Charles M. *The Destructive Achiever, Power and Ethics in the American Corporation.* Reading, MA: Addison-Wesley. 1988.

Kreps, Gary L. *Organizational Communication*, 2d ed. New York: Longman, 1989. Chapter 12.

Martinson, David L. "Enlightened Self-Interest Fails as an Ethical Baseline in Public Relations." *Journal of Mass Media Ethics* 9, no. 2 (1994): 100–108.

Mathews, M. Cash. *Strategic Intervention in Organizations: Resolving Ethical Dilemmas.* Newbury Park, CA: Sage, 1988.

McElreath, Mark P. *Managing Systematic and Ethical Public Relations.* Dubuque, IA: Brown Benchmark, 1993. Chapters 9 & 10.

Metzger, M., D. R. Dalton, and J. W. Hill. "The Organization of Ethics and the Ethics of Organizations: The Case for Expanded Organizational Ethics Audits." *Business Ethics Quarterly* 3, no. 1 (1993): 27–44.

Michalos, Alex C. *A Pragmatic Approach to Business Ethics.* Thousand Oaks, CA: Sage, 1995.

Nash, Laura L. *Good Intentions Aside: A Manager's Guide to Resolving Ethical Problems.* Boston: Harvard Business School Press, 1990.

Newsom, Doug, Allan Scott, and Judy Vanslyke Turk. *This is PR: The Realities of Public Relations*, 5th ed. Belmont, CA: Wadsworth, 1993. Chapter 8.

Nicotera, Anne Maydan, and Donald P. Cushman. "Organizational Ethics: A Within-Organization View." *Journal of Applied Communication Research* 20 (November 1992): 437–62.

Pastin, Mark. *The Hard Problems of Management: Gaining the Ethics Edge.* San Francisco: Jossey-Bass, 1986.

Pepper, Gerald L. *Communicating in Organizations: A Cultural Approach.* New York: McGraw-Hill, 1995. Chapter 7.

Piper, Thomas R., et al. *Can Ethics be Taught? Perspectives, Challenges, and Approaches at the Harvard Business School.* Boston: Harvard Business School Press, 1993.

Porter, James E. "The Role of Law, Policy, and Ethics in Corporate Composing: Toward a Practical Ethics for Professional Writing." In *Professional Communication: The Social Perspective*, Nancy Roundy Blyler and Charlotte Thralls, eds. Newbury Park, CA: Sage, 1993, pp. 128–43.

Pratt, Cornelius B. "Applying Classical Ethical Theories to Ethical Decision Making in Public Relations: Perrier's Prudent Recall." *Management Communication Quarterly* 8 (August 1994): 70–94.

Rentz, Kathryn C., and Mary Beth Debs. "Language and Corporate Values: Teaching Ethics in Business Writing Courses." *Journal of Business Communication* 24 (Summer 1987): 37-48.

Riley, Kathryn. "Telling More Than the Truth: Implicature, Speech Acts, and Ethics in Professional Communication." *Journal of Business Ethics* 12 (1993): 179–96.

Rion, Michael. *The Responsible Manager: Practical Strategies for Ethical Decision Making*. New York: Harper and Row, 1989.

Rubens, Philip M. "Reinventing the Wheel? Ethics for Technical Communicators." *Journal of Technical Writing and Communication* 11 (1981): 329-40.

Seibert, Donald V., and William Proctor. *The Ethical Executive*. New York: Simon and Schuster, 1984.

Shea, Gordon F. *Practical Ethics*. New York: American Management Association, 1988.

Shimberg, H. Lee. "Ethics and Rhetoric in Technical Communication." *Technical Communication* 25 (4th Quarter, 1978): 16-18.

———. "Technical Communicators and Moral Ethics." *Technical Communication* 27 (3rd Quarter, 1980): 10-12.

Shockley-Zalabak, Pamela. *Fundamentals of Organizational Communication*. New York: Longman, 1988. Chapter 10.

Sims, Ronald R. *Ethics and Organizational Decision Making: A Call for Renewal*. Westport, CT: Quorum Books, 1994.

Steinberg, Sheldon, and David T. Austern. *Government, Ethics, and Managers*. Westport, CT: Praeger, 1990.

Toffler, Barbara Ley. *Tough Choices: Managers Talk Ethics*. New York: Wiley, 1986.

Trevino, Linda Klebe. "Ethical Decision Making in Organizations: A Person-Situation Interactionist Model." *Academy of Management Review* 11 (1986): 601-17.

Victor, Bart, and John B. Cullen. "The Organizational Bases of Ethical Work Climates." *Administrative Science Quarterly* 33 (1988): 101-25.

Walton, Clarence. *The Moral Manager*. Cambridge, MA: Ballinger, 1988.

Walton, Richard, and Donald P. Warwick. "The Ethics of Organizational Development." *Journal of Applied Behavioral Change* 9 (1973): 681-98.

Watson, Charles E. *Managing With Integrity: Insights from Americas' CEOs*. New York: Praeger, 1991.

Walzer, Arthur E. "The Ethics of False Implicature in Technical and Professional Writing Courses." *Journal of Technical Writing and Communication*, 19 (1989): 149–60.

Wicclair, Mark R., and David K. Farkas. "Ethical Reasoning in Technical Communication." *Technical Communication*, 31 (2d Quarter, 1984): 15-17.

Wilcox, Dennis L., Philip H. Ault, and Warren K. Agee. *Public Relations: Strategies and Tactics*, 2d ed. New York: Harper & Row, 1989. Chapter 6.

Wilkins, A. L. *Developing Corporate Character: How to Successfully Change an Organization Without Destroying It*. San Francisco: Jossey-Bass, 1989.

Windt, Peter Y., et al. *Ethical Issues in the Professions*. Englewood Cliffs, NJ: Prentice Hall, 1989.

Wright, Donald K. "Philosophy of Ethics." *Public Relations Journal* 38, no. 12 (1982): 13, 16-17.

Formal Codes of Ethics

Blake, Eugene Carson. "Should the Code of Ethics in Public Life Be Absolute or Relative?" *Annals of the American Academy of Political and Social Science* 363, no. 1 (January 1966): 4-11.

Bruun, Lars. ed. *Professional Codes in Journalism*. Prague: International Organization of Journalists, 1979.

Bowie, Norman E. "Business Codes of Ethics: Window Dressing or a Legitimate Alternative to Government Regulation?" In *Ethical Theory and Business*, Tom L. Beauchamp and Norman E. Bowie, eds. Englewood Cliffs, NJ: Prentice-Hall, 1979, pp. 234-39.

Christians, Clifford G. "Self-Regulation: A Critical Role for Codes of Ethics." In *Media Freedom and Accountability*, Everette E. Dennis, Donald M. Gillmor, and Theodore L. Glasser, eds. Westport, CT: Greenwood Press, 1989, pp. 35-53.

Cooper, Thomas W., Clifford G. Christians, Frances Ford Plude, and Robert A. White, eds. *Communication Ethics and Global Change*. New York: Longman, 1989.

Crable, Richard E. "Ethical Codes, Accountability, and Argumentation." *Quarterly Journal of Speech* 64 (February 1978): 23-32.

DeGeorge, Richard. *Business Ethics*, 3rd ed. New York: Macmillan, 1992. Chapter 18.

Dennis, Everette E., and John C. Merrill. *Basic Issues in Mass Communication: A Debate*. New York: Macmillan, 1984. Chapter 12.

Frankel, Mark S. "Professional Codes: Why, How, and with What Impact?" *Journal of Business Ethics* 8 (1989): 109–15.

Gorlin, Rena A., ed. *Codes of Professional Responsibility*, 2d ed. Washington, DC: Bureau of National Affairs, 1990.

Johannesen, Richard L., "What Should We Teach About Formal Codes of Communication Ethics?" *Journal of Mass Media Ethics* 3, no. 1 (1988): 59–64.

Jones, J. Clement. *Mass Media Codes of Ethics and Councils: A Comparative International Study on Professional Standards*. New York: Unipub, 1980.

Journal of Mass Media Ethics 1 (Fall/Winter 1985–1986), entire issue.

Kintner, Earl W., and Robert W. Green. "Opportunities for Self-Enforcement Codes of Conduct." In *Ethics, Free Enterprise, and Public Policy*, Richard T. DeGeorge and Joseph A. Pichler, eds. New York: Oxford University Press, 1978, pp. 248-63.

Kultgen, John. "The Ideological Use of Professional Codes." *Business and Professional Ethics Journal* 1 (Spring 1982): 53-69.

———. "Evaluating Codes of Professional Ethics." In *Profits and Professions: Essays in Business and Professional Ethics*, Wade L. Robison, Michael S. Pritchard, and Joseph Ellin, eds. Clifton, NJ: Humana Press, 1983, pp. 225-64.

———. *Ethics and Professionalism*. Philadelphia: University of Pennsylvania Press, 1988. Chapter 10.

Levy, Charles S. "On the Development of a Code of Ethics." *Social Work* 19 (March 1974): 207-16.

Mathews, M. Cash. *Strategic Intervention in Organizations: Resolving Ethical Dilemmas*. Newbury Park. CA: Sage, 1988, pp. 51-82.

Meyer, Philip. *Ethical Journalism*. New York: Longman, 1987. Chapter 2 and Appendix III.
Molander, E. A. "A Paradigm for Design, Promolgation, and Enforcement of Ethical Codes." *Journal of Business Ethics* 6 (1987): 619–31.
Neelankavil, James P., and Albert B. Stridsber. *Advertising Self-Regulation: A Global Perspective*. New York: Hastings House, 1980.
Nordenstreng, Kaarle, with Lauri Hannikainen. *The Mass Media Declaration of UNESCO*. Norwood, NJ: Ablex, 1984. Chapters 9 and 10.
Olen, Jeffrey. *Ethics in Journalism*. Englewood Cliffs, NJ: Prentice-Hall, 1988. Chapter 2.
Rogers, Priscilla S., and John M. Swales. "We the People? An Analysis of the Dana Corporation Policies Document." *Journal of Business Communication* 27 (Summer 1990): 293–313.
Rivers, William L., Wilbur Schramm, and Clifford G. Christians. *Responsibility in Mass Communication*, 3rd ed. New York: Harper & Row, 1980, pp. 273-75, 289-350.
Rivers, William L., and Cleve Mathews. *Ethics for the Media*. Englewood Cliffs, NJ: Prentice-Hall, 1988, pp. 198-213, 235-96.
Schultze, Quentin J. "Professionalism in Advertising: The Origin of Ethical Codes." *Journal of Communication* 31 (Spring 1981): 64-71.
Stevens, Betsy. "Analysis of Corporate Ethical Code Studies: 'Where Do We Go from Here?'" *Journal of Business Ethics* 13 (January 1994): 63–70.
Swain, Bruce M. *Reporters' Ethics*. Ames: Iowa State University Press, 1978, pp. 85-96, 111-34.
Weller, S. "The Effectiveness of Corporate Codes of Ethics." *Journal of Business Ethics* 7 (1988): 389–95.

Feminist Contributions

Brabeck, Mary M., ed. *Who Cares? Theory, Research, and Educational Implications of the Ethic of Care*. New York: Praeger, 1989.
Card, Claudia, ed. *Feminist Ethics*. Lawrence: University Press of Kansas, 1991.
Evans, Judith. *Feminist Theory Today*. Thousand Oaks, CA: Sage, 1995.
Gilligan, Carol. *In a Different Voice: Psychological Theory and Women's Development*. Cambridge: Harvard University Press, 1978.
Gilligan, Carol, Jamie Victoria Ward, and Jill McLean Taylor. *Mapping the Moral Domain*. Cambridge: Harvard University Graduate School of Education, 1988.
Hanen, Marsha, and Kai Nielsen. *Science, Morality, and Feminist Theory*. Calgary, Alberta, Canada: University of Calgary Press, 1987.
Held, Virginia. *Feminist Morality: Transforming Culture, Society, and Politics*. Chicago: University of Chicago Press, 1993.
Jaggar, Alison M. "Feminist Ethics." In *Encyclopedia of Ethics*, 2 vols., Lawrence C. Becker and Charlotte B. Becker, eds. New York: Garland, 1992, pp. 361–70.
Kittay, Eva Feder, and Diana T. Meyers, eds. *Women and Moral Theory*. Totowa, NJ: Rowman and Littlefield, 1987.
Larrabee, Mary Jeanne, ed. *An Ethic of Care*. New York: Routledge, 1993.
Lassner, Phyllis. "Feminist Responses to Rogerian Argument." *Rhetoric Review*, 8 (Spring 1990): 220–31.

Lerner, Harriet Goldhor. *The Dance of Deception: Pretending and Truth-Telling in Women's Lives*. New York: HarperCollins, 1993.
Manning, Rita C. *Speaking from the Heart: A Feminist Perspective on Ethics*. Lanham, MD: Rowman and Littlefield, 1992.
Michell, Gillian. "Women and Lying: A Pragmatic and Semantic Analysis of 'Telling It Slant.'" *Women's Studies International Forum* 7, no. 1 (1984): 377–83.
Noddings, Nel. *Caring: A Feminine Approach to Ethics and Moral Education*. Berkeley: University of California Press, 1984.
———. *Women and Evil*. Berkeley: University of California Press, 1989.
Rich, Adrienne. *On Lies, Secrets, and Silence*. New York: Norton, 1979.
Schaef, Anne Wilson. *Women's Reality: An Emerging Female System in the White Male Society*. Minneapolis: Winston Press, 1981.
Sichel, Betty A. "Women's Moral Development in Search of Philosophical Assumptions." *Journal of Moral Education* 14 (1985): 149–61.
Starhawk. *Dreaming the Dark: Magic, Sex, and Politics*. New Edition. Boston: Beacon Press, 1988. Chapter 3.
Steiner, Linda. "Feminist Theorizing and Communication Ethics." *Communication* 12 (1991): 157–74.
Sullivan, Patricia A., and Steven R. Goldzwig. "A Relational Approach to Moral Decision-Making: The Majority Opinion in *Planned Parenthood v. Casey*." *Quarterly Journal of Speech* 8 (May 1995): 167–90.
Tronto, Joan C. *Moral Boundaries: A Political Argument for an Ethic of Care*. New York: Routledge, 1993.
Welch, Sharon D. *A Feminist Ethic of Risk*. Minneapolis: Fortress Press, 1990.
Wood, Julia T. *Who Cares? Women, Care, and Culture*. Carbondale: Southern Illinois University Press, 1994.

Intercultural and Multicultural Communication

Asuncion-Landé, Nobleza C., ed. *Ethical Perspectives and Critical Issues in Intercultural Communication*. Falls Church, VA: Speech Communication Association, n.d.
Bineham, Jeffrey L. "From Within the Looking-Glass: The Ontology of Consensus Theory—Bineham's Rejoinder." *Communication Studies* 40 (Fall 1989): 182–88.
Benhabib, Seyla. *Situating the Self: Gender, Community and Postmodernism in Contemporary Ethics*. New York: Routledge, 1992.
Byrd, Marquita L. *The Intracultural Communication Book*. New York: McGraw-Hill, 1993.
Condon, John C. "Values and Ethics in Communication Across Cultures: Some Notes on the American Experience." *Communication* 6, no. 2 (1981): 255–66.
Cooper, Thomas W. "Communion and Communication: Learning from the Shuswap." *Critical Studies in Mass Communication*, 11 (December 1994): 327–45.
Cortese, Anthony. *Ethnic Ethics: The Restructuring of Moral Theory*. Albany: State University of New York Press, 1990.
Gutmann, Amy. "The Challenge of Multiculturalism in Political Ethics." *Philosophy and Public Affairs*, 22 (Summer 1993): 171–206.
———, ed. *Multiculturalism: Examining the Politics of Recognition*. Princeton: Princeton University Press, 1994.

Johannesen, Richard L. "The Ethics of Plagiarism Reconsidered: The Oratory of Martin Luther King, Jr." *Southern Communication Journal* 60 (Spring 1995): 185-94.

———. "Diversity, Freedom, and Responsibility in Tension." In *Communication Ethics in an Age of Diversity*, Josina Makau and Ronald C. Arnett, eds. Champaign: University of Illinois Press, 1966.

Kale, David W. "Peace as an Ethic for Intercultural Communication." In *Intercultural Communication: A Reader*, 7th ed., Larry A. Samovar and Richard E. Porter, eds. Belmont, CA: Wadsworth, 1994, pp. 435–40.

Kirkwood, William G. "Truthfulness as a Standard for Speech in Ancient India." *Southern Communication Journal* LIV (Spring 1989): 213–34.

May, Larry, and Shari Collins Sharratt, eds. *Applied Ethics: A Multicultural Approach*. Englewood Cliffs, NJ: Prentice Hall, 1994.

Nardin, Terry, and David R. Mapel, eds. *Traditions of International Ethics*. NY: Cambridge University Press, 1992.

Optow, Susan. "Moral Exclusion and Injustice: An Introduction." *Journal of Social Issues* 46 (1990): 1–20.

Sitaram, K. S., and Roy T. Cogdell. *Foundations of Intercultural Communication*. Columbus, OH: Chas. E. Merrill, 1976. Chapter 10.

Case Studies of Theory and Practice

Andrews, James R. "Confrontation at Columbia: A Case Study in Coercive Rhetoric." *Quarterly Journal of Speech* 55 (February 1969): 9-16.

Archibald, Samuel J., ed. *The Pollution of Politics*. Washington, DC: Public Affairs Press, 1971.

Bailey, F. G. *Humbuggery and Manipulation: The Art of Leadership*. Ithaca, NY: Cornell University Press, 1988.

———. *The Prevalence of Deceit*. Ithaca, NY: Cornell University Press, 1991.

Baker, Lee W. *The Credibility Factor: Putting Ethics to Work in Public Relations*. Homewood, IL: Business One Irwin, 1993.

Baskerville, Barnet. "The Illusion of Proof." *Western Speech* 25 (Fall 1961): 236-42.

———. "Joe McCarthy: Brief-Case Demagogue." *Today's Speech* 2 (September 1954): 8-15. Reprinted in *The Rhetoric of the Speaker*, Haig Bosmajian, ed. Boston: D. C. Heath, 1967, pp. 62-75.

Bennett, James R. "Corporate sponsored Image Films." *Journal of Business Ethics* 2 (February 1983): 35-41.

———. "Doublethink and the Rhetoric of Crisis: President Reagan's October 22, 1983 Speech on Arms Reduction." In *Oldspeak/Newspeak: Rhetorical Transformations*, Charles W. Kneupper, ed. Arlington, TX: Rhetoric Society in America, 1985, pp. 54-66.

Benoit, William L. "Richard M. Nixon's Rhetorical Strategies in his Public Statements on Watergate." *Southern Speech Communication Journal* 47 (Winter 1982): 192-211.

Bergen, Maj. John D. "Military Language: Barometer or Booby Trap?" *Military Review* LV (June 1975): 19-25.

Bineham, Jeffery L. "Some Ethical Implications of Team Sports Metaphors in Politics." *Communication Reports* 4 (Winter 1991): 35–42.

Blythin, Evan. "Improbable Claiming." *Western Journal of Speech Communication* 41 (Fall 1977): 260-65.

Boeyink, David E. "Casuistry: A Case-Bound Method for Journalists." *Journal of Mass Media Ethics* 7 (1992): 107–20.
Bolinger, Dwight L. *Language, the Loaded Weapon: The Use and Abuse of Language Today*. New York: Longman, 1980.
Booth, Wayne. *The Company We Keep: The Ethics of Fiction*. Berkeley: University of California Press, 1989.
Bormann, Ernest G. "The Ethics of Ghostwritten Speeches." *Quarterly Journal of Speech* 47 (October 1961): 262-67. For a letter to the editor criticizing Bormann's view and for Bormann's reply, see *Quarterly Journal of Speech* 47 (December 1961): 416-21.
———."Huey Long: Analysis of a Demagogue." *Today's Speech* 2 (September 1954): 16-19.
Bosmajian, Haig. *The Language of Oppression*. Washington, DC: Public Affairs Press, 1974.
Bowyer, J. Barton. *Cheating: Deception in War and Magic, Games and Sports, Sex and Religion, Business and Con Games, Politics and Espionage, Art and Science*. New York: St. Martin's Press, 1982.
Burke, Kenneth. "The Rhetoric of Hitler's 'Battle.'" In *The Philosophy of Literary Form*, Rev. abridged ed., Kenneth Burke, ed. New York: Vintage Books, 1957, pp. 164-89.
Bursten, Ben. *The Manipulator*. New Haven, CT: Yale University Press, 1973.
Carson, Thomas L., Richard E. Wokutch, and Kent F. Murrmann. "Bluffing in Labor Negotiations: Legal and Ethical Issues." *Journal of Business Ethics* 1 (February 1982): 13-22.
"Cases and Commentaries: Larry Speakes—He Did Not Check With the Chief." *Journal of Mass Media Ethics* 3 (Fall 1988): 73-77.
Cirino, Robert. *Don't Blame the People: How the News Media Use Bias, Distortion, and Censorship to Manipulate Public Opinion*. New York: Vintage Books, 1972.
Crossen, Cynthia. *Tainted Truth: The Manipulation of Fact in America*. New York: Simon & Schuster, 1994.
Davison, W. Phillips. "Diplomatic Reporting: The Rules of the Game." *Journal of Communication* 25 (Autumn 1975): 138-46.
DeBakey, Lois, and Selma DeBakey. "Ethics and Etiquette in Biomedical Communication." *Perspectives on Biology and Medicine* 18 (Summer 1975): 520-40.
Delia, Jesse G. "Rhetoric in the Nazi Mind: Hitler's Theory of Persuasion." *Southern Speech Communication Journal* 37 (Winter 1971): 136-49.
Dieterich, Daniel, ed. *Teaching About Doublespeak*. Urbana, IL: National Council of Teachers of English, 1976.
Dittmer, Lowell, and Chen Ruoxi. *Ethics and Rhetoric of the Chinese Cultural Revolution*. Studies in Chinese Terminology No. 19. Berkeley: Center for Chinese Studies, Institute of East Asian Studies, University of California, 1981.
Dowling, Ralph E., and Gabrielle Marraro. "Grenada and the Great Communicator: A Study in Democratic Ethics." *Western Journal of Speech Communication* 50 (Fall 1986): 350-67.
Erickson, Keith V., and Wallace V. Schmidt. "Presidential Political Silence: Rhetoric and the Rose Garden Strategy." *Southern Speech Communication Journal* XLVII (Summer 1982): 402-21.
Ethics: Easier Said Than Done 1 (Spring/Summer 1988). Entire issue on ethics in government.

Felknor, Bruce. *Dirty Politics*. New York: Norton, 1966.
Flynt, Wayne. "The Ethics of Democratic Persuasion and the Birmingham Crisis." *Southern Speech Journal* 35 (Fall 1969): 40-53.
Freedman, Monroe H. *Lawyers' Ethics in an Adversary System*. New York: Bobbs-Merrill, 1975.
Freeman, Douglas N. "Contemporary Applications of Orwell's Concept of Newspeak in 1984: An Analysis of Intentionally Misleading Political Rhetoric." In *Oldspeak/Newspeak: Rhetorical Tranformations*, Charles W. Kneupper, ed. Arlington, TX: Rhetoric Society of America, 1985, pp. 38-53.
Freeman, Patricia Lynn. "An Ethical Evaluation of the Persuasive Strategies of Glenn W. Turner of Turner Enterprises." *Southern Speech Communication Journal* 38 (Summer 1973): 347-51.
Gaske, Paul C. "The Analysis of Demagogic Discourse: Huey Long's 'Every Man a King' Address." In *American Rhetoric from Roosevelt to Reagan*, Halford Ross Ryan, ed. Prospect Heights, IL: Waveland Press, 1983, pp. 49-67.
Glazer, Myron, and Penina Glazer. *The Whistle-Blowers: Exposing Corruption in Government and Industry*. New York: Basic Books, 1989.
Golden, James L. "Ethical Implications of the Watergate Hearings." In *Rhetorical Studies in Honor of James L. Golden*, Lawrence W. Hugenberg, ed. Dubuque, IA: Kendall-Hunt, 1986, pp. 97-121.
Goodin, Robert E. *Manipulatory Politics*. New Haven, CT: Yale University Press, 1980.
Green, Mark, and Gail MacColl. *Reagan's Reign of Error: The Instant Nostalgia Edition*. Expanded and Updated. New York: Pantheon, 1987.
Gross, Larry. "The Contested Closet: The Ethics and Politics of Outing." *Critical Studies in Mass Communication* 8 (September 1991): 352–88.
———. *Contested Closets: The Politics and Ethics of Outing*. Minneapolis: University of Minnesota Press, 1993.
Hahn, Dan F. "Corrupt Rhetoric: President Ford and the Mayaguez Affair." *Communication Quarterly* 28 (Spring 1980): 38-43.
Haiman, Franklyn S. "The Rhetoric of the Streets: Some Legal and Ethical Considerations." *Quarterly Journal of Speech* 53 (April 1967): 99-114.
———. "The Rhetoric of 1968: A Farewell to Rational Discourse." Reprinted in Richard L. Johannesen, *Ethics in Human Communication*, 2d ed. Prospect Heights. IL: Waveland Press, 1983, pp. 177-190.
Herman, Edward S. *Beyond Hypocrisy: Decoding the News in an Age of Propaganda, Including the Doublethink Dictionary*. Boston: South End Press, 1992.
Hilgartner, Stephen, Richard Bell, and Rory O'Connor. *Nukespeak: Nuclear Language, Visions, and Mindset*. Sierra Club Books, 1982.
Herzog, Arthur. *The B. S. Factor: The Theory and Technique of Faking It in America*. New York: Simon and Schuster, 1973.
Huxley, Aldous. *Brave New World Revisited*. New York: Harper & Row, 1958.
Iezzi, Frank. "Benito Mussolini, Crowd Psychologist." *Quarterly Journal of Speech* 45 (April 1959): 166-70.
James, Gene G. "Whistleblowing: Its Nature and Justification." In *Profits and Professions*, Wade L. Robison, Michael S. Pritchard, and Joseph Ellin, eds. Clifton, NJ: Humana Press, 1983, pp. 287-304.
Johnson, Barbara M. *Cheating: Maintaining Your Integrity in a Dishonest World*. Minneapolis: Augsburg Fortress, 1989.

Johnstone, Christopher Lyle. "Dewey, Ethics, and Rhetoric: Toward a Contemporary Conception of Practical Wisdom." *Philosophy and Rhetoric* 16, no. 3 (1983): 185-207.
Katz, Stephen B. "The Ethic of Expediency: Classical Rhetoric, Technology, and the Holocaust." *College English* 54 (March 1992): 255-75.
Kessler, Ronald. *The Life Insurance Game*. New York: Holt, Rinehart, and Winston, 1985.
Kominsky, Morris. *The Hoaxers: Plain Liars, Fancy Liars, and Damned Liars*. Boston: Brandon Press, 1970.
Kreps, Gary L., and Barbara C. Thornton. *Health Communication: Theory and Practice*, 2d ed. Prospect Heights, IL: Waveland Press, 1992. Chapter 8.
Lieberman, Jethro K. *Crisis at the Bar: Lawyers' Unethical Ethics and What to do About It*. New York: Norton, 1978.
Logue, Cal M., and Howard Dorgan. eds. *The Oratory of Southern Demagogues*. Baton Rouge: Louisiana State University Press, 1982.
Logue, Cal M., and John H. Patton. "From Ambiguity to Dogma: The Rhetorical Symbols of Lyndon B. Johnson on Vietnam." *Southern Speech Communication Journal* 47 (Spring 1982): 310-29.
Lomas, Charles W. *The Agitator in American Society*. Englewood Cliffs, NJ: Prentice-Hall, 1968.
———. "The Rhetoric of Demagoguery." *Western Speech* 25 (Summer 1961): 160-68.
Luthin, Reinhard. *American Demagogues*. Boston: Beacon Press, 1954. Reprinted Gloucester, MA: Peter Smith, 1959.
Lutz, William. *Doublespeak: From Revenue Enhancement to Terminal Living: How Government, Business, Advertisers, and Others Use Language to Deceive You*. New York: Harper & Row, 1990.
McKerrow, Raymie E. "The Ethical Implications of a Whatelian Rhetoric." *Rhetoric Society Quarterly* XVII (Summer 1987): 321-328.
Mackey-Kallis, Susan, and Dan Hahn. "Who's to Blame for America's Drug Problem?: The Search for Scapegoats in the 'War on Drugs'." *Communication Quarterly* 42 (Winter 1994): 1-20.
MacRae, Duncan, Jr. "Scientific Communication, Ethical Argument, and Public Policy." *American Political Science Review* 65 (March 1971): 38-50.
Markie, Peter J. *A Professor's Duties: Ethical Issues in College Teaching*. Savage, MD: Rowman & Littlefield, 1994.
Miller, Keith D. "Martin Luther King, Jr. Borrows a Revolution: Argument, Audience, and Implications of a Secondhand Universe." *College English* 48 (March 1986): 249-65.
Mitroff, Ian I., and Warren Bennis. *The Unreality Industry: The Deliberate Manufacturing of Falsehood and What It Is Doing to Our Lives*. Birch Lane Press, 1989.
Newman, Robert P. "Ethical Presuppositions of Argument." *The Gavel* 42 (May 1960): 51-54, 62-63.
Nilsen, Thomas R. "Confidentiality and Morality." *Western Journal of Speech Communication* 43 (Winter 1979): 38-47.
Oakes, Guy. *The Soul of the Salesman: The Moral Ethos of Personal Sales*. Atlantic Highlands, NJ: Humanities Press International, 1990.
Osborn, Michael. "The Abuses of Argument." *Southern Speech Communication Journal* XLIX (Fall 1983): 1-11.

Osborne, David. "Newt Gingrich: Shining Knight of the Post-Reagan Right." *Mother Jones*, November 1984, pp. 15-20, 53.

Parry, Robert. *Fooling America: How Washington Insiders Twist the Truth and Manufacture Conventional Wisdom*. New York: Marrow, 1992.

Pei, Mario. *Words in Sheep's Clothing*. New York: Hawthorn Books. 1969.

———. *Weasel Words: The Art of Saying What You Don't Mean*. New York: Harper & Row. 1978.

———. *Double-Speak in America*. New York: Hawthorn Books, 1973.

Quarterly Review of Doublespeak. Newsletter published by the Committee on Doublespeak of the National Council of Teachers of English.

Rank, Hugh. ed. *Language and Public Policy*. Urbana, IL: National Council of Teachers of English, 1974.

———. *The Pep Talk: How to Analyze Political Language*. Park Forest. IL: The Counter-Propaganda Press, 1984. Chapter 12.

Rasberry, Robert W. *The "Technique" of Political Lying*. Washington, DC: University Press of America, 1981.

Rasmussen, Karen. "Nixon and the Strategy of Avoidance." *Central States Speech Journal* 24 (Fall 1973): 193-202.

Rosen, R. D. *Psychobabble: Fast Talk and Quick Cure in the Era of Feeling*. New York: Atheneum, 1977.

Rosenfeld, Lawrence B. "The Confrontation Policies of S. I. Hayakawa: A Case Study in Coercive Semantics." *Today's Speech* 18 (Spring 1970): 18-22.

Rothwell, J. Dan. *Telling It Like It Isn't: Language Misuse and Malpractice/What We Can Do About It*. Englewood Cliffs. NJ: Prentice-Hall, 1982.

Schweitzer, Sydney C. *Winning with Deception and Bluff*. Englewood Cliffs, NJ: Prentice-Hall, 1979.

Siebers, Tobin. *The Ethics of Criticism*. Ithaca, NY: Cornell University Press, 1988.

Skopec, Eric Wm. "Ethical Implications of Thomas Reid's Philosophy of Rhetoric." *Pennsylvania Speech Communication Annual* XXXIX (1983): 5-14.

Smith, David H. "Stories, Values, and Health Care Decisions." In *The Ethical Nexus*, Charles Conrad, ed. Norwood, NJ: Ablex, 1993, pp. 123–48.

Smith III, Ted J. *Propaganda: Pluralistic Perspectives*. Westport, CT: Praeger, 1989.

Snider, Wm. D. *Helms and Hunt: The North Carolina Senate Race 1984*. Chapel Hill: University of North Carolina Press, 1985.

Sparke, William, Beatrice Taines, and Shirley Sidell. *Doublespeak: Language for Sale*. New York: Harper & Row, 1975.

Spero, Robert. *The Duping of the American Voter: Dishonesty and Deception in Presidential Television Advertising*. New York: Lippincott and Crowell, 1980.

St. Onge, Keith R. *The Melancholy Anatomy of Plagiarism*. Washington, DC: University Press of America, 1988.

Stewart, Charles J. "Voter Perception of Mud-Slinging in Political Communication." *Central States Speech Journal* 26 (Winter 1975): 279-86.

Swomley. John M. *Liberation Ethics*. New York: Macmillan, 1972.

Thompson, Ernest C. "A Case Study in Demagoguery: Henry Harmon Spalding." *Western Speech* 30 (Fall 1966): 225-32.

Vaux, Kenneth L. *Ethics and the Gulf War: Religion, Rhetoric, and Righteousness*. Boulder, CO: Westview Press, 1992.

Walzer, Michael. Political Action: The Problem of Dirty Hands. *Philosophy and Public Affairs* 2 (Winter 1973): 160-80.

Weaver, Richard M. *The Ethics of Rhetoric*. Chicago: Regnery, 1953.
Weigert, A. "The Immoral Rhetoric of Scientific Sociology." *American Sociologist* 5 (1970): 111-19.
White, James Boyd. "The Ethics of Argument: Plato's *Georgias* and the Modern Lawyer." *University of Chicago Law Review* 50 (1983): 849-95.
Wilshire, Bruce. *The Moral Collapse of the University*. Albany: State University of New York Press, 1990.

Ethics in Mass Communication

Adams, Julian. *Freedom and Ethics in the Press*. New York: R. Rosen Press, 1983.
Alley, Robert S. *Television: Ethics for Hire?* Nashville, TN: Abingdon, 1977.
Andren, Gunnar. *Media and Morals*. Stockholm: Akademilitterature, 1978.
———. "The Rhetoric of Advertising." *Journal of Communication* 30 (Autumn 1980): 74-80. For a criticism by John Heeren and a response by Andren, see *Ibid*., 31 (Autumn 1981): 218-21.
Baker, Richard M., and Gregg Phifer. *Salesmanship: Communication, Persuasion, and Perception*. Boston: Allyn and Bacon, 1966. Chapter 5.
Baker, Samm S. *The Permissible Lie: The Inside Truth About Advertising*. Boston: Beacon Press, 1971.
Beauchamp, Tom L. "Manipulative Advertising." *Business and Professional Ethics Journal* 3 (Spring/Summer 1984): 1-22.
Bedell, Clyde. *How to Write Advertising that Sells*, 2d ed. New York: McGraw-Hill, 1952, pp. 471-94.
Belsey, Andrew, and Ruth Chadwick, eds. *Ethical Issues in Journalism and the Media*. New York: Routledge, 1993.
Birkhead, Douglas. "An Ethics of Vision for Journalism." *Critical Studies in Mass Communication* 6 (September 1989): 283–94.
Black, Jay, Bob Steele, and Ralph Barney. *Doing Ethics in Journalism: A Handbook with Cases*. 2d ed. Boston: Allyn and Bacon, 1995.
Broadcast Financial Journal, September/October 1988. Entire issue.
Carson, Thomas L. "An Ethical Analysis of Deception in Advertising." *Journal of Business Ethics* 4 (1985): 93-104.
Casebier, Allan, and Janet Casebier, eds. *Social Responsibilities of the Mass Media*. Washington, DC: University Press of America, 1978.
Christians, Clifford G. "Fifty Years of Scholarship in Media Ethics." *Journal of Communication* 27 (Autumn 1977): 19-29.
———. "A Theory of Normative Technology." In *Technological Transformation: Contextual and Conceptual Implications*, E. F. Byrne and J. C. Pitt, eds. Dordrecht: Kluwer Academic Publishers, 1989, pp. 123-39.
Christians, Clifford G., Mark Fackler, and Kim B. Rotzoll. *Media Ethics: Cases and Moral Reasoning*, 4th ed. New York: Longman, 1995.
Christians, Clifford G., John P. Ferré, and P. Mark Fackler. *Good News: Social Ethics and the Press*. New York: Oxford University Press, 1993.
Christians, Clifford G., and Michael R. Real. "Jacques Ellul's Contributions to Critical Media Theory." *Journal of Communication* 29 (Winter 1979): 83-93.
Coakley, Mary Lewis. *Rated X: The Moral Case Against TV*. New Rochelle, NY: Arlington House, 1977.

Cooper, Thomas W. *Television and Ethics: A Bibliography*. Boston: G. K. Hall, 1988.
Cooper, Thomas W., Clifford G. Christians, Frances Ford Plude, and Robert A. White, eds. *Communication Ethics and Global Change*. New York: Longman, 1989.
Cullen, Maurice R., Jr. *Mass Media and the First Amendment*. Dubuque, IA: Wm. C. Brown Co., 1981. Chapters 2, 3, and 11.
Day, Louis A. *Ethics in Media Communications: Cases and Controversies*. Belmont, CA: Wadsworth, 1991.
Dennis, Everette E., and John C. Merrill. *Media Debates: Issues in Mass Communication*. New York: Longman, 1991. Chapters 12–16.
Durham, Taylor R. "Information, Persuasion, and Control in Moral Appraisal of Advertising." *Journal of Business Ethics* 3 (August 1978): 173-80.
Elliott, Deni T., ed. *Responsible Journalism*. Beverly Hills: Sage, 1986.
Ellul, Jacques. *Propaganda: The Formation of Men's Attitudes*. New York: Knopf, 1965.
———. "The Ethics of Propaganda." *Communication* 6, no. 2 (1981): 159-76.
Ferre, John P. "Contemporary Approaches to Journalistic Ethics." *Communication Quarterly* 28 (Spring 1980): 44-48.
Fink, Conrad C. *Media Ethics*, 2d ed. New York: Allyn & Bacon, 1995.
Geis, Michael L. *The Language of Television Advertising*. New York: Academic Press, 1982.
Goldstein, Toni. *The News at Any Cost: How Journalists Compromise Their Ethics to Shape the News*. New York: Simon and Schuster, 1985.
Goodwin, H. Eugene. *Groping for Ethics in Journalism*, 3rd ed. Ames: Iowa State University Press, 1994.
Gross, Larry, John Stuart Katz, and Jay Ruby, eds. *Image Ethics: The Moral Rights of Subjects in Photographs, Film, and Television*. New York: Oxford University Press, 1988.
Harrison, John M. "Media, Men, and Morality." *The Review of Politics* 36 (April 1974): 250-64.
Harvill, Jerry. "'Oikonomia': The Journalist as Steward." *Journal of Mass Media Ethics* 3, no. 1 (1988): 65-76.
Hausman, Carl. *Crisis of Conscience: Perspectives on Journalism Ethics*. New York: HarperCollins, 1992.
Henry, Jules. *Culture Against Man*. New York: Random House, 1963. Chapter 3.
Hiebert, Ray, Robert Jones, Ernest Latito, and John Lorenz, eds. *The Political Image Merchants: Strategies for the Seventies*, 2d ed. Washington, DC: Acropolis Books, 1975. Section VII.
Hulteng, John L. *Playing It Straight: A Practical Discussion of the Ethical Principles of the American Society of Newspaper Editors*. Chester, CT: Globe Pequot Press/ASNE, 1981.
———. *The Messenger's Motives: Ethical Problems of the News Media*, 2d ed. Englewood Cliffs, NJ: Prentice-Hall, 1985.
Johnson, J. Douglas. *Advertising Today*. Chicago: Science Research Associates, 1978, pp. 335-52.
Johnstone, Henry W., Jr. "Communication: Technology and Ethics." In *Communication, Philosophy, and the Technological Age*, Michael J. Hyde, ed. University: University of Alabama Press, 1982.
Journal of Mass Media Ethics (every issue).

Key, Wilson Bryan. *Subliminal Seduction: Ad Media's Manipulation of a Not So Innocent America*. Englewood Cliffs, NJ: Prentice-Hall, 1973.
———. *Media Sexploitation*. Englewood Cliffs, NJ: Prentice-Hall, 1976.
———. *The Clam-Plate Orgy and Other Subliminal Techniques for Manipulating Your Behavior*. Englewood Cliffs, NJ: Prentice-Hall, 1980.
Klaidman, Stephen, and Tom L. Beauchamp. *The Virtuous Journalist*. New York: Oxford University Press, 1987.
Lambeth, Edmund B. *Committed Journalism: An Ethic for the Profession*, 2d ed. Bloomington: Indiana University Press, 1992.
LeRoy, David J., and F. Leslie Smith. "Perceived Ethicality of Some TV News Production Techniques by a Sample of Florida Legislators." *Speech Monographs* 40 (November 1973): 326-29.
Lowenstein, Ralph L., and John C. Merrill. *Macromedia: Mission, Message, and Morality*. New York: Longman, 1990.
Martin, Thomas H., Richard D. Byrne. and Dan J. Wedemeyer. "Balance: An Aspect of the Right to Communicate." *Journal of Communication* 27 (Spring 1977): 158-62.
Martin, William C. "The God-Hucksters of Radio." *Atlantic* 225 (June 1970): 51-56.
Mason, Richard O., Florence M. Mason, and Mary J. Culnan. *Ethics of Information Management*. Thousand Oaks, CA: Sage, 1995.
McCulloch, Frank, ed. *Drawing the Line: How 31 Editors Solved Their Toughest Ethical Dilemmas*. Washington, DC: American Society of Newspaper Editor, 1984.
McKern, Joseph. "Media Ethics: A Bibliographical Essay." *Journalism History* 5 (Summer 1978): 50-53, 68.
Meiden, Anne van der. "Morality Beyond Society: Ethical Aspects of the New Media." *Communication* 9 (1986): 173-93.
Merrill, John C. *Existential Journalism*. New York: Hastings House, 1977, pp. 50-55, 129-38.
———. "The Press, the Government, and the Ethics Vacuum." *Communication* 6, no. 2 (1981): 177-92.
———. *The Dialectic in Journalism: Toward a Responsible Use of Press Freedom*. Baton Rouge: Louisiana State University Press, 1989.
Merrill, John C., and Ralph D. Barney, eds. *Ethics and the Press: Readings in Mass Media Morality*. New York: Hastings House, 1975.
Merrill, John C., John Lee, and Edward Jay Friedlander. *Modern Mass Media*. New York: Harper and Row, 1990. Chapter 14.
Merrill, John C., and S. Jack Odell. *Philosophy and Journalism*. New York: Longman, 1983. Chapters 4 and 6.
Meyer, Philip. *Editors, Publishers and Newspaper Ethics*. Washington, DC: American Society of Newspaper Editors, 1983.
———. *Ethical Journalism*. New York: Longman, 1987.
Michalos, Alex C. "Advertising: Its Logic, Ethics, and Economics." In *Informal Logic: The First International Symposium*, J. A. Blair and R. H. Johnson, eds. Pt. Reyes, CA: Edgepress, 1980, pp. 93-111.
Olen, Jeffrey. *Ethics in Journalism*. Englewood Cliffs, NJ: Prentice-Hall, 1988.
Packard, Vance. *The Hidden Persuaders*. New York: McKay, 1957. Chapter 23.
Paine, Lynda Sharp. "Children as Consumers: An Ethical Evaluation of Children's Television Advertising." *Business and Professional Ethics Journal* 3 (Spring/Summer 1984): 119-45.

Parker, Douglas. "Ethical Implications of Electronic Still Cameras and Digital Imaging in the Print Media." *Journal of Mass Media Ethics* 3 (Fall 1988): 47-59.
Patterson, Philip, and Lee Wilkins. *Media Ethics: Issues and Cases*, 2d ed. Dubuque, IA: Brown & Benchmark, 1994.
Phelan, John M. *Disenchantment: Meaning and Morality in the Media*. New York: Hastings House, 1980.
Pippert, Wesley G. *An Ethics of News: A Reporter's Search for Truth*. Washington, DC: Georgetown University Press, 1989.
Rivers, William L., Wilbur Schramm, and Clifford G. Christians. *Responsibility in Mass Communication*, 3rd ed. New York: Harper & Row, 1980.
Rivers, William L., and Cleve Mathews. *Ethics for the Media*. Englewood Cliffs, NJ: Prentice-Hall, 1988.
Rose, Ernest D. "Moral and Ethical Dilemmas Inherent in an Information Society." In *Telecommunications: Issues and Choices for Society*, Jerry L. Salvaggio, ed. New York: Longman, 1983, pp. 9-23.
Rotzoll, Kim B., James E. Haefner, and Charles H. Sandage. *Advertising in Contemporary Society: Perspectives Toward Understanding*. Cincinnati: South-Western Publishing Co., 1986. Chapter 9.
Rotzoll, Kim B., and Clifford G. Christians. "Advertising Agency Practitioners' Perceptions of Ethical Decisions." *Journalism Quarterly* LVII (Autumn 1980): 425-31.
Rubin, Bernard, ed. *Questioning Media Ethics*. New York: Praeger, 1978.
Samstag, Nicholas. *Persuasion for Profit*. Norman: University of Oklahoma Press, 1957, pp. 102-3, 187-95.
———. *How Business is Bamboozled by the Ad Boys*. New York: Heineman, 1966.
Sandage, C. H., and Vernon Fryburger. *Advertising Theory and Practice*, 8th ed. Homewood, IL: Irwin, 1971. Chapter 5.
Sandman, Peter M., David M. Rubin, and David B. Sachsman. *Media: An Introductory Analysis of American Mass Communications*, 3rd ed. Englewood Cliffs, NJ: Prentice-Hall, 1982. Chapter 2.
Santilli, Paul C. "The Informative and Persuasive Functions of Advertising: A Moral Appraisal." *Journal of Business Ethics* 2 (February 1983): 27-33.
Schmuhl, Robert, ed. *The Responsibilities of Journalism*. Notre Dame, IN: University of Notre Dame Press, 1984.
Schrank, Jeffrey. *Deception Detection*. Boston: Beacon Press, 1975.
Schudson, Michael. *Advertising. The Uneasy Persuasion: Its Dubious Impact on American Society*. New York: Basic Books, 1984.
Schwartz, Tony. *The Responsive Chord*. Garden City, NY: Anchor Books, 1972, pp. 18-22, 31, 31, 97.
———. "Ethics in Political Media Communication." *Communication* 6, no. 2 (1981): 213-24.
Smith, Samuel V. "Advertising in Perspective." In *Ethics and Standards in American Business*, Joseph W. Towle, ed. New York: Houghton Mifflin, 1964, pp. 166-77.
Swain, Bruce M. *Reporters' Ethics*. Ames: Iowa State University Press, 1978.
Taplin, Walter. *Advertising: A New Approach*, 1st American ed. Boston: Little, Brown, 1963. Chapters 4 and 6.
Thayer, Lee, assisted by Richard L. Johannesen and Hanno Hardt, eds. *Ethics, Morality and the Media*. New York: Hastings House, 1980.

Traber, Michael, ed. *The Myth of the Information Revolution: Social and Ethical Implications of Communication Technology*. Beverly Hills: Sage, 1986.
Ward, Hiley H. *Professional Newswriting*. New York: Harcourt, Brace, Jovanovich, 1985. Chapter 21.
White, Ralph K. "Propaganda: Morally Questionable and Morally Unquestionable Techniques." *Annals of the American Academy of Political and Social Science* 198 (1971): 26-35.
Wright, John S., and John E. Mertes, eds. *Advertising's Role in Society*. St. Paul, MN: West Publishing Co., 1974. Part VI.
Wright, John S., and Daniel S. Warner, eds. *Speaking of Advertising*. New York: McGraw-Hill, 1963. Chapters 37, 40, 42, 43, and 48.
Wrighter, Carl P. *I Can Sell You Anything*. New York: Ballantine Books, 1972.
Wurlinger, Gregory T. "The Moral Universe of Libertarian Press Theory." *Critical Studies in Mass Communication* 8 (June 1991): 152-67.

Index

Abdicated responsibility, 166
Abzug, Bella, 136
Acceptance of others, as an aspect of caring, 229
Accessibility, in organizational communication, 182
Accountability, in Ethical Values and Principles in Public Service, 212
Action, influencing character, 11, 300, 303
Actual and ideal, tension between, 2–3
Adler, Mortimer J., 297, 299
Advertisers
  attitudes of, 76
  responsibilities of, 102
Advertising
  See also Commercial advertising; Political advertising
  Advertising Principles of American Business (American Advertising Federation), 204
  American Association of Advertising Agencies code of ethics, 203–4
  Better Business Bureau Code of Advertising, 204–5
  Christian ethical guidelines for, 102–3
  as commercial poetry, 130
  cultural factors in, 112
  ethical obligations of, 47
  influencing patterns of evaluation as well as choice, 119–20
  intentional ambiguity in, 125
  legal and ethical not synonymous, 110, 112
  legally innocent prevarication in, 112
  and politics, 111–13
  poor taste to be distinguished from immorality, 137
  practices in poor taste, 138
  puffery, 112
  religious perspectives on, 102–3
  suggestive, 47
  as symbols of human aspiration, 130
  truth defined for, 112
  undermining human rational capacity, 47
Advertising Principles of American Business, 204
Advertising tactics, judging, 47–48
Advertising techniques, defending on basis of symbolism, 49–50
Agnew, Spiro T., 135
Albert, Ethel, 40
Alderman, Harold, 297
Alinsky, Saul, 90, 91, 92, 334
Allen, Jodie, 268, 274, 279
Alter, Jonathan, 296, 308, 314

Altheid, David, 192
Altman, Andrew, 255
Ambiguity. *See* Intentional ambiguity and vagueness
American Advertising Federation, Advertising Principles of American Business, 204
American Association of Advertising Agencies
 code of ethics, 203–4
 Code of Ethics for Political Campaign Advertising, 213
Andersen, Kenneth, 148
Anecdotes
 ethically questionable use of, 275
 misuse of, by Reagan, 272–73
 as pseudoproof, 275
Apel, Karl Otto, 163
Appreciative understanding, human need for, 48
Appropriateness
 essential to ethical communication, 53
 judging, 67
Ardener, Shirley, 230
Argumentation, arguers as lovers, 74–75
Aristotle, 11, 47, 292, 297, 304
 Principle of the Golden Mean, 5
 view of human nature, 46
Arnett, Ronald, 159
Aronoff, Craig E., 210
Attentiveness, as an ethical element of care, 228
Audience
 as active participants in communication, 146
 appropriate feedback required from, 147–48
 considering ethical criteria of, 3
 dialogical relationship with, 75
 ethical responsibilities of, 146–48
 ethics of adaptation to, 4–5
 for public relations, 187
 reasoned skepticism required of, 146–47
 rhetorical lover's attitudes to, 75
 rhetorical rapist's attitudes to, 75
 rhetorical seducer's attitudes to, 75
 sharing responsibility with communicators, 146–48
 speakers' attitudes to, 74
 unilateral relationships with, 75
Audience adaptation
 and Principle of the Golden Mean, 5
 seeking ethical balance point, 4–5
Authentic interpretation, as alternative for objectivity, 142
Authenticity, characteristic of dialogue, 67

Bach, George, 161
Bailey, F. G., 38, 305, 306
Baker, Howard, 270
Barber, James David, 273, 275, 289, 307, 310
Barnes, Richard, 159, 160
Barnlund, Dean, 157, 243
Barone, Michael, 268, 274, 279
Barrett, Harold, 161
Barron, Frank, 270
Baskerville, Barnet, 275
Baskin, Otis W., 210
Batchelder, Robert, 184
Bate, Barbara, 221
Bates, Don, 188
Beauchamp, Tom L., 12, 17, 302, 313
Beck, Joan, 296
Becker, Lawrence C., 297
Behavior, role of ethical character in, 299–301
Bell, Linda, 226
Benhabib, Seyla, 54, 251
Bennett, Milton, 244
Bennett, W. Lance, 142, 291
Bentham, Jeremy, 11, 107, 297
Berlo, David, 4
Better Business Bureau Code of Advertising, 204–5
Biden, Joseph, 308, 309

Bitzer, Lloyd, 310
Black sham, distinguished from white sham, 163
Blum, Lawrence, 249
Boeynik, David, 263
Bok, Sissela, 14, 122, 123, 124, 143, 231
Booth, Wayne, 10, 75, 76, 267
Bormann, Ernest, 25, 166, 166
Bosmajian, Haig, 253
Bovée, Warren, 120
Bowyer, J. Barton, 123
Boyte, Harry, 334
Bradley, Bert, 87
Brembeck, Winston, 108, 111, 120, 128, 137
Brockriede, Wayne, 74, 75, 77, 75, 77, 107, 286
Brown, Charles, 78, 79
Brown, Peter, 201
Brown, William, 79
Brummett, Barry, 56
Buber, Martin, 64, 66, 69, 71, 73, 164, 224, 302
Buddhism, religious perspectives offered by, 106
Burger, Warren, 110
Burke, John P., 287
Burke, Kenneth, 3, 49, 181, 320
Buursma, Bruce, 104, 105
Byrd, Marquita, 250, 256

Campbell, Karlyn, 54
Cannon, Lou, 274
Care
　See also Ethic of care
　devaluation of, 230
　ethical elements of, 228–29
　liberating, 230
　as an ongoing process, 228
Care-givers, valued qualities of, 229
Carey, James, 140
Caring
　care-giving, 228
　care-receiving, 228
　caring about, 228
　defined, 165
　done disproportionally, 227
　in Ethical Values and Principles in Public Service, 211
　phases of, 228
Carpenter, J. R., 130
Carter, Jimmy, 306
Categorical Imperative. *See* Kant's Categorical Imperative
Chapman, Stephen, 312
Character
　actions shaping, 12, 300, 303
　assessing ethical character, 13
　and ethics, 11–13
　guiding behavior, 11–12
　influence of ethical character, 11
Character-depiction function of formal codes of ethics, 202–3, 302–4
Character ethics, 11
　See also Ethical character
　importance of, 297
　in organizations, 177–78
　as viable approach to ethics in organizations, 314
Charen, Monica, 74
Cheney, George, 181, 182, 183
Christian ethic for persuasion, 99-100
Christian evangelism, 103–6
Christian morality, 101–2
Christians, Clifford, 148, 236, 320, 321
Christian situation ethics, 89–90
　See also Situation ethics
　considered defective, 102
Church, G. J., 274
Citizenship, in Ethical Values and Principles in Public Service, 211
Civility, imperative of, 57–58
Civilizing values, 57
Clinton, Bill, 6, 296
Cochran, 300, 302, 304
Code of Advertising of the Better Business Bureau, 204–5
Code of Ethics for Political Campaign Advertising of the Ameri-

can Association of Advertising Agencies, 213
Code of ethics for televised political campaign advertisements, proposed, 214–18
Code of Ethics of Sigma Delta Phi, 140
Code of ethics of the International Association of Business Communicators, 205–6
Code of Professional Standards for the Practice of Public Relations, 206–10
Codes of ethics. *See* Formal codes of ethics
Coercion, 161
Coffey, 309
Cogdell, Roy, 245
Commercial advertising
  See also Advertising; Political advertising
  as a poetic game, 130
  ethical criteria appropriate for attention-getting advertising, 130–31
  ethicality to be assessed by effect on receivers, 131
  to prove a claim, 129–31
  truth considered irrelevant as standard for, 130–31
  truth standard in, 129–31
Committee on Decent Unbiased Campaign Tactics (CONDUCT) Code of Fair Campaign Practice, 213–14
Common Cause standards for assessing ethics of political candidates' campaigns, 212–13
Communication
  See also Human communication
  democratization of, 332–34
  and ethical character, 301–2
  existentialist ethic for, 54–55
  feminist view of, 232
  needing supervision from general public, 148
Communication behavior
  attempting to enforce ethical standards on, 113–14
  fostering values of democratic system, 24–25
  habit of justice, 24, 183
  habit of preferring public to private motivations, 24, 183
  habit of respect for dissent, 24–25, 183
  habit of search, 24, 183
Communication competence, and ethical responsibility, 165–66
Communication consultants, ethical guidelines for, 187
Communication consulting and training, ethics for, 186–87
Communication ethics
  See also Communication; Ethics
  absolute or relative standards for, 117–18
  a contextual interpersonal ethic, 159
  as a function of context, 109
  Condon's interpersonal ethic, 158–59
  criteria for, from social utility perspective, 109
  degree of rationality approach to judging, 25–27, 46
  democratic liberal tradition not typical, 40
  dialogical perspectives for evaluating, 64–66
  ethical operation of third-generation cable systems, 330–32
  an ethic for everyday conversation, 160–61
  an ethic for interpersonal trust, 159–60
  ethics shared by world religions, 107
  extreme situational perspective criticized, 87–88
  to guide relations between communicators, 234–35
  human nature framework for assessing in Sartre's work, 54
  for intercultural communication, 243–47

judging ends and means separately, 120
justice and solidarity as fundamental principles, 54
keeping the conversation going, 163–65
and lying. *See* Lying
male and female moral voices in, 223
maximum or minimum standards for, 118–19
in other political systems, 39–40
significant choice as political perspective for judging, 27–30
social utility approach to, 108–9, 244
in Soviet communist perspective, 39
standards varying between fields of discourse, 129
study of, 16–17
suggestions for making judgments, 17–18
truth standard in commercial advertising, 129–31
Communications technology
ethical operation of third-generation cable systems, 330–32
media biased toward space and time in particular ways, 323
Communication techniques
consideration of, required by Christian ethic, 100
fostering significant choice, 27–30
judged by degree of rationality, 25–27
Communication trainers, guidelines for, 186–87
Communicative competence, 52–54
and ideal speech situation, 53
Communicators
adapting to audiences, 4–5
attitudes of, 73–75
attitudes revealed verbally and nonverbally, 79
choosing techniques, contents, and purposes, 16
considering ethical criteria of audience, 3
ethical relationship with audience, 14
ethical responsibilities of, 9, 266–67
ethical standards for, 24–25
functioning as catalysts or facilitators, 55
goals of, 120
image improved by ghostwriting, 138–39
monological attitudes shown by, 74
motives of, 2
neutral, evil, and noble speakers, 74
obligated to follow better of two good criteria, 118–19
pedant, advertiser, and entertainer, 76
promoting conflict, unrest, and tension, 93–94
questions for, 24–25
requiring appropriate feedback from receivers, 147–48
rhetorical rapists, seducers, and lovers, 75
rhetorical stance of, 75–76
sharing responsibility for outcomes of transactions, 165–66
sharing responsibility with receivers, 146–48
and sincerity and intent, 10–11
using unethical techniques with audience approval, 88
viewing appeals differently from receivers, 127–28
viewing truth and values as relative, 90
warned against intentional ambiguity and vagueness, 276
Community building, relationship with protest movements, 334
Compassion, and persuasion, 52
Competence, as an ethical element of care, 228
Computer communication, responsibility for ethicality of, 197–98

Condit, Celeste Michelle, 292, 294
Condon, John, 128, 158, 243
Condon's interpersonal ethic, 158–59
Confucianism, religious perspectives offered by, 106
Congruence, 65, 66
Connolly, Frank, 197
Conversation
    See also Human communication
    blocking or distorting, 164–65
    ethic for, 160–61
    ethic for everyday conversation, 231
    importance of mutual understanding in, 164
    keeping the conversation going, 163–65
    manner of presentation in, 161
    maxims to guide, 160–61
    practices blocking or distorting, 164–65
    quality and quantity of information in, 160
    relevancy of information in, 160–61
Convivial technology, 328–29
Convivial tools, 328–29
Cooper, Thomas, 106, 243
Cortese, Anthony, 2
Crable, Richard E., 189, 201, 200, 208
Critical condemnation, 161
Critical thinking, culture bound, 128
Cultural conceptions of rationality, 128
Cultural continuity
    differentiation and integration at work in, 326
    seen in historical terms, 326
    and technological activities, 325–27
    technology specific operating principles, 327–28
Cultural conceptions of rationality, 128

Cultural factors, in advertising, 112
Cultural imperialism, imposed by satellite technology, 329–30
Cultural norms, functioning as universals, 128
Cultures
    approved norms in, 128–29
    critical thinking methods culture bound, 128
    different meanings of sincerity in, 11, 112
    differing concerns in, 128
    expressing different logics, 128
    organizations as, 176
    variability of standards for assessing rationality, 128
    Western cultural assumptions not universal, 112
Cunningham, Stanley, 299, 301
Cynicism, in organizational communication, 193

D'Angelo, Gary, 157
Dargatz, Jan, 105
Davies, Jacqueline MacGregor, 237
Day, Dennis G., 32
Deception
    See also Lying
    characteristic of leaders, 38, 305–6
    distinguishing between white sham and black sham, 163
    habit of, shown by presidents Johnson and Reagan, 307
    intentional deception and intentional lying distinguished, 122
    in interpersonal communication, 121, 163
    necessity of argued, 124
    practices considered unethical by Aristotle, 47
    presidential obligation to avoid, 279–80
    resulting from Reagan's misstatements, 280
Deetz, Stanley, 163, 164
Defensive communication, in small group communication, 72–73

DeGeorge, Richard, 12, 110, 137, 199, 298
Degree of rationality, 25–27
Demagogues, 134–35
Democracy. *See* Democratic system
Democratic debate, as a procedural ethic, 32–33
Democratic system
  ability to understand nature of democracy basic to welfare of, 24
  communication behavior fostering values, 24–25
  ethical principles essential to, 6
  values and procedures central to, 27, 287–88, 304
  values basic to welfare of, 23–25
Democratization of media, 332–34
Dennis, Everette, 140, 141
Denton, H. H., 269, 275
Deontelic ethics, 8–9
Deontological ethics, 8
Des Jardins, Joseph, 314
Dialogical attitudes, 64
  in public and written communication, 73–76
Dialogical communication
  characteristics of, 63
  in small group communication, 72–73
Dialogical perspectives
  characteristics of dialogue, 66–68
  characteristics of monologue, 68–70
  conditions and contexts for dialogue, 72–73
  dialogical attitudes in public and written communication, 73–76
  dialogical ethics and significant choice, 78–79
  dialogue and persuasion, 71–72
  dialogue vs. expressive communication, 66
  toward an ethic for rhetoric, 76–78
  focusing on participant attitudes, 64–66

  guidelines for applying dialogical standards, 79–80
  humans as persons and objects, 70–71
Dialogical relationship
  characteristics of, 64–65
  and therapy, 65–66
Dialogue
  authenticity characteristic of, 67
  characteristics of, 66–68
  characteristics of echoed in an ethic of care, 224–25
  choosing to open ourselves to, 73
  in concept of desirable human communications, 64
  conditions and contexts for, 72–73
  confirmation characteristic of, 67
  essential movement in, 65
  and ethical character, 302
  focus of, 64–66
  inclusion characteristic of, 67
  involving genuine concern for the other, 66
  not always possible, 71
  not the same as expressive communication, 66
  and persuasion, 71–72
  possibility of in different fields and settings, 73
  presentness characteristic of, 67
  privacy desirable but not necessary for, 72
  in small group communication, 72–73
  spirit of mutual equality characteristic of, 67–68
  supplementing persuasion, 78
  supportive climate characteristic of, 68
  time needed for maturation of, 72
  views of, 63, 78
Dickinson, Emily, 230
Diggs, B. J., 89, 120
Dissent, habit of respect for, 24–25, 183
Doublespeak Award, 270
  Reagan receiving, 269–70
Dowling, Ralph E., 264, 291

Drucker, Peter, 11
Dynamic autonomy, as an aspect of caring, 229

Edelman, Murray, 285, 291
Ehninger, Douglas, 77, 286
Eisenberg, Eric, 192
Electronic media, truth considered irrelevant as standard for, 130–31
Ellul, Jacques, 132, 321, 324
Emmet, Dorothy, 251
Emotional appeals
　castigated, 26–27
　ethicality depending on technique used, 129
　ethicality of, 46–47, 127–29
　guidelines for evaluating, 129
　in interpersonal communication, 127
　justification of, 88
　pseudo-proof ethically suspect, 129
　in public communication, 26, 27
　and rationality, 127–29
Empathy
　in organizational communication, 183
　valued in care-givers, 229
Ends and means
　assessing ethicality of, 58–59
　end as justification of means, 119–21
　end exalted over means in public communication, 25
　ends not justifying unethical means, 46
　humans to be treated as ends, not means, 50, 57
　judging ethics of separately, 120
　rules for making ethical judgments of, 91–92
　suggestions for judging ethicality in relationship, 120–21
Engrossment, central to a caring relation, 224
Entertainer, attitudes of, 76
Epistemic ethic for communication, 55–57

Epistemology, 55
Ethical behavior
　characteristics and values associated with, 303–4
　citizen concern with, 5–6
　importance of role models, 178
Ethical character
　See also Character ethics
　assessing, 13
　and assessment of political candidates, 311–12
　and communication, 301–2
　descriptions of, 298–99
　and dialogue, 302
　focused on, in presidential campaigns, 308–9
　functions of, 299–301
　guiding behavior, 11–12
　humanizing application of abstract rules and principles, 301
　importance of, in political candidates, 314
　influencing choices and actions, 299–300
　nature of, 298–99
　potential for changing thinking about politics, 305
　qualities necessary for a president, 312
　reasons for scrutiny of, 312–13
　role in political communication, 304–5
　and roles played in life, 300
　sensitizing function of, 300
　virtues associated with, 302
　virtues playing a role in, 298
　vision central to, 299
　weakened by lying, 299
Ethical climate, in organizations, 176–77
Ethical conduct, ethical ideal as guide for, 225
Ethical contracts, implied, 13–14
Ethical dilemmas, defined, 179
Ethical guidelines
　for applying dialogical standards, 79–80
　for assessing character of political candidates, 312

based on capacity to generate knowledge, 56–57
based on Sartre's philosophy, 55
Christian ethical guidelines, 102–3
for communication consultants, 187
for communication trainers, 186–87
derived from "Groupthink," 169–70
for developing formal codes of ethics, 199–200
for evaluating emotional appeals, 129
for evaluating presidential secrecy, 144–45
for intercultural communication, 256–58
for interpersonal ethics, 158–59
from Russell's philosophy, 51
for small group discussion, 167–68
for writing moral standards into law, 114
Ethical habits for organizations, 180–81
Ethical ideal, as guide for conduct, 225
Ethical issues
  defined, 179
  in human behavior, 1
  inherency of, in communication, 2–3
  relevancy of, 1
  in social protest situations, 93–96
Ethicality
  to be appraised separately from sincerity, 267
  to be judged separately from sincerity, 275
Ethical judgments
  derived from Rogge's analysis, 88
  exclusive to human beings, 2
  of profanity and obscenity, 93
  rules for judging means and ends, 91–92
  sincerity affecting, 275

unique human capacity for making, 99–100
Ethical norms, and persuader's role, 89
Ethical responsibilities of non-participants, 148
Ethical responsibilities of receivers, 146–48
Ethical responsibility. *See* Freedom and responsibility; Responsibility
Ethical sensitivity, as a leadership function, 168–69
Ethical standards
  absolute and relative, 117–18
  for advertising, 102–3
  American value system not widely shared, 243
  and audience acceptance of persuasion, 89
  based on human symbol-using capacity, 48–50
  for communication in organizations, 181–85
  compared with value standards, 1
  Context bound nature of, 117–18
  and degree of rationality, 25–27
  derived from Kant's Categorical Imperative, 50
  derived from utilitarianism, 107–8
  elements of ideal speech situation serving as, 53
  evaluating in communication transaction, 3
  examples of, 1
  and human rational capacity, 46–48
  for interpersonal communication, 158–66
  maximum and minimum, 118–19
  metaethic needed, 243
  objectivity as an ethical standard for journalism, 140–43
  for presidential secrecy, 144–45
  for public communication, 24–25
  questions to consider, 17–18
  relating to purpose, 118

376 Index

for rhetoric, 76–78
of right and wrong, 1
search for global commonalities for journalistic ethics, 243–44
transcultural ethical standards, 251–52
Western cultural assumptions not universal, 118
Ethical systems, necessity and practical functions of, 6
Ethical Values and Principles in Public Service, 210–12
Ethic for everyday conversation, 231
Ethic of care
   application to public political and social contexts, 227–28
   central dimensions of, 224–25
   characterizing female moral voice, 223
   contrasted with male ethic of justice, 223
   criticized for forcing dichotomy between natures and abilities of men and women, 229–30
   criticized for limitation to private sphere, 229
   echoing Martin Buber's characteristics of dialogue, 224–25
   ethical ideal as guide for conduct, 225
   focused on individual relationships, 225–26
   grounded in human nature ethical perspective, 224, 226
   needed together with ethic of justice, 227–28
   needing relevance to both public and private spheres, 227
   principles and rules rejected as guides for ethical behavior, 5
   purposes of rules and rights within, 227
   universality of some aspects of, 225
   version developed for the public sphere, 227–28
Ethic of justice
   appropriate in some situations, 227
   characterizing male moral voice, 223
   contrasted with ethic of care, 223
   needed together with ethic of care, 227–28
Ethic of narrative. *See* Narrative ethic
Ethics
   See also Morals
   avoiding rigidity in, 258
   character ethics. *See* Character ethics
   in communication. *See* Communication ethics
   for communication consulting and training, 186–87
   defined, 298
   and the demagogue, 134–35
   deontological, 8
   distinguished from morals, 1–2
   ethnic ethics, 250–51
   exclusive to human beings, 2
   feminist ethics. *See* Feminist ethics
   and ghostwriting, 138–39
   importance of, 5–6
   of lying, 121–24. *See also* Lying
   need to consider, 2–3
   new ethics of pluralism advocated, 258
   and nonverbal communication, 135–37
   and personal character, 11–13. *See also* Character ethics
   of photojournalism, 136–37
   and propaganda, 131–34
   in public relations, 187–90
   reasons given for avoiding consideration of, 2
   and tastefulness, 137–38
   technology seen as antithetical to, 321–22
   teleological, 8
   virtue ethics, 11
   working against greed, 193
Ethics of persuasion. *See* Persuasion

Ethnic ethics, 250–51
Eubanks, Ralph, 57
Evans, R., 278
Evil speaker and evil lover, 74
Excellence, in Ethical Values and Principles in Public Service, 211
Existentialist ethic for communication, 54–55
Expressive communication, not the same as dialogue, 66

Fackler, P. Mark, 320
Facts, misstatement and misuse of, by Reagan, 267–72
Factual truth, differentiated from impressionistic truth, 102
Fairness
  basic to welfare of democratic system, 24
  in Ethical Values and Principles in Public Service, 211
  substituted for objectivity, 142
False lover-persuaders, 104
Feedback, 147–48
Female and male moral voices
  in communication, 223
  essential for moral conduct of politics, 305
Feminism, 221
Feminist ethics
  applied to mass communication, 235–36
  challenging male-dominated ethical traditions, 221–22
  challenging mass media to change, 235–36
  challenging standard image of moral agent, 222
  challenging treatment of mass media subjects as objects, 236
  characteristics of, 235–36
  emphasizing interpersonal ethics, 222
  focusing on degrees of rightness and wrongness, 235
  focusing on commitment to equality and respect for life, 221
  focusing on interpersonal ethics, 222
  importance of, 239
  providing ethical grounds for condemning pornography, 237
  reacting against male standards as universal, 223
  seeing persuasion as violence, 232
  seen as an ethic of care, 222–30
  and the silencing of women, 238
Ferre, John P., 320
Festa, Regina, 333
Fidelity
  as a touchstone for narrative paradigm, 288–89
  in Ethical Values and Principles in Public Service, 211
Finan, Ted, 35
Fisher, Walter R., 13, 77, 278, 279, 284, 285, 286, 288, 291, 292, 293, 299
Fleishman, Joel L., 266
Fletcher, Joseph, 89, 90, 101
Flirt, 104
Flynn, Lawrence, 46, 133
Formal codes of ethics
  Advertising Association Codes, 203–5
  American Advertising Federation: Advertising Principles of American Business, 204
  American Association of Advertising Agencies code of ethics, 203–4
  argumentative function of, 201–2
  attitudes to, 197
  character-depiction function of, 202–3, 302–4
  clarity of language essential, 199
  Code of Advertising of the Better Business Bureau, 204–5
  code of ethics for Political Campaign Advertising, 213
  Code of Ethics of Sigma Delta Phi, 140
  Code of ethics of the International Association of Business Communicators, 205–6

codes for political campaign communication, 212–14
Committee on Decent Unbiased Campaign Tactics (CONDUCT) Code of Fair Campaign Practice, 213–14
and computer communication, 197–98
contractual approach suggested, 200–201
criticisms of, 198–99
depicting desirable virtues of character, 303–4
to be developed through participation of all group members, 200
distinguishing between ideal goals and minimum conditions, 199
to be enforceable and enforced, 200
Ethical Values and Principles in Public Service, 210–12
focusing on specific functions of group, 199
to be founded on clear moral principles, 200
guidelines for developing, 199–200
for individual organizations, 200–201
National Religious Broadcasters' Code, 104–5
proposed by Common Cause for political campaign communication, 212–13
proposed code for televised political campaign advertisements, 214–18
protecting public as well as group members, 199
providing a comparative standard, 201
providing ethical guidance for profession as a whole, 191–200
providing visible and impersonal standard, 201
provisions to be logically coherent, 199

Public Relations Society of America code, 206–10
reasonableness required, 199
recommended for organizations, 176
stimulating continued discussion and reflection, 199
useful functions of, 201
Foss, Sonja, 233, 234
Freedom
ethical use of, 8
of participants in invitational rhetoric, 234
responsible exercise of basic to welfare of democratic system, 24
restriction of, 161
Freedom and responsibility
See also Responsibility
in human communication, 6–9
increase in freedom bringing increase in responsibility, 7
in interpersonal communication, 162–63
in journalism, 8–9
with respect to photojournalism, 136–37
tension between, 8
and UNABOM manifesto, 7–8
Freezing participants, in conversation, 164–65
Freund, Ludwig, 267
Fried, Charles, 121
Froman, Lewis, 126
Fromm, Eric, 64
Fryburger, Vernon, 138
Frye, Northrop, 75, 76
Fuller, Buckminster, 330

Gadamer, Hans-Georg, 164
Garrett, Thomas, 47
Gearhart, Sally Miller, 232, 233
Gelman, R., 280
Gentleness, and persuasion, 52
Genuine speech, distinguished from bastard speech, 76
Gergen, David, 272, 275, 290
Germond, Jack, 272, 273, 274, 275, 289

Ghandi, Mahatma, 73
Ghostwriting
  communicators claiming responsibility for, 139
  ethics of, 138–39
  improving communicator's image, 138–39
  knowledge of, 138
  reasons for using, 139
Gibb, Jack, 64
Gibson, Walker, 75, 76
Giffin, Kim, 4, 159, 160
Gilligan, Carol, 223, 229, 302, 305
Gingrich, Newt, 6, 264
Glazer, Myron, 185
Glazer, Penina, 185
Goebbels, Joseph, 39
Golden Rule, 5
  Platinum Rule offered to replace, in international communication, 244
  as possible principle for intercultural communication ethics, 244
Goldwater, Barry, 276
Goldzwig, Steven, 95
Goss, Blaine, 125
Gouran, Dennis, 35, 168, 168
Governmental communication, ethical standards for, 34–36
Governmental secrecy, 144. *See also* Secrecy
Government officials, using obscure or jargon-laden language, 10, 267
Graham, Donald E., 8
Green, Mark, 264, 268, 269, 274, 307
Greenfield, Meg, 275, 280, 290, 296
Gregg, Richard, 55
Grice, H. P., 160, 231
Griffin, Cindy, 233, 234
Griffin, Emory, 75, 103, 104, 106
Gross, Larry, 320, 321
"Groupthink," 169–70

Guardedness, in organizational communication, 182
Gulley, Halbert, 167
Gusdorf, Georges, 64
Gutmann, Amy, 251

Habermas, Jürgen, 52, 53, 54, 163
Habit of interacting responsibly, 180
Habit of justice, 24
Habit of modeling integrity, 180–81
Habit of practicing personal integrity, 181
Habit of preferring public to private motivation, 24, 183
Habit of respect for dissent, 24–25, 183
Habit of search, 24, 183
Habit of sharing organizational purposes and directions, 181
Habit of solving ethical problems directly and reflectively, 180
Habit of valuing shareholder perspectives, 181
Habit of justice, 183
Hackett, Robert, 140
Haiman, Franklyn, 25, 26, 33, 46, 94, 114, 137, 255
Halperin, Morton, 145
Hammarskjold, Dag, 9
Harrington, Walt, 174
Hart, Gary, 308
Haselden, Kyle, 100, 101
Hate speech. *See* Racist/sexist language and hate speech
Hauerwas, Stanley, 298, 299, 300, 302
Hayakawa, S. I., 119, 141
Hearn, Thomas, 108
Heidegger, Martin, 322, 324
Held, Virginia, 222
Henry, Jules, 112
Hitler, Adolf, 10, 39
Hoffman, David, 145
Holmes, Oliver Wendell, 269

380 Index

Homer, 304, 305
Honesty
  See also Truth
  in Ethical Values and Principles in Public Service, 211
  in organizational communication, 184–85
  required by Christian ethic, 100
Hook, Sidney, 30, 31, 32, 93, 93
Horowitz, R., 273
Howe, Reuel, 64
Howell, William S., 108, 111, 120, 128, 137, 244
Hudson, Stephen, 296, 297, 300
Human attributes
  ability to use language, 51
  capacity for reason, 51
  capacity to persuade and be persuaded, 51–52
  language use, 51
  rational capacity uniquely human, 46–48
  symbol-using capacity, 48–50
  used to assess ethics of communication, 45–46
Human behavior
  ethical evaluation of, 90
  role of ethical character in, 299–301
Human beings
  to be treated as ends and not means, 57
  to be treated as subjects, not objects, 54–55
  need for others a quality of, 48
  obligations of, 47
  obligation to behave rationally, 47
  as persons and objects, 70–71
  as persuaders, 182
  promoting primacy of the person, 57
  seen as objects by rhetorical rapist, 75
  sharing fundamental human spirit, 246–47
  as story-tellers, 285, 288
  uniquely human capacity for ethical judgment, 99–100
Human communication
  See also Communication ethics; Rhetoric
  achieving maximum ethicality, 80
  adaptation to audience, 3, 4–5
  assessing ethicality of means and ends, 58–59
  assumptions underlying, 53
  attitude of dialogue in, 66. See also Dialogue
  basic elements of, 15–16
  to be judged in light of situational factors, 89–90
  communicative competence in, 52–54
  concept of dialogue at heart of, 64–66
  developing discerning receivers and consumers of, 17–18
  dialogical standards for assessing ethics of, 78
  end as justification of means in, 119–21
  end exalted over means, 25
  epistemic ethic for, 55–57
  ethical analysis of, 15–18
  and ethical character, 301–2
  ethicality of emotional appeals in, 46–47
  ethical standard based on symbol-using capacity, 48–49
  ethics of audience adaptation, 4–5
  existentialist ethic for, 54–55
  freedom and responsibility in, 6–9, 162–63
  genuine speech and bastard speech distinguished, 76
  human attributes used to assess ethics of, 45–46
  and human symbol-using capacity, 48–50
  ideal speech situation, 53
  intercultural communication, 243–49, 256
  interpersonal communication. See Interpersonal communication
  justifying avoidance of consideration of ethics, 2–3

mass communication. *See* Mass communication
maximum participation desired, 56–57
monologue as, 68–70
multicultural communication, 249–56
objectifying communication usually undesirable, 70–71
person-centered view of, 65
persuasive purpose inherent to, 3–4
potential ethical questions always present in, 2–3
and principle of dialogue, 64. *See also* Dialogue
to produce cooperation rather than conflict, 51
responsibility for integrity of language, 9
Sartrean ethical guidelines for, 55
seeking ethical balance point in audience adaptation, 4–5
shaping audience, 119
sincerity and intent in, 10–11, 266–67
situational factors of, 16
striving for good consequences, 57
superogatory ethical communication, 119
trust in sources essential to, 37
Humanistic ethic for rhetoric, 58–59
Human moral development, 223–24
Human nature
  Aristotle's view of, 46–48
  as grounding for ethic for international communication, 246–47
  questioned as basis for ethical norms, 45–46
Human nature perspectives
  communicative competence and the ideal speech situation, 52–54
  concentrating on a single attribute, 45
  an epistemic ethic, 55–57
  for ethic of care, 224, 226
  an existentialist ethic for communication, 54–55
  focusing on essence of human nature, 45–46
  human capacity for value judgment, 57–58
  humanistic ethic for rhetoric, 58–59
  human rational capacity, 46–48
  humans as persuaders, 51–52
  human symbol-using capacity, 48–50
  inherently biased against women, 236–37
  Kant's Categorical Imperative, 50
  reason and language, 51
Human personality, intrinsic worth of, 25, 27
Human rational capacity, 46–48
Human relationships
  I-It and I-Thou, 64–65
  involving both monologue and dialogue, 72
Human society, ethical principles essential to, 6
Human symbol-using capacity, 48–50
  as foundation for definition of man, 49
  power of, 48

Ickes, Harold, 268
Ideal speech situation, 53
Identification, power of, 181–82
I-It relationship, 64
Illich, Ivan, 320, 328, 329
Image, in political campaigns, 310
Implied ethical contracts, 13–14
  assumptions of, 14
  illustrated, 15
Impressionistic truth, 102
Inclusiveness, to guide relations in communication, 234
Individuals, as moral agents, 17
Innis, Harold, 323
Integrity
  in Ethical Values and Principles in Public Service, 211

habit of modeling, 180–81
Integrity of others, respect for essential, 56
Intent, relationship with responsibility, 10–11, 266–67
Intentional ambiguity and vagueness
  in advertising, 125
  balanced view of ethics of, 125
  communicators warned against, 276
  considered unethical in most cases, 125
  ethics of, 125–27, 276
  justified in political communication, 126, 276
  not to be equated with untruthfulness, 125
  Reagan using, 267–68, 275–79
  sometimes appropriate in international communication, 277
Intercultural communication
  See also Multicultural communication
  Golden Rule as possible principle for, 244
  human nature ethic proposed for, 246–47
  Kant's Categorical Imperative as possible principle for, 244
  proposed code of ethics for, 245–46
  search for global commonalities for, 243–44
  and social utility approach, 244
International communication
  ethical principles grounded in human nature, 247
  intentional ambiguity and vagueness sometimes appropriate in, 277
Interpersonal communication
  See also Human communication
  attitudes to be encouraged, 78
  deception in, 163
  definitions of, 157
  dialogical perspectives applied to, 78–79, 157–58
  dialogical standards for assessing ethics of, 78
  emotional appeals in, 26–27, 46–47, 88, 127
  ethical issues emerging in, 158–59. *See also* Interpersonal ethics
  ethically irresponsible tactics in verbal conflict, 161–62
  ethically objectionable techniques for, 161
  ethical responsibility and communication competence, 165–66
  individual responsibility in relational communication, 162–63
  keeping the conversation going, 163–65
  openness in, 162
  privacy in, 162–63
  protectiveness in, 163
  rhetorical perspective on interpersonal ethics, 161
  tension between candor and restraint, 163
  tension between freedom and responsibility in, 7, 162–63
  trust among participants essential to, 159–60
Interpersonal ethics
  Condon's interpersonal ethic, 158–59
  contextual approach to, 159
  ethically irresponsible tactics in verbal conflict, 161–62
  an ethic for everyday conversation, 160–61
  an ethic for interpersonal trust, 159–60
  feminist ethics focusing on, 222
  guidelines for, 158–59
  rhetorical perspective for, 161
Intracultural communication
  examples of, 250
  guidelines for, 256–58
Invitational rhetoric, 233–35
  change not intent of, 233
  compared with conquest/conversion model of rhetoric, 232–34
  nonjudgmental character of, 233–34

safety, value, and freedom of participants in, 234
Islam, religious perspectives offered by, 106–7
Issues, created for political campaigns, 309
I-Thou relationship, 64–65

Jabusch, David, 165, 166
Jackall, Robert, 174, 175
Jaggar, Alison, 221, 222
Jamieson, Kathleen Hall, 30, 311
Janis, Irving, 169
Jargon, ethically irresponsible use of, 10, 267
Jaspers, Karl, 64
Jensen, J. Vernon, 107, 185
Johannesen, Richard L., 197, 265, 266, 276, 279, 280, 302, 304, 309
Johnson, David, 64
Johnson, Haynes, 268, 269, 273
Johnson, John, 192
Johnson, Lyndon, 307
Johnstone, Christopher Lyle, 45, 58
Johnstone, Henry W., Jr., 38, 51, 52, 77, 182, 233, 264, 265
  Basic Imperative of, 52
Jonsen, Albert, 263, 297
Jourard, Sidney, 64
Journalism
  freedom and responsibility in, 8–9
  making as objective as possible, 141–42
  objectivity as an ethical standard for, 140–43
  relevance of feminist ethic for, 236
Journalistic ethics
  Code of Ethics of Sigma Delta Phi, 140
  ethical considerations for photojournalism, 136–37
  Mexico Declaration, 142
  search for global commonalities for, 243–44
Journalists
  imperatives of freedom for, 8
  responsibility to provide information about political candidates, 313
Justice, 54
  See also Ethic of justice
  habit of, 24, 183
  in organizational communication, 184–85

Kale, David, 246, 247
Kant, Immanuel, 11, 50, 70, 297
Kant's Categorical Imperative, 50, 70
  forms of, 50
  as possible principle for intercultural communication ethics, 244
Katz, John Stuart, 321
Kauffman, Charles, 278
Keller, Paul, 78, 79
Keniston, Kenneth, 94
Kennedy, Edward, 134
Kierkegaard, Soren, 103
Klaidman, Steven, 12, 17, 302, 313
Knickerbocker, B., 276
Knowledge, human capacity to generate and transmit, 56
Kohlberg, Lawrence, 223
Kolenda, Konstantin, 314
Korzybski, Alfred, 141
Kreps, Gary, 183, 184
Kruger, Arthur, 26
Kruschwitz, Robert B., 296
Kultgen, John, 199
Kupfer, Joseph, 122, 298
Kupperman, Joel, 296, 297, 300

Lambeth, Edmund, 142
Langer, Susanne, 49
Language
  ethical implications of, 253–54
  ethicality of vague language, 126
  ethics of ambiguous language, 125–27

humans alone able to use, 51
need for respect for, 9
not neutral and objective, 3–4
only the best required by Christian ethic, 100
persuasive dimension of, 4
racist/sexist language and hate speech, 253–56
and reason, 51
reflecting prejudices of society, 253
sermonic dimension of, 3–4
undermined by loss of trust, 37
used by women, 230
used to exclude and demean, 253–54
used to influence others, 51
Leahy, P.J., 268
Lear, Norman, 324
Lebacqz, Karen, 12, 202, 298, 302, 303
Legalistic lover, 104
Legally innocent prevarication, 112
Legal perspectives
   enforcing standards through legislation not possible, 110
   general nature of, 110
   legal and ethical not synonymous, 110, 112
   legality and ethicality made synonymous, 110
   in politics and advertising, 111–13
   problems with, 113–14
Legislation, 110–111
Leiser, Burton, 112
Lescaze, L., 268, 271
Levitt, Theodore, 49, 50, 130
Levy, Charles, 203
Lewis, William, 290, 291, 292
Liars, damage done to by lying, 298–99. *See also* Lying
Liebman, L., 266
Lilla, Mark T., 305
Littlejohn, Stephen, 165, 166
Logical fallacies, used by rhetorical seducer, 75

Logicality of reasons, testing, 286–87
Longino, Helen, 237
Love, as only ethical criterion in situation ethics, 89–90
Lover-persuaders, in Christian evangelism, 103–4
Lucaites, John Lewis, 292, 294
Ludwig, Arnold, 135
Luthin, Reinhard, 135, 275
Lying
   See also Deception; Secrecy; Truth
   affecting liar and deceived, 122–23
   affecting trust, 122
   communicated nonverbally, 135
   considered always wrong, 121
   determining whether justifiable, 123–24
   ethics of, 121–24
   excuses offered for, 123
   forced on women, 238
   impact of, on trust, 238
   intentional deception and intentional lying distinguished, 122
   in interpersonal communication, 161
   in interpersonal relationships between women, 238
   Jews and Christians admonished against use of, 99
   making ethical judgments of, 121
   moral presumption against, 122–23
   moral prohibition against, 14
   nature and boundaries of, 121–22
   necessity of deception argued, 124
   negative effect on the liar, 298–99
   negative ethical presumption against, 143
   occasions for ethical lying by the president, 145
   pornography as, 237
   potential harm from, 122–23, 124
   presidential lying, 37

"telling it slant," 230–32
weakening moral character, 299
withholding truth not seen as, 121

Macauley, Stewart, 35
MacColl, Gail, 264, 307
Machiavelli, Niccolo, 306
MacIntyre, Alasdair, 285, 297, 298, 300, 301, 304
Makay, John, 79
Malanchuk, Oksana, 311
Male and female moral voices
  in communication, 223
  essential for moral conduct of politics, 305
Male moral voice, characterized by ethic of justice, 223
Manley, Marshall, 312
Manning, Rita, 222, 226, 226, 227
Margolis, Joseph, 287, 309
Marietta, Don, 70
Marketing tactics, judging, 47–48
Marraro, Gabrielle, 264, 291
Marston, John, 119
Maslow, Abraham, 64
Mass communication
  feminist ethic applied to, 235–36
  guidelines for exploring ethical issues in, 101–2
  need for public ethic in, 113
Mass media
  as centralized oligopolies, 332
  challenged to change by feminist ethic, 235–36
  and Christian morality, 100–102
  and move towards participatory media, 332–34
  treating subjects as objects, 236
Matson, Floyd, 64, 72
May, William, 178
Mayerhoff, Milton, 64
Mayo, Bernard, 300
McCarthy, Colman, 269
McCarthy, Joseph R., 275
McCarthy, Thomas, 54
McDonald, Donald, 141

McGee, Michael Calvin, 292, 310, 311
McLuhan, Marshall, 128, 323, 330
McMillin, John, 102
Meaning, denial of, in conversation, 165
Means, humans never to be treated as, 50, 57, 70
Means, Richard, 2
Means and ends. See Ends and means
Media
  biased toward space and time in particular ways, 323
  democratization of, 332–34
  ethical operation of third-generation cable systems, 330–32
  truth considered irrelevant as standard for electronic media, 130–31
Meilaender, Gilbert C., 299, 300
Merrill, John, 8, 87, 140, 243, 244
Metaethic, need for, 243
Michell, Gillian, 230, 231, 298
Mill, John Stuart, 11, 113, 297
Miller, Arthur H., 311, 312
Miller, Casey, 253
Miller, Gerald, 157
Mitchell, Terence R., 314
Model of Organizational Integrity, 180–81
Modified universalism, 25–252
Mondale, Walter, 5
Monological arrogance, in written communication, 74
Monological attitudes, 64
Monological communication
  features of, 63
  in small group communication, 72–73
Monologue
  characteristics of, 68–70
  considered always unethical, 70
  disguised as dialogue, 69
  equated with persuasion, 71
  manipulative nature of, 68–69

nonpersonal and impersonal nature of, 68
not always avoidable, 69–70
as one form of persuasion, 72
treating humans as means, 70
Monsma, Stephen, 322, 327
Montagu, Ashley, 64, 72
Moore, Mark H., 266, 287
Moral character. *See* Ethical character
Moral education
condemned, 17
criticized for silence on virtue, 315
Moral exclusion, manifestations of, 252–53
Morality, 250–51
Moral judgments, 223
Moral pluralism, 251
Moral purpose, sacrificed to technical excellence, 324
Morals
See also Ethics
defined, 298
distinguished from ethics, 1–2
Moral standards, guidelines for writing into law, 114
Moral voices, 223, 305
Motivation, habit of preferring public to private motivations, 24, 183
Motivational displacement, central to a caring relation, 224
Multicultural communication
See also Intercultural communication
definition of, 249–50
ethnic ethics, 250–51
examples of, 250
guidelines for, 256–58
modified universalism, 251–52
moral exclusion, 252–53
moral pluralism, 251
racist/sexist language and hate speech, 253–56
transcultural ethical standards, 251–52
transcultural norms, 251
Murphy, Patrick, 178

Muted group theory, 230

Name-calling, ethics of, 133
Narrative
considered central to human belief and action, 285
functions of, 292, 293
Narrative adequacy, 292
Narrative ethic, 285–94
Narrative paradigm
concept criticized, 293–94
fidelity as a touchstone for, 288–89
probability as a touchstone for, 288
Reagan's rhetoric judged using, 290–91
subsuming rational world paradigm, 288
National Religious Broadcasters' Code, 104–5
Neibuhr, H. Richard, 267
Nelson, John S., 292
Neutral speaker and neutral lover, 74
Neutral technology. *See* Technology
News, in view of feminist ethic, 235–36
News reporting, types of stories, 142
Nielsen, Kai, 45
Nilsen, Thomas R., 3, 27, 28, 29, 73, 78, 119, 127, 167, 266, 287
Nimmo, Dan, 128, 135
Nixon, Richard M., 79
Noble speaker and noble lover, 74
Noddings, Nel, 224, 225, 226, 229, 237, 302
Non-lover
in Christian evangelism, 103–4
equated with neutral speaker, 74
Non-participants
affected by communication, 148
ethical responsibilities of, 148
Nonverbal communication
ethical implications of silence, 135

ethical standards for, 136–37
ethics of, 135–37
ethics of electronic manipulation of material, 135–36
indicating lying, 135
revealing communicator attitudes, 79
silence as, 237–38
subtly violent techniques, 161
unintentional or semiconscious, 137
Nonviolence, in organizational communication, 182–83
Normative technology, 325–27
See also Technology
North, Oliver, 12, 314
Nyberg, David, 124

Objectifying communication, 70–71
Objectivity
as a goal never perfectly achieved, 141–43
as an attitude, 141
authentic interpretation as alternative for, 142
considered largely achievable, 141
constraints on, 141
as an ethical standard for journalism, 140–43
fairness substituted for, 142
views of, 140–41
Obligation, distinguished from responsibility, 228
Obscenity and profanity
considered unethical by Christian ethic, 100
ethical judgment of, 93
function served by, 93
used in protest situations, 93
Odell, S. Jack, 6
Olasky, Marvin, 208, 209
Olbrechts-Tyteca, L., 278
O'Leary, Stephen D., 306
Olen, Jeffrey, 14
Olsen, Tillie, 230
Oliver, Robert, 120
Openness

defined, 165
limiting in interpersonal communication, 162
and persuasion, 52
Opotow, Susan, 252
Oran, Daniel, 126
Organizational communication
accessibility important to, 182
character and virtue ethics in, 177–78
cynicism and relevance in, 193
empathy essential to, 183
and ethical climate, 176–77
ethical standards to guide, 182–85
ethics for communication consulting and training, 186–87
ethics in public relations, 187–90
ethics rooted in values of honesty, avoiding harm, and justice, 183–85
examples of ethical problems, 190–93
framework for analyzing ethics of, 179
model of organizational integrity, 180–81
role of guardedness in, 182
use of "we" in organizational messages, 182
whistleblowing, 185–86
Organizational purposes and directions, habit of sharing, 181
Organizations
assessing ethical responsibility in, 174–75
assessing individual responsibility advised, 175
character and virtue ethics in, 177–78
character of individual employees affecting, 178
commitment of resources demonstrating concern for ethics, 177
communicator roles within, 173
as cultures, 176
elements of ethical systems in, 179
ethical climates in, 176–77

ethical virtues important for individuals in, 178
facilitating unethical or immoral conduct, 174–75
formal code of ethics recommended, 176
framework for analyzing ethics in, 179
instilling a sense of ethics, 177
model of organizational integrity, 180–81
negative attitudes of public to ethical standards of business, 173–74
organizational factors in, 179
seen by the public as not trustworthy, 173–74
top management to set ethical tone, 176
Orman, John, 37, 144, 145
Ottoson, Gerald, 193

Pacey, Arnold, 322, 323, 326
Pacification, in conversation, 165
Palmour, 305
Partiality, valued in care-givers, 229
Participant attitudes and behavior in dialogue, 64–65
    indicating ethicality of communication, 64
Participation, to guide relations in communication, 234–35
Pathos. See Emotional appeals
Patience, as an aspect of caring, 229
Patton, Bobby, 4
Pauly, John, 329
Pearsall, Marilyn, 236
Pedant, attitudes of, 76
Pennock, J. Roland, 267
Perelman, Chaim, 278
Personal character. See Ethical character
Persuaders
    and characteristics of demagogues, 134–35
    humans as, 51–52
Persuasion

See also Rhetoric
appealing to values, 278
Christian ethic for, 99–100
conquest/conversion model of, 232–33
desired and needed by human beings, 72
and dialogue, 71–72
dialogue supplementing, 78
dialogue to be substituted for, 78
duties of resoluteness, openness, gentleness, and compassion, 52
ethical criteria for, 33–34
ethical standards for assessing instances of, 52
human capacity to use, 51–52
monologue as one form of, 72
monologue equated with, 71
propaganda as, 131–32
responsible use of, 51–52
role of dialogue in, 71–72
role of identification in, 181–82
seen as violence, 232
spirit of love in, 52
standard for judging ethics of, 26–27
Persuasive techniques
    ethics evaluated from perspective of significant choice, 28–30
    judged by effectiveness of results in Nazi Germany, 39
Phelan, John, 320
Photojournalism, ethical considerations for, 136–37
Pichler, Joseph, 110
Pinckaers, 301
Pincoffs, Edmund L., 9, 267, 297, 298
Plagiarism
    condemned as theft of an idea, 248
    culturally variable attitudes to, 247–49
    focused on, in presidential campaigns, 308–9
    as fraud or deception, 248
    indicating character flaws, 308–9
    linked to print orientation, 248

linked to view of words and ideas as private property, 248
Plain folks technique, ethics of, 133–34
Platinum Rule, to replace Golden Rule in international communication, 244
Plato, 11, 297, 304
Political advertising
  Code of Ethics for Political Campaign Advertising of American Association of Advertising Agencies, 213
  Committee on Decent Unbiased Campaign Tactics (CONDUCT) code of fair campaign practice, 213–14
  Common Cause standards for assessing ethics of political candidates' campaign, 212–13
  proposed code for televised advertisements, 214–18
  truth considered irrelevant as standard for, 130–31
Political argument, ethical, 30
Political campaigning
  character, image, and issues in, 309–12
  and character issue, 308–9
  content viewed as free speech, 111
  issues created for, 309
  issues vs. images, 309–11
  legislation to control not successful, 111
  personal qualities for assessing candidates, 311–12
  persuasive techniques evaluated, 28–30
  standards for minimal disclosure established, 111–12
Political candidates
  evaluation of, 309–12
  guidelines for assessing character of, 312
  reasons for scrutiny of character of, 312–13
Political communication
  See also Public communication
  intentional ambiguity justified in, 126
  rational world ethic compared with narrative ethic for, 285–94
  role of ethical character in, 304–5
  and single-issue politics trend, 126
  values guiding ethical scrutiny of, 287
Political controversy, ground rules for, 30–32
Political leadership, deception characteristic of, 38
Political perspectives
  communication behavior fostering values, 24–25
  degree of rationality approach, 25–27
  of differing systems of government, 23
  and presidential secrecy, 144–45
  scope of, 23
  significant choice as, 27–30
  used to examine Reagan's rhetoric, 266
  values basic to welfare of democratic system, 23–25
Political values
  of a political system, 23
  generating criteria for examining communication ethics, 266
  used as criteria for evaluating ethics, 23
Politicians, lying and deception expected of, 305–6
Politics
  and advertising, 111–13
  male and female moral voices both essential to moral conduct of, 305
Pool, Ithiel de Sola, 40
Pope Gregory XV, 131
Pornography, 237
Powell, John, 64
Power tactics, rules for using, 92–93
Presentness, characteristic of dialogue, 67

Presidential communication
  obligation to accuracy and fairness, 307
  obligation to avoid deception, 279–80
Presidential lying, 37
Presidential secrecy, 144–45
  See also Secrecy
Preston, Ivan, 112, 128
Principle of the Golden Mean, 5
Privacy
  desirable but not necessary for dialogue, 72
  distinguished from secrecy, 162–63
  essential in interpersonal communication, 162–63
Probability, as a touchstone for narrative paradigm, 288
Procedural ethics, democratic debate as, 32–33
Profanity. *See* Obscenity and profanity
Promise-keeping, in Ethical Values and Principles in Public Service, 211
Propaganda
  as campaign of mass persuasion, 131–32
  definitions of, 131–32
  destroying sense of history and philosophy, 132
  ethicality depending on definition of, 131–32
  and ethics, 131–34
  ethics of name-calling, 133
  as self-justifying process, 132
  threatening total human personality, 132–33
  traditional devices of, 133–34
  undercutting conscious choice making and interpersonal communication, 132–33
  viewed as inherently unethical, 132
Protest movements, relationship with community building, 334
Protest rhetoric
  arguments for, 94
  effectiveness of, 94
  need for ethical standards to evaluate, 96
  reasons for use of, 94–95
  rules for using power tactics, 92–93
  seen as sometimes necessary, 95
  using obscenity and profanity, 93
Pseudoproof
  anecdotes as, 275
  ethically suspect, 129, 133
Public communication
  See also Political communication
  claimed inadequate by protesters, 94–95
  consequences of weakening of public trust, 37–38
  dialogical attitudes in, 73–76
  emotional appeals in, 26, 27
  end exalted over means, 25
  ethical guidelines for examining, 31
  ethically suspect techniques in, 113
  ground rules for political controversy, 30–32
  judging using degree of rationality criterion, 25–27
  judging using significant choice criterion, 27–30
  means and ends to be considered, 25
  primary ethical standard for judging, 32–33
  problems with legal attempts to enforce standards, 113–14
  rational world ethic compared with narrative ethic for, 285–94
  tendency to distrust, 38–39
  unethical practices in, 25–27, 30
  weakened public confidence in, 36–39
Public context, application of ethic of care in, 227–28
Public relations
  as a management function, 188
  audiences for, 187

Code of Professional Standards for the Practice of Public Relations, 206–10
  dialogical ethic desirable for, 72–73
  ethics in, 187–90
  phases of, 189–90
Public Relations Society of America code of ethics, 206–10
  responsibility to help build and maintain ethical behavior, 188
Puffery, false by implication, 112

Quality, as a guideline for interpersonal conversation, 160, 231
Quantity, as a guideline for interpersonal conversation, 160, 231
Quine, W. V., 29

Racist/sexist language and hate speech
  to be condemned on ethical grounds, 255–56
  dehumanizing others, 255–56
  psychological harm caused by, 254, 255
  speech codes to prohibit, 254–55
Rainie, Harrison, 296
Rakow, Lana, 234
Rasmussen, Karen, 79
Rationality
  biased against women when used as an ethical standard, 236–37
  cultural variability of standards for assessing, 128
  differing concepts of, 128
  emotional appeals considered in the light of, 127–29
Rational world ethic, compared with narrative ethic, 285–94
Rational world paradigm
  fundamental presuppositions of, 286
Reagan warranting ethical condemnation when judged by, 289–90
  reflected in values and procedures central to representative democracy, 287
  subsumed in narrative paradigm, 288
  testing logicality of reasons, 286–87
Rawlins, William K., 7, 162
Rawls, John, 11, 297
Reagan, Ronald, 289, 290
  continuing habit of deceit, 307
  ethically irresponsible, 275
  intentionally employing ambiguity and vagueness, 267–68, 275–79
  making appeals to values, 277–79
  misstating facts, 268–72
  misusing anecdotes, 272–73
  motives suspect, 273–74
  not concerned for accuracy, 274, 307
  playing fast and loose with facts, 267, 268–75, 307
  stories faulted in light of narrative paradigm, 290–91
  warranting ethical condemnation when judged by rational world paradigm, 289–90
Reagan rhetoric
  criteria appropriate for judging, 265
  damaging trust between government and people, 280
  judging ethicality of, 279–80
  viewed from political perspective, 266
Reality, rhetoric functioning to create, 55
Reason
  human capacity to use, 46–48, 51
  and language, 51
Reasoned skepticism, required of receivers, 146–47
Receivers. *See* Audience
Reciprocity
  central to a caring relation, 224–25

to guide relations in communication, 235
Redding, Charles, 174, 186
Redford, Emmette S., 266, 287
Reich, Robert B., 294
Relation, as a guideline for interpersonal conversation, 160–61, 231
Relational communication. *See* Interpersonal communication
Relativism, 56, 56
Relevance, in organizational communication, 193
Religiousness, source of, 99
Religious perspectives
  on advertising, 102–3
  Christian ethic for persuasion, 99–100
  derived from sacred writings, 99
  an ethic for Christian evangelism, 103–4
  examples from oriental religions, 106–7
  general nature of, 99
  mass media and Christian morality, 100–102
  National Religious Broadcasters' Code, 104–5
  shared perspectives of world religions, 107
Rescher, Nicholas, 10,
Resoluteness, and persuasion, 52
Respect for worth of others
  basic to welfare of democratic system, 23–24
  as basis for ethical communication, 167–68
  in Ethical Values and Principles in Public Service, 211
  required by Christian ethic, 100
Responsibility
  See also Freedom and responsibility
  abdicated, 166
  of communicators, 9, 266–67
  distinguished from obligation, 228
  elements of, 9, 266–67
  ethical, 166
  as an ethical element of care, 228
  increasing as freedom increases, 7
  irresponsibility, 166
  judgment an essential element of, 9, 266–67
  relationship with intent, 10–11, 266–67
  sense of, a necessary condition for self-respect, 9
  in tension with freedom, 6–9
  unshared, 166
Responsiveness to others, as an ethical element of care, 228–29
Reston, James, 274
Rhetoric
  See also Persuasion; Reagan rhetoric
  Aristotle's ethical standards for, 46–47
  assessing ethicality of content of, 59
  broad view of, 55
  capacity for rationality necessary part of, 46
  conceptions of, 55–57
  conquest/conversion model compared with invitational rhetoric, 232–34
  ethic for, 51–52
  toward an ethic for, 76–78
  functions of, 49, 55–57
  invitational rhetoric, 233–35
  male-dominated model of, 232
  protest rhetoric, 94–96
  spirit of love in, 52
  as subtle form of Might Makes Right, 232
  viewed as advocacy of realities, 56
  womanization of, 232–33
Rhetorical lovers
  in Christian evangelism, 103–4
  dialogical stance towards audience, 75
  kinds of, 74–75
  non-lover, evil lover, and noble lover, 74
  relationship with audience, 75

Rhetorical narrative, tests of, 292
Rhetorical perspective, for interpersonal ethics, 161
Rhetorical rapist, 75
Rhetorical seducer
  in Christian evangelism, 104
  unilateral attitude to audience, 75
Rhetorical stances, 75–76
Rhetoric-as-epistemic view, 55–57
Rhetoric as love, 74–75
Rhetoric-as-persuasion, criticized, 232
Rich, Adrienne, 238
Richards, I. A., 49
Roberts, Oral, 105
Roberts, Robert C., 296
Robertson, Marion "Pat," 308
Roderick, Lee, 268
Rogers, Carl, 64, 65
Rogge, Edward, 33, 88
Rokeach, Milton, 2
Role models, encouraging ethical behavior, 178
Roosevelt, Franklin D., 139
Ross, Mark, 162
Ross, Raymond, 161
Rotfeld, Herbert, 193
Rothwell, J. Dan, 93, 93
Rowan, Carl, 74
Rowan, H., 268
Rowland, Robert C., 46, 47, 284, 293, 294
Rowley, S., 268
Ruby, Jay, 321
Ruesch, Jurgen, 118
Rules
  functions of, 327–28
  need for grounding, 328
Russell, Bertrand, 51

Safford, E. S., 113
Safire, William, 272, 275, 289
Sandage, C. H., 138
Santoro, Luiz, 333
Sartre, Jean-Paul, 54–55

Satellite technology
  as a nonconvivial instrument, 329
  engineering criterion unacceptable, 330
  serving cultural imperialism, 329–30
Scapegoating, 161
Schramm, Martin, 269, 270
Schwartz, Tony, 130, 131
Scott, William G., 314
Scott, Robert, 56, 57, 58,
Search, habit of, 24, 183
Secrecy
  See also Lying; Presidential secrecy
  desirability of control over personal secrets, 143
  discretion necessary for judging ethicality, 143
  distinguished from privacy, 162–63
  harm caused by, 143
  neutral view of, 143
  policy should be debatable, 144
  relationship with power, 143–44
Seducer, 104
Self-respect, sense of ourselves as responsible necessary condition of, 9
Sensitivity to others, as an aspect of caring, 229
Sermonic dimension of language, 3–4
Sheehy, Gail, 307, 310, 313, 314
Sherman, Nancy, 13, 296
Shibles, Warren, 14
Shockley-Zalabak, Pamela, 183, 190
Shorris, Earl, 136
Shostrom, Everett, 64
Sichel, Betty, 300, 301
Significant choice
  and dialogical ethics, 78–79
  as ethical touchstone for communication, 27–30
Silence

ethical implications of, 135, 237–38
situations in which women are silenced, 238
Sincerity
to be judged separately from ethicality, 267, 275
different meanings in Western and Eastern cultures, 11
essential to ethical communication, 53
and ethical judgments, 275
and ethical responsibility, 10–11, 266–67
and misstatement and misuse of facts, by Reagan, 267–75, 307
Single-issue politics, 126
Sitaram, K. S., 245
Situational perspectives
Alinsky's situational perspective, 90–93
criticized, 87–88
Diggs's situational perspective, 89
ethical issues in protest situations, 93–96
factors relevant in, 87
Fletcher's situational perspective, 89–90
making judgments in light of each different context, 87
Rogge's situational perspective, 88
Situation ethics
See also Christian situation ethics
love the only ethical criterion for, 89–90
Slander, Jews and Christians admonished against use of, 99
Small group discussion
ethical sensitivity as a leadership function, 168–69
"Groupthink" ethic for, 169–70
guidelines for ethical communication in, 167–68
political perspective for, 166–67
respect for worth of others, 167–68
Smith, David H., 263

Smith, Samuel, 27
Smother lover, 104
Social change, use of video as a tool, 332–34
Social protest situations, ethical issues in, 93–96
Social utility approach, 108–9
cultural-specific nature of, 109
as possible principle for intercultural communication ethics, 244
Solidarity, 54
Solomon, Robert, 178, 238, 258
Sommers, Christina Hoff, 17, 300, 315
Speakes, Larry, 269, 272
Spear, Joseph, 264
Spero, Robert, 111, 214
Spirit of mutual equality, characteristic of dialogue, 67–68
Sproule, J. Michael, 37
Steiner, Linda, 235, 236
Stevenson, Adlai E., II, 139
Stewart, John, 70, 71, 157
Stone, I. F., 38
Subjectification of experience, in conversation, 165
Subjects and objects
human beings not to be treated as objects, 54–55
pornography treating women as objects, 237
Suggestive advertising, demeaning effect of, 47
Sulzberger, Arthur, Jr., 8
Superogatory ethical communication, 119
Supportive climate, characteristic of dialogue, 68
Supportive communication, in small group communication, 72–73
Swift, Kate, 253
Sylvester, Arthur, 120
Symbols
guiding ethical use of, 48
power of use of, 54

Symbol-using capacity
  as a fundamentally human characteristic, 48–50
  not confined to human beings, 49
Szasz, Thomas, 6–7

Tact, 137–38
Taking care of, 228
Taoism, religious perspectives offered by, 106
Task analysis, ethics of, 189
Task identification, ethics of, 189
Task performance, ethics of, 190
Tastefulness
  as an ethical criterion, 137–38
  poor taste to be distinguished from immorality, 137
Taylor, Paul, 314
Technical excellence, moral purpose sacrificed to, 324
Technology
  as a cultural activity, 322–23
  considered value-laden, 323–24
  convivial technology, 328–29
  cultural continuity as controlling aim of, 325–26, 327
  more sophisticated understanding needed, 322
  normative technology alternative to neutral technology, 324
  not merely a tool, 322
  not value-neutral, 322–23
  presumed neutrality allowing escape from responsibility, 323
  presumed neutrality promoting technological determinism, 323
  proceeding out of human experiences, 323
  seen as antithetical to ethics, 321–22
  socially responsible, 327–29
  technologies taking on a life of their own, 324
  virtuosity values of, 323
Teleological ethics, 8
Television, inspired by cult of large audiences, 324
"Telling it slant"
  categorized as lying, 230–31
  problems of, 231
  seen as ethically excusable and justifiable, 231
  and truth, 231
Thatcher, Margaret, 292
Therapy, dialogical relationships in, 65–66
Third-generation cable systems, 330–32
  to be made available according to need, not ability to pay, 331
  envisioned as a social necessity, 331
  public ownership suggested for, 332
Thompson, Dennis, 175
Tofler, Barbara, 179
Tompkins, Phillip, 181, 182, 183
Topical avoidance, in conversation, 165
Torrence, Donald, 51
Toulmin, Stephen, 17, 263, 297
Tournier, Paul, 64
Transcultural norms, 251
Trevino, Linda Klebe, 191
Tronto, Joan, 227, 228, 229
Truman, Harry, 133
Trust
  affected by lying, 122
  consequences of weakening, 37–38
  damaged by Reagan's misstatement and misuse of facts, 280
  essential for communication, 159–60
  impact of lying on, 238
  in interpersonal relationships between women, 238
  lacking in institutional settings, 174
  needed between government and people, 280
  public not trusting organizations, 174
  public trust protected in Ethical Values and Principles in Public Service, 212

relationship destroyed by violating, 161
stimulating trust, 160
Truth
  See also Lying
  approximating as closely as possible, 29–30
  as a print ethic, 131
  in communication, 29
  considered irrelevant as standard for electronic media, 130–31
  defined as not legally false, 112
  essential to ethical communication, 53
  ethical demand for truthfulness, 58
  expectation of, 14
  factual truth and impressionistic truth, 102
  and intentional ambiguity and vagueness, 275–79
  and misstatement and misuse of facts, 267–75, 307
  reaching an approximation of, 29–30
  and telling it slant, 231
  withholding truth not lying, 121
Truth of the situation, 28
Truth telling, in voluntary and involuntary relationships, 124
Tuchman, Gaye, 140

Ullian, J. S., 29
UNABOM manifesto, 7–8
Unconditional positive regard, in therapy, 65–66
Unethical techniques, justifying use of, 88
Unlabeled hyperbole, 88
Unshared responsibility, 166
Utilitarianism
  evaluation of consequences test of, 107
  standard for ethical rhetoric derived from, 107–8
Utilitarian perspectives
  general nature of, 107–8
  social utility approach, 108–9

Vagueness. *See* Intentional ambiguity and vagueness
Value of participants, in invitational rhetoric, 234
Value judgment, ethical standards stemming from human capacity for, 57–58
Values
  assessing ethicality of appeals to, 278–79
  capacity to create, sustain, and apply, 57
  central to Reagan's image of America, 278
  civilizing, 57–58
  as criteria for choices and judgments, 1
  emotive view of, 323
  human capacity for value judgment, 57–58
  Reagan making appeals to, 277–79
  and technology, 322–25
Value standards, compared with ethical standards, 1
Vander Kooi, Daryl, 99, 100
Veenstra, Charles, 99, 100
Veracity, ethical demand for, 58
Verbal conflict, unfair tactics in, 161–62
Verbal elements, revealing communicator attitudes, 79
Vibbert, Steven L., 189, 200, 208
Video, use of, as a tool of social change, 332–34
Violating a trust, in interpersonal communication, 161
Virtue ethics, 11
  in organizations, 177–78
Virtues, 298
  as described by ethicists, 11
  Machiavelli's conception of, 306
  as sole criterion for leadership, 306
Vision, central to moral character, 299

Wagman, R. J., 268, 275
Wall, J. M., 268, 273, 280
Wallace, Doug, 180
Wallace, George, 134
Wallace, Karl R., 23, 24, 25, 32–33, 166, 166, 183, 287
Walter, Otis, 48, 49
Walton, Clarence, 47, 297, 314
Warnick, Barbara, 55, 284, 293
Warwick, Donald P., 287
Watson, R., 274
Wattenberg, Martin P., 311
Weaver, Richard M., 3, 72, 74, 320
Weber, Max, 325
Wellman, Carl, 6, 121
Westerstahl, Jorgen, 140
Whistleblowing, 185–86
White, Julie Belle, 180
White, Robert, 333
White sham, distinguished from black sham, 163
Wieman, Henry, 48, 49
Wilbur, James B., III, 300, 314
Will, George, 276
Williams, Harold, 112
Williams, Lee, 125
Williams, Oliver, 178
Wise, David, 280
Witcover, Jules, 272, 273, 274, 275, 289

Wolf, John, 105
Womack, Deanna, 46, 47
Women
  See also Feminist ethic
  silencing of, 238
  Western male-dominated cultural tradition biased against, 236–37
Wood, Julia, 221, 229, 230
Words. *See* Language
Words and ideas, as private property or communal resources to be shared, 248–49
World religions, ethical standards for communication held in common by, 107
Wright, R. George, 255
Written communication
  dialogical attitudes in, 73–76
  monological arrogance found in, 74
  tough, sweet, and stuffy style used in, 76
Wyden, Peter, 161

Yoos, George, 121
Yousef, Fathi, 128
Yulgok, 106

Ethics in human communication /

30000410